FIELDING'S
KENYA

Fielding Titles

Fielding's Amazon
Fielding's Australia
Fielding's Bahamas
Fielding's Belgium
Fielding's Bermuda
Fielding's Borneo
Fielding's Brazil
Fielding's Britain
Fielding's Budget Europe
Fielding's Caribbean
Fielding's Europe
Fielding's Far East
Fielding's France
Fielding's Guide to the World's Most Dangerous Places
Fielding's Guide to the World's Great Voyages
Fielding's Guide to Kenya's Best Hotels, Lodges & Homestays
Fielding's Guide to the World's Most Romantic Places
Fielding's Hawaii
Fielding's Holland
Fielding's Italy
Fielding's London Agenda
Fielding's Los Angeles Agenda
Fielding's Malaysia and Singapore
Fielding's Mexico
Fielding's New York Agenda
Fielding's New Zealand
Fielding's Paris Agenda
Fielding's Portugal
Fielding's Scandinavia
Fielding's Seychelles
Fielding's Southeast Asia
Fielding's Spain
Fielding's Vacation Places Rated
Fielding's Vietnam
Fielding's Worldwide Cruises
Fielding's Cruise Insider

FIELDING'S KENYA

Guide to Kenya's Best Hotels, Lodges & Homestays

by
Bridget Glenday
Susan Southwick
and
Joan Westley

Fielding Worldwide, Inc.
308 South Catalina Avenue
Redondo Beach, California 90277 U.S.A.

Fielding's Guide to Kenya's Best Hotels, Lodges & Homestays
Published by Fielding Worldwide, Inc.

Text Copyright ©1995 FWI

Maps, Icons, Illustrations Copyright ©1995 FWI

FIELDING WORLDWIDE INC.

PUBLISHER AND CEO **Robert Young Pelton**
PUBLISHING DIRECTOR **Paul T. Snapp**
ELECTRONIC PUBLISHING DIRECTOR **Larry E. Hart**
PROJECT DIRECTOR **Tony E. Hulette**
ADMINISTRATIVE COORDINATOR **Beverly Riess**
ACCOUNT SERVICES MANAGER **Christy Harp**

EDITORS

Linda Charlton   **Kathy Knoles**

PRODUCTION

Gini Martin   **Chris Snyder**
Craig South

COVER DESIGNED BY **Digital Artists, Inc.**
COVER PHOTOGRAPHERS — Front Cover **Manoj Shah/Tony Stone Images**
Background Photo, Front Cover **John Garrett/Tony Stone Images**
Back Cover **Robert Young Pelton/Westlight**
INSIDE PHOTOS **David Anderson, Bruce Coleman, Inc.,**
Robert Young Pelton/Westlight
ILLUSTRATIONS **Tuula Sotamaa, Pam Toh, Elizabeth Washburn**

Inquiries should be addressed to: Fielding Worldwide, Inc., 308 South Catalina Ave., Redondo Beach, California 90277 U.S.A., Telephone (310) 372-4474, Facsimile (310) 376-8064, 8:30 a.m.–5:30 p.m. Pacific Standard Time.

ISBN 1-56952-038-0

Library of Congress Catalog Card Number

94-068347

Printed in the United States of America

Dedication

We dedicate this book to the hospitable people of Kenya.

Letter from the Publisher

In 1946, Temple Fielding began the first of what would be a remarkable new series of well-written, highly personalized guidebooks for independent travelers. Temple's opinionated, witty, and oft-imitated books have now guided travelers for almost a half-century. More important to some was Fielding's humorous and direct method of steering travelers away from the dull and the insipid. Today, Fielding Travel Guides are still written by experienced travelers for experienced travelers. Our authors carry on Fielding's reputation for creating travel experiences that deliver insight with a sense of discovery and style.

World travelers Bridget Glenday, Susan Southwick and Joan Westley have lived in and traveled throughout Kenya for four years. During their 4-wheel drive, hot air balloon and camel journeys they have painstakingly reviewed every type of accommodation from the bustling tourist hotels to little–known private homes and even tented camps to create a colorful, opinionated guide for the independent traveler.The other half of the international team, Tuula Sotamaa, Pam Toh and Elizabeth Washburn, spent months creating the exquisite maps, line drawings and illustrations that give this book its special personality. Together with Fielding, they have created the only in-depth guide to every major safari camp, lodge and homestay in Kenya. In addition, our Quick Safari Guide is a helpful reference to Kenya's national parks, biospheres and nature preserves.

Today, the concept of independent travel has never been bigger. Fielding's policy of *brutal honesty* and a highly personal point of view has never changed; it just seems the travel world has caught up with us.

Enjoy your Kenyan safari with Bridget, Susan, Joan and Fielding.

RYP

Robert Young Pelton

Publisher and C.E.O.

Fielding Worldwide, Inc.

FIELDING SURVEY

The authors and publisher of Fielding's guide to Kenya would like to hear your opinion of hotels, lodges, homestays, campsites and tour organizations. Please be as candid as you like and feel free to send your expanded comments on the reverse. If your comments are used you will receive a free Fielding Guide of your choice. Be concise, creative and opinionated.

Fielding Survey

Name:

Address:

City, State, Zip:

Phone Number: (   )

Profession:

Date of visit to Kenya:

Please tell us your opinion of your tour operator:

Tour Operator:

Please tell us the restaruant hotel, lodge, homestay or campsite you stayed in and your opinion on them:

Location:

Location:

Fielding Survey

Location: _____

_____
_____
_____
_____
_____
_____
_____

Location: _____

_____
_____
_____
_____
_____
_____

Location: _____

_____
_____
_____
_____
_____
_____

Location: _____

_____
_____
_____
_____
_____
_____

If you are a member of the travel industry or someone with a vested interest in a property, feel free to wax poetic but do not expect to have your rating changed by sheer volume of mail. (We have spies you know). Please note that no Fielding author or inspector ever asks for compensation, free services or any favors. So don't use this form to scam freebies!

Fielding Survey

Name:

Address:

City, State, Zip:

Phone Number: (   )

Profession:

Date of visit to Kenya:

**Please tell us your opinion of
your Tour Operator:**

Tour Operator:

**Please tell us the restaruant hotel, lodge, homestay or campsite you
stayed in and your opinion on them:**

Location:

Location:

Location:

Fielding Survey

Location:

_____
_____
_____
_____
_____
_____
_____
_____

Location:

_____
_____
_____
_____
_____
_____
_____

Location:

_____
_____
_____
_____
_____
_____
_____

Location:

_____
_____
_____
_____
_____

Location:

_____
_____
_____
_____
_____

TABLE OF CONTENTS

LIST OF MAPS

BEGINNINGS

Although we have lived in Nairobi for several years, we first arrived with conflicting images and expectations of Kenya. Like most people we were drawn by the excitement of wildlife, "Out of Africa" romantic adventure, and warm coral beaches. However, like many first-time visitors, we were also concerned about personal security and health and about how welcome we would feel. We have written about what we have found, and we hope our experience will give you a good perspective for planning your trip to Kenya.

For the tourist, the extraordinary beauty of this country, its friendly people, and its sophisticated tourist industry can provide an experience of a lifetime, a unique and wonderful holiday. It is no surprise that many who visit keep returning, and those of us lucky enough to live here for a while are deeply saddened at the thought of leaving.

WHY KENYA?

Living here, we have discovered much about this diverse, modern, yet ancient land. Why come to Kenya? Here's a "short" list:

Magnificent wildlife • See the big five (lion, elephant, rhino, buffalo, leopard) along with graceful giraffe, and herds of zebra and gazelle in their spectacular natural setting—conservation issues take on new meaning.

Amazing landscape • From the snows of Mts. Kenya and Kilimanjaro to the great Rift Valley with its string of unusual lakes; from open savannah with no apparent horizon to mountain ranges with strange inselbergs and mesas; from plantations of coffee, tea, and coconut palms to tropical gardens lush-green and brilliant with flowers and colorful birds.

Beautiful lakes • Lake Victoria, almost an inland sea; lakes ranging from emerald green to flamingo pink; lakes with land and water birds galore…an ornithologist's heaven.

1

Tropical coastline • Miles of white sandy beaches, waving palms, and coral reefs bright with exotic fish. Big game fishing, windsurfing, snorkeling.

Strong ethnic traditions • Masai and Samburu herdsmen with lion spears, red cloaks, and beadwork; Kisii soapstone carvers; Akamba wood carvers; Swahili coastal villagers with their strong Arabic influence; and more.

Hospitality • You have many choices: highland ranches, some dating back to first European settlements; relaxed and spacious coastal resorts; historic hotels such as the Norfolk, the Aberdare Country Club, and the Mt. Kenya Safari Club. You will love the traditional Kenyan welcome—a big smile and a tropical drink.

Weather • Generally sunny and warm, with occasional showers—practically perfect vacation weather, amazing blue skies with an astonishment of clouds, and right on the Equator.

Food • Tropical fruits, highland vegetables, fresh beef and lamb, freshwater Nile perch and highland trout, every kind of seafood (try the Swahili preparations), wines and spirits from local vineyards, Europe, and South Africa.

Handicrafts, some fine, some useful, some amusing • Wood and soapstone carvings, handwoven fabrics, gemstones (especially tsavorite and tanzanite), ethnic and modern jewelry, leatherwork, embossed chests and mirrors, handwoven carpets, baskets, baskets, baskets.

Pre-history • The Leakey family and others study early man in 5-million-year chunks of time—see the Turkana Boy (5 million years young) in the Nairobi Museum.

There is something about Kenya—perhaps it truly is the birthplace of mankind, and we all feel a returning, that the land is not unknown to us.

It's Not Perfect...

Kenya is a fairly new nation on the modern scene. There will be some aspects of being here that you may not "enjoy" or even find "shocking":

• Bone-jarring potholes in highways and city streets.

• Trucks and buses loaded to bursting with cargo and passengers and belching clots of black smoke.

• Nairobi streetboys begging with hungry looks and a ready curse if their expectations are not met.

• Brash young vendors, pushing their wares on the beach, in the markets, and sometimes on the street.

• Gecko lizards, sometimes on walls and ceilings, with a scary swift slither (in reality a true mosquito-eating friend).

• The slow pace of bureaucracy, especially if you are in a hurry.

• Telephones which only connect after the tenth dialing.

Other things that may "disturb"...

- No working elevators, walkways, or escalators at the international airport...luggage carts that creak and lack paint.

- Old women carrying impossible loads of wood on their backs.

- Men straining to pull handcarts laden like pickup trucks.

- Fruit stands that are little more than shacks, but with jewel-toned fruits in beautiful display.

- Market stalls created by spreading a cloth on the ground.

- Homes in the country handmade of sticks, grass, mud, and dung.

- The occasional metal roof shines as a mark of status.

- Farming with hand implements.

- Brilliant bougainvillea blossoms camouflaging webs of barbed wire.

- Public bathrooms you wish you had never entered...keep some tissues handy.

- Strange smells, not all of them pleasant.

Weathering it all is part of enjoying and learning the difference of a foreign place. It is challenging to see beyond what seems grimy and grim to the real beauty of Kenya and to the real charm of the Kenyan people.

So, no problem, HAKUNA MATATA.

Be ready to enjoy all of Kenya, even the "salt." Take heart—the tourist industry is well-developed and major, dedicated to making visitors from other lands COMFORTABLE.

WHY THIS BOOK?

We were keen to discover as much of this splendid and varied country as possible. Guides, friends and travel agents were quick with recommendations: go to the game parks, go to the coast, go to the mountains, go to this or that accommodation.

However, we were amazed to find no comprehensive guide to help independent travelers like us decide where to spend weekends and holidays on sometimes limited resources. Since we were spending several years in Nairobi, we decided to visit every corner of Kenya where tourists go and to record our impressions of Kenya and Kenya's best hotels, lodges and homestays.

QUEST FOR THE BEST

We felt well-qualified for the task ahead. All of us have traveled widely in the world, and as a group have a variety of skills, experiences, and perceptions which were invaluable in creating this book.

Each of us has moved from place to place as part of families connected with different institutions and organizations: the U.S. Department of State, Harvard University's Institute for International Development, U.S. Agency for International Development, the Finnish Foreign Service, or American International Schools.

We traveled around Kenya and gathered first-hand information. Our quest was to discover the best that this country had to offer. In reviewing accommodations, we defined "best" as being places which were special in some way—they might have magnificent views, outstanding buildings, or captivating histories; or they might offer wonderful, memorable experiences. They would all have to meet a certain standard of accommodation.

Such lodgings and the people who run them can be as much a part of the travel adventure as experiencing firsthand the wonder of the Rift Valley or the drama of the Great Wildebeest Migrations.

Armed with hotel brochures, tips from friends, and advice from people experienced in the Kenya travel business, we set off. We travelled by 4-wheel drive, by train, by planes of all sizes, by boats of all sorts, by steam tractor, by balloon, by horseback, by camel.... We stayed in big, bustling tourist hotels, tented camps, mountain lodges and small private homes and ranches.

Everywhere we were charmed by the friendliness and courtesy of the people we met. To do justice to all we had learned on our travels, we describe what we feel is important or unique about a place, giving you sufficient information to decide whether or not it appeals to you. We hope you enjoy reading *Fielding's Guide to Kenya*, and we wish you wonderful adventuring.

TRAVEL TIPS

GETTING READY

Most travelers to Kenya come from Europe, North America, or Asia. This involves some serious travel, preparing for international formalities, and being ready for some cultural differences.

When to come: The main tourist seasons are December–January and July–August, responding to international vacation schedules. The Great Migration of Wildebeest and Zebra usually reaches Kenya's Masai Mara during July–August. October–January is the best time for a beach holiday, as there is less seaweed.

Residents love the rest of the year as well—fewer tourists, brilliant green of new tropical growth, cooler temperatures, and lower rates everywhere. Temperatures are temperate all year. Day temperatures are typically between 20–30 C. or 65–85 F. The rainy seasons are usually in April–May and November.

International Travel: Most people travel to Nairobi by air. It is not possible to fly directly to Nairobi from North America. You must connect with a flight leaving from London, Amsterdam, Paris, Geneva, Rome, or Zurich.

Reputable travel agents or the various airlines flying into Nairobi or a connecting European city can sometimes find bargain fares, but beware of time and refund restrictions. Book in advance to be sure of a seat, especially at peak travel times. Be aware that there will be a $20 departure tax levied when you leave Kenya.

Passport & Visas: Passports should be current and valid for at least six months after your stay in Kenya. Visas are required. Before you travel, you should request your visa from any Kenyan embassy, consulate, or high commission, or from any British embassy in countries where there is no Kenyan embassy. Visas take at least 24 hours to process plus mailing time if you live at a distance. You need to send two passport photos with the application and your passport, along with proof of your ability to leave Kenya such as an air ticket.

Although visitors are usually given a six-month visa, the length of stay granted at the airport may be less. It is important to know what is granted so that you can renew your length of stay if necessary. It is also possible to purchase a visa on arrival at the airport. We do not recommend this.

Money: The number of Shillings to the U.S. Dollar varies often, but follows the Central Bank of Kenya exchange rates which are quoted daily in the local newspapers. U.S. Dollars and Pounds Sterling are easy to exchange as are travelers' checks, which can be replaced if stolen. Kenyan Shillings are a soft currency.

Major Credit Cards: Also accepted by many hotels, travel agencies, car rental companies, airlines, restaurants, and city shops. Cash, especially in lower denominations, is needed in a bargaining situation.

Immunizations: The U.S. Department of State recommends that you carry up-to-date immunization records of the following:

- Tetanus boosters
- Polio boosters
- Typhoid shots
- Gamma-globulin shots (against hepatitis A)
- Yellow Fever Vaccination*
- Cholera Vaccination*

*(Most doctors will provide these even if they feel the shots are unnecessary.)

Interpreting Travel Advisories: The U.S. Department of State has issued warnings to travelers based on danger from tourist-related crime. You may also read sensational news stories of unfortunate crimes against tourists. Bear in mind, however, that thousands of tourists visit Kenya with no such unfortunate incidents. Before canceling or postponing a trip to Kenya, check with your travel agents, the airlines, or the Department of State to get more information about the basis of the warning. You should not disregard such warnings, but sometimes the actual danger is not as serious as it sounds.

Luggage: Traveling by air, you are allowed two bags to check and one carry-on bag. Leaving Europe or Kenya, you may be subject to overweight charges if a checked bag weighs more than 20 kilograms or 44 pounds.

Try to plan your packing to allow for the possibility of repacking a smaller bag with clothes for a particular safari. Sometimes there isn't a lot of room for luggage in a small airplane or a safari vehicle.

CLOTHING

You will need comfortable clothes that are cool, but that can layer up to keep you warm at night or at higher altitudes. Casual is fine for daywear, but you may want some possibilities for more dressy dinners and evenings. Traditional "camouflage" colors are best when near wildlife. More rugged clothing would be necessary for camping, hiking, or riding.

- Bring a sweater or a light jacket for early morning game drives.
- Lightweight, comfortable walking shoes are sufficient for most safaris.
- Pack a bathing suit. Don't forget a hat or your sunglasses.

We advise to pack lightly. It is possible to get clothing washed and ironed.

OPTIONAL EQUIPMENT

You may also like to bring:

- Camera equipment (extra film; video recorders are great for game)
- Field binoculars (lightweight)
- Snorkel and mask
- All-purpose knife, with corkscrew
- Flashlight (extra batteries)
- Pocket calculator
- Alarm clock
- Large and small plastic bags (for storage, against dust)
- Notebook and pens for safari journal
- Reading material
- Guides and maps
- Sugar substitute (if desired)
- Decaf coffee (if desired)
- Humor
- Patience

TAKING CARE OF YOURSELF

First Aid Kit: Most drugstore items are available and inexpensive in Kenya. Consider including for your safaris:

- Sunblock (bring lots)
- Chapstick
- Moisturizers/lotions (bring plenty: hot sun, low humidity)
- Insect repellant
- Acetaminophen, aspirin, or ibuprofen for pain or fever
- Antimalaria tablets for prophylactic or attack
- Antidiarrheal agents
- Antibiotics (for lower bowel problems and for broad spectrum use against infections.
- Antihistamines for allergic reaction
- Antifungal powder
- Antiseptic ointment
- Alcohol swabs for clean wounds or insect bites
- Band-Aids, gauze dressings, tape
- Thermometer
- Lens solution for contact lenses
- Small packs of tissue (for allergy "noses" or "rest-stop" emergencies)
- Handi-Wipes

Hospitals & Doctors: Major hotels have some kind of medical officer. Nairobi Hospital is considered well-equipped. The Flying Doctors service the more remote areas. You can buy traveler's insurance for medical evacuation from them or from international companies in advance or after your arrival. There are American and European trained doctors and dentists in Nairobi.

Malaria: A mosquito bite can kill. Take appropriate precautions. Follow updated medical advice on which prophylactic to take, and remember to complete the dose when you get back home. If you do get sick, especially with flu-like symptoms of fever, headache, or stomach problems, be sure to tell your doctor you were in a malaria area.

These malarial mosquitoes tend to bite in the evening and at night. You can help protect yourself in the evenings by using mosquito repellant and by covering arms and legs. Most hotels and lodges in malaria areas do their bit to help protect you. They often provide mosquito nets, spray the rooms, leave a sachet of mosquito repellant by your bed.

Malaria is more prevalent in low-lying areas. The coast, the game parks, and Lake Victoria are the most affected areas.

Aids: Come for the animals, come for the sun, come for the panoramas. Don't come for "sex."

Water: As a rule of thumb, don't drink the tap water. Most hotels/lodges provide a thermos or flask of drinking water in the rooms or tents. You can also buy bottled mineral water—local or imported. Carbonated club soda is an inexpensive alternative.

Food: Most travellers are impressed by the quantity and diversity of food offered in Kenya. Even when you are deep in the bush and miles from any agricultural or commercial center, you are almost always assured of finding a buffet groaning with appetizing-looking food including many salads. These elaborate "Safari Buffets" usually look better than they taste and become repetitive after several times through the line. It is relatively safe to try most of the food offered by hotels and lodges which cater to international tourists.

Rays: Beware the tropical sun. Wear sunblock. Bring a hat, or better, two. You burn faster at high altitudes and near the Equator.

Highs and Lows: In Kenya, altitudes range from sea level to over 5000 meters. Be alert to the fact that quick altitude changes can be dangerous to your health. Mountain climbers—beware!

Rain or Shine: Kenya is not all hot, or all dry.

Early morning game drives in an open vehicle can be very cold—come prepared. There is snow on the summits of Mt. Kenya and Mt. Kilimanjaro. Staying in the vicinity of the mountains or on the highlands can be very cold, especially at night.

Kenya's seasons are classified by "rainy" and "dry." The "long rains" usually come in April and May, and the "short rains" in November. The rains are not always neatly confined to the months "allocated."

Exercise: The word safari means journey in Swahili. A "Safari in Kenya" sounds like such an outdoor, healthy activity. It connotes exercise (perhaps strenuous) and possibly hiking boots. A false impression. For most tourists, game-watching safaris in the major game parks mean game drives in vehicles, vast amounts of food in the form of generous buffets, perhaps a siesta, and sitting around the campfire. Hardly great for those abdominal muscles.

Many game lodges are now realizing the popularity of game walks. There is a move to offer more personal interactive experiences with the African bush. Because of park regulations, this is easier for places outside of game park boundaries. Ranches and homestays often specialize in this kind of interaction.

Ironically, it is easier to get more exercise at the coast. There is always swimming, perhaps disco dancing at night, and long walks along the beach. However, sun and humidity, the languid pace, big meals, and good beer also mean that exercise might not feature in your coastal holiday. You can always return to your aerobic classes when you get home.

Security: Kenya has had more that its share of bad press, particularly relating to security issues. While theft and violence are real concerns, they represent an escalating problem in most countries of the world.

Nairobi is still safer than hundreds of other major cities. Travelers should exercise good sense and take some reasonable precautions:

- Don't parade valuable jewelry.
- Desist from strolling the streets at night.
- Catch cabs rather than walk in strange areas.
- Don't carry lots of money and important papers.
- Don't take valuables to the beach.

Culture Shock/Stress: Although Kenya is one of the wealthier countries in Africa, there is still a great deal of poverty. Visible poverty. Poor mothers with babies beg in the streets, makeshift shacks mushroom next to modern buildings, trash heaps never completely disappear.

Life goes on in public—hairdressers ply their craft under a tree, sewing machines sing on sidewalks, furniture makers display their wares in the sun.

Kenya jars and excites with color and chaos, vibrant life and the unexpected. It can be an exhilarating, eye-opening cultural experience.

If you come from a fast and efficient life-style, you may feel frustrated by the slow pace and the inefficiencies. Humor works better than anger. Surely, slowing down and appreciating a different culture is part of what makes a holiday.

Remember one of the most common Swahili expressions: "Hakuna Matata"—no problem.

Vendor Vigilance: You may be pestered by local souvenir vendors. Bargaining is the order of the day. Bartering is an option—T-shirts and pens are popular. Remember! Use humor and don't be dismayed at persistence.

Photo Ops: Photograph landscapes, photograph animals, but ask permission before taking photos of people, and be prepared to pay for the privilege in some instances.

Creepy Crawlies: You will see less of these than you expect. They do of course exist. You should not walk around at night, or in the bush, without shoes. Hopefully you will be lucky enough to see some brightly colored lizards or perhaps the odd chameleon. (P.S. Most of us who have lived here for years have yet to see a snake.) Don't forget your insect repellant.

Our Furry Friends: The animals are wild. They are not paid to entertain the guests. Respect them, and keep your distance. The fact that hippos are grazing next to your tent at night does not mean you can pat them. Hippos are very dangerous. So are lions, elephant, buffalo, rhino, crocodiles, monkeys, teddy-bear-like hyrax.... It is just not prudent to pet...

The Big Five are lion, elephant, rhino, leopard and your choice of buffalo or hippo. Remember, each animal is more than an addition to a list. It is fun to see how individuals react with each other, in groups, and with the environment.

Favorites of the Tiny Five: a scarlet nit, an iridescent emerald fly, and the walking stick.

PLANNING YOUR STAY IN KENYA

Most tourists coming to Kenya for the first time are surprised by the variety of experiences the country has to offer. Not only is there a great range of topography, scenery and wildlife, but there is also an amazing choice of ways in which you can enjoy these attractions. It is worthwhile to decide exactly what you want to do and see, and in what style you want to do it.

Your memories of Kenya could include:

• Eating breakfast under a thorn tree with Mt. Kenya in the distance and a herd of giraffe nearby.

• Lying in a hammock at the beach after a feast of fresh crab.

• Looking up at the moon through a mesh tent after an exhilarating day on your camel safari.

Your memories of Kenya could also include:

• Long bumpy and dusty rides in a minivan crowded with other tourists.

• Queuing for the third consecutive day for the same buffet lunch.

• Blocking the sound of the disco as you try to go to sleep at your beach hotel.

THE CHOICES ARE YOURS

Don't feel that the only way you can see Kenya is with a package tour. Kenya's tourist industry is quite sophisticated. There are many experienced travel agents and private tour operators who can tailor a holiday to meet your needs and preferences.

You have many options:

- Vehicle rentals—often come with the service of a driver who is familiar with the country and the roads.

- Flying in small planes—although pricey, can save a lot of time, give you marvelous views of the country, and can often land very close to your destination. Many private homestays have a landing strip and even planes of their own.

- Special interest tours—focus on fishing, photography, bird watching, anthropology, mountain climbing, horseback riding, hiking, and camping. There are even camel safaris.

This Fielding guide can help you plan a holiday tailor-made for you.

TOUR OPTIONS

These range from roughing it to exclusive up-market tours. You could travel from lodge to lodge in a minivan or be flown in small planes from one private homestay to another. You could enjoy the pampering and service of a deluxe tented safari, or save money with a more basic "participation" camping trip where you do some of the camp work. You could make up your own private group and travel with a professional safari guide, or you could join a bus load of other tourists and have the local driver doubling as your guide. Besides offering standard tours, most tour operators will also custom-tailor tours for clients. Although the descriptions below focus primarily on camping or bush safaris, most operators and agents can also organize beach holidays.

PRIVATE UPMARKET SAFARI GUIDES AND OUTFITTERS

Almost all of the tour guides on these safaris have a great deal of experience in Africa and with wildlife. Generally, their safaris are based on personal leadership and charisma. Most have rugged safari vehicles with professional drivers. Some are pilots and own their own planes to fly you from place to place. Many have exclusive rights to pitch their luxury camps in out-of-the-way scenic spots. Some also cater to special interests such as horse riding, fishing, ornithology or walking.

In previous years some of the guides were "great White Hunters" and can thrill you with tales of adventure. Some are more at home in the bush than entertaining people and others are smooth, chatty hosts—nearly all are characters you will enjoy and remember. On many of these safaris you will spend some of the time in tented accommodations and some of it in lodges, hotels, or home-stays.

Daily rates are usually per person and vary by the size of the group. They generally include all meals, park fees, game drives, and in some instances drinks. Rates range from $400 to $1000 per day.

International telephone codes for Nairobi: ☎ *254 02.*

Allen Safaris

> *Box 14712, Nairobi.* ☎ *& FAX: 521538*
> London: ☎ *071-9372937.*

Or U.S. contacts:

Anton Allen, Austin, Texas
☎ *(512) 858-7045, FAX: (512) 264-2862.*

Joanna Allen, New York, NY
☎ *(212) 772-7720, FAX: (212) 772-6223.*

60+ years experience. Exclusive and customized photographic and sightseeing safaris. Hosted by David Allen or associate. Travel by light aircraft.

Ron Beaton

> *c/o Wilderness Trails,*
> *Box 56923, Nairobi,* ☎ *506139, FAX: 502739 REKERO.*

Ron hosts guests at his Rekero Farm adjacent to the Masai Mara. Best known for his walking safaris.

Carr-Hartley Safaris

> *Box 59762, Nairobi,* ☎ *882453, FAX: 884542.*

Or U.S. contact:

Mr. John Take or Ms. Sandy Sullivan

> *Convention Planning Services Inc.*
> *5422 Carrier Drive, Suite 203, Orlando, Florida 32819*
> ☎ *(407) 351-5333, FAX: (407) 351-1784.*

Cheli & Peacock Ltd.

> *Box 39806, Nairobi,* ☎ *(0154) 22551, FAX: (0154) 22553.*

Luxury customized tented safaris

Chrissie Aldrich

> *Box 82, Nanyuki, Kenya,* ☎ *(176) 22053, FAX: (176) 23302.*

Long time lady guide. Custom and special safaris.

Clive Lee Private Safaris Ltd.

> *Box 55905, Nairobi,* ☎ *882271, FAX: 714628,*

UK contact:

"Fairfield", *St. Mary's Rd., Portishead, Avon BS20 9QP*
☎ */FAX: (0275) 847017.*

Custom and special interest safaris.

Four by Four Safaris Ltd.
Box 24397, Nairobi, ☎ *567251, FAX: 564945.*

Upmarket customized safaris.

Iain MacDonald Safaris
Safcon Travel Services, Box 59224, Nairobi, ☎ *503265, FAX: 506824.*

Experienced small company offering flexible safaris: luxury tented, lodge safaris, sporting safaris.

Ker & Downey
Box 41822, Nairobi, ☎ *556466, FAX: 552378.*

Oldest established safari specialists in Africa with a "sterling reputation" and "unsurpassed in their knowledge of the bush and wildlife" (*New York Times*, March '93). Ker and Downey run luxury camping safaris and a wide range of special interest safaris. Experienced host/guides are shareholders in the company and attract their own clientele. The following guides come highly recommended: Alan Binks, Derek Dames, Allan Earnshaw, Nigel Dundas, James Robertson, Tony Seth-Smith, John Sutton (has also hosted location camps for crews of *Out of Africa, Gorillas in the Mist, Mountains of the Moon* and others), Bill Winter, Dave Williams, Don Young (American-born expert on Richard Burton the explorer, and fireside storyteller supreme).

Mark C. Ross
Box 60157, Nairobi, ☎ *338041, FAX: 338072.*

Or U.S. agent:

Table Mountain Travel
14062 Denver West Pkwy, Ste 100, Golden, Co. 80401, ☎ *(800) 999-1580, FAX: (303) 277-1589.*

American, offers flying safaris. Knowledgeable ornithologist.

Richard Bonham Safaris Ltd.
Box 24133, Nairobi, ☎ *882521, FAX: 882728.*

Or U.S. contact:

Frontiers International Travel
Box 959, Wexford, PA 15090, ☎ *(800) 245-1950, FAX: (412) 935-1570.*

Richard has an exclusive lodge in the Chuluyu Hills, Ol Donyo Wuas; leads walking safaris in Tanzania, and is a pilot.

Tor Allan Safaris
Box 15114, Nairobi, ☎ *891190, FAX: 890142.*

Tor customizes upmarket tented safaris. Snippets from the *New York Times* (March 1993). "Sterling reputation…spares no extravagance…staff cater to every whim…unsurpassed in the knowledge of the bush and wildlife."

Tropical Ice Ltd.
Box 57341, Nairobi. ☎ *740811 FAX: 740826.*

Adventure safari company specializing in mountaineering expeditions. Iain Allan is the experienced guide.

OTHER TRAVEL PROFESSIONALS

There are many companies and individuals in Nairobi who offer a wide range of travel services. These can include booking and operating standard itineraries, general accommodation bookings and transport services, and customized adventure safaris. Most Kenyan travel professionals can direct you to experts in special interest safaris.

Abercrombie & Kent International (A&K)

Box 59749 Nairobi, ☎ *334955, FAX: 335442.*

Or U.S. Headquarters:

1420 Kensington Rd., Oakbrook, Illinois 60521, ☎ *312/954-2944 or 800/323-7308.*

A&K offer lodge tours and more exclusive tented safaris. Well-known—been in the business since 1962.

Across Africa Safaris

Box 49420, Nairobi, ☎ *332744, FAX: 332419.*

Variety of tours: road, air, special interest. Mainly mini-bus package safaris.

Archer's Tours & Travels Ltd.

Box 40097, Nairobi, ☎ *223131, FAX: 212656.*

Tailor-made holidays in established upmarket lodges and homestays.

Bateleur Safaris Ltd.

Box 42562, Nairoibi. ☎ */FAX: 891007.*

Or U.S. contact:

Sporting International Inc.

13201 Northwest Freeway, Suite 880-C, Houston, Texas 77040, ☎ *(800) 231-6352.*

Special interest safaris: walking, ornithology.

Big Five Tours and Safaris Ltd.

Box 10367, Nairobi, ☎ *229803, FAX: 337965.*

From package group tours to private safaris. Bookings and car hire.

Bookings Limited

Box 56707, Nairobi, ☎ *225255, FAX: 216553.*

Well-established tour operator offering variety of excursions and safaris. Car rentals.

Bruce Safaris Ltd.

Box 40662, Nairobi, ☎ *227311, FAX: 223647.*

In the business 40 years. Can customize adventure safaris and book standard itineraries.

Bunson Travel Service
> *Box 45456, Nairobi,* ☎ *221992, FAX: 214120.*

Offers wide range of safari services.

Bushbuck Adventures
> *Box 67449, Nairobi,* ☎ *212975, FAX: 218735.*

Specialize in safaris for the more adventurous—from basic to more luxurious. Special interest safaris. Actively involved in conservation.

Flamingo Tours Ltd.
> *Box 45070,* ☎ *600900, FAX: 502566.*

U.S. address:

Flamingo Tours of East Africa Inc.
520 North Michigan Ave. Suite 1016, Chicago. Ill. 60611.

Wide range of tours, most by minibus.

Gametrackers
> *Box 62042, Nairobi,* ☎ *338927, FAX: 330903.*

Less expensive and special interest safaris: camel, canoe, foot, mountain bike, mountaineering...

Just the Ticket
> *Box 14845, Nairobi,* ☎ *741755, FAX: 740087.*

Full-service travel agency.

Kenya Wildlife Trails Ltd.
> *Box 44687, Nairobi,* ☎ *228960, FAX: 214532.*

Tours and car hire.

Let's Go Travel
> *Box 60342, Nairobi,* ☎ *340331/213033, FAX: 336890.*

Several branches in Nairobi, publish updated rate sheets for most hotels and lodges, rent vehicles.

Muthaiga Travel Ltd.
> *Box 34464, Nairobi,* ☎ *740034, FAX: 750035.*

Full-service travel agency.

Prestige Safaris Ltd.
> *Box 43987, Nairobi,* ☎ *227977, FAX: 333669.*

Wide range of services and tours—standard and customized.

Pollman's Tours and Safari Tours
> *Box 45895, Nairobi,* ☎ *337952, FAX: 337171.*

Range of minibus tours

Rhino Safaris Ltd.
> *Box 48023, Nairobi,* ☎ *332372, FAX: 338427.*

Well-established tour operation offering range of lodge safaris and tours as well as budget camping safaris.

Safari Camp Services Ltd.
Box 44801, Nairobi, ☎ *228936, FAX: 212160.*

Range of safaris from budget to exclusive.

Safaris Unlimited (Africa) Ltd.
Box 24181, Nairobi, ☎ *891168, FAX: 891113.*

Camping and special interest safaris, especially horseback. In the business for 21 years.

Safcon Travel Services Ltd.
Box 59224, Nairobi, ☎ *503265/503267, FAX: 506824.*

Full-service travel agency, private safaris.

Smart Tours & Travel Ltd.
Box 42830, Nairobi, ☎ *225850, FAX: 216293.*

Classic or special interest safaris.

Somak Travel
Box 48495, Nairobi, ☎ *337333, FAX: 218954.*

United Touring Co. (U.T.C.)
Box 42196, Nairobi, ☎ *331960, FAX: 331422.*

Or U.S. address:

United Touring International
400 Market St. Suite 260, Philadelphia, Pennsylvania 19106, ☎ *(800) 223-6486.*

Large operation offering wide range of safari and package options.

Universal Safari Tours (U.S.T.)
Box 49312, Nairobi, ☎ *221446, FAX: 218686.*

Large tour operator.

Wilderness Trails (K) Ltd./Bush Homes of East Africa Ltd.
Box 56923, Nairobi, ☎ *506139, FAX: 502739.*

Booking agent for many homestays and ranches.

SOME U.S. COMPANIES DEALING WITH AFRICA

Abercrombie & Kent International (A&K)
(see above)

Bush Homes of East Africa
1786-A Century Blvd. Atlanta, Georgia 30345, ☎ *(404) 325-5088, FAX: (404) 315-9809.*

Exclusive safaris, specializing in Homestay accommodations

CATS (Custom African Travel Services, Inc.)

30 Shepard Street, Cambridge, MA 02138, ☎ *(617) 491-1678, FAX: (617) 491-1042.*

Upmarket, customized safaris, often with an adventurous or exotic touch.

Safariworld!

425 Madison Ave., New York, N.Y. 10017, ☎ *(212) 486-0505, (800) 366-0505, FAX: (212) 486-0783.*

Upmarket safaris.

TRAVCO - Travel Corporation of America

P.O. Box 2630, Newport Beach, California 92658, ☎ *(714) 476-2800 or (800) 992-2004, FAX: (714) 476-2538.*

Upmarket safaris, well-established, cover much of Africa.

CHOOSING A SAFARI

- If you have a guide, check on his/her experience and background. Does the guide have any special expertise? Is the guide familiar with the local people and the region you will visit?
- Any of the larger 4-wheel drive vehicles is better than a mini-bus.
- The driver should be experienced.
- Find out what safety measures are planned for your safari.
- A small group costs less than going by yourself. If the group is too large it is cumbersome. Six to eight people in two vehicles is ideal.

TRAVEL OPTIONS WITHIN KENYA
CAR RENTAL

Various car rental companies operate in Nairobi, Mombasa and Malindi. A valid driver's license (from country of residence, or an International license) is required. Driver must be between the ages of 25 and 70 and have held a license for a minimum of two years.

Major credit cards are accepted. Car rentals and the price of petrol are high by U.S. standards. Saloon/sedan cars as well as 4-Wheel drive safari vehicles can be rented (ranging from $100 to $460 for a one day all-inclusive rate—daily cost can drop to about half of this if you keep the car for a week). Many routes and circuits require 4-wheel drive, especially in the rains. Driving is on the left side of the road. Parks and Reserves are open to private and rented vehicles.

Many travellers prefer to rent a car with a driver. Driving in Kenya is hard work. Having an experienced Kenyan driver who knows the country, the roads, and often a lot about the wildlife, can add to your relaxation if not your privacy. The added expense of a driver is usually very reasonable.

Here is a partial list of car hire agencies. More are listed in the Nairobi Yellow Pages.

Apollo, *Box 42391, NBI,* ☎ *333606/337534, FAX: 214026.*

Avis, *Box 49795, NBI* ☎ *336794/334317, FAX: 215421.*

Budget, (Abercrombie & Kent), *Box 59749, NBI,* ☎ *334904, FAX:332033.*

Central Rent a Car, *Box 49439, NBI,* ☎ *222888, FAX: 339666.*

Concorde Car Hire, *Box 25053 NBI,* ☎ *448653.*

Hertz - UTC, *Box 42196, NBI,* ☎ *331960/331973, FAX: 216871.*

Let's Go Travel, *Box 60342, NBI,* ☎ *340331/213033, FAX: 214713.*

Rasuls, *Box 18127, NBI,* ☎ *558234, FAX: 540341.*

The Car Hire Company, *Box 56707 NBI,* ☎ *225255, FAX: 216553.*

DRIVING

Driving in Kenya is a challenge. Drivers are frequently impatient and incautious. Many vehicles are old, and emission standards unheard of. Most notorious are the Matatus—brightly painted, invariably overloaded minivan taxis who all seem to think they are "king of the road" and totally invincible.

You frequently have to slow down for jolting and often unmarked speedbumps. You may also encounter police check points where you have to wind between lethal metal spikes. Usually only commercial vehicles are made to stop at these check points. Goats in the road, a herd of cattle on the highway or even a real "zebra" crossing may well liven up your trip. Try to make sure you reach your destination before nightfall—driving at night is even worse than in the day and not advisable.

You also have to contend with bad roads. Many tarred roads are in poor repair with potholes and ragged edges. Dirt roads often require 4-Wheel drive, especially on rocky slopes and during the rainy seasons. Travelling from one place to another generally takes longer than you would expect from the projected mileage. It can also be a lot more uncomfortable and dusty than you bargained for.

There are two ways to deal with these problems. Either you can embark on road travel with a sense of adventure, admire the scenery, ride the bumps, brush off the red dust, and think "this is certainly more fun than rush hour traffic at home!" or—you can fly. We suggest flying for at least part of your safari if you can afford it. Game drives will give you a taste of bumps and dust.

FLYING

Jomo Kenyatta Airport in Nairobi, and Moi International Airport in Mombasa are both international airports, but are also used for some in-country flying.

Kenya Airways is the National airline and flies out of Jomo Kenyatta airport in Nairobi. It services Kisumu, Mombasa and Malindi in Kenya. Its reputation for tardiness has improved somewhat. Remember to confirm your booking a day in advance to avoid being bumped. Reservations: ☎ *210771*, Departures/Confirmation: ☎ *229291.*

Wilson Airport is one of the busiest small plane airports in the world. There are regularly scheduled commercial and charter flights and a lot of private planes. Listed below are some of the airlines which operate out of Wilson Airport.

Air Kenya operates scheduled flights from Nairobi to the Masai Mara, Nyeri, Nanyuki, Samburu, Amboseli and the coast (Mombasa, Malindi, Lamu and Kiwayu). Private charters are also available. ☎ *501421/2/3, FAX: 500845.*

Prestige Air/Safari Air Services Ltd. has scheduled flights from Nairobi to the Masai Mara, Nanyuki, and Samburu. It also services Mombasa, Malindi, Lamu and Kiwayu at the coast. Charter flights also available. ☎ *501211/2/3, FAX: 503024.*

Africair/Boskovic Air Charters Ltd. offers charter flights on a variety of different small planes. ☎ *501210/501226, FAX: 505964.*

Excel Aviation Ltd. offers charter flights. ☎ *501751, FAX: 501751.*

Charter rates are usually based on the size of the airplane and the distance to the destination.

There is an Airport Tax of 100ksh for all flights within Kenya.

KENYA RAILWAYS

The only train trip frequently used by tourists is the overnight sleeper between Nairobi and Mombasa. Although some consider this one of the world's great railway journeys, the equipment is old and the romance is dusty. Since most of the journey is at night, you see little from your train window, but save on a night's accommodation. Train meals are for the adventuresome. The first sitting is cleanest. NBI office hours ☎ *221211* outside office hours ☎ *210851*, Mombasa ☎ *(011) 312221.*

TAXIS

Many taxis do not have working meters. Make sure you agree on a price before you start. In town, you might bargain your own deal for a half day or day's tour. Some Nairobi taxi companies:

Archer Cabs ☎ *220289/221935.*

Avenue Car Hire Ltd. ☎ *221666/336442.*

Kenatco ☎ *338311/221561/221523.*

London Taxi ☎ *225123.*

Mini Cabs & Tours ☎ *226944/220743.*

ACCOMMODATION OPTIONS

Kenya has an amazing variety of accommodation types. Hotels range from city high-rises to sprawling thatched beach "villages." You can stay in private homes in the middle of a ranch/game sanctuary or in an "Arabian Nights" Swahili-style house in a fishing village. You can stay in tents in the bush or grass shacks on the beach.

HOMESTAYS

A homestay gives you the closest relationship with the country. You stay in private homes and very often the owners are your hosts and guides. The homes range from up-country colonial game ranches and homey farm houses to elegant villas by sea or lake.

Many of our favorite places to stay in Kenya are the private homestays. When we began our research on this book, we had no idea that there were so many homestay options, or that staying at such places would be so wonderful.

Some of the main features of homestays include:

- Being hosted by people who are willing to share their love and knowledge of Kenya with you. Many host families date back to early European settlement days. There are still some Lords and Ladies among them!

- Personalized and individual treatment—you are one of a "select few" rather than part of a "tourist crowd."

- Staying in some very beautiful homes and ranches—some with fascinating histories and many in stunning and unspoiled settings.

- The opportunity to experience Kenya in a very personal and interactive fashion—you might go on a game walk or a horse ride on a ranch, go fishing or sailing with your host at the coast.

- Enjoying food and service which are often superior to most larger establishments.

- Being free to do what you want in your own time. Don't hesitate to say if you just want to relax and enjoy the view.

TENTS

Most established tented camps in Kenya have very fancy tents which bear no resemblance to most people's mental image of a "tent." They are not cramped, dark, uncomfortable, or a way of roughing it. Often more luxurious than most hotel rooms, some tents even have bidets and four-poster beds. You can even stay in a tent with a beautiful wooden floor and a big bathtub. On the other hand some tents offer more adventure with bucket showers and no electricity. They all tend to be completely enclosed with a floor attached to the sides—to keep out unwanted reptiles or insects. Mesh windows let in light and air, but canvas blinds can be zipped shut for privacy.

Try sleeping in a tent in Africa—it has a certain magic.... feels like an adventure. You hear the night sounds, and you know you are somewhere special.

GRASS SHACKS ON THE BEACH

See "Tents:" but substitute thatch and *makuti* (woven palm leaves) for canvas and put the shack on sand.

In the accommodation section, the descriptions can help you get a good idea if you would enjoy a place or not. The choices are yours.

SAFARI OPTIONS—ON THE MOVE

All the places described in the accommodation section have fixed sites. There are other safari options which involve moving from one campsite to another. These are typically up-market private accompanied safaris offered by well-known guides and small companies. There are also more modest alternatives which involve a greater degree of "roughing it."

You can travel on foot, by four-wheel drive vehicle, on camels, on horses, by ox wagon, by air...These safaris can be focused on wildlife, bird watching, bird shooting, fishing, photography, mountain climbing, anthropology...Check with your travel agents for details.

BALLOON SAFARIS

Early morning hot air balloon trips take off from several places in the Masai Mara (including Little Governor's Camp, Mara Serena Lodge, Mara Safari Club, Fig Tree Camp, and Masai Mara Sopa Lodge). Transportation can be arranged to take you from other lodges and camps to the nearest balloon launching site. These trips are extremely popular and very pricey ($300+ per person, including breakfast).

The Masai Mara has become one of the busiest hot air ballooning centers in the world. While out on early morning game drives in the Mara, you are bound to see one or more brightly colored balloons majestically rising at about the same time as the sun. They look so silent and romantic.

When you splurge on this unique adventure, the excitement starts while it is still dark. Loud, bright flames roar as they heat the air filling the colorful skin of the balloon. Up to 12 passengers climb into the basket grinning in fear-tinged anticipation tinged with a little fear. White knuckles grip the basket edge. You lift up, the burners roar loud and close. You float over forests, savannah, river and game—sometimes soaring way up high, sometimes brushing branches of trees, and sometimes just skimming the tops of termite mounds. Herds of animals scatter below you, a bull elephant with a long shadow crosses a field, there are hippo humps in the curve of the river. It is warmer than you expect—you don't feel the wind when you travel at wind speed. It is also noisier than imagined—the burst and flare from the burners punctuate the commentary of the pilot.

You land for a champagne breakfast in the bush—holding tight to the sides and ducking down as the basket tips and is dragged along the ground. The sides are well-padded and passengers inelegantly crawl out to emerge laughing. A full breakfast is cooked over the balloon burners, animals dot the scene, large hawks fly down for tidbits, and there is a sense of camaraderie among the passengers. Champagne glasses clink—a memorable adventure, complete with your own souvenir flight certificate.

WALKING, HIKING, TREKKING IN KENYA

Another way to experience the adventure of the Kenyan bush is to put one foot in front of the other as directed by knowledgeable guides. Usually designed to make the most of Kenya's spectacular scenery and wildlife, these foot safaris give you the feeling of being part of the life of the bush. Very often, the hiking is combined with game drives either after a lunch in camp or when an early morning hike is designed to rendezvous with camp vehicles at a prearranged place.

Depending on the guide or safari company you choose, you can be totally pampered in camp or you can be responsible for a certain amount of camp life, such as putting up your own tent. Typically, as with other kinds of adventure camping in Kenya, a new camp is set up every day, with the supplies and equipment being transported by camp staff in camp vehicles.

The pace for most walking safaris is considered suitable for hikers of average fitness. However, clients are encouraged to ride the camp vehicles for a rest day or to enjoy staying in camp if the camp is to remain in one place for several days. All hikers are encouraged to have adequate medical insurance before coming to Kenya, and most companies require that a waiver form is signed before the beginning of the safari.

Rates range from $38 to more than $1000 per person, depending on what supplies and services are provided, how many people are included in the safari, and how long the safari lasts.

FOR WALKING SAFARIS CONTACT

1. **Tropical Ice**
   Box 57341, Nairobi. ☎ *740811, FAX: 740826.*

   These are upmarket safaris ranging from mountain treks to slow walks along the remote Galana River in Tsavo. They are led by expert and renowned naturalists such as Clive Ward, author of *The Mountains of Southern Africa* and photographer for *Snowcaps on the Equator,* and Iain Allan, author of *Guide Book to Mount Kenya and Kilimanjaro* and *Snowcaps on the Equator.* Prices cover everything including park fees, rangers, fresh food, beer, sodas and wine. Alcoholic drinks and tipping are extra.

2. Ron Beaton - Off the Beaton Path
c/o Wilderness Trails (K) Ltd./Bush Homes of East Africa Ltd. Box 56923, Nairobi, ☎ 506139, FAX: 502739 REKERO.

Ron Beaton will tailor his adventure safaris to suit. Very often a five-day walking safari will be incorporated into a private homestay at his Rekero Farm at the edge of the Masai Mara. (See accommodation section.)

3. Richard Bonham Safaris Ltd.
Box 24133, Nairobi, ☎ 882521, FAX: 882728.

Richard Bonham will organize unusual safaris to suit. Walking safaris are a specialty of his.

4. Bushbuck Adventures
Box 67449, Nairobi, ☎ 212975, FAX: 218735.

Walking in the hills and plains around their "Out of Africa" camp near the Masai Mara. Maasai guides. Possible to spend nights away from camp in fly camps.

5. Tribal Treks & Wildlife Walks Kentrak Safaris Ltd.
Box 47964, Nairobi, ☎ 441704, FAX: 441690.

These safaris seem a little more basic, with more set itineraries to choose among.

6. Bike Treks: Walking & Cycling in Kenya
Box 14237, Nairobi, ☎ 446371, FAX: 336890.

These are organized by Nigel Arensen, a third generation Kenyan, who also specializes in cycling safaris. Prices range up to $720 per person for a six-day walk.

7.   Hiking & Cycling Kenya Ltd.
Box 39439 Nairobi, ☎ 218336/8, FAX: 224212.

or

Sobek's International Explorers Society
Box 1089 Angel's Camp California 95222 USA, ☎ 800-777-7939.

These trips seem very basic, often using public transportation to and from safari points.

8.   Savage Wilderness Safaris
P.O. Box 44827, Nairobi, ☎ 521590, FAX: 501754.

or

USA Office
925 31st Avenue, Seattle, Washington 98122 USA, ☎ 206-323-1220.

CAMEL SAFARIS

Several different camel safaris are offered in the drier Northern parts of Kenya. They range from regularly scheduled safaris to trips customized to meet the size and time schedule of your group. Typically only four to 12 clients would be on a camel safari at any one time, usually for about five nights. Camel safaris are suspended during the rainy seasons. Prices tend to vary by group size and duration of the safari.

In most cases, camels are used primarily as pack animals to move camp from one site to the next. You can also ride camels if you like, or you can walk. Camels are rather bad tempered and not especially comfortable to ride—many clients spend more time on foot than on the camels. Typically, you walk through dramatic, unspoiled scenery with your guides. You may encounter wild animals or occasionally come across Samburu herdsmen or small tribal settlements. You don't have to be particularly fit for these safaris. The pace and amount of walking will be geared to the group. You usually reach the new campsite around midday, rest after lunch and take an optional late afternoon game walk. Each night a tented camp is set up in a preselected spot. Dinner is prepared for you, a camp fire is lit, and water is warmed for a bucket shower. The night noises of the bush surround you. Above are brilliantly star-spattered skies.

Simon Evans Ewaso River Camel Safari Bookings Ltd.
Box 56707, Nairobi, ☎ *225255, FAX: 216553.*

Highly recommended. Departs from Colcheccio Ranch, north of Rumuruti. All trips customized. Minimum of five clients. Most safaris are guided
by Simon or a relative. Beautiful campsites next to the Ewaso Nyiro River.
Good food and thoughtful service. $150 per person per day. Transport
from Nairobi and back $640 for a nine pax vehicle. "Our young teenagers
had the time of their lives...we saw elephant, kudu and buffalo...airy mesh
tents allowed us to watch the full moon from our beds...each campsite was
more remarkable than the last...possibly the best thing we've done in
Kenya." (quote from long-term Kenya resident).

Kenya Camel Safaris Let's Go Travel
Box 60342, Nairobi, ☎ *340331, FAX: 336890.*

Recommended. Departs every Monday from Nairobi. The group meets in
Isiolo town (north of Timau, south of Samburu) and is transported from
there to the base camp. These safaris cater from four to 20 people, last for
three or five nights, and are usually guided by Malcolm Destro and/or his
wife. Campsites are near the Ewaso Nyiro river. When the weather is dry,
clients often sleep under mosquito netting rather than in a tent. Cost is
$560 per person for a five night safari and $450 per person for a three night
safari. Optional transport from Nairobi is $100 per person return.

Desert Rose Camels Ltd.
Box 44801, Nairobi, ☎ *228936, FAX: 212160.*

Known for being more adventurous than other camel safaris. All trips customized—several choices of where to start from: Samburu, Mathews
Range, Maralal. Minimum six days. Usually 4–8 clients. Guides Helen
Douglas Defreshne, Emma or Yoav Chen. Cost $500 for the group and
then $65 per person, per day.

Yare Safaris Co. Ltd.
Box 63006, Nairobi, ☎ *214099, FAX: 213445.*

Weekly departure on Saturdays from Nairobi to Maralal for five night camel
safari. Typically 2–6 clients. Campsites are moved by Land Rover and set up
near the Ewaso Nyiro river. Clients have a Samburu guide and ride camels
or walk. Total cost (including transport) $300 per person. Bring your own
sleeping bag... Mixed reviews.

DONKEY SAFARIS

Samburu Trails Trekking Safaris
Box 40, Maralal.

or

Wilderness Trails (K) Ltd./Bush Homes of East Africa Ltd.
Box 56923, Nairobi, ☎ *506139, FAX: 502739.*

Although donkeys carry all the supplies and gear, these are essentially walking safaris for the fit, the adventurous and lovers of wild and remote places of beauty. The trails wind and climb through magnificent landscapes in the northern region of Kenya—around Losiolo (near Maralal). Clients are likely to see wild animals and many species of birds. These safaris typically include at least four nights camping under the stars in comfortable but unpretentious style—there are camp beds, safari showers, and meals cooked over the campfire. Hosted by Peter Faull and his wife.

HORSEBACK SAFARIS

Experienced horseback riders can enjoy the unique experience of exploring some spectacular wild savannah and bush on even terms with the wild animals. You begin your ride from a base camp or ranch house to follow game trails cross-country on horseback. There is no sign of modern roads or even telephone poles, just space and freedom for the four-to-six-hour ride to the saddle safari camp, usually set near a shady waterhole.

The rides begin in the early morning, which is also the best time for viewing wildlife. There are stops for drinks and lunch. You arrive at the day's camp in time for tea and hot showers, with everything all set up and waiting for you. The "syces" or grooms attend to the horses as well as provide additional protection at night. You can relax or take a walk around camp before sundown and later enjoy your meal around the traditional campfire.

Saddle safaris usually use specially designed English trekking saddles (there are no Western saddles) and Anglo-Arab Somali ponies. The camp moves daily by truck along bush roads that the main group avoids. Some saddle safaris combine horseback and four-wheel drive photographic segments, some are "no frills" with riders taking care of some of their own camp needs, some include a "rest" at a house on the beach. There are several different itineraries to choose from, and some trips are offered on a guaranteed departure basis with the price changing depending on the numbers of riders who actually go on the trip.

As a rider you must have your own accident and medical insurance before arriving in Kenya. Only riders confident at all paces are accepted. You must have suitable riding attire including warm clothing and a waterproof jacket, coat, or poncho in case of rain.

For those horsemen who wish to ride as a relaxing form of exercise or to add an extra dimension to their stay at a ranch, lodge, or hotel, there are a number of places offering guests opportunity. There are some where the trail ponies are even suitable for beginners. See accommodation section for details.

For a horseback safari in Kenya contact the following:

I.   Safaris Unlimited (Africa) Ltd.
P.O. Box 24181, Nairobi, ☎ *891168/890435, FAX: 891113/882723.*

or

FITS Equestrian
685 Latin Road, Solvang, California 93463 USA, ☎ *805-688-9494, FAX: 805-688-2943.*

Organized by Tony Church, this was the first saddle safari company in Kenya. Prices for a full safari range from $804 to $4630 depending on number of days and numbers of riders on safari. Prices cover ground transfers only, and bottled drinks are supplied on a Pay Bar basis. There are no safaris scheduled for the April-May rainy season.

2.   Offbeat Safaris Ltd.
P.O. Box 56923, Nairobi, ☎ *506139, FAX: 502739.*

or

Equitour Worldwide Riding Holidays
Bitterroot Ranch, Box 807, Dubois, Wyoming 82513 USA, ☎ *800-545-0019, FAX: 307-455-2354.*

Directed in Kenya by Tristan Voorspuy, who was trained by Tony Church.

3.   Richard Bonham Safaris Ltd.
P.O. Box 24133, Nairobi, ☎ *882521, FAX: 882728.*

Richard Bonham is known for arranging unusual safaris. He will work with riders to create riding safaris suitable to their skills. He knows many areas of Kenya well, including the Chyulu Hills.

CYCLING SAFARIS

This is the newest form of adventure safari in Kenya. It follows the idea of meeting experiences in the wild as a participant. Most of the organized trips use a combination of cycling, walking, boating and traveling by vehicle to camps that follow a set itinerary with you.

Some companies pamper you and do all the camp work, some ask you to participate in camp chores. Again, prices vary depending on numbers of cyclists and number of days required for the safari. They range from $360 per person for three days to $720 per person for six days. If you do not bring your own, a mountain bike is provided.

For further information contact:

1. **Bike Treks: Walking & Cycling in Kenya**
   P.O. Box 14237 Nairobi, ☎ 446371, FAX: 336890.

   These are organized by Nigal Arensen, a third generation Kenyan, who specializes in cycling safaris.

2. **Hiking & Cycling Kenya Ltd.** *P.O. Box 39439, Nairobi, ☎ 218336/8, FAX: 224212.*

   or

   Sobek's International Explorers Society
   P.O. Box 1089, Angel's Camp, California 95222 USA, ☎ 800-777-7939.

   These trips seem very basic, often using public transportation to and from safari points.

3. **Gametrackers**
   P.O. Box 62042, Nairobi, ☎ 338927, FAX: 330903.

WHITE WATER RAFTING

Depending on water levels, White Water Adventures can give you rafting trips ranging from 40 to 400 miles, from one day to several weeks, and all at a level of luxury designed to suit you. Rafts are put in on the Tana or the Athi River. You can see plenty of bird life and wildlife along the shore. Class III to V rapids are interspersed with calmer water.

For longer trips, you camp along the river. Rafting trips can be combined with caving in the Chyulu Hills or game drives in Tsavo or Amboseli National Parks. You are required to sign a release and assumption of risk before making the trip.

Savage Wilderness Safaris Ltd.
   P.O. Box 44827, Nairobi, ☎ 521590.

USA Office
   925 31st Avenue, Seattle, Washington 98122 USA, ☎ 206-323-1220.

BIRD SHOOTING SAFARIS

According to Mr. Charles W. Waring, III, of Charleston, South Carolina, bird shooting is good in Kenya, especially on safari with Joe Cheffings of Bateleur Safaris Limited, who has organized personal safaris for more than 25 years.

One of Kenya's best professional hunters, Joe also offers photographic safaris throughout Kenya, though he specializes in bird shooting. He makes certain you are far, far away from other tourists. His favorite haunt is located in arid acacia woodlands over 100 miles south of Nairobi and roughly 40 miles north of the Tanzanian border.

The private camp is set up in the traditional East African style with a shower tent, a toilet tent, mess tent, and sleeping tents with camp beds. There are lots of friendly staff to look after laundry and the day to day running of the camp. All meals, beer, and soft drinks are included, and the food in camp is delicious.

The day begins early with tea or coffee delivered to your tent. You can have breakfast before you go out or after you come back; it is up to you to set the schedule. After you arrive at the waterhole, expect flocks of sandgrouse and doves. They come by the hundreds. The limits are generous: 20 per person per day for sandgrouse, 25 for doves, and 15 for a mixed bag of ground birds. Not only can you expect very challenging shooting, you may also see magnificent Mt. Kilimanjaro!

The rest of the day will include lunch back in camp and naps to avoid midday equatorial heat. Perhaps you might request a game drive at nearby Amboseli National Park. Afternoon ground bird shooting includes guinea fowl, spurfowl, and francolin. Sundowners in the cool of the evening and safari stories by the warm campfire are the traditional finish to an exciting day.

Walking around camp you can be sure of seeing plains game and perhaps a rare lesser kudu. You can hear lion roaring at night. You will be amazed at the quantity and brightness of stars in the East African sky. With Bateleur Safaris, you will experience the beauty of one of the last pieces of "old Africa."

Prices: $350 per person per day (exact amount depends on the number of clients) plus 10% more per shooter per day plus cartridges and spirits at cost.

For the most current information about guns and licenses, contact Joe or Sporting International direct.

Joe Cheffings, Bateleur Safaris Ltd.
Box 42562, Nairobi, ☎/FAX: 254-2-891007.

or his agent:

Sporting International Inc.
13201 Northwest Freeway, Suite 880-C, Houston, Texas 77040,
☎ 1-800-231-6352.

Bird Shooting Safaris are also offered by the following:

Guy Grant of El Karama Ranch
  c/o Let's Go Travel, P.O. Box 60342, Nairobi, ☎ *340331, FAX: 336890.*

Richard Bonham Safaris Ltd.
  P.O. Box 24133, Nairobi, ☎ *882521, FAX: 882728.*

FISHING IN KENYA

Mr. Charles W. Waring, III, of Charleston, South Carolina, reports that fishing in Kenya is as good as the finest anywhere, depending on what you are after and the time of the year. While Kenya is best known for big game fishing, you can also fish for trout, bass, nile perch and tiger fish.

BIG GAME FISHING

From Ernest Hemingway to European royalty, all have found the challenge of landing a big marlin, sailfish, shark, or yellowfin tuna to be worth the trip. Chartering a boat is not inexpensive, but it is very reasonable in terms of international standards ($500–$650 per day and $350–$465 per half day) includes everything for up to four fishermen except tips).

The main centers for big game fishing are Lamu, Malindi, Watamu, Mombasa, and the Pemba Channel Area (Msambeweni, Funzi Island, and Shimoni). While many hotels can arrange big game fishing, many serious fishermen place high value on the Pemba Channel Inn (formerly the Pemba Channel Fishing Club). Hemingways in Watamu is one of the best fishing hotels. Both Hemingways and its middle grade neighbor hotel, Ocean Sports, sponsor fishing tournament weekends as well as chartering fishing boats.

All of the coast hotels are well-known, and booking should be made as far as a year in advance for peak high season fishing in February–March. Some captains are highly recommended and can be booked privately. Mr. Andrew Wright, captain of the Snowgoose, is one of these. He can be reached through **Baharini Ventures**, *P.O. Box 124, Malindi, (FAX: 31650 or* ☎ *20879).*

The more adventurous fisherman can hire outfitters such as Mike Carr-Hartley of **Carr-Hartley Safaris**, *P.O. Box 59762, Nairobi (*☎ *882453/882810 FAX: 884542)* or the Paul family of **Kingfisher Safaris**, *P.O. Box 29, Malindi* (☎ *21168).* The most productive sailfishing is at the remote northernmost tip of the Kenyan Coast, and the outfitter sets up a private camp very close to where you will be fishing.

You should decide what fish you would like to try for before you go out to avoid disappointment. If you stay close to shore you are likely to get bonito, dorado (dolphin), yellowfin, sailfish, or kingfish. If you want big marlin, say so. Your captain will take you far out to concentrate on spots known to hold the big ones. You risk finding nothing, but you may get the chance to have the fight of your life with one of the giants of the sea.

Many captains will use light tackle at your request, which can add tremendous sport to bringing in a good fighter, even one which may not be that big. Remember, you have chartered the boat and have the right to add your direction to the trip. A "tagged release" policy is encouraged for willing fishermen. You will receive a certificate verifying your catch.

TROUT

If trout are your prey and you enjoy beautiful mountain scenery, you will love the Aberdare Mountains. Since there are few tourists in the area, it is peaceful and quiet. Although the fish are not large, they are plentiful, despite the bait fishing of temporary residents.

A map of the area is a good investment regardless of how far you wish to go off the beaten track, but an easy trip for beginners is the Fisherman's Camp in the Aberdare National Park. Check with the Kenya Wildlife Service (KWS) about road conditions and book one of the bandas at the camp through them. KWS can also help you to obtain a fishing license. You should always fish with a companion in the Aberdares as wild animals (including lion) and slippery paths and rocks can be dangerous. It is also a good idea to take two reliable four-wheel drive vehicles on the trip.

The Chania River is very near the camp and holds significant numbers of trout. Above the bridge is a very narrow stretch of water, but you can pull out many trout in a very short period of time. (You won't have much space to cast, but if you practice on the wide stretch below the bridge, you'll be ready.)

Below the bridge are some lovely pools full of trout, and if you continue to hike along the river, you will find some very large pools with larger fish. Roll casting is best here due to overhanging branches. Depending on whether fishing conditions are dry or wet, the best flies to use are the Adams Irresistible, Kenya Bug, Mrs. Simpson, and Royal Coachman. **Kenya Trout and Salmon Flies Limited (☎ *569790*)** of Nairobi is a good place to buy your flies. With three or four days advance ordering, they can tie a few dozen for you for an extremely reasonable price.

Another good place for the beginner is the Aberdare Country Club. The Club stocks the stretch of the river running along the boundary of the Club's property, and the friendly staff at reception will gladly direct you to the best fishing spots. If you walk for about two kilometers upstream, you will find a very large pool that looks like a fisherman's dream. It is. If you fish this pool, you will very likely have your own fish for breakfast!

LARGER TROUT

For the experienced fisherman, the more remote streams in the Aberdares hold what you would expect: larger fish. Verify your route with a warden before going, but the largest fish caught in the Aberdares are often a result of long hikes through beautiful terrain. The bamboo line is mainly below the boundary of the park and has some very difficult-to-reach streams, but the trout there are the largest in all of the Aberdares.

The streams on Mt. Kenya are also worthwhile. If you are very fit, a seven-hour hike to Lake Alice will produce five- and six-pound rainbows. This requires camping for the night at 12,000 feet. Bring a warm sleeping bag!

It is easy to find the Sirimon River on the northwestern side of Mt. Kenya. About 15 kilometers past Nanyuki, a sign on the right points to the Sirimon

Gate. The unmarked road on the left leads to the river. After turning off the main road, take the first right to an open area below the road (only 10 minutes from the highway). Park. Walk upstream. You will find many pools with over-hanging branches to test your patience and skill.

The Cherangani Hills are known to hold the biggest brown trout in all of Kenya, but it is a long drive from Nairobi. Nearby bandas may be booked in Nairobi, and the proprietor will gladly give directions to fishing spots.

Many dams in the highlands also hold fish, but the best ones are on private property, so getting written permission is a must. The Kericho Area is very accessible to the beginner, with the streams and dams controlled by the **Kericho Sotik Fishing Association**, *P.O. Box 281, Kericho.*

For a day trip from Nairobi, try the stream on top of the Rift Valley escarpment on the road to Lake Naivasha. After you go under the overpass (about 40 minutes from Nairobi), take your first right. Turn right again and follow the road to a village. Ask for directions to the river. For a small tip, you can hire a guide who knows exactly where the good pools are. You should always bring a guard to stay with your car while you are fishing.

Trout fishing in Kenya is always changing. Some places are better at different times of the year. Mr. John Lyal of **Bookings Limited in Nairobi** (☎ *220365/225255*) is a reliable contact. As a fisherman himself, he can advise on where to go for any type of fishing in Kenya. He can make bookings for lodges and hotels at the coast and elsewhere, and he is the agent for Mr. Mike Carr-Hartley, one of Kenya's best fishermen and outfitters.

NILE PERCH

If you are after nile perch, you can go to Lake Turkana or to Lake Victoria. Going to Lake Victoria is the easier trip, and there are several luxurious fishing lodges on various islands, where fish over 100 pounds are brought in regularly.

Lake Turkana has tiger fish in addition to perch, but a rough two-day drive or a chartered flight are the only ways of reaching the lake. You can try fly fishing for perch, but Mike Carr-Hartley is probably the only one who can guarantee your success in this most challenging venture. The lodges around the lake and on Central Island are very Spartan, and a private tented safari is the better way to go, though pricey.

BASS

Bass fishing is not exceptional in Kenya, but if you are visiting Lake Naivasha, why not try it? Some fish are more than five pounds, and some boats have brought in as many as 50 fish.

Four hours from Nairobi, Mr. Clive Aggett has a ranch near Rumuruti with dams holding bass and rainbow trout. You can book a cottage on his largest dam. Commercial duck shooting could be combined with fishing. Ask for details if this appeals. Write him at P.O. Box #2, Rumuruti.

Across Kenya, there are many small ponds, dams and streams which may be worth trying. Mr. Waring has visited and proven all the places listed above. However, any fisherman knows catching a fish is never a sure bet. No matter what the catch, however, fishing in Kenya always takes you to beautiful settings which never fail to lure anglers back to Kenya.

SMOOTHING YOUR WAY

A potpourri of safari tips:

- If you want a double bed, ask for it when booking, make sure it is noted on your voucher, and ask for it again when checking in! Sometimes they are available.

- Ask for a description of special activities. Maybe there is a game walk or a snorkeling trip that is not mentioned at check-in.

- Overseas telephone calls are very expensive—plan ahead.

- Game park fees: often an extra. Be prepared.

- Decaffeinated coffee & sugar substitutes are not readily available. Bring your own.

- Bush stops: Easier in a skirt. Carry tissue or T.P.

- Washcloths: Bring your own. There will be towels.

- Cucumber slices: Cucumber slices are great naturally pH-balanced skin wipes, very cooling on all exposed skin and soothing to tired eyes as well. Cucumber slices are also very thirst quenching! Don't forget your pocket-knife.

- Bottled water: Carry some.

- Beer: Try different brands. They are good and inexpensive.

- Baridi sana: What to say if you want your drinks cold.

- Bargains: Fresh flowers including roses and orchids; massages and manicures, sodas, most handicrafts, cashews and macadamia nuts, coffee and tea.

- Expensive items: Gasoline (petrol), wine, photography, boutique fashions.

- Frustrations: Telephones that don't work, power failures, water shortages, time spent waiting, bad roads, manic traffic (including roundabouts).

- Sunblock, insect repellent, a hat: Carry these.

- Electricity: Don't count on it everywhere you go. Some lodges and camps don't have it or don't have it 24 hours a day.

- Solar heated showers: Best taken at the end of a sunny day. The water won't be hot the next morning.

- Laundry services • Remember many hotels, lodges, and camps have these.

- Morning game drives need windbreakers; some evenings need warm wraps.

- Bathrooms go under these aliases: W.C., choo, loo, long-drop, cloakroom, restroom.

HOW TO USE THE
ACCOMMODATION SECTIONS

These sections have been divided geographically. Each chapter deals with a different part of the country. The map below defines the areas covered in the different chapters.

Each chapter has a brief introduction to the area. After each introduction we discuss the hotels, lodges, homestays, tented camps, ranches and grass shacks in that area. These have been grouped according to the symbols that follow below.

Hotel/Lodge

 Tented Camp

 Grass Shacks/Tents on the Beach

 Homestay

 Ranch/Sanctuary

Our favorites appear first in each group, and we have devoted more detail to these places. In smaller print is a brief description of other places we visited (or know of) in the area. Where we have no clear preferences, we have alphabetized our listings.

We make no claims to have a comprehensive list of all tourist accommodations, and we are well aware that new places are opening all the time, while others are closing. Since there is a frequent turnover of chefs and even managers, food and service change. So, except where there is an established and reliable history of good food or service, we have focused our attention on the more enduring aspects of a place—location, design, history, ambiance.

HATS OFF

We have marked our favorite places with traditional safari hats (topis). "Three Hats" is our highest rating. This means that all three of us agreed that this place was special and stood out from the rest. Our hat awards are personal and were often influenced by ambiance, location, and activities. The "best" in our view was not necessarily a function of facilities or amenities. Sometimes it was the lack of them that made a place special. Our hats have no particular relationship to any Kenyan or international star system. The hats and our descriptions tell you how it feels to be in a place rather than how it measures up to any set criteria. "Phantom" hats have been awarded to places which were not yet operational when we visited.(See "Top Topis" list at end of the book.)

MONEY BAGS REQUIRED

Prices in Kenya tend to vary according to season and market conditions. There are frequent promotional specials, package rates, and often discounts for residents, families, diplomats, conferences, and tour groups. Because of extremes in variation, we have not included specific tariffs for each listing. Instead, we have classified hotels by the number of "moneybags" it would require to stay there based on the 1995 double occupancy, high season rates.

💰 = $100	**Per Double**
💰💰💰💰	**OVER $400**
💰💰💰💰	**$300—$399**
💰💰💰	**$200—$299**
💰💰	**$100—$199**
💰	**UNDER $100**

Most tariffs in Kenya are now quoted in American dollars (used above) or British pounds sterling.

Except for city and coastal hotels, most rates include full-board. Some tariffs also include additional extras such as watersports, game drives, horse riding etc. which could add substantially to the basic price if purchased separately. It is to your advantage to check out all options and activities being offered by a hotel since they are not always advertised.

In Kenya, a voucher system is frequently used for confirmation and advance payment of bookings. You often need to show this voucher for entry into the property. If you pay for any extras, be sure they are listed on the voucher. Although you may request certain rooms, you have no real guarantee of getting them. Your chances improve if you contact the hotel directly.

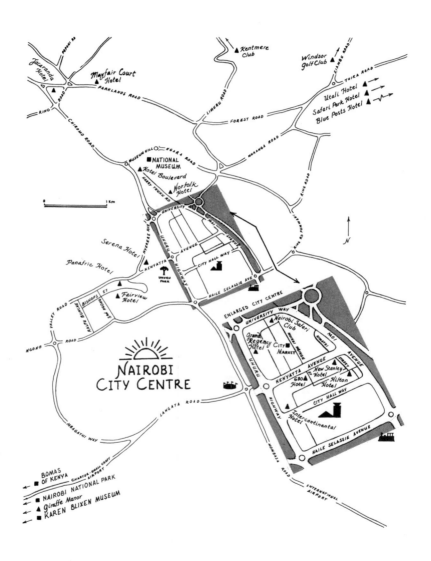

NAIROBI

Nairobi is the largest city in East Africa. It began as a shanty town depot of the East African Railroad in 1899. In a little over 90 years it has become one of the major cities of modern Africa and a headquarters of the United Nations. It is a vibrant and growing city—a mosaic of many races and cultures.

Most of the many tourists to Kenya only spend about one or two nights in Nairobi. From a variety of sightseeing options, we recommend:

The Nairobi National Game Park

(11,300 hectares). The Park is not far from the city center, but gives you a real bush experience. You'll see the most game except elephant. This is possibly your best chance of seeing rhino. Stay in your vehicle.

AFEW Giraffe Center

In Langata. See giraffe eye to eye and feed them by hand—long, sticky, blue tongues and giant eyelashes. Fun for children and adults. Tea room, gift shop and nature trails. Operated by African Fund for Endangered Wildlife.

Karen Blixen Museum

Pleasant house and gardens. Worth a visit if you read the book. The nearby Karen Blixen Coffee Garden, gallery and gift shop echo themes of the museum.

Bomas of Kenya

Tribal dancing in an amphitheater and displays of traditional Kenyan home-steads (boma). Many tour groups and heavy-duty souvenir selling.

National Museum

There is alot to see, famous for Leakey pre-history discoveries and tribal artifacts.

Tourist time in Nairobi is also often spent shopping—searching out Kenyan mementoes and gifts to take home. There are soapstone carvings, wonderful ethnic jewelry, many wooden carvings, colorful cloth *kanga* and *kikoi*. Most hotels have souvenir shops. African Heritage shops (downtown and on the airport road) have a broad selection and good displays. If you are more adventurous, try the block of small blue *duka* across the road from the Nairobi City Market Building. Leave behind your valuables, but take your humor, patience and bargaining skills and have fun. Downtown Nairobi is full of souvenir shops. Farther out in the suburbs are Utamaduni (an up-market craft center) and Kazuri Beads (original ceramics) in Karen, and the Craft Market and Undugu (co-op store) in the Westlands area.

WHERE TO STAY

Hotels in the Nairobi area are either in the city center, just beyond the center, or in the city suburbs. Price is not necessarily linked to location. Many of these hotels could be anywhere in the world and most are acceptable rather than exceptional.

City Center Hotels tend to be high-rises on city streets—lots of shops, activity and noise. They are handy for those conducting business in the city and good for tourists who want to be in the "hub" of Nairobi.

Beyond City Center Hotels tend to have gardens, are usually low-rise and have less traffic noise. Some are a short walk or an inexpensive taxi ride into town.

City Suburb Hotels tend to have a more defined character and extensive grounds. Most are 15 or more minutes from downtown and farther from the airport.

CITY CENTER HOTELS

As this book goes to press, there appears to be a "race for renovation" among the leading city hotels. None too soon. A great many of the rooms looked tired and tawdry. Fabrics, overwhelmingly in browns and greens seem to be wearily serving overtime. To make matters worse, the large new suburban hotels are wooing away tourist trade, and a brand new high-rise hotel has just opened in the city center. In addition, international tourism has been affected by world recession. Many downtown hotels have not kept pace with the business demands of today. Huge function/conference rooms are not enough: business centers with fax machines and modern electronics are needed.

So...it's "time to renovate." We heard of proposed state-of-the-art telephone/communication systems. We saw beautiful and elegant interior decor in "sample" guest rooms. We learned of applications for casino licenses, plans for lobby face-lifts, and the introduction of business services. After renovations, there could be some very attractive hotel options in the city center. Since no city center hotels currently qualify as "best" hotels, we have simply listed them alphabetically.

HOTEL INTER-CONTINENTAL NAIROBI
Hotel Inter-Continental, Box 30353, Nairobi
☎ *335550, FAX: 214617*

The Hotel Inter-Continental Nairobi is part of the international chain and is located in downtown Nairobi, bordering on the Uhuru Highway and convenient to the Kenyatta Conference Center. This large seven-story hotel with 440 rooms has a wide range of services and facilities.

The spacious lobby with its hand-painted faux-marble pillars and scattered seating has a bustling international air. There are tourists in khaki shorts clutching binoculars, African businessmen in pinstriped suits, European aircrews, and even a Japanese courtesy desk. Phones are ringing, luggage is being stacked, and the doorman is trying to untangle a traffic jam.

There are three restaurants. The Chateau Bar and Restaurant on the top floor with windows right around, is popular for its views over Nairobi and dancing in the evenings. On the ground level are the Pool Terrace Restaurant, which overlooks the pool, and a coffee shop.

Two heated pools (one for children) are in a huge patio area with many loungers and chairs around umbrella tables. Food and drinks can be served outside, and landscaping and planters add color.

The guest rooms are off claustrophobic passageways which seem to stretch on and on. There are definite plans to rehabilitate the room decor which is unacceptably tired and worn at the moment. We saw a sample guest room which had been beautifully and stylishly furnished with many luxurious and comfortable touches. Hooray! Some rooms have pleasant views across a park and towards the Parliament Buildings.

In a city with major parking problems, the Inter-Continental is constructing a multistory car park. This will be a particular boon when the hotel has large functions in the evening.

Accommodations

All rooms have air conditioning, TV with in-house videos, phones and minibar stocked on request. There are a handful of suites including a very large executive suite which can include three bedrooms.

Other Facilities

Bank, shopping arcade, travel agencies, large function and conference rooms, business center and services, pool, beauty salon, health spa, casino, Six Continents Club Lounge, airport shuttle service.

GRAND REGENCY HOTEL

Grand Regency Hotel, Box 40511, Nairobi
☎ 211199, FAX: 217120

This new and fancy 300-room hotel combines executive sophistication with modern comfort. Located in Nairobi's newest up-market business area, this white-wash and solar glass high-rise overlooks Uhuru Park.

The hotel center is a soaring multi-story atrium. A gleaming glass mosaic suggests ethnic bead work as it rises in swirls of color to rooftop skylights many floors above. Local marble and granite are softened by hanging plants. Brass and mirrors multiply light and space. Glass elevators to room levels give panoramic views of the atrium bar, restaurant and piano lounge below. (Shades of Hyatt Regencys!)

A very large outdoor terrace has a roofed pool, glass windshields and views of the park and Nairobi skyline. The hotel boasts the largest ballroom/conference room in Kenya. Shimmering with the cut glass of ceiling chandeliers, it can accommodate 1500 guests.

Nairobi has waited and wondered about this hotel. Ownership changed hands while it was being constructed, and its opening kept being delayed. When it finally did open with advertising heralding its modernity and luxury, it got unplanned front-page media attention as well when ownership changed once again—this time seized by the Central Bank of Kenya. No doubt there will be a new owner soon.

Accommodations

Rooms are on open levels around the atrium. Each has a sitting area including a desk. Rooms are carpeted, have mahogany furniture and large windows. All have TV, video, telephone and minibar. Bathrooms are well-equipped with bath/shower, bidets, hairdryers, guest robes and a telephone. There are 40 suites and one Presidential Suite.

Other Facilities

À la carte restaurant, 24-hour coffee shop, health center, Reuters business center, parking for 180, customer service counter, private Summit Club with restaurant and rooftop lounge, shopping arcade, casino, airport shuttle.

NAIROBI HILTON

Nairobi Hilton, Box 30624, Nairobi
☎ *334000, FAX: 339462*

The distinctive circular tower of the Nairobi Hilton is a landmark in downtown Nairobi. It can accommodate more than 600 business travellers and tourists. Its ground floor covers a small city block, with a row of shops, offices and restaurants lining all sides. A massive makonde wood sculpture seems to teem with life at the main entrance to the hotel, echoing the sidewalk crowds and frontage street flooded with "London" taxis, tourist group mini-buses, and other vehicles of all descriptions. Through the main doors of the hotel, the reception area is full of activity and the impression of people on the move. However, thick carpets, cool granite friezes high on the walls, and high ceilings reaching up two floors or more have a calming effect.

Most of the rooms are located in the cylindrical tower and have at least one curved wall with big picture windows, many with panoramic views of Nairobi. Room decor is pleasant, but not distinctive, even rather tired. However, like many of Nairobi's downtown hotels, the Hilton has major plans for remodeling and redecorating.

The Hilton has extensive meeting and conference rooms, including a very large and newly redecorated ballroom. Most of these are on the Mezzanine level which can be reached from the lobby via the grand curving stairway. The Hilton's Residents' Lounge is wonderful—reminiscent of an Edwardian living room. There are comfortable groupings of sofas and wingback chairs; polished wood bookcases, desks, and overhead beams; and accents of brass in lamps and at the bar. The lighting is good, but not harsh, and the fireplace is warming. It is truly inviting, a home away from home.

The Hilton has a wide range of restaurants and bars. You can choose from an informal pizzeria, Pool Terrace snack bar, English-style pub, and the Mara Restaurant, which is open all day. For more elegant dining, the Amboseli Grill is open for lunch and for dinner, when there is also dancing.

Accommodations

Standard rooms have either twin beds or a queen-sized bed. Suites have sitting and dining areas and one or two bedrooms, and there are six parlor rooms with space for a sitting area. There are also 24 more spacious rooms with French doors opening onto the pool terrace. All rooms have ensuite modern bathrooms with plenty of hot water from the Hilton's own wells. Guest rooms also have air conditioning, direct-dial telephone, radio, electronic safe, mini-bar stocked on request, hair dryer, and color television.

Other Facilities

Business Center, health club with gym, doctor/dentist, packaging service, travel agency, airlines office, parking, boutiques, beauty and barber shop, drugstore, newsstand, photo shop, and East African Wildlife Office and Shop.

NAIROBI SAFARI CLUB

The Nairobi Safari Club, Box 43564, Nairobi
☎ 330621, FAX: 331201

The Nairobi Safari Club is an all-suite hotel managed by Pullman International with the promise of comfort and privacy for every guest. The hotel is a striking white circular tower rippling with vertical rows of bay windows and balconies. It is located on University Way across from the University. The entry is elegant with broad white marble steps and facade, a dramatic cascade of tropical plants and a handsome brass plaque announcing The Nairobi Safari Club.

A doorman in caped livery greets you with pomp and smiles. The circular reception area is somewhat dark with wood panelling. You are almost overwhelmed by the thick carpets, chandeliers, brass friezes of African bush themes, leather armchairs and striking arrangements of tropical flowers. A circular fountain with sheets of falling water is a dramatic focal point.

The hotel is run as a social club, with hotel guests having temporary memberships. In the center of the hotel, the Kirinyaga Lounge gives residents a private club lounge and reading room furnished with more leather armchairs and cut-glass mirrors, lamps and barware. Down the hall, the Kirinyaga Restaurant serves an à la carte menu in a room heavy with mirrors, linen, crystal and silver. Both rooms are somewhat dark and stuffy with no windows, but certainly recall the more formal traditions of London clubs.

In contrast, the Brasserie and Safari Bar bring in the light with floor to ceiling windows. The Brasserie is open for snacks and meals, and the Safari Bar serves snacks and drinks on two airy levels overhung with ferns.

There are 146 suites in the hotel including four luxurious penthouse suites with plenty of space for entertaining and very beautifully furnished. Other suite sizes vary, and some are very small. Furnishings in all but the penthouse suites are somewhat tired. However, suites have comfortable and separate sitting areas which could be desirable for those of you that wish to have a longer stay.

Accommodations

All suites have sleeping, sitting, and eating areas or rooms. There are three telephones, TV, mini-bar, 24-hour room service, and ensuite bathrooms, some with bidet.

Other Facilities

Outdoor swimming pool with sun terrace and snackbar, conference facilities, health center with exercise room, airport shuttle, parking, boutique, gift and sundry shop.

NEW STANLEY HOTEL
Sarova Hotels Ltd., Box 30680
☎ *333248, FAX: 211472*

Located on the corner of Kimathi Street and Kenyatta Avenue, the New Stanley Hotel has been a central landmark of Nairobi since 1906. It was first opened to cater to the needs of Kenya's fledgling railroad staff. Today it can accommodate more than 400.

Over the years, young travelers have made a tradition of visiting the hotel's famous sidewalk Thorn Tree Cafe. The young Ernest Hemingway and other famous travelers liked to talk and people watch there. The cafe today does not live up to the romance of its history. However, left messages, which sometimes wait months for pick-up, are still fastened to the trunk of the cafe's live thorn tree spreading its branches above.

Compared to the size of the hotel, the New Stanley's lobby seems small, dark, and crowded with guests coming and going. There are dark leather furnishings and wood panelling. However, the place feels lively, and the rather dim corridor beyond reception beckons with glass shop fronts displaying fine jewelry and gifts.

On the first floor, the Safari Bar overlooks the colorful crowds of Kenyatta Avenue through floor to ceiling glass walls. You feel you are suspended in air. The Tate Room, the hotel's main restaurant, serves an à la carte menu and is open for lunch and dinner. The grand ballroom has been recently redecorated.

There is a wide range of room sizes in the hotel. Room decor is very tired, with colors and furniture that have seen better days. Hallways seem dingy and dark. However, Sarova Hotels plan extensive redecoration for the New Stanley in the near future.

High on the fifth floor of the hotel with views over Nairobi is a strikingly tiled swimming pool, large enough for recreation and laps.

SIX EIGHTY HOTEL
Six Eighty Hotel, Box 43436, Nairobi
☎ *332680, Telex: 22513*

This hotel, built in 1972, has 340 rooms on 10 floors. Now, it needs a face-lift. The hotel is rather unwelcoming and unexciting, with tired linoleum floors and carpeting. Guests may use the pool at the Boulevard Hotel, as there is none at the "Six-Eighty."

BEYOND CITY CENTER HOTELS

THE NORFOLK HOTEL

Lonrho Hotels Kenya Ltd., Box 58581, Nairobi
☎ *216940, FAX: 216796*

The Norfolk Hotel's international reputation for hospitality and excellence began with its opening on Christmas Day in 1904. It soon became a gathering place for new arrivals, men and women of affairs in business, in land development, and in government. Big Game Hunters with safari clients such as Theodore Roosevelt, aristocrats eager to experience the new Kenya, authors, adventurers and actors, all came to the Norfolk with its promise of stone-built coolness, quiet tile roofs, good food and baths. It was an island of civilized comfort in the early wild and dusty days of country and capital. Now it is among "The Leading Hotels of the World."

The Norfolk has evolved into an unusual collection of half-timbered turrets, terraces, wings and walks. These are loosely grouped around an interior grassy courtyard which has rambling gardens, aviaries and a display of vintage rickshaw, oxcart and cars. On arrival at the cobblestone entry, you are greeted by a beaming doorman in top hat and livery. Passing through the high-arched gateway, you are reminded of horse and buggy days. To one side is the Lord Delamere Terrace and Bar where people gather to meet friends or take time out from safari or business schedules. This popular spot to enjoy a quick meal is always a lively swirl of activity. It is open on one side to a street busy with traffic and London-style taxi cabs.

The small lobby is low-ceilinged, dark with wood paneling, and sometimes crowded with baggage. Although the Norfolk can accommodate approximately 200 guests, there is a sense of intimacy, and reception staffers make an effort to learn your name.

The Norfolk is possibly most remarkable for its history. The name conjures images of romance, adventure and camaraderie of a bygone era. In its heyday, many guests were regulars and knew each other well. They came for long stays with leisure to drink and dine in style, to plan safaris, business deals or swindles. Today, however, most international tourists come to this famous hostelry for one-night stays. They can have good service and pleasant surroundings, but the leisurely magic of those early days is a memory.

Accommodation wings have been added, rebuilt or refurnished, and many rooms have now become typical superior hotel rooms. The exceptions are in the 1937 Wing and the Cottage Wing. These rooms have charm and character—they overlook the courtyard and, more than the other rooms, they allow you to savor the historic, homey atmosphere of this gallant old hotel.

The excellence of Norfolk cuisine has figured in the hotel's reputation since it first opened its kitchens with a French chef from the Waldorf Astoria Hotel of New York. One of the best places to eat in Nairobi today is the Ibis Grill, a cozy little à la carte restaurant. Diners can enjoy world-class cuisine created by Norfolk Head Chef Eamon Mullan, winner of many international awards. Emphasis is placed on local ingredients, and main courses are served under shiny silver salvers. Many tables are drawn up to comfortable banquettes and are set to perfection with heavy linen and silver. Ibis tapestries on the walls bring the restaurant's namesake to life. Visible through a wall of tall Palladian windows, other tables are set on the cool courtyard terrace shaded by broad vine leaves on the overhead trellis. Locals and guests can enjoy a quiet lunch or dine by candlelight and piano music during the dinner hours.

The Lord Delamere Restaurant serves breakfast, lunch and dinner. The outdoor Lord Delamere Terrace serves a varied menu. There is also a poolside terrace and bar near the pool which is reached down one of the hotel's access alleys.

The Norfolk continues to play an active role in the community by hosting various events in a series of Function rooms. Occasionally there are even Music Hall or dramatic productions featuring imported and local talent.

Accommodations

Most accommodations are grouped in wings around the central courtyard. The four 1937 Wing studio suites have a garden entrance, spacious bedrooms, high ceilings, a separate dressing room and, best of all, a private little veranda overlooking the central courtyard. The Cottage Wing is all homey luxury: each cottage has a private garden veranda, living room with sofa and easy chairs, and either one or two bedrooms.

After recent renovations, there are several wings of the "typical modern hotel room" with two beds, two armchairs, luggage bureau unit, and modern ensuite bathroom. Some of these rooms are also considered mini-suites when space permits a larger sitting area. Some of the newly renovated rooms are upstairs over the main public rooms and overlook a noisy street; others are in wings built behind the main courtyard and at some distance from the heart of the hotel. *Our Favorites:* 1937 and Cottage Wings.

Other Facilities

Travel desk, gift shops, beauty salon.

Off-Notes

There is no comfortable lounge for hotel guests that is not a restaurant or bar.

Safari Journal

Thursday – late

The Ibis pianist swooped into his dreamy version of "Somewhere My Love", the candles gave the room a soft glow, there was a muted buzz of conversation . . . He helped me with my wrap. It was hard to leave. The head waiter presented me with a perfect pink carnation and a box of Ibis Grill truffles.

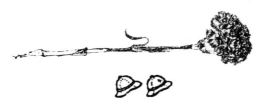

NAIROBI SERENA HOTEL

Serena Lodges & Reservations, Box 48690, Nairobi
☎ *710511, FAX: 718103*

The Nairobi Serena is a beautiful garden hotel just a 10-minute walk from the city center. The hotel's clean white silhouette rises at the edge of Nairobi's extensive Central Park. Surrounded by its own tropical garden, the hotel's rather stark lines are softened by cascades of plants and flowers growing on terrace areas and individual balconies. From the gardens, terraces, swimming pool, and many of the rooms, there is a striking view of modern Nairobi's distinctive skyline, especially beautiful at night.

The Serena can accommodate more than 300 guests in 192 luxurious double rooms. It has been accepted as a "Leading Hotel of the World." You are met by a liveried doorman wearing white gloves and fresh carnation boutonniere. The Serena's beautifully appointed lobby is rich with colorful tile borders on walls and floors. Carved cedar paneling and brass accent pieces glow under skylights set off by a profusion of indoor tropical plants. A raised lounge area invites with velvet Swahili-style sofas. From there, you can look through wall-sized windows to the garden beyond.

Throughout the hotel there is an abundance of natural light from windows and skylights. Many plants create the welcome effect of bringing the garden indoors, and you often hear the running water that is part of the landscaping. This enhances and unifies Serena decorative themes which have been drawn from all over Africa.

The Mandhari is one of Nairobi's finest à la carte restaurants. The elegance of the food, fine linens and silver is perfectly complemented by the inspired use of Kisii stone from western Kenya. Square columns are faced in hand-polished stone tiles and framed in cedar. The skylight overhead is edged in hanging plants. Appropriately, since "mandhari" means landscape in Swahili, one whole wall is hung with a unique Kisii stone mural carved into an African landscape. On the other side of the restaurant, the windows and dining terrace overlook the Serena's panoramic view of Nairobi.

The popular and more informal Cafe Maghreb is North African in style with arched recesses displaying pieces of brass or copper, and colorful tapestry screens separating tables. The Bambara Lounge has wood carvings and designs from West Africa.

The Kisima Bar is decorated to reflect the importance of water themes in Swahili coastal life. "Kisima" means watering hole in Swahili. There are low divans and stools, Swahili implements and murals on the walls. The elaborate health and fitness center, one of Nairobi's best, is named "Maisha", which means life in Swahili. Both the fitness center and the sparkling outdoor swimming pool are decorated in Arabic style tiles.

Accommodations

Rooms at the Serena are fairly uniform luxurious doubles. Although the rooms are not spacious, each has a wall-size picture window with garden or city view. The furniture is the typical two bed, two chair, baggage and bureau combination, but has been crafted and carved from African wood in African designs. African fabrics brighten beds and windows.

Modern ensuite bathrooms have both bathtubs and showers. Each room has a stocked mini-bar, direct-dial telephone, electronic private safe, radio and TV.

There is an additional suite more elaborately furnished with separate sitting and dining area, bedroom, kitchen and bath. Thirty junior suites can be created on demand by opening connecting doors between double rooms and furnishing one as a sitting room.

Other Facilities

Business center, conference rooms, boutique, gift shop, hairdresser, book shop.

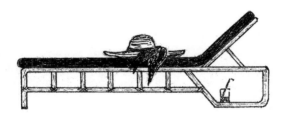

MAYFAIR COURT HOTEL

The Mayfair Court Hotel, P.O. Box 74957, Nairobi
☎ *748278, FAX: 746826*

Near the center of the busy Westlands suburb, the Mayfair Court Hotel bustles with activity and recalls the crisp accommodation and service of an old English country inn.

Built in 1949, the hotel closed and spent some years as a university site. Completely renovated for its reopening as a Horizon Hotel (part of the Windsor Group) in February, 1994, the hotel intrigues with half-timbered, tile-roofed, and old-brick charm. The lobby and reception glow with brass fixtures, wood paneling, and shiny Kenyan marble underfoot. The many windows let in lots of light and views of gardens beyond. Tall bay windows light the paneled stairway leading to the second floor, and flowing plants accent the deep window ledges.

The hotel has 108 rooms and is built in several wings rambling under mature trees. The central garden areas are traversed by pathways, some covered. Fish ponds, fountains, two swimming pools, and some outdoor terrace dining areas accent the new landscaping. At present, complimentary breakfast and all hotel dining is in the new Mischief Bar and Grill where an extensive menu of snacks is available all day. Interesting memorabilia ranging from antique music scores to old safari gear add a certain charm to this room. A new hotel dining room is under construction and will feature breakfast, lunch and dinner buffets.

Accommodations

Standard rooms are simple but quite spacious with a tasteful nod at an English country decor. Most have twin beds, though there are a few with one queen-sized bed. Rooms have parquet floors, spacious bathrooms, and TV featuring CNN and two video channels. A superior luxurious wing of 66 rooms is under construction.

Other Facilities

Superior gift shop, laundry, scheduled courtesy bus circuit to downtown Nairobi. Under Construction for June 1994 Opening: Conference facilities, casino with restaurant and bar, health club, beauty shop, second boutique/shop.

Off-notes

Street noise can be a problem since the hotel is right on a major suburban street. Landscaping except for trees is not yet established. Views of less-than-scenic neighboring lots are not yet camouflaged by landscaping. Bus loads of tour groups can fill up the tables in the dining room.

FAIRVIEW HOTEL

Fairview Hotel, Box 40842, Nairobi
☎ *723211, FAX: 721320*

The Fairview bills itself as "the country hotel in town." This family owned hotel, which has been operating since the 1930s, offers good value to guests. The hotel is a huge rambling old stone house with two garden cottages on two hectares of grounds. There are big trees, wide lawns, flower beds, and the sound of birds. Although it is just over a kilometer from the city center, the hotel feels like a calm oasis after the hustle and bustle of downtown Nairobi. It has a sense of history and individuality.

The Fairview attracts a wide range of clientele, from international consultants to up-country Kenyan residents. Many guests stay several days. Large tour groups are unlikely to be there. The atmosphere is friendly and relaxed—continuing the image of a traditional English country hotel.

A new addition and some upgrading was completed in 1991, giving the hotel entrance an elegant appearance with gleaming stone floors, curved stairway and skylight. There is a rather clubby lounge with a central fire-place and a small, hideaway bar with character and attractive decor. The sunny and spacious dining room has lovely big Palladian windows and opens out onto the garden. At the front of the hotel is a newly built out-door dining terrace which serves à la carte meals. The main dining room serves both set/buffet and à la carte meals and is a popular lunch spot for Nairobi businessmen. A traditional African lunch buffet is served two days a week with the food attractively presented in ethnic clay pots.

There is a large bright room which can be booked for conferences or re-ceptions. There is no swimming pool or health spa. Guests have free access to the pool at the nearby Panafric hotel. The Fairview has its own genera-tor and borehole to ride out the vagaries of Nairobi's water and power sup-plies.

The hotel can house almost 200 guests in a wide variety of rooms rang-ing from singles to family units. As the executive assistant informed us proudly, "This hotel is not standardized anywhere." Each of the rooms has an individual character.

The tariff at the Fairview includes bed and breakfast. There is quite a variation in rates to match the range of room types and sizes. The Fairview is known for being good value for the money.

Accommodations

In general, the decor is rather old-fashioned and functional. Some rooms have nice oriental-style rugs and unusual chandeliers. Although the rooms do not feel updated, they do have an appearance of being well kept and maintained. In general, they are bright, clean, spacious, and comfortable. Most of the rooms have bathrooms ensuite—some with tub and shower and others with shower only. There are televisions (including a video chan-nel), telephones and radios.

Most accommodations are in the main house where two rooms have balco-nies and several have lovely restful views over the gardens. You could also choose to stay in one of the garden cottages or "Annexes," where the room variations are even more extreme. In Annex #1 there is a large family unit with bay window, 1950's decor and a children's room. In Annex #2, which is a historical building with corrugated iron roof and a big veranda, there are six rooms with shared bathrooms and no TV. Just across a small road from the hotel are the Fairview Flats—a rectangular concrete-looking building without the charm of the main hotel or cottages. The upper floors are leased out for long term lets but the ground floor is used as part of the hotel with spacious family units leading out to a large lawn.

Please Note

Deposit required, no credit cards accepted, no air conditioning, no pool on grounds (free access to pool at neighboring hotel), 24-hour room service, mosquito nets, park.

THE JACARANDA HOTEL
Block Hotels, Box 47557, Nairobi
☎ *335807, FAX: 340541*

This is the Nairobi-based Block Hotel and is located in the suburb of Westlands, only a few minutes drive from downtown. It is a fairly middle-of-the-road tourist and business hotel. There is a swimming pool set in quite attractive gardens and facilities for mid-sized conferences. Westlands has many shops and a selection of restaurants. There is a hotel shuttle bus to downtown Nairobi.

BOULEVARD HOTEL
Hotel Boulevard, Box 42831, Nairobi
☎ *227567, FAX: 334071*

Located right at the foot of Museum Hill, this no-frills hotel is only a 10-minute walk to the city center. It has 70 small guest rooms on three floors, each with ensuite bathroom and private balcony. Public areas are furnished in a functional '50s style. There are conference facilities. The hotel gardens overlook the Nairobi River on one side, and rooms with garden view are less noisy than those on the street side. The Boulevard has a pool and a tennis court.

PANAFRIC HOTEL
Sarova Hotels Ltd., Box 30680
☎ *333248, FAX: 211472*

The Panafric Hotel can accommodate approximately 350 guests. You drive through an Agip Gasoline Station to reach the entrance of this modern concrete structure. Set on a rise near Nairobi's Central Park, the hotel has an oblique view of the city skyline, which is just a few minutes away by car. In addition to single and double rooms, the hotel has six suites and 42 service apartments suitable for longer stays. There are comprehensive conference facilities. The outdoor pool is larger than most in city hotels.

The decor is very plain and tired. The public rooms tend to be dark and need refurbishing. However, the Panafric has recently been sold to the Sarova Hotel Chain. Complete renovations are planned throughout to appeal to business travelers and tourists.

CITY SUBURB HOTELS

WINDSOR GOLF AND COUNTRY CLUB

Windsor Hotels International Ltd., Box 74957, Nairobi
☎ *219784, FAX: 217498*

The Windsor Golf and Country Club is a larger-than-life Victorian extravaganza newly built in the Nairobi suburbs. There is nothing to prepare you for the overpowering impact of this hotel. It seems to be in the middle of nowhere. You drive past some suburban houses and through coffee fields and then....

The imposing main building follows the Grand Victorian style. It is built of stone and crowned by ochre tiled peaks and cupolas. The soaring entrance concourse has Victorian street lamps and shop fronts. There are dramatically high windows, miles of curtaining, wide stairways—everything is on a grand scale. The hotel was designed to recall the early days of Kenya's aristocratic British pioneers, to compare with the elegance and service of the Savoy Hotel or Claridges in London, and to create a setting for world-class golf to rival the renown of Gleneagles in Scotland. With all of its "nouveau" splendor, there is also a chic resemblance to Hollywood's Rodeo Drive.

The decor is reminiscent of a grand English country hotel. There is a huge copper fireplace in the vast ballroom. There are countless armchairs and sofas in richly woven fabrics. You see lots of etched glass, polished brass, wood and leather. Ornate draperies billow around towering small-paned windows and there are many cozy drawing rooms and bars set at different levels. Throughout the hotel, original works of art have been hung to compliment the decor.

Most of the public rooms and the expansive open-air terrace below command wonderful wide views over the golf course with its forests and ponds. The sky seems to stretch forever, and there are hills and mountains in the far distance. The separate accommodation buildings and cottages stride out to each side of the main complex, lining the first and last holes—a frame for this beautiful, world-class golf course.

The club has been designed and equipped in grand style, and there is a whole directory of services and facilities. They have tried to include everything including a shopping arcade, a full-service health and beauty spa, a huge baronial banquet hall, conference and business facilities, a variety of club-like lounges, several bars and restaurants, a state-of-the-art kitchen gleaming with all the latest imported equipment, and sophisticated up-to-date electronic audio and visual systems. There are also special "Butler Service" stations for every so many bedrooms. It all seems so ambitious and rather incongruous in its setting. However, the hotel is still too new to gauge its ambiance and operation. When it has mellowed a bit, has a smooth operation, and the huge rooms are filled with animated guests, this might become a very special place. Effort and expense have certainly been expended to create something of quality and stature.

Quotes from Visitors:

> *"The golf course is magnificent. It ranks with the best."*

> *"It's like a grand Victorian Railway Station with some Tudor thrown in."*

Accommodations

The hotel can accommodate 230 guests in a choice of rooms, studio suites or cottages. The accommodation has been arranged in a series of separate buildings which stand along the edge of the golf course to each side of the main hotel. The buildings look rather grand with their large red tiled roofs and high chimneys. They all offer woodland or golf course views.

Rooms are furnished to resemble an English country-style hotel or inn. All have a full bathroom ensuite and a seating area. They are well equipped with direct dial telephone, hairdryer and electronic digital safe. Guests have the convenience of parking near individual rooms.

The "Windsor Butler Service" on each floor is designed to help guests with everything from laundry to hiring cars, from getting newspapers to reserving golf tee times.There are 15 cottages. A central living room with fireplace is flanked on each side by a double room with full bath. There is an outdoor terrace. *Our Favorites:* Cottages overlooking the first fairway.

The 20 studio suites are situated on the top floor of each guest wing. They feature fireplaces, a sitting area with sofa and chairs, cathedral ceilings with exposed beams and a separate dressing area.

The 80 standard rooms, called superior doubles, are on the bottom two floors of the guest wings. They have one double or two larger-than-twin beds. Rooms on the bottom floor also have garden access doors.

Recreation

18-hole Golf Course (putting green, golf tuition, golf driving range), heated swimming pool, tennis courts, squash courts, bowling green, croquet lawn, jogging trails through forest, fishing for Tilapia and Black Bass in three lakes on the grounds, bird and nature walks with ornithologist, beauty and health spa with aerobics and exercise machines.

Other Offerings

Shopping (wide selection of shops including fashion, gifts, African arts and crafts, sports equipment); excursions (local trips and major safaris can be arranged); car hire, Nairobi shuttle every two hours, doctor.

SAFARI PARK HOTEL

Safari Park Hotel, Box 45038, Nairobi
☎ *802493, FAX: 802477*

The Safari Park Hotel is an exciting 25-hectare hotel and convention complex that feels like a resort. About 15 minutes from downtown, it has dramatic architecture and a complete range of facilities spread out in beautifully landscaped grounds.

There is a relaxed holiday atmosphere, and the hotel feels like a theme park version of "larger-than-life exotic Africa." You are greeted at the entrance by imposing Masai morans in red shuka and beads. The thatched roof of reception soars above you. Inside is a life-sized sculpture of an elephant, exotic Lamu-style furniture from the coast, and a sign to the Hemingway bar upstairs: a potpourri of African images.

At the Safari Park Hotel you can be as sporty or as decadent as you like—play squash or have a massage, go shopping or gambling, lie by the pool or read on your private balcony. Also, there are a whole host of restaurants, specializing in various cuisines and offering different atmospheres and price ranges.

The many restaurants and facilities of this complex are scattered around the grounds. You are never far from lovely gardens and the sounds of birds.

In the center of the grounds is an amazing swimming pool, reputed to be the largest in Africa. The pool has a rock water-slide and islands; it meanders through tropical gardens and is crossed by footbridges. A second, more traditional pool is set off to one side and there are floodlit tennis courts and a squash court. A brand new fitness center has saunas, jacuzzi, gymnasium and beauty parlor. There is a posh gambling casino. With your winnings, you might choose to browse through the shops and boutiques which sell a selection of curios and clothing.

The Safari Park Hotel is a popular place for conferences and exhibitions. The large, up-to-date Jambo Conference Center has recently been completed. This can accommodate up to 1000 people and is fully equipped with audio visual and communications equipment. Multilingual translation facilities and secretarial services are also offered. There are separate sub-committee rooms and a business lounge equipped with fax facilities. The hotel prides itself on its ability to organize and cater for various events and conferences.

A wide variety of international cuisine is represented in the restaurants including Korean, Japanese, Chinese, African, Italian, French, and Indian. Some of the restaurants are small and intimate with very elegant decor, while others are larger and more relaxed. You can have a classy, French gourmet meal, or opt for a quick bite at the Cafe Kigwa which is open until 4 a.m. You might like to sample some game meat while watching African dancing or select vegetarian dishes at the Indian Mamta Restaurant. There is a pizzeria and a British pub with live music. During the day you can be served drinks and snacks around the pool. The main Le Bougainvillea restaurant spills out onto a wide stone patio where chairs and tables are set up under an enormous spreading tree.

At the moment, the Safari Park Hotel can accommodate **400** guests. However, there are plans for almost doubling this capacity. There is a choice of rooms, suites and cottages. The rooms are in two-story, thatched buildings which are spread out among lawns and trees. The Safari Park Hotel seems constantly to be expanding and updating. There is a sense of quality and attention to detail. Experts have been employed in the hotel's design and landscaping. It shows.

Accommodations

Each room has a private veranda or balcony with a garden view. The well-equipped rooms are bright and spacious with big windows, Lamu furniture and four-poster beds. The ensuite bathrooms have marble, gold fittings and hairdryers. There are a variety of suites with special extras such as oriental carpets and two balconies.

Special Offerings

Pool, tennis, squash, complete health spa, casino, free shuttle bus to town, shops and boutiques, conference and business facilities.

UTALII HOTEL
Utalii Hotel, Box 31067, Nairobi
☎ *802540*

This pleasant modern hotel eight kilometers from the city center acts as a practical training unit for students at Utalii College. Students work with the hotel's professional staff to learn the hotel industry. With all those students learning to help you, the service and food are great. Utalii is good value for money.

The three-story hotel has 43 double rooms and seven suites with kitchenettes. All have been recently redecorated and have ensuite bathrooms, large windows, and balconies. Rooms on the highway side of the hotel have air conditioning to block out the noise, but we prefer the rooms on the garden/pool side.

Although the Utalii Hotel is tastefully decorated, it has no real African character—the hotel could be anywhere. However, the gardens around the pool and pool bar are very inviting, and the pool is one-half Olympic size. There are two tennis courts and guests can golf at the Muthaiga Golf Course.

Other Facilities
Free shuttle to city center, conference rooms, boutique, TV, direct-dial telephone, room service, mini-refrigerator, English breakfast included.

THE KENTMERE CLUB
The Kentmere Club, Box 39508, Nairobi
☎ *(0154) 41053*

The grounds and country setting are the best features of the Kentmere Club. This small hotel nestles on the side of a hill in the Tigoni Highlands about 20 kilometers from Nairobi. There are colorful gardens all around and lush green tea in the distance.

The club is like an English country inn. There is a large dining room with Tudor beams and red tablecloths. The club bar is wood panelled. Lunches are served on the veranda and in the garden—if you can afford the wait.

There are 16 double rooms in several garden cottages. Each room has its own bathroom, fireplace and veranda. The beds and decor are both tired.

Guests at the Kentmere Club are welcome at the nearby Limuru Country Club for golf, tennis and swimming.

THE BLUE POST HOTEL
The Blue Post Hotel, Box 42, Thika
☎ *(0151) 22241*

Just off the Thika Road (A2) approximately 40 kilometers from Nairobi, the Blue Post Hotel still attracts a mixed cross-section of Kenyan residents. The hotel was built in 1906 on a promontory where the Chania and Thika Rivers meet to form the Thika and Chania Falls. Early settlers stopped there for tea and talk and to see the falls from the hotel's garden. Today the falls are quite wide, but rather muddy with more than a whiff of industry.

The hotel has seen better days. It still has expansive grounds with outdoor eating areas, viewpoints for the falls, and an outdoor market where local crafts are made and sold. There are large conference facilities. Except for the Blue Post Hotel and the Del Monte Company, Thika has little appeal for the tourist.

THE GIRAFFE MANOR

The Giraffe Manor, Box 15004, Langata, Nairobi
☎ *891078*

Staying at the exclusive Giraffe Manor is a unique and special experience. This mellow old stone house has an appealing history which is kept alive today. It was home to Daisy, the famous Rothschild giraffe. Today her grandchildren eat the flowers in the manor's extensive gardens. It's hard to believe Nairobi is only minutes away.

The manor house was built in 1932 in Langata, part of the Karen suburban area of Nairobi. It became the home of Jock Leslie-Melville and his wife Betty in 1974. They founded the African Fund for Endangered Wildlife (AFEW) and moved five babies of the endangered Rothschild giraffe to this property. They were successful at raising these giraffe, who have since grown and had their own offspring. Now, your hosts at the Giraffe Manor are Betty's son, Rick Anderson, and his wife Bryony—an energetic and charming couple who bring a great deal of professionalism to this role. Rick is active in continuing and expanding AFEW. Thanks to him and AFEW, there are still giraffe on the grounds of the manor today. You are quite likely to have a giraffe peer in at you through the front door or amble up to be hand-fed.

Giraffe Manor is only a short drive from downtown Nairobi. However, when you turn into the gates and bump along the dirt road winding through bush and riverine forest, you feel that you are far away from civilization. Warthogs run by, and there are giraffe among the trees. Your first, full frontal view of the manor is particularly impressive. It is an imposing double-story stone building with gables, tall chimneys, and red tiled roof. The house is set on large open grounds with acacia trees and gardens reduced to those flowers which the giraffe will not eat. Off to one side you can see the distinctive knuckle-shaped peaks of the Ngong Hills.

The high-arched front door leads to a grand entrance hall with a fireplace and a wide stairway. There is a generous living room arranged with chairs and sofas. With its old rugs, bowls of flowers, books, family photos, and piano, the room feels old-fashioned and lived-in. Through an archway is a long sun-room bright with big arched windows looking towards the Ngong Hills. Decorated with ferns and floral fabrics, this room is cheerfully elegant. It is here that lunch is served. The main dining room is formally paneled in wood with a huge table and chairs covered in rich fabrics. At Giraffe Manor, a great deal of emphasis is placed on elegant, gourmet dining. In fact, when there are no guests staying at the manor, it is possible to arrange for a group of six or more to be served sumptuous meals in this grand setting.

You are paying for exclusivity when you stay at Giraffe Manor. There are seldom more than six guests at a time, and they are usually all from one party. However, there are expansion plans to accommodate a few more guests without sacrificing the manor's personal or exclusive atmosphere.

This is meant to be a home, not a hotel. The bedrooms vary considerably in size and grandeur. Three bedrooms have bathrooms ensuite while two smaller rooms have no adjoining bathroom. The master bedroom has a fireplace and a huge bed. The walls are covered in bright striped fabrics. In the black and white tiled bathroom, water spouts into the bath from a lion's head. Another room has some of Karen Blixen's original furniture. The smaller rooms are rather ordinary. The upstairs is not as impressive as the lower floor—the beds look rather saggy.

As Rick says, the "whole point of this place is to relax." Guests are free to wander in the extensive grounds, feed and photograph the giraffe and warthogs, or go on a nature walk in the adjoining forest. There are more than 170 species of birds, and you might also see bushbuck or dik-dik. You are encouraged to make yourself completely at home in the manor—settle down and read a book, admire the view, help yourself to a drink.

Right next door, and in view of the manor is the popular and successful AFEW Giraffe Center. Here visitors can come to feed the giraffe, take the Nature Walk, and learn more about wildlife and conservation.

Your full-board fee for staying at Giraffe Manor, which also includes wine and cocktails, is a donation to AFEW, and may be tax deductible. The money goes to save endangered species and for educating African school children about conservation. The manor has been visited by a host of famous people—Margaret Mead, Bobby Kennedy, Brooke Shields, and Hal Prince, just to name a few.

Safari Journal
August

BLAST! None of us remembered a camera and this scene
should be recorded. Framed in silhouette against the bright light
outdoors was an enormous giraffe, her legs splayed and
her long neck and head peering in through the high arch
of the front door. Joan giggled as the gooey, long, blue
tongue curled around the food pellets she held out
in her hand.

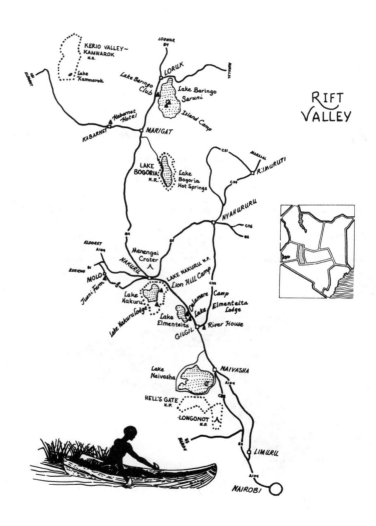

RIFT
VALLEY

THE RIFT VALLEY

The Rift Valley is the greatest valley in the world, a continental fault system which stretches from the Dead Sea all the way to Mozambique. In Kenya, the valley forms a great rift through the middle of the country beginning from Turkana in the north to Lake Magadi in the south. In between are a series of other lakes: Baringo, Bogoria, Nakuru, Elmenteita, and Naivasha. Only two of these lakes (Naivasha and Baringo) are fresh water lakes. The others are shallow soda lakes.

Dozens of volcanoes erupted in and around the Rift Valley. Most of them are now extinct, but have left their mark on the landscape in the form of half-submerged islands, giant calderas, and the distinctive cone shapes which dot the landscape. The Rift Valley evokes a sense of immense mystery and the power of time.

Most visitors to Kenya first see the Rift Valley when travelling on the Nairobi-Naivasha road. This first view is almost always a stunning surprise. After driving through cool conifer forests suddenly you are at the edge of the Rift. The land drops way down to the dry and dusty plains below, and the distinctive volcanic shape of Mt. Longonot dominates the scene. Forty-eight kilometers across rises the dark blue escarpment of the other side of the valley. At the viewpoints, persistent souvenir salesmen force you back to reality.

The Masai have been in the Rift Valley for centuries. Today, the most popular tourist areas in the Rift Valley are around Lakes Naivasha, Nakuru, and Baringo. All of these lakes have several accommodation options and are linked by relatively good tarmac roads. The lakes are known for their exceptional birdlife, especially the pink flocks of flamingos which feed in the soda lakes. National Parks have been established around Lakes Nakuru and Bogoria.

LAKE NAIVASHA AREA

Lake Naivasha, 83 kilometers from Nairobi, is the highest of the Rift lakes. Surprisingly, Lake Naivasha (1888 meters) is at a higher altitude than Nairobi (1670 meters). This beautiful freshwater lake has large floating islands of papyrus, a mysteriously fluctuating water level, a healthy hippo population, and wonderful and diverse birdlife (340 species). Its shores are lined with yellow-barked fever trees and horticultural farms and vineyards. There is a yacht club on Crescent Island for sailing and windsurfing. Fishing is popular and there are even fresh water crayfish in the lake. There are a whole host of places to stay around the lake, ranging from bustling hotels to catered homestays.

Naivasha's proximity to Nairobi makes it ideal for a weekend (or longer) getaway. There is much to see and do in the area:

Crescent Island: This small island in Lake Naivasha is the outer rim of a submerged volcano. There is a private game sanctuary on the island, and it is safe to walk among wild animals (no big cats or elephant).

Hell's Gate National Park: Entrance Fee. The geological formation of this park is particularly impressive with soaring red cliffs, isolated volcanic plugs, spreading grasslands dotted with game, and a deep gorge where visitors can walk. There is a geothermal project at the far end of the park.

Elsamere Conservation Center: This former home of Joy Adamson of *Born Free* fame is now a residential conservation center. It is open to visitors for afternoon teas (3–6pm). Entrance Fee.

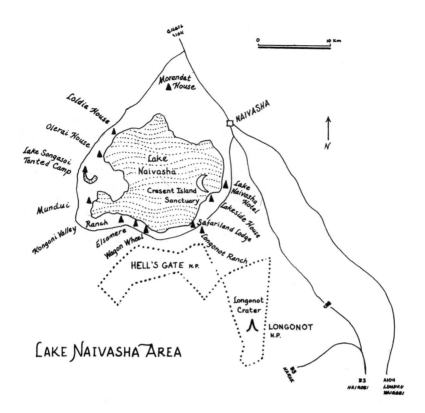

LAKE NAIVASHA AREA

Crater Lake Sanctuary: A vivid green lake has formed in the caldera of an extinct volcano. This is a peaceful and remote spot with lovely views. Entrance Fee.

Mount Longonot: This extinct volcano (2776 meters) has a path to the top and around the rim. There are magnificent views. Security is an issue.

Cordon Bleu Ox-Wagon Safari: Variety of day or overnight trips available.

Elmenteita Weavers: Attractive and colorful handwoven items (kikoi, cushion covers, shawls etc.) as well as other locally produced handicrafts. Located next to the Lake Naivasha Club.

Bee's Herb Garden: It is possible to visit this herb garden with advance arrangements.

La Belle Inn: This popular and relaxed restaurant in Naivasha town serves surprisingly good food at reasonable prices. The long outdoor veranda overlooks a street busy with trucks.

LAKE NAIVASHA CLUB
Block Hotels, Box 47557, Nairobi
☎ *335807, FAX: 340541*

This beautiful old hotel was Kenya's international air terminal just after World War II. The flying boats of British Overseas Airways landed there as they followed the Nile south and on to South Africa. Today, only glimpses of Lake Naivasha are visible through tall acacia trees at water's edge.

The hotel is centered on an elegant old house with the charm of wood floors, French doors and a long covered veranda leading to the lawns. Several wings and clusters of rooms and cottages are set in 12 hectares of cool lawns, shaded by spreading fever trees and accented by colorful gardens. Rustic wooden chairs and benches invite the traveler to relax and listen to birds and watch the grazing waterbuck. Meandering walkways lead down to a wooden gazebo built over the water, perfect for watching birds, water-life, or sunsets.

The hotel is a popular overnight transit point and is often busy with international tour groups. It provides an easy weekend getaway from Nairobi. It is also a convenient base for exploring the many attractions in the Naivasha area.

The public rooms are elegant and relaxed. The comfortable residents' lounge has a magnificent fireplace and large bay windows. The bar area is inviting with its mural of Lake Naivasha and color-washed walls with floral stencils. Located at one end of the commodious veranda, the dining room is light and bright, with a panoramic view of the grounds. On holidays and weekends lunch buffets are served on the lawns. Day visitors are required to pay a hefty club membership fee to enter the grounds.

The Lake Naivasha Club is the most convenient place on the lake for exploring Crescent Island. There is a jetty and several boats. You can be ferried to the island where you can wander freely among wild animals, or you can go on longer lake trips to enjoy the birdlife and spot hippo.

Accommodations

The hotel has 51 rooms in separate one-story wings and garden cottages. Each room has a private entrance and a small veranda with a view of the grounds. There is variation in room sizes and decor, but all have been attractively furnished, many in an English country style, some with Lamu-style beds. All have clean and pleasant bathrooms (many with bathtubs only). Each room is available for at least double occupancy. Most have two twin beds, a few have a double bed. There are mosquito nets.

An extravagant and private Lake View Cottage sits at the edge of the lake. This delightful cottage is reached by a raised wooden walkway and has a wraparound porch with panoramic views of the lake. There are two bedrooms and a spacious central living room. The decor is rustic: wooden furniture, throw rugs, and baskets of dried flowers. *Our Favorites:* Rooms 17 and 23 (for size, Lamu-style furniture and bathrooms with both tub and shower); The Lake View Cottage.

Special Offerings

Swimming pool and children's wading pool, conference/function room, souvenir and sundry shop, massage, boats and fishing rods for hire, hotel ferry service to Crescent Island, environmentalist-guided boat trip, Lake Cruiser with bar, bird walks led by an ornithologist, indoor board games, videos (wildlife and classics), excursions to local attractions.

Off Notes:

The hotel can be crowded with tour groups coming and going.

ELSAMERE CONSERVATION CENTER

Elsamere, Box 1497, Naivasha
☎ *(0311) 30079*

Elsamere was once the home of Joy Adamson of *Born Free* fame. Several pleasant and bright cottages have been built on the grounds near the main house for guests. As this is a residential conservation center, guests are required to be members of a conservation society, and the rates have been kept very reasonable.

The conservation center is beautifully situated under huge old trees on a grassy slope at the edge of Lake Naivasha. There are lovely views through the trees and across the water. In the main house there is a Joy Adamson memorial room and a separate video room with an extensive library of conservation and wildlife videos. Communal meals are taken in the main house at long tables. You might find yourself sitting next to someone doing research on the lake or the nearby Hell's Gate National Reserve. There are areas for relaxing and reading, a wide veranda, and lots of conservation magazines and materials.

It is particularly relaxing and pleasant sitting out on the lawn, listening to the birds, and watching the resident troupe of black and white Colobus monkeys cavorting in the grounds. There are nature trails along the edge of the lake and on higher ground across the road, where you can see many wildflowers and get good views of the lake. It is possible to rent boats to explore this end of the lake.

Elsamere can handle 15–18 guests in three cottages. Each cottage has a veranda and faces towards the lake. The rooms are bright and attractive and have ensuite bathrooms. Our Favorites: #6 and #8 for space and view. Guests may also stay in the main house in the Joy Adamson bedroom.

In addition to overnight guests, Elsamere attracts day visitors who may come for lunch or a traditional tea on the lawn. They are invited to watch the film "The Joy Adamson Story" and to visit the memorial room. Lunches should be booked in advance. There is a gift shop. No pool.

SAFARILAND CLUB, LTD.

Safariland Club Ltd., Box 72, Naivasha
☎ *(0311) 20241, Telex: 39051 Safarclub*

Safariland is the only other large hotel on the shores of Lake Naivasha. It has a fine setting overlooking the lake. A wide range of rooms and cottages are scattered over the spacious grounds. Most cry out for maintenance and decor. Hotel staff spoke of renovations and expansions to come, including a golf course and health spa. At the moment there is a pool, an unkempt tennis court, an aviary, horses for riding, boats for hire and conference facilities. Safariland Club can accommodate 114, and there is a campground next door.

CRATER LAKE OR LAKE SONGASOI TENTED CAMP

Let's Go Travel, Box 60342, Nairobi
☎ *340331, FAX: 336890*

This small tented camp is within the Crater Lake Sanctuary near Lake Naivasha. A basic mess tent and a row of six simple double tents (with hot showers and flush toilets) are in the lush vegetation at the edge of the unusual green waters of Crater Lake. To reach the tents you walk through high rocks and down a steep and narrow path. The walls of the crater encircle the camp and the lake, giving an enclosed sense of privacy and isolation. There is a Swiss-trained chef, who plans and produces cordon bleu meals for the camp.

From the camp you can take game walks around the lake where you are likely to see colobus monkeys, waterbuck and fish eagles. For an unusual and unique experience, you might book an ox-wagon safari. You sit in a shaded wagon and are slowly pulled through the bush by a team of 14 oxen while you keep an eye out for game. It is possible to book ox-wagon safaris with a lunch or tea even if you are not staying in the camp.

KONGONI GAME VALLEY RANCH

Kongoni Game Valley Ranch, Box 41759, Nairobi
☎ *338838, FAX: 218939*

You become one of the "privileged few" when you stay at the Kongoni Game Valley Ranch. This is a 5600 hectares paradise stretching from the shores of Lake Naivasha to the high plateau of the Masai Mara. The elegance of the Brighetti ranch house and its dramatic setting make this a very special place.

The Kongoni Game Valley Ranch has been home to the Bruno Brighetti Family for the last 25 years. The ranch house is on a hilltop overlooking Lake Naivasha and the surrounding volcanic peaks. The romance of the place begins in 1901 with a French Marquis who built this home in Africa for his new American bride. They lived there happily until the early 1940s. They are both buried in a secluded part of the garden where the view they loved is absolutely breathtaking.

When Bruno Brighetti brought Gianna Bellingeri Zasio to Africa as his new bride, the newlyweds fell in love with Kenya and decided to make the Kongoni Game Valley their home. Their very personal interest in Kenya has fostered their desire to protect the land, the people and the animals.

When you come to Kongoni Game Valley Ranch, you come as Gianna's personal guests. She welcomes you to her home with grace, warmth and enthusiasm. She takes pleasure in the fact that she herself has personally decorated every room. There is an eclectic mix which creates a harmonious and interesting effect. You want to browse slowly through her home looking at everything: Lamu furniture from the coast, Oriental rugs, impala trophies, brass pots filled with dried grasses, books piled on low tables, and shell collections. Watch for the Kongoni motif—the distinctive outline of this rather peculiar looking antelope—which is repeated here and there on firescreens, ashtrays and glassware.

The long, low stone house, with its ochre-tiled roof stands in a wide expanse of mowed lawns and tended gardens. It all feels very established and well-cared for—there is an aura of quality. The house is built around a central courtyard. The communal living and dining rooms overlook the lake and open out to a wide veranda furnished with commodious wicker furniture and cushions. Guests are encouraged to relax in this restful spot and enjoy the magnificent view.

Below, shining beyond its fringe of acacia trees is the lake framed by extinct volcanoes and the soaring sides of the Rift Valley. A forest of primeval euphorbia contrast with the clipped lawns and English style flower beds of the garden.

Meals at Kongoni are memorable: intimate tables, garden flowers, views from the sunroom at breakfast, cozy candlelight inside at night. The food is wonderful. You can smell the bread baking; pizza arrives fresh from the oven. The emphasis is on gourmet Italian cooking, and the pasta and ice cream are homemade.

Gianna jokes that the "Big Five" at Kongoni Valley Ranch are parmesan cheese, olive oil, capers, risotto, and pasta—mouth-watering.

At Kongoni, you set your own pace, choose what you would like to do. Gianna's lively descriptions and enthusiasm help you to plan your day, and there are many options. You can go for game drives into the unspoiled ranch highlands. You can take guided walks among herds of plains game. Day-long treks with box lunches can be planned, and there are horses for experienced riders. The high grassland savannas rise to hilltops which open up vistas of range after range of mountain peaks and volcanic remains.

Other choices are a walk at lake shore or boating. You are likely to see a wide variety of birds and perhaps a wide-open toothy yawn from a hippo. You may decide simply to sit on the veranda in cushioned comfort and absorb the beauty and peace.

Quotes

"In this beauty we have to be silent."—Gianna leading early morning game walk.

Accommodations

Kongoni can accommodate up to 26 guests. Every guest room has been furnished by Gianna. The many personal touches remind you that you are in a private home...a squash racquet in a cupboard, a family photograph on the wall. The bedrooms each have a different atmosphere, a unique "theme"; all are attractive and comfortable. Each room has a rather charming and old-fashioned bathroom, many with turn-of-the-century European fixtures, including bidet. Most rooms open onto the central courtyard, but some are in separate cottages or have private outside entrances. Some have fireplaces, and one even has an ensuite sauna.

Kongoni Valley Ranch has recently opened another house very near the lake with beautiful water views. Though separate, this house is still on ranch property and can accommodate a private party of up to seven guests in one single and three double bedrooms. It is fully catered and can enjoy all the activities and facilities of the ranch.

LOLDIA HOUSE

Musiara Ltd. (Governor's Camps) Box 48217, Nairobi
☎ *331871, FAX: 726427*

This old-fashioned stone house with views across Lake Naivasha has a supremely peaceful setting sheltered by giant wild fig trees and surrounded by lawns and flowering shrubs. Loldia House is on the cattle ranch of Rick and Bette Hopcraft and was built in the 1940's by Rick's grandfather with the help of Italian prisoners of war.

Today Loldia House is open to guests and run by Musiara Ltd. (Governor's Camps)—perfect hosting, wonderful food, and attention to every comfort. One of the senior members of the Musiara team is your host. The attentive resident manager, Peter Njoroge, who was described in Country Living as "probably the world's best butler," makes sure you are extremely well-cared for throughout your stay.

Loldia House is built of rough-hewn lava rock around a central grass courtyard in the up-country Kenyan style. There is a wide, welcoming veranda along the lake side of the house. From its shady coolness you have wonderful views across the long sweep of the lawn and the shimmering lake with Mt. Longonot rising dramatically beyond. On the lawn comfortable chairs are set out under trees and a croquet set beckons.

Inside the house, there is an aura of earlier days. The paneled sitting room is cozy and rather dark with comfortable sofas and chairs, a fireplace and a grand piano. A large abstract mural adds interest to the dining room.

In the main house, there are two double bedrooms with ensuite bathrooms and two singles. The master bedroom is spacious and has views of the lake. Enjoy the old-fashioned claw-foot bathtub. There are two more double rooms in a small guest cottage near the main house. The cottage is surrounded by flowers and also has good views of the lake. The rooms have been attractively decorated and are cool and pleasant with high ceilings and lovely old windows. Together, the house and cottage can accommodate up to 10 guests.

In addition, guests have the choice of staying in a luxurious but rustic rondavel-style cottage built high on a cliff, near the home of Rick and Bette Hopcraft and a short drive up the hill behind Loldia House. Up to six guests can stay here and have the option of complete privacy—they can even take their meals here if they wish. This large rondavel is beautifully and imaginatively built of local stone and timber. The sitting room has a high vaulted papyrus ceiling, a large fireplace and opens out onto a veranda which has dramatic views of the lake. There are two large bedrooms downstairs, each with ensuite bathroom and one loft bedroom upstairs with no loo, but a simply marvelous view.

Loldia never feels crowded, and activities and meal schedules can be arranged to suit the guests. The meals we sampled were delicious and beautifully presented and served.

There are a variety of activities to choose from, both on the ranch or further afield. A very knowledgeable ornothologist/botanist can take you on walks and will accompany you on boat rides on the lake. Loldia owns two motorized boats—a canoe with a shade canopy and a colorfully painted sailboat.

> *"Being out on the water is supremely peaceful and beautiful. Wonderfully shaped hills and extinct volcanos ring the lake and there is an amazing variety of bird life. A goliath heron stands motionless, coots busy about, and a flock of pelicans lift themselves heavily into formation. The water heaves and a hippo snout comes into view, then another, and a third. The lake changes color and mood with every shift in the light and the weather. At times it is a blue mirror reflecting puffy clouds, at others it is mud-colored and wind-whipped. Mt. Longonot can transform from floating mauve mirage in the heat of the day to sharply etched reality, every crevice accentuated in the clear evening light." (Safari Journal)*

A Loldia vehicle, complete with gourmet picnic, can take you on day trips to Hell's Gate near Naivasha, Lake Nakuru National Park, the forested Aberdares or Lake Bogoria. If you are feeling particularly athletic you might opt to climb Mt. Longonot. You could choose to ride Loldia's horses or go on escorted game walks. There are still wild animals on the ranch—buffalo, antelope, ostriches—hippo regularly graze on the lawns at night. Perhaps you'd like to do a spot of fishing, or end a perfect day with sundowners on the lake.

There is an airstrip suitable for a twin-engine plane.

MUNDUI

Wilderness Trails (K) Ltd./Bush Homes of East Africa Ltd.
Box 56923, Nairobi
☎ *506139, FAX: 502739*

Past the southern end of Lake Naivasha, on the adjoining small lake, lies the elegant and beautiful Mundui Estate. The long dirt road leading to the house is ablaze with bougainvillea. The main house and grand two-story cottage are fronted by wide lawns partly shaded by trees with enormous spread. There is bright color in the shrubs and gardens which reach to the shimmering lake. Coming upon this scene for the first time leaves you silent or running for a camera. Mundui offers the best shore view of Lake Naivasha waters we've found.

This is the home of Sarah and Andrew Cole, the Lord and Lady of Enniskillin. (Yes, dig into your "Out of Africa"—the Cole family has played quite a role in Kenya's history.) Lady Sarah greets with a welcoming smile—you are at ease. An immensely artistic and capable woman, she is the main force behind the beauty of Mundui and its relaxed perfection. She has created rooms with taste and flair, adding the artistic decorative paint effects herself. Hats and books abound, pale cream colors predominate. There are wonderful wooden floors, colorful hand-made quilts, and an impressive collection of elephant statuary in various sizes and colors.

Guests stay in the "Cottage" adjacent to the main house. This lovely double story building with its rather flat and formal facade was originally built by an Austrian as a hunting lodge for his friends. On the upper floor are two bedrooms and bathrooms. Below, an enormous living room is light and airy with high ceiling and huge fireplace. Guests have the whole cottage exclusively to themselves. The Coles do not combine different parties of guests.

"This is a home and they are houseguests," says Sarah, "but they can spend as much or as little time with us as they wish."

There is a swimming pool, croquet and badminton—no discos. Early morning tea is served in bed or outside so you can enjoy the birds. Breakfast is on the veranda, perhaps after an early morning walk in the private Mundui game reserve. Mundui has 1200 acres of mainly open, rolling grasslands dotted with thorn trees. Plains game is plentiful, and 218 species of birds have been identified here. Views are spectacular all around—extinct volcanos, the Rift Escarpment and the lake. You can putter about in a quiet boat, siesta before enjoying an English tea with scones, or arrange for something more active like a trip to Hell's Gate Game Reserve, Elsamere, or Crater Lake. You might end the day with drinks under a full moon, a three-course dinner with wine, and neighbors invited for good conversation and to add more local color to the table. (A 900 meter private airstrip is a boon to fly-in guests) Exclusivity, elegance, and beauty at a price.

LONGONOT RANCH HOUSE

Safaris Unlimited (Africa) Ltd., Box 24181, Nairobi, Kenya
☎ *891168, FAX: 891113*

Longonot Game Ranch is on the slopes of Mt. Longonot near Lake Naivasha in the Rift Valley. This private ranch of 32,000 hectares is home to a wide variety of wild animals. The traditional ranch house, with its long verandas and central courtyard, sits on the top of an open hill. There are views all around and a sense of wonderful space and distance. On one side rises the dormant volcano, Longonot, and on the other, you look into the distance towards shimmering Lake Naivasha.

As you drive away from the lake and up the long dusty road to the ranch house, you leave cultivation and civilization behind. There are gazelle at the side of the road, and the grass is bleached and dry. The ranch house is dramatically sited on top of a rise. There are few trees around the house, and the veld grass has been cut to create a wide open area and to reveal a natural sunken rock garden filled with cactus and aloes. Beyond, the veld continues—waving yellow grass and thorn trees. It is peaceful and isolated, a place to take a deep breath and feel on top of the world.

Quotes

"This place is heaven for landscape junkies."

"I saw two cheetah on the dirt road."

The ranch house is at 2134 meters above sea level. It is currently owned by Tony Church and was originally built by Martha Gellhorn, one of Ernest Hemingway's wives.

The ranch can cater to a maximum of twelve people. It is very personalized, relaxed and casual. Guests stay either in the main ranch house (four double bedrooms) or in the separate cottage (two double bedrooms). The rooms are attractively decorated in country floral prints, and each has a bathroom ensuite. The living/dining room is friendly with a large stone fireplace and comfortable chairs. Most of your time, however, will be spent outdoors—walking, riding horses, or eating out on the veranda.

Horse riding is one of the main attractions of Longonot Ranch. Day groups even come here just for riding. There are stables and plenty of mounts. You ride over hills and down on to plains, practically touching giraffe and herds of antelope. The scenery is stunning—you have views of Hell's Gate Gorge, Lake Naivasha and mountains in the distance. There are also escorted game walks with a Park Ranger. Side trips to Hell's Gate or around the lake can be arranged. You set the pace and choose the activities.

Although this is a private Ranch house, it is not someone's permanent home. You will be hosted by your tour operator or, if you are travelling independently, by the ranch manager. The ranch feels as though it belongs to you and your group.

OLERAI HOUSE
Oria Douglas-Hamilton, Box 54667, Nairobi
☎ 334868

This charming, flower-covered farmhouse is the former home of Oria and Ian Douglas-Hamilton (renowned elephant conservationists). In its wide expanse of emerald lawn, the house is partly shaded by the enormous acacia trees for which it is named. Olerai is the Masai name for the Naivasha Acacia Tree. Although the house is quite a distance from Lake Naivasha and the water obscured by reeds, the setting is bucolic, timeless, and peaceful. There is a wonderful sense of space and green. The distinctive volcanic shape of Mt. Longonot, purple and blue with distance, adds a certain African drama.

This is a place to unwind, rest, read and enjoy your companions. The house, which easily sleeps up to ten people, is ideal for a large family or a group of friends. The living/dining room is spacious and comfortable, with a cozy fireplace, casual cushioned seating areas and a big round dining table. There are homey touches of fresh flowers, magazines on tables, a drinks table set up in the evening.

Quotes

> *"We wanted to create true Kenyan hospitality—it's like coming to a homestead..."* Oria Douglas-Hamilton.

"My family would love it here. What a perfect weekend break from Nairobi."

Safari Journal

Wednesday ~ lunch

Feeling warm and lethargic and at peace with the world.
I can hear bees buzzing and cows mooing. Everything looks
green and slightly hazy, and there is such a "telephoto" expansiveness
in the distance. i "zoom" back to the foreground ~ a long table
spread with a patterned cloth, a vase of bright flowers,
platters of food and glasses of red wine catching the sun.
And friends ~ women in floppy straw hats ~ we should be
part of a Fellini movie set

Four separate double bedrooms are arranged around a central garden courtyard. Two of these rooms are on split levels with charming upstairs lofts and extra beds. All four have bathrooms. The Douglas-Hamiltons plan to add a couple more cottage bedrooms in the garden. Since this was a family home, it retains its feeling of comfort and individual character. There are dramatic murals in some of the bathrooms, and there is something whimsical about the loft bedrooms with their mosquito netted beds and casement windows. You feel as though you have come to a weekend getaway cottage—casual and informal.

Olerai House offers complete privacy. There is no "host" hovering or joining you for meals. However, very capable and unobtrusive staff make sure you are completely comfortable. The meals are memorable and are served when and where you want them—lovely to eat outdoors under those giant trees. There are wonderful fresh soups, tempting pastas, roast lamb and decadent desserts. Not the place for a diet weekend!

If you feel the need to work off some of this lazing about and eating, you can go on walks. There is someone to guide you in the surrounding hills, and you can go for a bird walk near the lake. You come back to a fire and tea and more irresistible food.

The Douglas-Hamiltons now live in Sirocco House which was built in the early 1930s by Oria's parents. This unique art deco house is only a short walk from Olerai House. It is possible to make arrangements to visit Sirocco House for tea or sundowners.

You can buy soda and beer, but remember to bring your own wine and spirits.

When you leave Olerai House you can stock up on fresh farm produce.

Special Offerings

For an additional charge you can have farm walks with breakfast, tea or cocktails at Sirocco House, walks in Crater Lake Sanctuary with picnic or cocktails, ox-wagon ride and lunch, picnic lunch at Hell's Gate National Park, Mt. Kenya morning or evening flights.

Off Notes

Being near a lake and on a farm, insect life abounds. No lake view or access.

LAKESIDE HOUSE

Lakeside House, Box 1262, Naivasha
☎ *(0311) 20908,* ☎ *(02) 56742*

Lakeside House is a small home near the turnoff onto Moi South Lake Road. The grounds and gardens are not very grand, but you can look toward the papyrus at the edge of Lake Naivasha from the veranda. June Shaw is the hostess: she treats her guests like family. Hospitality seems part of the decor in the dining room and in the blue and chintz sitting room.

Guests sleep in one double room in the main farmhouse and in a nearby cottage. The cottage rooms have ensuite shower bathrooms. The rooms are very small and rather crowded with furnishings. There are some homey touches such as books, magazines and instant coffee/tea trays.

June and her family can help guests locate boats and horses to rent and plan day excursions in the area. June says you can walk to Crescent Island through the adjoining property.

MORENDAT HOUSE

Morendat House, Box 299, Naivasha
☎ *(0311) 20041*

Just off the main Nakuru Road, this gracious old Lake Naivasha house of whitewashed stone is the home of Giulia Bisleti. It has a convenient position between Lake Naivasha and Lake Nakuru. She wants her guests to feel that Morendat House is their own home base in Kenya.

The huge garden is fragrant with orange trees; the veranda is cool with overhanging plants; the living room is spacious with elegant arches. She has furnished her home with many polished antiques, and objets d'art. A central stone fireplace gleams with copper pots and utensils. Her decor is eclectic with an enriched country elegance.

There are two double bedrooms in the house, both graciously furnished, both with private bathroom including bidet. A third double bedroom is in a private cottage at the side of a pleasant swimming pool.

All meals are included, but guests are asked to bring their own wines and spirits. Because of the antique glass and a serious commitment of quiet relaxation, younger children are not invited. Although the property extends to the shore of Lake Naivasha, there are no views of the lake from the house.

THE WAGON WHEEL

Safcon Travel Services, Ltd., Box 59224, Nairobi
☎ *503265, FAX: 506824*

At The Wagon Wheel, you are the personal guests of Millicent Morson. Her two-story home is framed by an absolutely splendid garden, probably one of Kenya's best, and all Mrs. Morson's own work. It is laid out English fashion, with rambling walks through multilevel beds and shady trees. There are delightful floral surprises at each turn of the path. Many species of birds make it their home.

The Morson family have been in Kenya since 1904 when Lord Delamere encouraged two brothers to open Kenya's first sawmills in Limuru. After logging until 1976, they stayed in Limuru to raise tea and horses for racing. Later Millicent and her husband, Kitch Morson, retired to The Wagon Wheel, a small farm on the shores of Lake Naivasha.

The house is homey and furnished in a pleasing "country cottage" style. There are robust green plants in glazed clay pots and a collection of antique china. Comfortable sofas and chairs in cool chintz are arranged near the fireplace. Colorful small rugs are scattered on wood floors; there are polished brass farm implements and bowls of flowers.

The "country" theme is carried through to the two guest bedrooms. Each bedroom has an ensuite bathroom and a private door to that marvellous garden.

Furnishings throughout the house reflect Mrs. Morson's interest in gardening and the family's history in Kenya. Some very special antiques have been passed down from earlier days and glow with the care the Morsons have given them. Various pieces have been used in period films produced in Kenya such as *Out of Africa.*

Guests can take walks to the lake, and Mrs. Morson can arrange for bird watching from a boat or for excursions to the other attractions of the area.

GILGIL

There is not much of interest for the tourist in this small town between Naivasha and Nakuru.

RIVER HOUSE

Bunson Travel Service Ltd., Box 45456, Nairobi
☎ *221992, FAX: 723599*

This private country house in Gilgil belongs to the Barratts. River House is
best known for its cuisine—Nann Barratt is a trained cordon bleu chef.

River House is surrounded by well-tended lawns and flower beds. Indigenous
forest edges a stream which runs through this 20 hectares property and there are
shady paths for pleasant walks. The vegetable gardens are amazing—ordered
rows of healthy produce just waiting to be transformed into the most memorable
of dishes.

Guests stay right in the house. There are two double bedrooms each with private bathroom. The living room has a huge fireplace which is lit on cool nights.
Pictures by a talented family member grace the walls and dog baskets line the
wide passage. There are oriental rugs, family antiques, frills, and memorabilia.
You are treated as a family guest. Nann is a warm and friendly person who loves
to talk and make you welcome.

Golf and tennis are available nearby. River House can be used as a base to explore the Rift Valley lakes or the Aberdares. You can also arrange to go to River
House for lunch if you are en route to somewhere else.

LAKE ELMENTEITA

Most of this shallow soda lake is on private land—part of the Delamere Estate's Soysambu property. There is game in the bush around the lake, and flamingos and pelicans congregate along the shores.

LAKE ELMENTEITA LODGE

Lake Elmenteita Lodge, Box 70559, Nairobi
☎ *224998, Telex: 22658 Tariff Pending*

A new lodge is due to open on a hill overlooking Lake Elmenteita. Ox-wagon safaris will be offered between this lodge and its sister hotel, Lake Nakuru Lodge.

Lake Elmenteita Lodge will have 70 beds in cottages and executive suites. There are plans for a swimming pool, sauna, and tennis courts. In addition to the ox-wagon safaris, there will be horse riding and game walks.

DELAMERE CAMP

Delamere Camps Ltd., Box 48019, Nairobi
☎ *335935, FAX: 216528*

Just one hour by road from Nairobi, Delamere Camp has one of the most beautiful sites in Kenya. A small tented camp, it is located within the Soysambu Wildlife Sanctuary on the shore of Lake Elmenteita, deep in Kenya's Great Rift

Valley. The lake is often pink with thousands of Lesser and Greater Flamingos, and the near and far skyline is mysterious and beautifully primeval with the weathered remains of broken volcanic peaks. The surrounding forest and bush are very green; they tend to soften the harshness of the volcanic rock and ash that are part of this setting.

Because the sanctuary is located within the vast estates of the current Lord Delamere (Hugh, the Fifth Baron), the camp feels very private, separate from outside life. It is a birder's paradise: besides flamingos, there are also Great White Pelicans and scores of other water and land birds. You can go on game or botanical drives in the camp's open-air four-wheel-drive vehicles. Camp guides or naturalists will help you to spot and identify game. They will also identify plants and trees and show how they are used by the local people (the sap from an aloe-like plant seemed to heal my cut finger in just a few hours!). Guides can lead you on walks and take you for night game drives in search of bush baby, aardvark and zorilla. You may also have a close-up view of elusive game and birdlife from several camp game blinds nearby.

On a cliff rising above the lake, natural stone benches and tables create the perfect place for grand views of the lake and the volcanoes—especially spectacular at sunrise or sunset. This high view point is perfect for sundowners with hot brochettes of gazelle cooked over an open fire. You could also arrange to have brunch or a picnic there.

The camp's 12 tents and main lodge are spread out on a shallow hillside sloping down to the lake. The main lodge is a rather utilitarian concrete and wood structure with one side open to view the lake. Small tables are arranged in the dining area at one end; a small bar is at the other. Rush sofas and chairs form a lounge area around a central fireplace, which smokes a bit as it tries to fight off the chill night breezes. When you check in, be prepared to sign a waiver releasing the camp from any liability for theft or injury.

Accommodations

The individual tents are raised on large concrete pads with very large concrete shower bathrooms attached to the rear of the tent. The tents are spacious with plenty of room for two—good twin beds, wardrobes, desks, shelves. Windows are large with zip covers over screens. Tents are sprayed at night, but there are no mosquito nets. Floors are unpainted concrete: the effect is utilitarian but comfortable. Safari chairs furnish the outdoor cement porch. Hammocks have been rigged in shady spots (Bliss...zzz). *Best views*: tents # 6, 8, 10, 12. Seven kilometers away is a treehouse which sleeps four in bunk beds—no electricity, no ensuite bathrooms. There is a small waterhole below, an open deck on the roof, and a battery-powered spotlight for night game viewing—a private adventure.

Other Facilities
Souvenir and Sundry Shop, Safe at Reception.

NAKURU

Nakuru is the capital of the Rift Valley Province and is the fourth largest town in Kenya. It is noisy, dusty and chaotic. Tourists go to this area for the Lake Nakuru National Park which is best known for its flamingos. There are also large flocks of pelicans. The parkland surrounding the lake has acacia and euphorbia forests as well as areas of grassland and rocky cliffs. It is home to many animals including waterbuck, leopards, and Rothschild giraffe. Surrounded by an electric fence, the park is also a sanctuary for black rhinos brought here from other areas. Outside the park, on the other side of the town, rises Menengai, a huge extinct volcano. Hardly recognizable as such from below, the view when you reach the top is breathtaking. You can drive to a lookout point and gaze down over an expanse of black lava and bush in the massive caldera.

LAKE NAKURU LODGE
Lake Nakuru Lodge, Box 70559, Nairobi
☎ *224998, Telex: 22658*

High on a hilltop in the southeast corner of Lake Nakuru National Park, this small lodge enjoys a particularly commanding view of the lake. Although the lodge has room for 120 guests, it can fill up fast with tour groups. A new all-suite deluxe wing is very private and has sweeping views from individual verandas. Older standard rooms in small bandas may be disappointing. Your first impression of the lodge is color—rampant bougainvillea lines all the stone pathways, and the many resident birds flit iridescent feathers.

From reception (cool drinks, a natural decor of rough wood and stone), you walk down more garden pathways with guest bandas on each side. The heart of the lodge is the dining area, view terrace, and swimming pool. The view is wonderful—you look down the hill and across a good bit of the park to the lake with its fluffy edging of pink flamingos. Frequently, other park animals are also on view. They often come right up to the low rock wall at the edge of the lawn.

Accommodations

Standard rooms in little peaked-roof bandas with ensuite bathrooms are sparsely furnished for double occupancy. Beds are hard, bathrooms have seen better days, but work. Rooms are sprayed, beds have mosquito nets. Standards of cleanliness are not high. *Our Favorites*: New deluxe wing suites.

SAROVA LION HILL
Sarova Lion Hill, Box 30680, Nairobi
☎ *333248, FAX: 211472*

Sarova Lion Hill is in Lake Nakuru National Park. Its location on a small plateau gives views of the lake. You can sit outside on the terrace of the rustic Rift Valley Bar to enjoy the gardens or the lake view—there is even a telescope for up-close viewing. From the Flamingo Restaurant patio, which overlooks the swimming pool, you also have views of the lake and the hills beyond.

Accommodations

In contrast to the surroundings, the lodge buildings are disappointingly stark and functional. The lodge can accommodate up to 150 guests in two-room units scattered on the hillside near the main lodge. Each room has ensuite bathroom and private veranda, some with panoramic views of the lake. The rooms are not outstanding. There are six nonsmoking rooms and a surprisingly elegant honeymoon suite with two bedrooms. *Best Choice for View of the Lake*: #60–65 on the hilltop.

Special Offerings

The lodge has a sauna, boutique, conference center for 80 and dancers to entertain the guests at night.

Off Notes

You are likely to share your safari buffet with noisy tour groups.

RONGAI AND MOLO

Traveling northwest of Nakuru you pass Rongai before climbing the western escarpment of the Rift Valley to Molo. Approximately 2500 meters high, the garden-green town of Molo has highland meadows and flocks of sheep. Molo lamb is known throughout Kenya for its fine quality.

DELORAINE

Wilderness Trails (K) Ltd/ Bush Homes of East Africa Ltd.
Box 56923, Nairobi
☎ *506139, FAX: 502739*

Deloraine is a grand colonial home built in 1920 by a prominent settler, Lord Francis Scott. Until her death in 1992, Pamela Scott, a well-known livestock breeder lived in the house. Today, Deloraine is the home of Tristan and Lucinda Voorspuy, who are best known for their riding safaris, and who have opened their home to small safari groups. Both are accomplished riders and polo players, and Lucinda is a pleasant and accommodating hostess.

Situated at 6000 ft. on the western side of the Rift Valley at Rongai, Deloraine is in the middle of a 5000 acre commercial farm. The imposing double-story stone building has a shaded veranda running the full length of the upper story and tall stone archways leading from the lower veranda to steps which descend to broad lawns and lovely gardens. There is a croquet lawn and a tennis court.

On the farm are about 40 horses—some of which are used on the riding safaris. There are also polo ponies which Deloraine guests can ride if they want to explore the farm or the surrounding hillsides.

The Voorspuys have been slowly redecorating the interior of Deloraine. The house has charm and some lovely features. It exudes a sense of the faded grandeur of Colonial Kenya—a shabby chic. The ground floor is the best feature of the house, with spacious living and dining rooms. The living room has high timbered ceilings, a large fireplace, comfortable chairs and sofas and many prints hanging on cheerful yellow walls. There are six double bedrooms with bathrooms. Some of these rooms will need further renovation before they match the imposing exterior.

The Voorspuy's first love and primary interest is in the private riding safaris which they operate under their company name "Offbeat Safaris". Although they will host nonriding guests at Deloraine, their preference is for keen riders.

JUANI FARM

Kesana Ltd., Box 39672, Nairobi
☎ *749062, FAX: 741636*

"Juani" means a place in the sun, and Juani Farm enjoys sunshine most days of the year. Situated near Molo, this is the home of Jean and Michael Skinner, the last White Kenyan farmers remaining in the Molo area. In their beautiful surroundings, they live the gracious life of a bygone era. When you stay at Juani, you are their guests, and sample a slice of this life.

One of the most memorable features of Juani is the magnificent garden. A breathtaking series of English flowerbeds, profuse with blooms, curve through thick green lawns. Beyond is the base of the Rift Valley with the opposite escarpment rising sheer on the horizon. During the day, meals are served outdoors in this lovely garden setting.

The farmhouse is rather charming. Several rooms have been added on over the years and outdoor passageways link some of the rooms. There are three guest bedrooms, each with fireplace and a private bathroom. These spacious rooms, although a little musty, are cozy with collected knickknacks, bowls of wonderfully arranged flowers, and thoughtful touches such as cigarettes, drinking water and hand lotions. In the evening you join your hosts around the fire in their large and comfortable living room. An English-style home-cooked dinner is elegantly served.

Jean Skinner envelops you with a genteel hospitality. Great attention is paid to your comfort—baths can be drawn for you, a covered hot water bottle warms your bed, and morning tea or coffee is served in your room. Michael Skinner is happy to express his views on Kenya and tells of his experiences leading private safaris.

Juani Farm is very self-sufficient. As Michael says, "We make our own water and our own light." Water is heated by wood fires, and the generator goes off before midnight.

Juani is a convenient location for exploring Lake Nakuru, and it is an easy drive to Lakes Bogoria and Baringo. If you have no transport, side trips with the Skinners can be arranged.

LAKE BARINGO

Lake Baringo is a freshwater lake. It is particularly well known for its amazing variety of birds (448 species) and is a popular destination for birders.

As is true with all the Rift Valley lakes, Baringo has its own unique character. Surrounded by harsh dry countryside, the lake has an isolated peacefulness. The water is heavily silted with soil. It is an unusual muddy-brown color which takes on dramatic tones depending on the light and weather. There are several rocky islands, and mountain ranges are visible in many directions. There is a sense of incredible space and a stark wild, beauty.

The lake is home to many hippo and crocodiles. The local tribesmen, the Njemps, fish there. You can often see them paddling in their small precarious-looking canoes made from branches of the Ambatch tree. They reckon the Baringo crocodiles are not dangerous.

It is usually extremely hot in this area. Go well prepared with hat and sunblock and take swimwear. This is a malaria area.

Most visitors to Baringo combine their stay with a trip to the neighboring Lake Bogoria National Reserve. This side trip is well worth it. Bogoria is best known for its impressive hot springs and its flamingos. This long narrow lake is beautiful—unspoiled, dominated by high steep hills and, when inhabited by thousands of flamingos, ringed with an amazing pink border. You might also be fortunate enough to see a herd of the Greater Kudu here.

ISLAND CAMP

Lonrho Hotels Kenya Ltd.
Box 58581, Nairobi
☎ *216940, FAX: 216796*

There is something unique and special about Island Camp—a sense of adventure and timeless Africa.

The adventure starts when you have to leave the civilized tarmac road at the Baringo Club Hotel. You then follow an unlikely and rocky track winding up to a headland parking spot. Here you leave your vehicle in the care of a Camp askari. Grab your bag, hang on to your hat, and hop aboard a motorized canoe for the 20 minute boat ride to the island.

The lake looks like mud, an unrelenting brown. The boat passes hippo—humps in the water or perhaps a pink yawning mouth and small eyes. There are several islands; your destination is Ol Kokwe, which means "place of rocks." You can see for great distances, and all around tower magnificent high hills and extinct volcanoes—ridge after ridge in dark, smoky tones of blue, purple, and grey, like an Oriental watercolor. In the middle of all this water it feels dry. And hot. You'll be pleased you brought a hat.

From the Visitor's book:

> *"Superb Africa"*

> *"Slowed down to a stop. A wonderful place to be at peace."*

When you land you are greeted by shade and a welcome drink. Because the camp is built on a hill, to reach the various tents and communal places, you walk and climb along winding stone paths. There are spreading trees, exotic vegetation, bright lizards and scores of different birds. You feel the whole camp is in harmony with its setting—walls are made of round yellow and tan stones, roofs are high thatch and the tents a faded green.

There is a lot of climbing along paths and up steps. At the highest point of the camp is the swimming pool. We vote this the best positioned pool in Kenya and, in this extremely hot place, one of the most necessary. From this high vantage point, you have views across the lake to the mountains beyond. You can marvel for hours at the play of light and the movement of weather over the land and water. There is great drama about this place—an awesomeness which reminds you of man's insignificance.

Around the pool there are comfortable loungers under creeper-covered trellises. There is a large open-sided thatched lounge and bar at this level—you don't have to move for a cold drink in the heat of the day. Afternoon tea is also served here, and the place is small and intimate enough for guests to strike up conversations.

If the spirit takes you, you can be more active. The camp is at the end of quite a big island, and you can take lengthy walks—to see birds, to visit the local Njemps Village, or to hike to the hot springs at the far end of the island. Island Camp is a paradise for bird-watchers—their enthusiasm is contagious.

Popular and well worth doing are the boat trips to the marshes and up the mouth of the Molo River. These are offered morning and evening and are accompanied by a guide to help identify the birds. You will see flocks of spectacular birds, and up the river, crocodiles suddenly slither out of the reeds to sink invisibly into the brown water.

Those who like water sports will also find plenty to do. There is waterskiing and windsurfing. Plans are afoot to expand water sports at Island Camp.

The dining locations at the camp are more memorable than the meals served. When you sit in the main thatched dining area, you are at the height of tree tops. Unhindered by walls or glass, you can enjoy the breezes and look down across the lake. Sometimes, on fine evenings, barbecue dinners are served alfresco around the pool area. With candlelight, the stars above, and the haunting notes of a Njemps reed pipe being played under a tree, there is a feeling of magic, of timelessness.

You come to Island Camp for its unique and unusual beauty, not for fancy accommodation. The tents are perfectly adequate, but are not of the same standard as luxurious tents found in some tented camps. The best thing about Island Camp tents is their position. Most have spectacular views over the lake and a nice sense of privacy. It is difficult to believe there are as many as 23 tents scattered around the camp property. Some are on the side of a steep rocky hill, some are tucked under trees, others perched on a rocky outcrop.

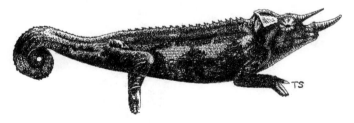

Accommodations

The tents have thatched shelters to help keep them cool and provide a shady veranda where you can sit on safari chairs and admire your view. Behind each tent is a solidly built functional bathroom with a flush toilet and solar heated shower. To get there you must unzip your tent and open the bathroom door. *Best bets*: #15 has a double bed, a great view, and is very private. Tents # 1 & 2 are private and have a good view.

Special Offerings

Boat trips, bird walks, walk to hot springs, waterskiing, windsurfing, pool, sundowners on neighboring island, traditional Njemps dances. Residents (on special rates) pay extra for boat ferry to island.

Off Notes

Not easy for people who would have difficulty climbing. Some people may not enjoy the host of insects and reptiles living on the island.

SARUNI

Chartered Expeditions Kenya Ltd. and Utalii Tours and Safaris Ltd. Box 61542, Nairobi
☎ *333285, FAX: 228875*

Saruni is the newcomer to the Lake Baringo area. It is a small tented camp built on the opposite end of Ol Kokwe Island from Island Camp. You reach Saruni in the same manner as Island Camp—by boat from the same jetty on the mainland.

Saruni is much wilder and more private than Island Camp. At present the entire camp consists of only eight tents and a simple mess area. The tents each face a lake view and are set in the natural bush, far enough apart that you feel you are all alone. The mess area is a flat space of pounded dirt under a big acacia tree with safari chairs and tables facing marvellous views of the lake and the mountains beyond. Next to it is a simple and functional bar and dining area with a cement floor, papyrus roof, and walls of netting to keep out the bugs but not the view or the fresh air.

"Saruni" means "a rescue place"—here you find peace and privacy in an unspoiled natural setting. At Saruni you are "roughing it" in style. There is no running water (no flush toilets) and no electricity. But, the tents are wonderful—large and light with many mesh windows and nicely furnished with a Zanzibar chest and handwoven fabrics. Even the rustic aspects have been dealt with in style. The long-drop toilets are ensuite in a large bright bathroom, and have a comfortably familiar toilet shape. A big container of water placed high outside the back of each tent provides truly solar-heated showers. Although there is no electricity, over 150 hurricane lamps are placed along the paths to light your way at night.

It is hot here—often oppressively hot with a dry enervating heat. In the middle of the day all seems limp and still. Such a relief to sit in the shade with a cold drink and ice—quite a feat for this remote island spot with no electricity. It would be wonderful to cool down in a swimming pool. Hopefully, that will soon be a reality. There are plans to build a pool on a high point, which should give lovely views. At the moment, if you want to swim, you are offered the lake. Apparently many do swim in these muddy waters. While contemplating the cove below the tent, a snout on eyes glided by. An inhabitant of the island claimed that no one has been attacked by crocodiles in this lake. We'll hold out for the pool.

Unfortunately we did not stay long enough for a meal, but a glance through the visitors' book revealed frequent praise for the food.

The camp is managed by Wilson Lemeriai who grew up in the area and is an accomplished bird man. He claims to know 461 species of birds and says there are 200 species on the island and more along the shores of the mainland. He leads bird walks and boat trips. Not far from the camp are the hot springs—the steam and gurgling sounds make you truly appreciate that you are on the floor of the great Rift Valley.

From the Visitor's Book:

> *"Paddling in crocodile infested waters is a wonderful way of building up an appetite for breakfast."*

> *"Now this is island living!"*

> *(Guest from Hawaii!)*

LAKE BARINGO CLUB

Block Hotels, Box 47557, Nairobi
☎ *335807, FAX: 340541*

The Lake Baringo Club is most memorable for its beautiful gardens. After driving through the parched and rocky countryside, the club feels like an oasis of green and color. Spread along the shore of Lake Baringo, it faces lovely grounds and the lake. In the wide lawns stand big exotic trees ablaze with flowers. A profusion of brilliant bougainvillea cascades over trellises and walls. Sturdy wooden tables with groupings of chairs are scattered around the lawns and under trees. It is all so still and hot and bright. Nothing moves except a big monitor lizard and the air busy with the sounds of birds.

The birds! They are the main attraction of this area. Some 448 species are found on and around the lake. The Baringo Club, with its resident ornithologist, is well organized to make the most of this natural attraction. Bird walks are led around the hotel grounds and on the nearby rocky cliffs. There are boat trips on the lake and to the marshy mouth of the Molo River—marvelous for water birds. Each evening a slide show on birds is presented.

Birds are not the only wildlife. There are lots of hippos in the lake. During the day you can see parts of hippos sticking out of the muddy water—backs, twirly ears, a yawning mouth. In the evening and at night, however, you might see the whole beast—grazing on the hotel lawns. You can ask for a "hippo call"—to be called when there are hippos outside. The big signs in the grounds which read "Wild Animals Are Dangerous" are there for a very good reason. Hippos are extraordinarily ornery and account for many deaths in Africa. Don't venture close.

Baringo Club has a relaxed and friendly air. The buildings are low and unobtrusive, and have been designed to take advantage of the view. With bedrooms on each side of the main building, it all looks a bit like a glorified motel covered in bougainvillea.

There is a small but pleasant swimming pool edged with stone paving. In the intense heat of this area, the pool is a real blessing.

Although the club is right on the shores of Lake Baringo, you are not conscious of being on the lake in the same way as when you stay on Ol Kokwe Island. The lovely garden, with its mature trees, obscures the wide stark vistas across the lake and hides the drama of the mountains beyond. When you stay at the club, the strange beauty and isolation of the area seems tamed and softened. Make sure you walk out to the jetty to appreciate the distances. Better yet, go on a boat trip—add some adventure.

Accommodations

There are a total of 52 bedrooms, most of which are in the "new wing." The rooms here are simple and functional with linoleum floors and high ceilings. Most have twin beds which can both be enclosed by a huge mosquito net. Each has a small bathroom with shower. There are ceiling fans and a private veranda facing the lake. The old wing is on the other side of the main building, near the swimming pool. Rooms in this wing are less uniform. The bathrooms tend to be bigger and some have bathtubs. These rooms are somewhat darker and more enclosed with lower ceilings and deeper verandas.

Special Offerings

Bird walks, boat trips, pool, games room, camel rides in the grounds, visits to the local Njemps fishing village, trips to Lake Bogoria. In the camp-ground next to the club is a shop selling colorful hand printed cotton items made by a local company called "Dry Season."

Designated as a "club," this hotel charges an entrance fee to casual visitors.

KABARNET

The small town of Kabarnet has a spectacular setting on top of the Kamasia Massif with views in one direction down over the Rift Valley towards Lakes Baringo and Bogoria, and in the other direction down into the plunging Kerio Valley.

Kabarnet is the home town of President Arap Moi. An unusually good road winds up to Kabarnet from Marigat.

KABARNET HOTEL
African Tours & Hotels, Box 30471, Nairobi
☎ *336858, FAX: 218109*

This is the main hotel in Kabarnet. It is fairly new, modern in design, and is operated by African Tours and Hotels Ltd. The only striking aspect of the Ka-barnet hotel is the dramatic view over the Kerio Valley. The hotel has 30 rooms, a conference center, and a swimming pool.

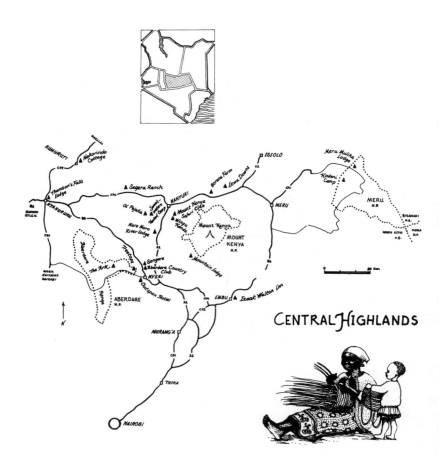

CENTRAL HIGHLANDS

CENTRAL HIGHLANDS (MT. KENYA AREA)

The Central Highlands of Kenya are an amazing geography of contrasts. The deep green of cultivated farmland gives way to the purple-gray scrub grass of high ranches where cattle, sheep and plains game graze. Mountain ranges are covered in forests with hidden trout streams. These highland streams flow to swift moving rivers that suddenly burst out and down into dramatic falls of water. Other mountains stand stark and dry, broken and weathered into moonscapes and mesas. Climbing a small rise can yield a panoramic vista of plains and plateaus rising to range after range of distant mountains. In the center, Mt. Kenya dominates.

With a base diameter of more than 150 kilometers and a height 5189 meters, Mt. Kenya is among the world's largest free-standing volcanic mountains. The equator crosses its northern slopes at 3350 meters with the mountain's twin snowcapped peaks, Batian and Nelion, brushing the sky some 17 kilometers south. Mt. Kenya has many moods—Wisping clouds can cloak the peaks in mystery. Thunder and lighting can rage. Falling rain can obscure and hide even the lower slopes with curtains of water. Glinting sunshine can illuminate the peaks.

TRAVELING IN THE CENTRAL HIGHLANDS

At the equator, slight variations of altitude create enormous changes in both climate and landscape. This means that the traveler can enjoy diverse experiences and surroundings without having to cover great distances. In just a short drive you can pass from the cool, misty forest of the Aberdares to the dry Laikipia Plateau with its miles of open ranch land. When you drive around the western side of the mountain you are on a long straight road through dry, flat scrub lands. The road around the eastern side however, curves and dips in a roller-coaster course through green farms, red cliffs and rushing waterfalls.

The great variation in the scenery is also reflected in the many choices available to the traveler. There is a great range in the types of places where you can stay, as well as in the kinds of activities and experiences you can enjoy. In terms of accommodations, there are night game viewing lodges deep in indigenous forests, elegant colonial country-club type hotels, and huge private ranches where you can ride and walk among wild animals. There are even sanctuaries and National Reserves where you can stay in tents or bandas and go on game drives. You could also plan climbing or fishing trips.

There are three **National Parks** in this region:

The Aberdare National Park

The volcanic massif of the Aberdare Mountains is part of the eastern side of the Rift Valley. With steep hillsides and thick forests, these mountains have not been tamed into farmland. Leopard, buffalo, and elephant inhabit the forests, and on the high misty moorlands are lions and antelope. There are streams and waterfalls, magnificent views, and lots of rain. It is frequently cold and misty. Four-wheel drives are essential. The park is often closed during the wet season.

Mt. Kenya National Park

Mt. Kenya (5189 meters) is the second highest mountain in Africa. Although it is right on the equator, its peaks are snow-covered all year. There are four main routes to climb the mountain and a few basic cabins and mountain huts. You are likely to see wild animals and an amazing range of unusual vegetation. The peaks of the mountain are more often than not obscured by clouds. Your best chance of seeing them is in the early morning or just before sunset.

Meru National Park

Situated east of Mt. Kenya and over the high Nyambene Hills, this is one of the least visited National Parks in Kenya. With its many streams, and higher than average rainfall, the park is luxuriant and bushy. There is long grass, a swamp and riverine forests. Tall distinctive doum palms add an exotic touch and contorted termite creations dot the grasslands. It is more difficult to spot animals here than in the wide open panoramas of some of the other parks. But, as a bonus, you are unlikely to see other vehicles when you are out on a game drive. It was in this area that the lioness, Elsa, heroine of *Born Free*, was released back into the wild. The park is home to many of the species found in northern Kenya—reticulated giraffe, Grevy's zebra, and gerenuk. There are also elephant, lion and cheetah, and over 300 species of birds. Options for tourist accommodations are limited.

The extremely fertile soil in the Central Highlands Area has resulted in extensive cultivation, especially to the south and the east of Mt. Kenya. Here you will see small farms on almost every available piece of land, and fields carved out on the sides of incredibly steep slopes. There are a number of major towns in the Central Highlands.

Nyeri is the administrative headquarters of Kenya's Central Province. One of the largest towns in the Central Highlands, it has a lively market and architectural reminders of colonial days. It is in a very lush and intensely cultivated area. Nyeri is where many of Kenya's most renowned athletes first trained.

Nanyuki is just north of the Equator. It is a social and market center for the ranch lands of the Laikipia Plateau and the lower slopes of Mt. Kenya. North of Nanyuki, at Timau, there is a trout farm, Kentrout—good for a lunch stop under the trees and possible to stay overnight. Soon after Timau, the road drops down towards the semi-arid northern deserts which seem to stretch on without end to Lake Turkana.

Nyahururu is best known for Thomson's Falls which are formed by the Ewaso Narok River and plunge 72 meters to the dense forest below. It is one of the highest towns in Kenya.

Meru town is both an agricultural center and the beginning of any visit to the Meru National Park. Dense forests surround the town, and the high altitude means that it is often misty.

Embu is the provincial headquarters of Eastern Province and is located amongst hills on the southeastern slopes of Mt. Kenya.

None of these towns is a major tourist attraction. Most of the accommodations described for this region are in the countryside, not the towns.

NYERI – NANYUKI – BEYOND

THE ABERDARE COUNTRY CLUB

Lonrho Hotels Kenya Ltd., Box 58581, Nairobi
☎ *216940, FAX: 216796*

Most people only see the Aberdare Country Club because it is the departure base for the Ark, a night game viewing lodge. The minivans disgorge their international, camera toting cargo before lunch. After lunch, the dark green Ark buses roll out, heading for the Aberdare Forest. The crowds come back next morning, looking weary and disheveled, to be herded back into minivans and on to the next stop.

For those who have the time to stay, however, the Aberdare Country Club can be a supremely quiet and relaxing getaway. The main house, a romantic stone building with red tiled roof, was built in 1937 by the Lyon family from England. They named the house "Steep" because of its position on the side of a hill, commanding sweeping views in all directions.

The Lyons were part of the notorious "Happy Valley Set." Apparently some pretty wild parties were thrown at "Steep" during World War II—difficult to imagine debauchery in this rather staid, British house with its mullioned windows, dark wood paneling and heavy drapes. Today the windows are larger, but the lounge and bar are still dark with maroon carpeting, leather couches and big stone fireplaces, reminiscent of an old British club.

The beauty of the place is best enjoyed sitting out at tables scattered on shaded lawns in front of the house. From here you can see forever out over grassy banks which extend down the hill—tempting children to run or roll. Vivid bougainvillea brightens the scene, and the swimming pool is partly visible through flowering shrubs. The open-sided Karuru Bar next to the pool overlooks two tennis courts. On a clear day you can see Mt. Kenya. There is a nine-hole golf course—rather steep and often host to families of baboons.

Guests stay in grey stone cottages, most of which are nestled among wonderful gardens on the hill behind the main building. They have high pitched shingle roofs, fireplaces, big picture windows and private outdoor sitting areas. There is a feeling of peace and privacy, and the fireplace is welcome on the many cool and misty evenings up in these highlands.

The dining room occupies a large part of the main house. There are yards of dark wood paneling and big windows frame lovely views. Lunch and breakfast are self-serve safari buffets. Children under 12 are encouraged to eat early. Adult dining is candlelit with a set menu. We had excellent smoked trout and baked ham. Special dining arrangements such as barbecues or bush banquets can be made for safari groups or conferences.

Beyond the stables is a game sanctuary where guests can take a walk or ride the club horses. There are no lion, elephant or buffalo in this 1100 acre sanctuary, but you are likely to see giraffe, zebra, impala and eland at close range. You can go on night game drives in the sanctuary. It is also possible to go on game drives to the "Salient" (in the Aberdare forest) and to "Solio Ranch," a private ranch which is home to both black and white rhino.

Accommodations

There are accommodations for about 100. Guests stay either in the original "Nursery Wing" or in cottages. The Nursery Wing is a separate building with five rooms. Some of the rooms are very large, and #2 and #5 have fireplaces. The cottages each contain two double rooms (one with a double bed and one with twin beds). Each room has a fireplace and ensuite bathroom. If you want connecting rooms, you can book the whole cottage. For a view of Mt. Kenya choose Rooms #28 or #29. Golfers might prefer the cottages down the hill and close to the golf course.

Special Offerings

Conference facilities for 50, club membership available, nine-hole golf course, pool (unheated), tennis courts, horse riding, game sanctuary (1300 acres), game drives, trout fishing, superior gift shop.

Off Notes

Lunch-time can be busy and loud with the Ark crowd. Cottages are more impressive from the outside than inside.

MOUNT KENYA SAFARI CLUB

Lonrho Hotels Kenya Ltd., Box 58581, Nairobi
☎ *216940, FAX: 216796*

The Mount Kenya Safari Club, with its blend of romance, history and scenery, has become a Kenyan tradition. Built right at the equator, on a ridge facing Mt. Kenya, the site is truly magnificent—well worth a visit, just for the view alone. The grand main building gleams white against the green sweep of surrounding lawns, and there are dramatic views of the foothill forests rising to the peaks of Mt. Kenya.

The original building was designed as a dream home by Rhoda Prudhomme for her husband, Gabriel. As a wealthy New York matron of 50, Rhoda fell in love with the young French aviator who took her big game hunting on her safari in Kenya. She gave up all to marry and live with him in Njoro among the Happy Valley Set of the 1930s. The land had been owned by a Mrs. Wheeler who agreed to sell it to them as "only lovers should live there." The Prudhommes called the house they built *Mawingo*, Swahili for the clouds cloaking the slopes of Mt. Kenya.

The house, with its many guest rooms, became an inn in 1948 when it was purchased by Abraham Block. In 1959 William Holden and two friends rested there during a shooting safari. They fell in love with the place, bought it, and turned it into one of the most unusual and exclusive clubs in the world, the Mt. Kenya Safari Club. Sir Winston Churchill was a founding member, as were Lord Louis Mountbatten, Robert Ruark, U.S. President Lyndon Johnson, Conrad Hilton, Bob Hope, Bing Crosby and more. During the last 30 years, the Club's guest book has been signed by many of the rich and famous of the world. It is now a "Leading Hotel of the World."

The sense of history remains strong in the main building and the original "William Holden Cottages." There is an odd mix of colonial Kenya and the glitz and glamour of the Hollywood set. In the Trophy Lounge are big leather seats, and the walls sport antlers and mounted heads—the room oozes "hunting" and "gentlemen." In the nearby Mountain View Lounge zebra skins vie for wall space with glossy photos of film stars. It is not hard to imagine these rooms peopled with film stars and celebrities of earlier days.

Today, the Mount Kenya Safari Club is a large and complex organization. The grounds of over a hundred acres contain a wide and diverse range of accommodations. A whole host of sporting options are available, and there are conference facilities, shops and galleries. Hotel vehicles are even necessary to transport you from your cottage or villa to the main hotel! The fame and popularity of the club has meant expanding the accommodations and services to cope with the influx of tourists who visit.

The hotel maintains a tradition of upscale elegance. Jackets and ties are required for dinner, there is live music for dinner dancing, and children must eat separately. The manicured gardens encourage sedate strolls. There is a sense of formality harking back to an earlier era, a hint of snobbery and pretention. The Mount Kenya Safari Club operates as both a club and a hotel. Although anyone can stay here, there are also paid-up club members who get special attention.

It is the setting of the Mt. Kenya Safari Club which is so special, so memorable. The view is spectacular. You look across sweeping lawns, past the idyllic swimming pool to the dark evergreens of the foothill forests, and further up to the clouds and peaks of Mt. Kenya. Moving back and forth across the lawns is an amazing parade of enormous birds: marabous, peacocks, and cranes.

There is a varied selection of things to do here. You can browse through the excellent art gallery, ride horses through the forests, laze by the pool, have a massage, play a round of golf, visit the boutiques, shop for books or curios, wander through the aviary...the list goes on and on.

The accommodations at the Mt. Kenya Safari Club cover a wide range of styles, locations and prices. You can have quite a different experience here depending on which room you get. For example you can be social and feel steeped in history if you stay in one of the rooms or suites in the main building. On the other hand, if you want a more private experience, you can opt for one of the lavishly appointed newer cottages tucked down by the river. You can be in a rather functional room with small windows, or you can luxuriate in front of a massive stone fireplace in a grand cottage with stunning views of the mountain. The options are wide, varied and confusing. Perhaps our "Accommodations" section will help you make your selection.

Quotes:

> *"This is my favorite place for a romantic getaway."*
>
> *"I had to bring a tie and a jacket all the way to Africa just for this hotel. I came to see wild animals, not to dress up and see other tourists."*

Accommodations

The club has room for more than 250 guests. There are various types of accommodations.

Standard rooms: These are in the main building and the new wing annex. All have fireplaces and many have good views of the mountain and grounds. Rooms #62–65 have the best views.

Main building studios and suites: These rooms are older and have more character. Some have good views. *Our Favorites:* Presidential Suite, Royal Suite #34/35 and studios #44 and #46.

Garden Suites: These give a sense of privacy, but not much view. Curtains separate the bedroom from the living area. Some suites connect and are good for families.

Riverside Cottages: These modern, spacious cottages are tucked down by the river. They have cathedral ceilings, fireplaces, nice verandas, double beds and sunken bathtubs. They are private, but far from the main building. Each cottage has two studios, with a suite in the middle. *Our Favorites:* For the view—Suites #104 and #107, and Studios #103 and #108. For privacy near the river and trees #97 and #99.

William Holden Cottages: These older cottages are our favorite accommodations at the Mt. Kenya Safari Club. They are luxurious and private, and some have magnificent views. In each cottage there is a central living room with a large stone fireplace. Leading off this are two bedrooms each with a private bathroom. *Our Favorites:* for view #3 and #4.

Luxury Villas: There are three large villas; each has a kitchen, large living room, dining room, and jacuzzi. They are far from the main building, near the river and a pond.

Special Facilities

Nine-hole golf course, heated swimming pool, horseback riding on trails, tennis, bowling green, table tennis, museum of African art, tribal dances, fashion boutique, curio and gift shops, club souvenir shop, conference facilities, health and beauty treatments, doctor, transportation in grounds, gas pump.

Off Notes

Busy with tour groups and buses…Calling and waiting for transport from your cottage to the main building is tedious…. Children are to be seen and not heard…. You need to pack a tie and jacket.

NARO MORU RIVER LODGE

Alliance Hotels, Box 49839, Nairobi
☎ *337501, FAX: 219212*

Sixteen kilometers south of the equator on the rather flat and dry western side of Mt. Kenya is the Naro Moru River Lodge. This rustic "mountain" style lodge is set among trees along the banks of a rushing stream. The lodge serves as the most popular base for climbing Mount Kenya and offers a wide variety of accommodations.

Tree shaded lawns and the sound of the snow-fed stream create your first impression of Naro Moru—tranquility and refreshing coolness. The place seems well established—colorful gardens flourish, birds are all around, jasmine scents the air, and the wooden chairs and tables seem to be growing under the trees. The entire lodge is informal, comfortable and relaxed.

The original lodge, a two-story dark timber building, houses the main dining room and the Pt. Lenana Bar and Lounge. This spacious lounge is bedecked with mementos of successful ascents to the top of the mountain.

Rooms meander among terraced rock gardens that follow natural contours above the river. Beyond are larger self-service cottages and further on are bunk houses and a campsite. There are accommodations to suit every pocket and style.

On the rise above the lodge, an inviting swimming pool commands an impressive view of Mt. Kenya. A bright, contemporary restaurant with adjoining bar and lounge overlooks the pool and serves lunch, tea, snacks and sundowners.

There is a sense of sportiness and outdoor activity at Naro Moru. Many visitors come to climb the mountain, others come for bird-watching or trout fishing. There are many choices: tennis, squash, swimming, darts, and table tennis. A peaceful forest path winds along the riverbank.

The lodge specializes in safaris to Mt. Kenya and offers a wide range of options from one day hikes to week long treks. Guides, porters and equipment can be hired, and the lodge operates Met Station Cabins and Mackinders Camp on the mountain. Book in advance.

Quotes:

"*It's great value for the money—there's so much to do here.*"

Accommodations

There are a wide range of accommodations—from deluxe rooms to a campsite. Most rooms have private decks overlooking trees and the river. *Our favorites* are the deluxe rooms, which have cathedral ceilings, blond wood-paneling, a fireplace and generous balconies. They are decorated in attractive local fabrics and have large modern bathrooms with a bathtub and separate shower. From deluxe rooms #24 and #25 you might see Mt. Kenya in the morning.

Special Facilities
Mountain trekking safaris, hire of climbing and camping equipment, transport hire to Mt. Kenya, heated swimming pool, tennis (two new courts), squash, fishing (river stocked with trout), horseback riding, bird walks, sauna, indoor games, conference facilities (up to 40 participants), video room and laundry service.

Off Notes
Main lodge rather tired and dowdy. Poor maintenance in older sections.

OUTSPAN HOTEL
Block Hotels, Box 47557, Nairobi
☎ *335807, FAX: 340541*

The Outspan Hotel has a history of up-country colonial elegance. It was built in 1927 facing Mt. Kenya with the Aberdare Mountains rising behind and the Chania River tumbling below. The site was chosen by Sherbrooke Walker and his wife, Lady Bettie.

Walker had been Lord Baden-Powell's private secretary and first Boy Scout Commissioner. His travels took him to the West Indies, Eastern Europe and America, but it was his dream to build in Kenya. When the railroad was built to Lake Victoria, he and his wife wanted to construct a "proper hotel." It was to be a haven of convenience and luxury (first flush loos) for the up-country area opened for ranching and farming.

Outspan was named to suggest how early travelers prepared to rest at journey's end by unyoking or "outspanning" weary oxen from oxcarts.

The hotel stands solid, comfortable and elegant in well-tended rolling lawns accented by travelers' palms. Lush tropical gardens are laid out English style to frame distant views of Mt. Kenya. The hotel building itself has a certain graciousness that is now rather tired. The lively, elegant crowds of yesteryear have faded into the past.

Safari Journal — Saturday morning

We got up at dawn to see Mt. Kenya and to go for a walk before breakfast. The gardens were beautiful in the morning light. Sunbirds and turacos were as brilliant as the flowers. Everything seemed scented with sunshine. We were glad to find early breakfast in progress on the terrace. From our table, the top of Mount Kenya was still showing through the mist. We had to smile at the dishevelled appearance of the Treetops people. One lady was heard to say that she wished she had spent the night in comfort here at Outspan!

It is the lovely setting, established gardens and feeling of history which still make Outspan worth a visit today. When you sit on the veranda facing Mt. Kenya, you enjoy the bright flowers, the garden scents and the birds. You might also be treated to a performance by the elegant peacock who loves to shiver his tailfeathers in display.

Breakfast and lunch buffets are served on this open veranda with chippendale chairs and white linen. The set-menu dinner is in the baronial dining hall. Our dinner was unusually good and nicely presented. This room has a well-worn elegance—mellow wood in the moldings, parquet floors and cathedral roof beams. Candlelight makes each table an intimate little island.

The main lounge, sherry bar and snooker room have paneling, fireplaces, brass fittings and overstuffed chairs and sofas in soft pastels and chintz. There are full-length windows and glass doors, many of which open to the garden.

The hotel acts as the reception point for visitors to Treetops, the original night game viewing lodge. In fact most visitors to Outspan are on their way to Treetops and only stay for lunch. Except for the Treetops crowd, the hotel has a very quiet almost abandoned air.

Lord Baden-Powell, the founder of International Scouting, loved Outspan and its beautiful location. With the consent of his friends, the Walkers, he chose to live here during the last years of his life. "Paxtu," the two hotel rooms of his "cottage," have been set aside as a small museum of scouting.

Accommodations

Outspan can accommodate approximately 65 guests. The hotel's 37 rooms are spacious and airy, most with fireplaces and easy chairs, many with garden access, some with views of Mt. Kenya. Large connecting rooms, suites and garden cottages provide plenty of space for small groups or families. Unfortunately, many rooms are shabby and sparsely furnished. This is a particular shame because the beautifully proportioned rooms have such potential. *Our Favorites:* Suites & Cottages. Room #24 & 26, which are light and airy and have a large sitting area, fireplace, enclosed terrace, French doors opening onto garden lawns. Room #62, which is quite large, with access to the more private garden of the Baden-Powell Scout Museum.

Special Offerings

Bird and nature walks, river walk, Mt. Kenya hikes, Kikuyu dance group, golf, tennis, squash, billiards, table tennis, darts, trout fishing, video room, card room, pool, souvenir shop, conference facilities, and a visit to a nearby coffee plantation.

Off Notes

Room decor is not up to the elegance of the original construction or dimension.

THOMSON'S FALLS LODGE

Thomson's Falls Lodge, Box 38, Nyahururu
☎ *(0365) 22006, 22319*

In 1883 at the age of 25, Joseph Thomson made a journey commissioned by the Royal Geographical Society in London. It took him through the uncharted land that later became Kenya. He traveled through a mountain range he named Aberdare after the president of the Royal Geographical Society, and his name stuck in the case of Thomson's gazelle. He was the first to chart the falls of the Nyahururu River—now Thomson's Falls, near the present day town of Nyahururu in the Aberdare Mountains.

In 1930, a rambling brick lodge was built with garden views of the falls. Today the lodge is old, ramshackle and greatly in need of renovations. Unfortunately, the view of the falls is almost completely blocked by the many souvenir dukas lining the cliff.

NIGHT GAME VIEWING LODGES

Night Game Viewing Lodges are an alternative way to see wild animals. Instead of going in search of animals, you stay in one place and hope that the animals will come to you. There is a special excitement and magic about this late night game vigil. If you are lucky you will observe animals from close quarters and for long periods to appreciate more of their behavior and interaction.

We have visited five night game viewing lodges in Kenya. Three of them (The Ark, Treetops and Mountain Lodge) are in the Mt. Kenya Area, and the others are described in later chapters. Shimba Hills is near the South coast, and Salt Lick Lodge is in the Taita Hills Game Sanctuary.

Of the three night game viewing lodges in the Mt. Kenya area, the Ark probably offers the best chance of seeing the most game. Remember, it is always a matter of chance and luck—there are nights when you might only see one lone buffalo, and other times when elephant, rhino, buffalo and lion may all be "on stage" at once. Treetops, despite its famous history, is suffering the encroachment of man, and is no longer deep in the forest. Both the Ark and Treetops have rather spartan accommodations: small cabin style rooms, many with shared bathrooms. Of the three, Mountain Lodge is certainly the most comfortable, with its private bathrooms and larger bedrooms.

THE ARK FOREST LODGE

Lonrho Hotels Kenya Ltd., Box 58581, Nairobi
☎ *216940, FAX: 219212*

The Ark gives you a night passage into the secret wildlife world of the Aberdare forest. Visitors from all over the globe begin their Ark experience from the Aberdare Country Club. After check-in and a leisurely lunch admiring the Club's sweeping views, you board the Ark buses for the 30-minute drive into the Aberdare Forest. The first view of the Ark is across a valley—its high curving roof dramatic and in the forest.

A raised wooden walkway is the "gangplank" to the Ark. The forest spreads out on each side as you leave the everyday world to embark on your adventure.

Next comes a "mandatory" briefing on rules, facilities, and schedules: don't frighten the animals with loud voices or flash bulbs; a buzzer in your room will wake you if something new or exciting is spotted during the night, breakfast is...leave your packed bags...departure is...Finally you are allowed to find your room—not much to see there—and head to the end of the building which overlooks the waterhole and natural salt lick.

The game and the public viewing areas make the Ark special. You see animals from three different levels and can choose to be indoors or out. The ground level photo hide, with no glass in the windows, is brisk and exciting. A herd of elephant might be just feet away—you can hear and smell and see everything. Or you can sit in warmth and comfort with a cup of tea and look at the animals through big windows.

Safari Journal
Monday night

I squeezed my sister's arm — we exchanged silent smiles of amazed delight. Below us an incredible scene is unfolding: There was some charging and trumpeting from the elephant trying to assert dominance over the best area of the salt lick. The two rhino kicked up a bit of dust but have now settled down. A large lion family rests in a semi-circle on the grass .... the young lions are playing what we have christened "sniff-the-rhino's-bum game". They take turns sneaking up close behind the young rhino. The rhino suddenly turns and charges, sending the little lion racing back to the grassy area. Soon, another lion tries the same thing. Extraordinary to witness this interaction of the animals — had never imagined them playing together this way. My children will be green with envy — they saw nothing like this on our previous visit.

The light rain is cold, but my shivers are partly from excitement. We could go in and warm up by the fire, but we stay out here on the open deck, getting wetter, glued to the amazing scene flood-lit below. This memory will stay with us forever.

The main lounge has an impressive stone fireplace—a cheery warmth at this altitude. The mounted rhino head is a relic of a fatal fight with an elephant in front of the Ark. A log book records sightings of animals, and a naturalist is on hand to answer questions. Tea and cakes are served in the afternoon. With the late hours kept, the bar does brisk business.

The dining room has long communal tables. It does not overlook the waterhole. On a very active night, dinner may be quite an interrupted affair as guests rush out to see which new animal has made an appearance.

An expectant hush pervades the Ark. Conversations are whispered, and binoculars and video cameras abound. It can be very cold and damp standing outside trying to glimpse a leopard at midnight—so come well prepared with protective clothing. There is an early wake-up call—often a good time to catch a clear glimpse of snow-capped Mt. Kenya towering above the forest. After breakfast, it's time to return, rather bleary-eyed, to the Aberdare Country Club.

Accommodations

The cabin-like rooms are small, functional and rather dark with wood paneling and relatively small windows. All rooms have ensuite bathrooms with a shower. There are 46 doubles, five singles and eight triples. Each room has a buzzer to wake you (you can turn it off). To see what exciting animal prompted the buzz, you have to join the rush to the front viewing rooms.

Special Offerings

Photo hide, outside viewing terrace, bar, souvenir and sundry shop.

Reminders

No children under seven are allowed. Only small bags are permitted. Bring protective clothing (it can be cold and wet); cameras and binoculars (great video opportunities and good results with the strong night lights); warm and comfortable night wear (you are likely to spring out of bed and rush down the passage to see the game—your lacy negligee is hardly ideal).

Off Notes

You cannot see game from your room.... Regimentation.... A noisy crowd can disturb the animals.

MOUNTAIN LODGE

African Tours and Hotels Ltd., Box 30471, Nairobi
☎ *336858, FAX: 218109*

Mountain Lodge is located in indigenous forest 7200 feet up in the foothills of the Mt. Kenya National Reserve. You are likely to see elephant and buffalo along the scenic road which leads to the lodge. Unlike the Ark and Treetops, you can drive yourself to Mountain Lodge, and can arrive and depart when you choose. The lodge caters primarily to international tour groups.

The lodge, a four-story timber box-like structure, was built in 1970. It overlooks a natural waterhole and salt lick surrounded by dense forest. On a clear day you can see the jagged peaks of Mt. Kenya's summit through the trees. A boardwalk leads through dense forest from the parking area to the lodge. The lodge is rustic and natural. Walls are covered with yellow reeds, and there are timber columns and dim lighting. The atmosphere is casual, the service, friendly and attentive.

Each of the bedrooms faces directly over the waterhole. This is what makes Mountain Lodge appealing. You can view the game in the comfort and privacy of your own room—no need for a midnight dash to a public area in order to see the animals. Each room has a private bathroom and either an open balcony or a large picture window.

Game most frequently seen include: buffalo, elephant, rhino, forest hogs, suni, red duiker, spotted hyena, genet cat, and if you are lucky, a leopard or the big male lion who makes his appearance every now and then. Since the lodge was deliberately located beside a route animals travel between Mt. Kenya and the lowlands, it is not uncommon to see very large herds of animals. At night the waterhole area is lit by floodlights.

There are three public areas for watching game. The top floor is an open-sided, roofed viewing area without seating, there is a viewing balcony which leads off from the bar, and a very small subterranean photo hide with open grill windows.

Animal sightings are kept in a log book near the bar, and binoculars can be borrowed. There is a "game porter" who will supposedly wake you up during the night if animals you have specified appear. At 6:30 a.m. tea or coffee will be brought to your door.

The dining room is bright, cheerful and functional. Windows along both sides look out over the forest. Each table seats six with a window at one end. Trout (fresh from nearby trout farms) and turkey are specialties of the lodge.

Accommodations

The lodge has 42 bedrooms on three floors. There are three VIP rooms and 39 standard double rooms. Ground floor rooms are better for close up game viewing. VIP rooms have a comfortable sitting area, small fridge, phone, and bathtub with shower. Standard rooms have showers only, and most have one double bed and one single bed. Some rooms have narrow open balconies with a cushioned bench. The others have a large picture window with comfortable chairs for game viewing.

Special Offerings

Slide shows of animals, gift and sundry shop, telephone operator for long distance calls on the solar powered telephone.

Off Notes

There is poor soundproofing between rooms and floors, and the smell of mildew is pervasive.... Public rooms are not very inviting—there is no cozy fire.

Note

Children under eight are not allowed to stay at Mountain Lodge.

TREETOPS

Block Hotels, Box 47557, Nairobi
☎ *335807, FAX: 340541*

After leaving the colonial comfort of the Outspan Hotel, Treetops is a spartan contrast. Located just inside the gates to the Aberdare National Park, Treetops overlooks waterholes and a salt lick. You know you've left comfort behind as you trudge up the dirt path behind an armed escort.

Treetops rises straight and stark on stilts. It is solely dedicated to game viewing. Climbing the narrow open stairs, you commit yourself to a night of close quarters and cold decks. The possibility of seeing wild animals up close has drawn thousands over the last 60 years to create the Treetops tradition. Unfortunately, today's visitors are often disappointed since the forest has been denuded by elephants and buffalo, and game is less plentiful.

However, there are some unique aspects to the Treetops experience: there is a sense of history (it was here that Elizabeth II became Queen overnight); a lively lecture is delivered on animals of the park; and living tree trunks branch naturally through rooms and corridors. The lounge is friendly, with big picture windows and warm wood, and there is a roof deck with open viewing in all directions.

The narrow, dark paneled dining room features long communal tables and bench seating. The linen is crisp and white, the menu elaborate, the food disappointing. The tiny guest rooms, dark narrow passages and twisting stairways can contribute to a feeling of claustrophobia.

Accommodations

The 48 guest rooms, called "nests," are tiny bed closets with dark wood paneling, small windows and no bathrooms. Small communal shower bathrooms are down the hall or sometimes downstairs. Since Treetops "sells beds, not rooms," you may meet a new roommate. Rooms A and B, just as small, with shower, are called suites. In 1983 the Queen slept in "Suite A." *Our Favorite*: A room back at Outspan. Or Buckingham Palace.

SWEETWATERS TENTED CAMP

Lonrho Hotels Kenya Ltd., Box 58581, Nairobi
☎ *216940, FAX: 216796*

Sweetwaters is a luxury tented camp. Like Ol Pejeta Lodge, it is on the game ranch previously belonging to Adnan Kashoggi.

This Lonrho operated camp has 25 well-appointed double tents all facing towards a waterhole, with Mt. Kenya dramatic in the background. The tents are arranged in two rows on a huge expanse of cropped lawn. The back row tents are built up on platforms to see over the front row. Only a matter of meters in front of the lower tents is a deep ditch hiding an electric fence. This means that when you sit on your private canvas-covered veranda, or even lie in bed with the flaps open, you can see animals just a few meters away without any visual sense of something separating them from you. You are completely safe, but you are so close to that big elephant eating branches or the giraffe splayed long-legged to drink. Add a red sunset and a clear view of Mt. Kenya, and you know what makes Sweetwaters special.

The main building includes reception, a lounge and the dining area. The attractive lounge with big windows and a fireplace is cleanly decorated with white fabric on dark Lamu-style furniture. The dining area is part of the old gate house which existed on this site. Unfortunately, it feels rather enclosed and does not take advantage of the view. For better vistas there is a thatched treehouse viewing area. There, from a shaded vantage point, you can look down at the animals gathered round the water hole. Sweetwaters also has a pretty swimming pool which is unheated and requires strength of purpose.

Safari Journal
Saturday Sundown :

We've invited the Irish nurse to join us for a sherry on our veranda. The blood red glow in the sky is fading fast — so sudden, these equatorial sunsets. We are almost right on the equator and yet there is snow on Mt. Kenya and a chill in the evening air. There are two big elephant just over by the waterhole. They are so close we can hear their ears flap. The nurse had arrived the night before from Saudi Arabia where she is a sister in a major hospital. I needed break before burn-out, she said. Where would be a nice quiet place to get away from it all, she'd asked. And been directed to Sweetwaters. She took a sip and sighed in contentment.

You can take game drives in the 22,000-acre sanctuary and are bound to see reticulated giraffe, plenty of plains game, and hopefully elephant. In certain areas of the sanctuary you will also drive past small local villages and herders. Quite often you will see domestic cattle and goats side by side with wild plains game. You are not likely to meet many other tourists on the roads—another plus for Sweetwaters.

Rhinos are being brought into the area. In an enclosed sanctuary is Morani, the friendly Rhino who previously lived in an orphanage and is now quite happy to be petted and photographed up close. Camel walks, horse riding, and night game drives can be arranged from Sweetwaters. You might also like to set up a visit to see nearby Ol Pejeta Lodge which was Adnan Kashoggi's private home—a luxurious and interesting place, still with his furnishings.

Sweetwaters is very relaxed and low key. You will not see the volume or variety of game of the Masai Mara, nor will you see the dramatic mesas of Samburu, but it is not a bad drive from Nairobi, and the road is tarmac until the turnoff. Sweetwaters is a pleasant relaxing stop for a night or two.

Accommodations

We have a preference for the "front row" tents at ground level. Tent #7 has a particularly good view. Tent #1 has a four-poster Lamu-style double bed.

Please Note

It can be cold at night (hope they are still placing hot water bottles in the beds).... The long dirt road from the turnoff suggests 4-wheel advisability especially during the rains.

LEWA DOWNS

Lewa Downs is possibly the best known and most successful ranch/homestay in Kenya. A magical combination of thoughtful hospitality, unforgettable scenery, and abundant wildlife makes Lewa Downs deserving of this renown.

Located near Isiolo in the foothills of Mt. Kenya, Lewa Downs is a 45,000-acre cattle ranch and has been home to the Craig family for three generations. Emma and Will Craig welcome you almost as family-come-home. They are a warm and friendly couple—understated, relaxed, and easygoing. Like all the Craigs, Will was raised on Lewa Downs. Will and Emma have a thorough knowledge and deep understanding of this land and its animals. They are eager to share this with their guests. They will take you horse riding among the giraffe; drive you to ridge tops with views in all directions; and stop in a field full of prehistoric stone artifacts.

To reach Lewa Downs, you leave the tarmac between Timau and Isiolo. A dusty ranch road winds through rolling hills with wildlife and candelabra cactus. Finally you reach the main house which is built strongly of cut Kenyan lava-stone and softened by a thatched roof and clouds of white and fuchsia bougainvillea. There are three quaint guest cottages constructed of thatch and volcanic rock. Each rustic cottage has two guest rooms sharing a common rondavel-style living room with fireplace and huge veranda.

Guests join the Craigs for meals in the outdoor dining terrace reached by a natural stone stairway through rock gardens. Three open stone arches frame views down a steep gorge and up to the volcanic rock on the next hill. The food is memorable—fresh from the ranch and home-cooked. Sometimes there is wonderful bread, baked into loaves shaped like elephants and other animals. Conversation at the communal table is lively, and you have the feeling of getting to know the Craigs and their other guests. Lanterns light the way for dinner, which is accented by wine and candlelight. Sometimes the Craigs take guests for breakfast in the bush or for sundowners at a viewpoint.

Most activities at Lewa Downs center on experiencing the wildlife and scenery. The ranch horses are well trained and sedate—even novice riders can enjoy the proximity to wild animals which riding allows. You can practically touch giraffe! There is still a great deal of wildlife at Lewa Downs because the Craig clan is very conservation minded. They have helped to establish and protect the Ngare Sergoit Rhino Sanctuary on the property.

Guests go on game drives in customized four-wheel drive vehicles with open roof-hatches and seats covered in cavas or sheepskin. There are field guides, binoculars, and always a very knowledgeable driver/guide. Amazing how these vehicles tackle steep rocky hillsides with such gusto! It is wonderful to be out in these high hills. You may come close to elephant families, rhino and zebra. There are "tail-up" warthog, herds of impala, and buffalo. All around are spellbinding views of ridge after ridge stretching to blue distant mountains.

Night game drives are a specialty at Lewa. A guide sits on the roof with a hand-held searchlight to spot the elusive animals of the night. Brilliant stars and perhaps a flood of moonlight add to the excitement.

Lewa Downs is part of the area of Kenya where traces of some of the earliest humans have been found. You are free to search for their carved stones, hand-worked tools, and other artifacts. It is thrilling to hold something made by another human being thousands of years ago. It feels right to replace such items gently, for another to find.

Quotes:

> *"...A delightful experience in everything. The rides with patient horses, the excellent cuisine, the comfortable rooms, the views, the air, the company..."*

> *"...Lewa Downs is magical! The Craigs shared their paradise with all of us..."*

> *"...Great to return from a sunset ride and find a roaring fire, a bowl of hot popcorn, and a well-stocked bar waiting for us in our own living room!"*

Accommodations

There are six simple guest rooms with rustic decor. Booking two guest rooms gives you your own private cottage complete with veranda, living room and fireplace. Each room has a no-frills bathroom with shower and flush toilet.

Special Offerings

Children might enjoy a visit to the Craig's farmyard and vegetable gardens. You can visit the ranch spinning and weaving project and make orders for rugs, etc. You can also go on guided game walks at your own pace and inclination. A craft shop and a small swimming pool are located near the main house. There is an airstrip on the ranch.

Off Note

A lunchtime tour group may crowd your private experience.

NGARE NITI
Wilderness Trails (K) Ltd., Box 56923, Nairobi
☎ *506139, FAX: 502739*

In a separate location, Ngare Niti is a dream house designed by Will Craig. Here you have all the space and grandeur of Lewa Downs scenery plus the luxury of your own private and beautiful house. This unhosted gem is a two-story over-sized cottage—an ingenious English country creation using local African materials: lava rock, timber and thatch.

You arrive at the house after a drive across Lewa Downs Ranch. The road leads up a long but gentle slope through acacia savannah. A green oasis suddenly confronts you as you swing into the circular drive and see Ngare Niti. Flowers and climbing vines on the stone and thatch exterior give an intimacy to the entrance. However, when you pass through the house to the wide veranda and terrace, the scale dramatically changes. You feel you can see at a glance all the sky, land and mountains of northern Kenya.

The generous living room has a cathedral ceiling, a sculpted wood mantelpiece over the fireplace, and leather-cushioned chairs. It suggests cozy conversations with friends. Meals are taken in the dining room around a table for ten fashioned from a single piece of wood. From the entrance a wide rustic staircase sweeps to the upper floor. Here the spacious master bedroom has views in both directions with French doors leading to an outdoor balcony. There are papyrus-fronted cupboards, animal pictures, safari chairs and hand-woven carpets. A large bathroom and a child's bedroom also share this floor.

Arching over the entire house is the thatched roof. Inside the grasses are intricately woven to create a remarkable ceiling resembling a grand version of a Kenyan basket.

There are two separate double accommodations in cottages next to the main house. Although the cottage rooms are not as impressive as the master bedroom, they are engagingly decorated with simple fabrics making the cottages cozy and comfortable.

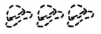

BORANA LODGE

Tandala Limited, Box 24397, Nairobi
☎ *567251, FAX: 564945*

Six luxurious suites in rustic cottages—a ridge top in the bush—staying at Borana Lodge is wonderful and relaxing. It is a wilderness immersion combined with surprising extravagance, elegance, privacy and homey comfort.

From its spectacular site on Borana Ranch (35,000 private acres), the lodge commands dramatic views of the high bush and mountain ranges of Mt. Kenya and the Laikipia Plateau.

Curving contours of hill and rock determine the unique shape of each structure. There are steep pathways, terraced rock gardens and lawns, and surprising lily ponds. A beautiful stone swimming pool is set right at the edge of the escarpment with views of distant mountains and a nearby waterhole below.

Walls are natural stone; plaited thatch forms tall rounded rooflines; and boulders are unusual points of interest in bathrooms, bedrooms, gardens and main lodge. Local cedar has been polished to frame floor-to-ceiling windows and to create unusual fireplace mantles. It is also used in ranch-made bedsteads and huge lounge chairs with leather cushions.

Each cottage has its own niche on the hill, with private view terrace and spacious rooms. Some cottages are high on the slope, some are lower, one has two levels, and one has two suites with shared terrace. Even bathrooms have huge windows. And privacy is assured, so many bathtubs are turned to enjoy the view. Beds are large and comfortable. Some are four-posters with canopies. Even the twin beds seem large enough for two. Each cottage has a sitting area with fireplace.

Due to sloping terrain and surrounding vistas, the central lodge is built on two levels at the very edge of the cliff. Since this high spot can be very windy, glass is used for protection, even on the open terrace.

Enormous windows curve to frame the panorama and fill the living room with light and space. A huge fireplace juts out from one wall and is open on three sides. The adjacent drawing room with its own big fireplace is perfect for pre-dinner drinks. The stuffed sofas and chairs are huge, and the atmosphere is cozy.

A staircase climbs to the dining room with its dramatic rosewood slab table. The crackling fire and candlelight give the feeling of a hospitable country manor, where every effort is being made to see to your comfort. By day, the dining room is bright with a whole wall of glass doors open to terraced lawns and gardens of indigenous plants.

Because it is small, Borana can cater to the individual desires of guests. From Laikipia, many activities are possible. You can make day or night game drives in an open Land Rover with high seating on two levels—not even a windscreen between you and the animals. Besides the ranch cattle, you can see elephant, lion, buffalo, and various plains game including the elusive Greater Kudu.

You can also go on guided game walks, ride horses, or swim, and a tennis court is planned. You can take camel safaris or an extravagant flying excursion to Mt. Kenya or to Lake Turkana for fishing.

OL PEJETA LODGE
Lonrho Hotels Kenya Ltd., Box 58581, Nairobi
☎ *216940, FAX: 216796*

Ol Pejeta was a private game ranch belonging to millionaire Adnan Kashoggi. The ranch in the dry savannah country on the west side of Mt. Kenya was used for game hunting—especially for buffalo. When Lonrho Hotels acquired the property, a 23,000-acre rhino sanctuary was created within the 110,000-acre ranch. The luxurious ranch house "Ol Pejeta" has kept all the original furnishings and operates as an exclusive and intimate lodge with health spa.

Staying at Ol Pejeta Lodge is like being invited to a luxurious private home. The main ranch house is light and airy, with a relaxed indoor-outdoor feel.

There are wide verandas with comfortable cushioned chairs, cool courtyards ablaze with bright bougainvillea, and enormous picture windows framing views of Mt. Kenya. Everything is outsized, extra large: you feel like a child sinking into the giant-sized chairs and couches, the fireplace is huge, large dramatic paintings fill the walls, and the beds in the suites are the biggest we've ever seen.

You are clearly in Africa—a luxurious, film-set, white-hunter Africa. The conservation-minded might balk at the impressive testament to earlier hunting safaris. Buffalo horns and heads of antelope, cheetah and leopard literally line the veranda and dining room walls. Gold-mounted ivory tusks stand here and there, stuffed rhino feet act as doorstops; there are lion-skin rugs with bared teeth intact—all seem quite in harmony with this slightly unreal place.

Safari Journal — The morning after.

We were lying in the vast wood-encased bath in

Mr. Kashoggi's suite, luxuriating in the imported Forest Pine Oil

and holding onto the handles so we wouldn't slip under the water —

our feet couldn't reach the end and my husband is six feet tall.

Two candles flickered among flowers at each end of the bath —

candles for romance and atmosphere, but also in anticipation

of the generator being switched off at midnight! From the bath,

which is raised and surrounded on three sides by mirrors, we looked

past two enormous elephant tusks that are mounted on the floor

and frame the bath, then over the head of the lion skin on the

floor and then across the 100 foot length of the suite.

I wonder what strange sights this bathtub has seen . . .

The house invites exploration and examination of the unusual and beautifully crafted furniture and trappings. There is an amazing console table made from small squares of cow horn, a large collection of pottery plates with yellow and brown abstract designs, old maps beautifully framed and a series of huge dramatic paintings with a sense of humor. In the seventies, this house must have boasted the latest and greatest of hi-tech equipment. There is a vast video library, VCR machines stand next to the main beds, in the study a big picture on runners slides aside to reveal a projection room.

The small number of guests at Ol Pejeta keeps the dining room intimate. Inside there are beautifully crafted wooden tables and leather chairs. Animal trophies watch you from the walls. Big sliding glass doors open to a veranda. You can choose to eat the breakfast and lunch buffets inside or out. Dinner is an elegant sit-down affair with candles. After dinner, coffee is served in the lounge where guests gather around the fireplace.

To savor Ol Pejeta in proper style, we strongly recommend staying in Mr. or Mrs. Kashoggi's suites. Pretend you are one of the rich and famous for a day as you get lost in the enormous bed, luxuriate in the imported bath oil in the family size bath, pad the expanse of your carpeted suite. Mrs. Kashoggi's suite is upstairs. You can look out a window as you lie in the bath. The headboard is an impossible creation of towering blue and white clouds. Mr. Kashoggi's suite, larger and more masculine with impressive woodwork, is on the ground floor with big sliding doors leading to a shaded veranda. There is a well-padded Lamu bed on the veranda—the height of delightful decadence.

Beyond the veranda, a sparkling swimming pool with a rock waterfall is surrounded by emerald lawns and imaginatively colorful gardens busy with birds. The outsized lounge chairs are made of soft interwoven leather. The outdoor whirlpool in the shade is an original jacuzzi. Beyond this is the spa wing with massage and exercise rooms. This seems more a spa for sitting and sipping your drink than working up a sweat. You can play croquet on the front lawn or try your hand at badminton. For the more energetic there are horses to ride and a tennis court.

Past the green lawns and tropical flower gardens you can see the dry bush country with its scattering of thorn trees. There is a water-hole to attract the animals, and the massive bulk of Mt. Kenya is a purple-blue backdrop. If you can tear yourself away from your intimate oasis of luxury, you can go on game drives; visit the tame Rhino, Morani; have sundowners in an elevated hide; or go for a game walk.

Quotes:

> *"Ours is a seven-roll bed. I could roll over seven times before I fell out the other side. It was so big, I couldn't find her in the night—so much for romance!" Guest*

Accommodations

Ol Pejeta can accommodate 12 guests. There are six deluxe suites—four in the main house, and two in Buffalo Cottage. Check current regulations regarding children. *Our Favorites:* Mr. and Mrs. Kashoggi Suites.

Special Offerings

Game hide, barbecue dinners, two swimming pools, two tennis courts, croquet, badminton, horse riding among wild animals, game drives, night game drives, game/bird walks, massage, sauna, jacuzzi.

Off Notes

Maintenance is needed on some facilities.

SEGERA RANCH

Wilderness Trails (K) Ltd.\Bush Homes of East Africa Ltd.
Box 56923, Nairobi
☎ *506139, FAX: 502739*

 At Segera your party has exclusive use of a spacious ranch house set in lovely grounds. You stay in relaxed and well-fed comfort with unspoiled bush in all directions and magnificent views of Mt. Kenya. You have the feeling of being way deep in Africa, close to the land and far from the tourist crowds.

Segera is a 50,000-acre cattle ranch northwest of Nanyuki in wide open, semi-arid country. In addition to cattle, the ranch is home to a range of wild animals, including many giraffe, zebra, antelope and elephant. The ranch is managed by a young couple, Giles and Ali Prettejohn, who live in a separate manager's house. Guests stay in the main ranch house, belonging to the originally American Fonville family.

This traditional old settlers' house has vanilla walls, green corrugated iron roof and wide veranda. It is surrounded by vast sweeps of lawn, imaginative cactus gardens and big old trees. There is an attractive swimming pool and a treehouse. Beyond the low hedges which border the garden, you can see dry bush and thorn trees stretching into the distance. On clear days Mt. Kenya fills the horizon, with the long slope of its shoulders culminating in craggy snow-covered peaks.

The house is relaxed and spacious. There are old leather safari chairs and a croquet set on the veranda. In the large living room zebra-skin carpets accent an eclectic mix of furniture including big old leather couches, an intricate sideboard for drinks, and a huge coffee table with carved Lamu-style legs. There are many windows and lovely wood floors. Crowded bookcases and magazines on tables add a homey touch, and each evening a fire is lit in the large fireplace. Dinners are served at a long table in the formal dining room. Breakfasts and lunches are often eaten on the veranda with its lovely view of the mountain.

The house can comfortably accommodate six or seven guests. There are three double bedrooms and a smaller single room in the main house. Two of the double bedrooms are set behind the veranda, and although good-sized, they are rather dark and share a large bathroom. The master bedroom, on the other hand, is very large and bright and has a private bathroom with shower, bidet and toilet. This wonderful suite has a separate sitting area with a fireplace, good views across the lawns and access to the veranda.

Only one group or party may stay at Segera Ranch at a time. Segera differs from a typical "hosted" homestay in that it is not somebody's permanent home and has no "live-in" hosts. Typically, guests are hosted by their tour operator. For unaccompanied clients, an experienced "professional" familiar with the area would be brought in to act as host. Residents who are able to provide their own transport and do not require a "host" may book Segera at reduced rates. They also have the option of bringing their own food with Segera staff to cook and clean.

In addition to the main house, there is a separate guest cottage with two bedrooms and a bathroom. The cottage is more basic than the main house. It might be used by the tour operator, or could be pressed into service if needed by a larger group of Kenya Residents.

There is a Toyota Land Cruiser which is adapted for game viewing. A large selection of well-groomed horses and ponies are available for riding. Accomplished riders can enjoy exhilarating rides among wild animals on the ranch. Novice riders can practice in the paddock under the watchful eye of a syce.

The small, exclusive nature of Segera Ranch means that guests get to do what they want, when they want. In addition to game drives and horse riding, guests can go on game walks with a tracker, and they can have picnic lunches near a waterfall or sundowners at a view site. Guests can also choose to relax on the open veranda with its wide distant views, or lie in comfort by the unusual free-form swimming pool which is painted in a dark color to attract and hold the sun's heat.

Most of the food at Segera is produced on the ranch and prepared by the very competent cook. There are home grown vegetables, freshly baked breads, and meat from the ranch—beef, lamb or even gazelle. We went to admire the vegetable garden and to see where an elephant had helped himself a couple of nights before. Big tracks through the rows of greens—exciting to know that there had been elephant that close. Reassuring to know that the house and main gardens are protected with an electric fence.

The ranch is almost 50 kilometers off the tarred road. A four-wheel drive is recommended, and is essential if there has been rain. In fact, a sign along the way proclaims: "No road when wet." Storm clouds threatened as we ate dessert. We didn't linger for coffee, but high-tailed it out in our "two-wheel drive" car before the sign became prophetic.

Quotes:

> *"We haven't done any real advertising. It's just word of mouth. Everyone who's stayed here absolutely loves it and wants to pass on the word...We want to stay small and exclusive."*
> Ranch managers

> *"We've just been out for a drive and saw three herds of elephant, some giraffe, and lots of game on the plain."*
> Guest

Special Facilities
Horse riding, game drives, game walks, pool, airstrip.

SANGARE
Safcon Travel, Box 59224, Nairobi
☎ *503265, FAX: 506829*

Just getting to Sangare is quite an adventure. It involves a gate (which you open with a key collected at the entrance to the Aberdare County Club), steep and winding roads, marvelous and varied views, and preferably a four-wheel drive. Sangare is situated on the Prettejohn's ranch. You first come to their delightful ranch house with its long veranda and colorful creepers. After a welcome, you will be guided to Sangare.

Sangare offers peace and privacy for a very small group. Staying here is a little like up-market camping in a remote spot with all the work done for you. Meals are provided, and camp fires are set. There is no electricity, but there is water. An experienced game person (with a gun) can accompany you on your game walks or horse rides. There is abundant game in the area, especially elephant, and a variety of buck...leopards, but no lion.

Sangare is designed to be very simple and basic. Three separate small buildings are set on the banks of a modest man-made dam. One building is the mess room—small and cozy with a fireplace. This room opens onto an outdoor veranda which faces the dam. A second compact structure houses the kitchen—no electricity, and wire-mesh for windows. Meals are prepared here, and everything is "homemade" using dairy products and vegetables from the farm. The third building, set at some distance from the mess room, is a basic banda which contains two rather spartan but pleasant bedrooms. The walls are lined with papyrus and the low windows face towards Mt. Kenya. Each bedroom has an adjoining bathroom with proper toilet and hot water.

Basically, you can decide how to spend your time. You could fish for trout, watch birds and game from the veranda, arrange to have picnics in the bush, go on a night game drive...Your "hosts," the Prettejohns, can pick you up from the Nanyuki airport, drive you into the Aberdare National Park, or even arrange overnight horse riding safaris. All is very personalized.

There is radio contact with the Prettejohn ranch house.

MOKORINDO COTTAGE

Mokorindo Cottage, c/o Clive Aggett,
Kifuku Est., Box 2, Rumuruti

Mokorindo Cottage is a quiet retreat in a rural setting. This two bedroom cottage is on the edge of a freshwater dam in the middle of a working cattle ranch of several thousand acres.

The cottage is fully equipped complete with a cook and food. It has a spacious sitting and dining room with a fireplace. There are two light and airy bedrooms, each with a private bathroom. Windows frame views of green lawns extending to the sparkling waters of the lake-like dam. A Mokorindo tree, from which the cottage gets its name, stands all alone by the water. The cottage is covered with golden shower vines, and bougainvillea climbs along the pillars of the lovely veranda.

There is abundant bird life surrounding the dam. You will see cormorants, Egyptian geese and sacred Ibis. There is ground bird and limited duck shooting. You can fish from the banks of the dam or go out in the fiberglass dinghy which is for guests. There is good largemouth bass fishing. The staff will prepare your freshly caught supper.

There are no wild animals on the ranch, so walking is perfectly safe. There are even walking sticks on a rack in the cottage!

Situated in the wide open spaces of the dry thorn tree country known as Laikipia, the beauty and seclusion of this farm with its 200 species of birds make this a very special place.

WINGU KENDA
Wingu Kenda, Box 321, Nanyuki
☎ *(0176) 22829, FAX: (0176) 32020*

Donna Hurt, ex-wife of the actor John Hurt, is opening her home to paying guests. This luxurious villa, close to the well-known Mt. Kenya Safari Club, has beautifully landscaped gardens with a magnificent view towards the peaks of Mt. Kenya. The house is called *Wingu Kenda* (Cloud Nine in Swahili)—an appropriate name for a dream house in this idyllic setting.

When you stay at Wingu Kenda you are Donna's guests, sharing her home. She has a relaxed American way and is very enthusiastic about this new venture.

Says Donna, "I love people. It'll be great fun. I always have visitors here...friends. I love entertaining people."

The house is one of a series of homes built along one rather incongruously suburban road near the gates of the Mount Kenya Safari Club. The houses are grand and tend to have owners who are rich, famous and interested in wildlife conservation.

Wingu Kenda is a rather modern ranch design and is built at the top of a ridge. It is long and rambling and is beautifully constructed and finished. There are big windows nicely encased in wood, wonderful tall stone chimneys, a huge veranda with grand wood posts supporting the high roof. The house is very well setup and equipped for guests. There are three guest bedrooms each with small bar fridge, modern bathroom and sliding glass doors leading out to a veranda.

When you stay at Wingu Kenda there are many attractive activities. On the five acre property are a lovely pool, a sauna, a tennis court and horses to ride. You can take walks or go riding in the forests, and golfing is also very convenient. For those who prefer indoor activities, or for evening entertainment, there is a room for playing pool, a separate and comfortable video room with an awesome video library and John Hurt on the walls.

The house is friendly, relaxed and full of personal memorabilia. There are jewel-colored tiffany style lamps, wonderful custom wooden furniture by Nairobi-based Marc Van Rampelberg, a gruesomely humorous flying monster by Jim Henson of Muppets fame, loads of photos, books, magazines and music. Settle yourself into the comfortable couch by the fire and feel right at home. Smokers will feel especially at ease here.

Activities and meal times are arranged to suit the guests. We sampled a delicious dinner around Donna's glorious large dining table. Breakfast and lunch are usually eaten on the veranda with Mt. Kenya dominant across the valley and a riot of color tumbling over walls and down steps in the terraced garden.

Animal lovers will enjoy staying at Wingu Kenda. In addition to the horses and the huge warthog who is usually confined in the paddocks, there are a host of dogs (mainly large rottweilers) and a bushpig called BP who likes the company of humans. Bushbabies play in a large outdoor cage close to the front entrance.

Staying with Donna is a rather unique experience in Kenya. Most other homestays are hosted by long-time Kenya residents who have a life-time's knowledge of the bush, the animals, and the country, and tend to offer a rather colonial experience. In contrast, Wingu Kenda feels more like a Hollywood view of Kenya. There is every luxury, comfort, and modern convenience, in a relaxed American ambiance. It provides a far more exclusive and personal experience than its busy and touristy neighbor, the Mt. Kenya Safari Club, which, like Wingu Kenda, also has beauty, style and more than a touch of Hollywood.

MERU – EMBU

MERU MULIKA LODGE
Msafiri Inns, Box 42013, Nairobi
☎ *330820, FAX: 227815*

This lodge looks directly over the Mulika swamp which attracts many animals. There are accommodations for 130 guests in a series of thatched bandas and a double-story complex. The main living and dining areas and all the guest rooms have lovely wide open views across the swamp with its scattering of doum palms. In the distance are the high ridges of the Nyambene Hills.

The lodge has pleasant gardens, many exotic trees and a small swimming pool. Guest rooms are threadbare and in need of refurbishing. There are mosquito nets and ensuite bathrooms with shower or bathtub. Each room has a private veranda. The lodge is seldom busy and has a rather deserted air.

KINDANI CAMP

Langwenda Safaris Ltd., Box 56118, Nairobi
☎ *445797, FAX: 443267*

Kindani is a small camp which has recently opened in a secluded spot in the seldom visited Meru National Park. The camp caters to a maximum of only 12 people. Instead of tents, guests stay in simple thatched rondavels.

This very basic camp is built on the banks of the narrow Kindani River and is surrounded by riverine forest. The appeal of Kindani Camp is its remote and natural setting. You know you are deep in the African bush, miles from any other tourists. There is a relaxed peacefulness here, rather than any scenic grandeur or excitement.

The managers want to maintain this unspoiled, rustic atmosphere. Roofs are thatched in raffia leaves, there are open-air showers, and there is no electricity. The concept is to provide a natural, bush experience while also catering to basic creature comforts—hot water, flush toilets and comfortable rondavels.

There are five spacious rondavels, each with three beds, mosquito nets, and a wash basin. Close to each rondavel is a toilet in a separate little stone out-house, and an open-air shower within a shoulder-high circular wall. The rondavels do not have verandas—guests gather in the main open-sided mess with its prime position on the river bank. Typically, only one group of guests are at Kindani at a time.

A mud-colored swimming pool has been built along the side of the river and is filled with river water. Besides relaxing at camp, guests can go on game drives. You are unlikely to see other vehicles. Four-wheel drives are essential—there are many streams to ford, and the earth roads are slippery after rain. There are two Land Cruisers at Kindani for game viewing. The bush is being cleared for a landing strip close to the camp.

IZAAK WALTON INN

Msafiri Inns, Box 42013, Nairobi
☎ *229751, FAX: 227815*

This small inn has 42 very basic double bedrooms each with private bath. It is set in eight and a half acres of lovely gardens and lawns, two kilometers from Embu town on the Nairobi–Meru Road. The inn was originally a farmhouse and is named after the famous English angler because there is good fishing in the mountain streams nearby. The hotel has a bar, lounge, dining room and conference/function rooms for up to 300. It is a convenient stop for tea.

NORTHERN KENYA

Northern Kenya is a vast expanse of scrub desert extending north from the foothills of Mt. Kenya to the emerald waters of Lake Turkana. It is also a magnificent wilderness with dramatic rock formations, towering mesas, and surprising green slashes of riverine forest to break the rolling flow of endless sun-scorched plains. This area begins at Isiolo where the tarmac ends: the paved road goes from Nairobi to Nanyuki at the foot of Mt. Kenya. From there it climbs through the mountain ranch lands of Timau, then across the northern shoulders of Mt. Kenya to plunge 900 meters in the 40-kilometer descent to the desert and Isiolo, where the unpaved highway north begins.

Unlike the more-traveled Samburu Area, the rest of northern Kenya is seldom included on Safari itineraries. The distances are great, the roads are rugged, and there are fewer places to stay. Traveling in this area requires a major time commitment and serious preparation. The stunning scenery is worth the effort.

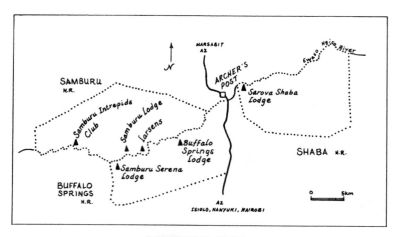

SAMBURU AREA

About 65 kilometers beyond Isiolo on the eroded dirt surface of the northern highway to Marsabit are the Samburu, Buffalo Springs, and Shaba National Reserves. As these reserves are essentially one area, you can make game drives in all three no matter where you stay. However, each has separate park fees.

SAMBURU NATIONAL RESERVE

The Samburu National Reserve extends for an area of 105 square kilometers north of the meandering Ewaso Ngiro or "Brown" River. It is part of a lava plain that includes a varied landscape of red dirt, thorn scrub, broken volcanic rock, dried river beds, steep hills, and rocky outcroppings, some large enough to be called mesas. Following the river curves, a riverine forest of doum palms, acacia, and tamarind is a magical contrast of cool green. It is attractive to the region's wildlife and visitors alike. There are elephant, hippo, crocodile, and leopard, as well as plains game, other small mammals and birdlife. The region is home to the rare Grevy zebra with large furry ears, gerenuk antelope standing on hind legs to feed, Somali ostrich with their distinctive blue legs, and the shy oryx beisa. Most of these can be seen near the tourist lodges and camps that have been built close to the river.

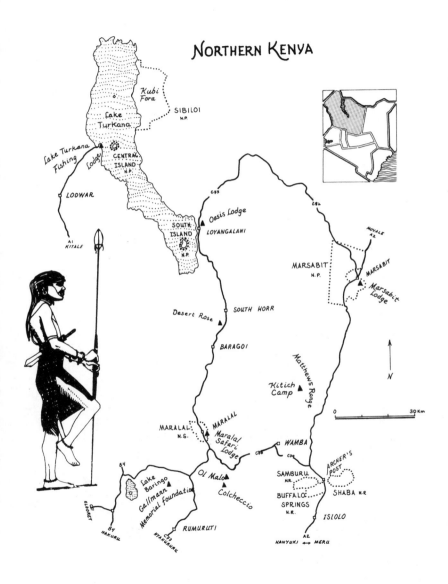

NORTHERN KENYA

Kubi Fora
SIBILOI N.P.
Lake Turkana
Lake Turkana Fishing Lodge
CENTRAL ISLAND N.P.
LODWAR
A1 KITALE
SOUTH ISLAND N.P.
Oasis Lodge
LOYANGALANI
C77
C82
MOYALE A2
MARSABIT N.P.
MARSABIT
Marsabit Lodge
Desert Rose
SOUTH HORR
BARAGOI
Matthews Range
Kitich Camp
N
0   30 Km
MARALAL N.S.
MARALAL
Maralal Safari Lodge
WAMBA
C78
C79
ARCHER'S POST
Lake Baringo Gallmann Memorial Foundation
Ol Malo
Colcheccio
SAMBURU N.R.
BUFFALO SPRINGS N.R.
SHABA N.R.
ISIOLO
B4
C51 ELDORET
B4 NAKURU
C77 NYAHURURU
RUMURUTI
NANYUKI A2 MERU

LARSENS

Block Hotels, Box 47557, Nairobi
☎ *335807, FAX: 340541*

Larsens is a small, luxurious, tented camp set in lush lawns at the edge of the muddy river. Everything is green canvas: tents, reception, bar, dining-room. However, the grounds give a sense of permanence and order: clipped and watered lawns stretch between the tents and down to the river; well-kept paths meander among the tall trees; and spacious tents sit on raised wooden decks.

Larsens was named in honor of Eric Larsen, a pioneer of camping safaris and founder of the United Touring Company. The present Larsens was rebuilt in 1988 by the camp staff. The first was washed away during severe floods only months after its initial construction. Those difficult days forged a strong bond among the staff. Together they provide efficient, personal, and friendly service. On arrival, you are greeted with a cold drink under the trees while the manager briefs you on meal times, hot water times, game-drives.

Staying at Larsens is a relaxing and private experience. With only 17 tents, there are no crowds, and children under 10 years are not allowed. There is a feeling of peace and tranquillity—the main sounds are birdsong and the flowing of the river.

Guest Quotes:

> *"We've come here many times. It's our favorite place in Samburu...and the food is really first class."*

*"We were just sitting on our deck looking towards the bend in the
river when two elephant came through the trees and waded right
across to the other side."*

This is camping in high style, a casual colonial elegance. Toweling gowns are
in your tent, the safari chairs have maroon leather seats, and complimentary sherry is served from a decanter at dinner. Brass mugs gleam above the bar, Eric Lars-
en's old cabin trunks and pith helmet add authenticity, and there are stacks of
games and wildlife books. At night you can sit companionably around the campfire listening to the sounds of the night bush, gazing at the Milky Way. In the
heat of the day you can relax on your private deck looking towards the river—monkeys play in the trees around you, and you might see animals drinking
on the opposite banks.

The mess tent, open on three sides, faces the river. Larsens takes pride in its
high quality cuisine. Dinner is served by candlelight. Tables are set with silver
and Larsens' china. The food is good and elegantly presented. Breakfast and a
barbecue lunch are buffet style, dinner a set-menu with choice of entree. Lunches are packed on request; dinner can be served in your tent.

Safari Journal

*The candles flicker, casting shadows on the green canvas
of the mess tent. There are only seven tables and
the feeling is intimate. I love the contrasts:
open sided mess tent and worn safari khaki next to
the charming elegance of candles, crystal, and
unobtrusive service. Feels as though I've stepped back
into an earlier and more gracious time.*

Accommodations

The 17 tents, arranged in a row, all face the river and are each named for a
bird. The tents have campaign-style furnishings and pleasant ensuite bathrooms. Hurricane lamps are hung on each private deck at nightfall. There is
generator-produced electricity in the early mornings and evenings for hot
showers.

Standard tents have twin beds. There are four tent suites each with one
double plus one twin bed. *Best Views*: Hornbills, Bateleurs, Curlews, and
Swifts.

Special Offerings

Transportation to swimming pool at Samburu Lodge, game drives.

SAMBURU INTREPIDS CLUB
Prestige Hotels Ltd., Box 74888, Nairobi
☎ *338084, FAX: 217278*

The Samburu Intrepids Club is like a fantasy tree house with decks built around trees, wooden walkways leading from one area to another and high thatched roofs towering above. The space is breathtaking.

Safari Journal — Monday

I've never seen anything like the space in this lodge.
The long vaulted corridor, the high log beams reach up... and up...
The thatched roof seems to brush the treetops. Everywhere
the light is touched with cool green as it filters gently
through the trees. How different this is from the pounding sun
of the desert surrounding us.

The main lodge stretches above sandy river banks. Shaded by thatch and trees, this soaring lodge is open to the air and river views. The decor is casual, and high quality—smooth leather and wood. You have a sense of harmony with your surroundings. The river flows muddily past, birds are everywhere, and you are likely to see monkeys and lizards. Across the river you may see Samburu tribesmen and their herds.

Beneath trees, high on the river banks are 25 luxury tents. They are furnished in African mahogany and have wooden decks with reclining chairs. There are four-poster beds, overhead fans, and double sinks. Luxuriant vegetation has been trained into lovely gardens near the tents.

Breakfast and lunch are served buffet style outside on wooden decks. Dinner is in the large dining area, open sided, roofed by thatch and lit by hanging gourds. There is an attractive swimming pool, and lounge chairs are placed under a creeper covered trellis.

Accommodations

There are 25 luxury tents, most with twin beds, five with double beds. *Our Favorites*—Best river views #2,#3 & #5. Best double bed tent, #10. The VIP Tent with living room, very special.

Special Offerings

Game drives, camel safaris, nature and bird walks, pool, souvenir and sundry shop, airstrip transfers.

Off Notes

Big game is rather sparse at this end of the Samburu National Reserve.

SAMBURU SERENA LODGE

Serena Central Reservations, Box 48690, Nairobi
☎ *71051, FAX: 718103*

The Samburu Serena Lodge is located across the river outside the Samburu National Reserve. The lodge is built mostly of natural stone and is surrounded by tall trees and lush established gardens. After driving the dusty roads and trails of the area, walking into reception with its rock garden and pool full of lily-pads gives you the feeling of stepping into another world. The shade is cooling, and there is the suggestion of age and permanence in the rock, the river, and the trees.

Symbols, implements and weapons of the Samburu people are used extensively in the lodge decor to bring guests closer to the life of this land and its people. There are murals on walls and on roofbeams of the dining area. Friendly staff will explain the symbols and subjects, and it is moving to learn that Samburu villagers provided drawings for the decorating artist to enlarge.

The dining area opens out to the terrace lounge overlooking the river. Below is the swimming pool, with several grassy game viewing areas descending down to the sandy river bank beyond. The whole area is a pleasant melding of shady old trees, mellow rock and flowers, sparkling water and sunshine. There are comfortable armchairs at the lounge level, deck chairs and loungers around the pool, and safari chairs scattered for game watching convenience along the lower terraces.

It is easy to watch wildlife from this lodge. You might see an elephant family stroll very close by on the other side of the river wall. You share the excitement with fellow guests when leopards are baited into floodlit view across the river. Crocodiles come up the bank practically at your feet to find their meat, and marabous and wild cats watch carefully for a chance to grab some too.

The lodge is popular with international tour groups and can accommodate up to 132 guests. Cottages have private verandas, most with river view; colorful bougainvillea climbs each high-thatched roof. The rooms are simply furnished and have clean whitewashed walls and bathrooms with shower. Bright local fabrics and natural matting have been used with imagination to create a pleasing decor. The pathways of natural stone are lined with plants and flowers, and on the walk to the main lodge you may spot game along the river or encounter monkeys.

All meals are served buffet style in the open-sided dining room. A Samburu tribesman protects the tables and buffet from monkeys and birds: they know he is dangerous to them as tourists are not! Kenyan folksingers perform during the dinner hour.

Quotes:

> *"We just came from London yesterday. This place is beautiful, very exotic and African. We love being right among the animals."*

> *"I liked learning that a Samburu warrior brushes his hair against things and people he loves. That's why the man's hair on the mural touches the hut...it's his home."*

Accommodations

There are two standard bedrooms per guest cottage, and all have private bathrooms with shower, ceiling fans, and small verandas. Most have twin beds; some have double beds. There are also six luxury family suites. *Our Favorites*: Standard Rooms #42, 43, 50 & 51 and Luxury Suites #14 & 17 with great river views from balconies.

Special Offerings

Game drives, wildlife lectures, swimming pool.

SAMBURU LODGE

Block Hotels, Box 47557, Nairobi
☎ *335807, FAX: 340541*

At this large established game lodge, you are greeted by a Samburu tribesman. The lodge is bustling with tour groups. It has a beautiful setting right on the river banks, with the popular Crocodile Bar almost overhanging the water. The dining room is open on the river side with long tables, long lines, and the usual safari buffets. The main lodge is polished stonework with high thatched roof.

Rooms for visitors are spread up and down the river in various sizes of cottages and bandas, with a confusing mixture of decor styles. A swimming pool is a welcome relief in the heat of the day. At night Samburu dancers perform, and there is leopard and crocodile baiting. There are daily bird walks, wildlife video shows, and outdoor barbecues twice a week. Four-wheel drive vehicles are available for game drives, and wildlife is usually plentiful in this prime area of the Samburu National Reserve.

Accommodations

All rooms have ensuite bathrooms. Some are quite a distance from the main lodge. Some have verandas. *Best River Views*: #60–63 (river deck), #32–33 (standard banda), and #5 & 6 (luxury cottages).

Other Offerings

Gas station, shop for souvenirs and sundries. There is a swimming pool, gas station, and a shop for gifts and sundries.

THE SHABA NATIONAL RESERVE

The Shaba National Reserve is south of the Ewaso Ngiro River, but across the Marsabit road from the Samburu National Reserve. It is 145 square kilometers of pristine wilderness full of more dramatic contrasts. There are intimidating flows of volcanic rock and ash; there are 32 kilometers of riverine forest; grasslands are idyllic with herds of wildlife and well-watered by four springs; and there is even a swamp. The towering Shaba Massif rises elegant and aloof above all, sheltering the wildlife of this desert Eden. The vistas are superb, but the rough tracks can be very difficult, especially after rains. The author, Joy Adamson, camped and was murdered in Shaba while working to return a young leopard to the wild.

SAROVA SHABA LODGE

Sarova Hotels Ltd., Box 30680, Nairobi
☎ *333248, FAX: 211472*

Sarova Shaba Lodge is a fantasy oasis of green luxury in the dry scrub and rocky hills of the Shaba Reserve. The bone jolting road leads through black lava flows and stunted trees surreal under their coating of white dust. Then you arrive.

The contrast is staggering. Clear water seems to be flowing everywhere—under little bridges, forming streams in the stone paving, widening into fish-filled pools, and finally cascading into the muddy waters of the Ewaso Ngiro River. The foliage is lush and green; the swimming pool, sparkling aqua; and the architecture, fantastic and fun—soaring thatch, dining area raised high in the trees—a whimsical blend of Africa, Polynesia, and the East. Small wonder the word "paradise" is mentioned so often in the visitors' book.

Safari Journal

afternoon —

The others went on a game drive. I played Esther Williams in the deserted pool. There were palms overhead and bright birds. The water was "postcard blue" ~ it seemed to flow away without end ~ as though it disappeared over a waterfall....

Sarova Shaba is near the *Born Free* camp site of Joy and George Adamson and close to natural springs which provide all of that wonderful flowing water. Local materials have been ingeniously used in the construction and furnishing of the lodge—rush chairs, stone floors, bold and colorful curtains. The overall effect is natural and bright.

The imaginative swimming pool deserves special mention. No geometry here; instead, the pool is shaped in a series of blue coves bordered by natural rock gardens and flowers. There is a romantic island with a thatched shelter and bentwood chairs—in one cove water cascades down high natural rock walls while you rest on an underwater ledge. You feel as though you are swimming in a private lagoon.

The dining area is built high on timber stilts and shaded by a series of peaked thatch roofs. It overlooks the river and the pool. Doum palms grow triumphantly through the roof. You can hear the relaxing sounds of birds and the rushing of the spring water below. All combine to create an atmosphere of natural tranquillity. Disney eat your heart out!

From your shaded table you can look across the river to the dusty white dryness of the reserve beyond. In the distance, dramatic sheer-faced mesas rise out of the heat. Samburu tribesmen in red herd goats on the opposite river bank.

Eighty-four guest rooms have been built in separate two-story units. Each room overlooks the river, with the upper levels looking beyond to the more distant rocks and crags of the desert.

Stone paths lead between palms and cactus and over streams to the rooms. Some are quite a hike. Rocks accent fantastic sculptured gardens of desert plants, especially dramatic under floodlights at night.

Accommodations

The rooms are colorful, and many natural products have been used with imagination. Although there is no air conditioning, there are ceiling fans and cross breezes. The bathrooms have marble counters and a proper bathtub.

There are standard rooms as well as larger junior suites. A separate fantasy cottage is set in a pond with lilies. A fabulous honeymoon splurge—king-size bed, sunken jacuzzi and bidet... *Best views*: Standard room #84, Suites #5 and #76.

Special Offerings

Conference/banqueting facilities (capacity for 170 theater-style in the "Doum Palm Room"—a beautiful and imaginative setting), pool, crocodile feeding, game drives, bird walks, evening entertainment, petrol station, souvenir and sundry shop.

Off-Notes

The food is not on a par with the setting.

BUFFALO SPRINGS NATIONAL RESERVE

The Buffalo Springs National Reserve makes up approximately 80 square kilometers south of the Samburu National Reserve across the Ewaso Ngiro River. Naturally much of the terrain is similar, but this reserve also includes a stretch of grassy lowland plains and the wonderfully clear Buffalo Springs.

BUFFALO SPRINGS LODGE
African Tours & Hotels, Ltd., Box 30471, Nairobi
☎ *336858, FAX: 218109*

This is the only lodge in the Buffalo Springs Reserve. Most of the original 40 tents have been converted to concrete bandas with makuti roofs. Bandas are small and tired, but adequate. The main lodge is cool and open to the view at one end. There is a small, poorly maintained swimming pool. Guests can walk down to game viewing areas near the springs. Although the lodge is beautifully sited with incredible vistas and the clear pools of the Buffalo Springs, the lodge does not do justice to its setting.

MARSABIT

To reach Marsabit you continue on the corrugated northern highway (A2) past Samburu. You drive through endless flat desert country; then you begin to climb towards Marsabit, a surprising cool, green and hilly oasis rising high above the dry heat of the desert lands. Marsabit means "place of cold," and the temperature can plummet at night. Marsabit is colorful with local Rendille people in their bright reds, beads and earrings. The Marsabit National Park has dense forests, crater lakes, many birds and a variety of wildlife, including elephant and greater kudu.

MARSABIT LODGE
Msafiri Inns, Box 42013, Nairobi
☎ *330820, FAX: 227815*

The lodge has a magnificent location two kilometers within the Marsabit National Park. It is in dire need of refurbishing. The rooms are very basic. Each room has a large picture window overlooking a water hole.

MATTHEWS RANGE

KITICH CAMP
Supoko Ltd., Kitich Camp, Box 14869, Nairobi
☎ *444288, FAX: 750533*

Kitich is a small tented camp situated in the remote Matthews Range north of Wamba. The best thing about Kitich Camp is its marvelous valley setting on the banks of the Ngeng River. Surrounded by dense vegetation and beautiful high hills, it is a peaceful, green refuge in the flat semi-desert of Kenya's northern districts—a welcome relief after a long, hot drive.

You go to Kitich Camp for its remoteness, its natural beauty, and the walking, not for luxurious accommodations or memorable cuisine.

The camp is small and simple. A central open-sided dining and bar area is flanked by ten tents which are well spread out along one side of the river. When we visited, the tents were very basic, with long drop toilets, safari showers and no electricity. Furnishings were rudimentary, with two small beds in each tent and a couple of safari chairs on the veranda. We hear that the tents and facilities have recently been upgraded.

As you eat your meal, you realize how far you are from food supplies. It seems that elephants are the primary beneficiaries of the vegetable garden.

Kitich is ideal for keen walkers. You can hike up to high rocks for a good view, walk to the deep natural swimming pool in the river and try your skill at swinging into the pool from a rope. You will be accompanied on your walks by Samburu guides armed with spears. This valley, which is a forest reserve, is home to many wild animals including buffalo and elephant. It is a haven for birds and butterflies and has some exotic vegetation such as prehistoric cycad palms. Each evening a leopard is baited across the river from camp.

Getting there: Driving: Kitich Camp is about 480 kilometers from Nairobi, through Isiolo and then Wamba. It can also be a stop on a safari from Samburu to Baringo. Flying: It is possible to fly to Wamba or to the rough strip somewhat closer to camp.

Kitich closes in April because of the rains.

RUMURUTI — WAMBA — MARALAL AREA

Several small, privately hosted places are opening up in northern Kenya. They will appeal to the well-heeled traveler with a yen for exclusivity and a desire for a more unique "hands-on" experience of

Kenya. There are two places of note south of the Wamba-Maralal road. They are built at the edge of the same high escarpment, and are only a 30-minute drive from each other. This is high country—too high for malarial mosquitoes.

Getting there: Driving: About five hours drive from Nairobi (through Nyahururu and Rumuruti) or a little longer if you go through Nanyuki. Flying: Both ranches have good landing strips for small planes.

OL MALO

Wilderness Trails (K) Ltd./Bush Homes of East Africa Ltd.
Box 56923, Nairobi
☎ *506139, FAX: 502739*

Ol Malo is located on 2020 hectares of land which used to be part of Colcheccio Ranch. Colin and Rocky Francombe, after many years of ranching in Kenya, purchased this magnificent piece of land for their dream home. They are also building three guest cottages to offer a very personal and exclusive "homestay" experience for up to four guests. They are warm, friendly hosts with a great deal of energy and a love and knowledge of the African bush.

Ol Malo is right at the edge of a steep escarpment with vast and sweeping views. There will be rather organic and very natural looking buildings with shapes determined by rocks and by the curve of ancient olive wood which has been used as wall beams. The Francombes are designing and building as they go along. There will be a separate living area and dining room, each with a fireplace for the cool evenings and big windows as protection from gusty winds. Guest cottages will be discretely nestled between the trees and rocks, facing the view. Each will have a living area and private terrace. A site has been chosen for an ambitious free-form swimming pool with natural rocks behind and a swim-up view. There is talk of a tennis court.

Already, there has been some amazing landscaping and gardening. There are cool green lawns in terraces between the rocks—such a surprise and contrast in this wild setting. There are also lovely rock gardens with exotic aloes and natural rock bird baths.

The Francombes plan to dine with their guests. However, if you desire complete privacy, meals could be served in your cottage. The emphasis is on exclusivity; only one party of guests would be booked at a time.

The Francombes are keen conservationists and are trying to attract an even greater number of wild animals to their protected piece of land. Ol Malo means "place of the greater kudu" and this area is known for its concentration of these animals, rarely found in other parts of Kenya. The same wide variety of game seen at Colcheccio will be found here. There will be guided walks, game drives, fly-camps that are set up near the river and the option of a camel safari with Simon Evans.

COLCHECCIO RANCH

Colcheccio Ranch, Box 50, Rumuruti
☎ *749280, Nairobi 882521*

 Colcheccio is a 26,000 hectare ranch belonging to Count Carletto Ancilotto. This enormous ranch is home to cattle and sheep and to a wide variety of wild animals including elephant, buffalo, giraffe, lion, leopard, kudu, zebras and other plains game. The Count's daughter, Luisa Ancilotto has supervised the renovation of what used to be a small lodge. It is built on the edge of a high escarpment with breathtaking views over plains to distant hills and ridges dominated by Mt. Kenya. These are views which inspire silence and humility.

A maximum of 10 guests can stay in simple but attractive bandas which are built right on the edge of the escarpment. The bandas are bright and airy with parquet floors, makuti thatched roofs, and dried papyrus walls. The ensuite bathrooms have bidets and are being lined in cedar. Best of all, each banda has a huge wooden veranda cantilevered out over the edge of the ridge to make the most of that vast and amazing view.

The lounge and dining area are in a large and rather functional looking building with a high papyrus thatch roof and cement floor. This was a part of the original lodge, and is also right at the edge of the escarpment—again with that grand view. It has a large living room with fireplace and comfy chairs, and a smaller room which serves as a card room and library. The windows in these rooms are rather small for that view. Not so in the big dining area which is completely open along the view side. Here you can sit on worn leather safari chairs and look out forever. Far below is a water hole; green grass at the side of a cliff signals a spring; huge rocks standing at the bend of a dry river bed invite exploration. Pan the view with binoculars—there are greater kudu camouflaged amongst the grey thorn bushes, a klipspringer bounces past, and above big birds glide on the thermals—Africa doing its thing—and you are the lucky spectator.

You can get out and be part of it too. There are horses for experienced riders, safari vehicles for day or night game drives and game walks with armed guides. You might walk to a big rock for a picnic breakfast, hike to Crocodile Jaws where the river suddenly disappears to appear 37 meters later in a huge whirlpool—the possibilities sound endless. Remember, you are walking where there are wild animals and will be required to sign an indemnity form.

Back on the home front is a good-sized swimming pool and a cement tennis court. Colcheccio's Italian cuisine will combine farm fresh produce and high quality imported ingredients.

OL ARI NYIRO RANCH

Gallman Memorial Foundation, Kenya
Box 45593, Nairobi, FAX: 521220

We hear that Kuki Gallmann, conservationist and author of "I Dreamed of Africa," is considering opening her ranch, Ol Ari Nyiro, to paying guests. This huge ranch, home to cattle and wild animals, is at the edge of the Laikipia Plateau, just east of Lake Baringo. There is talk of only a few guests and of cottages well spread out. Those who know her say that, if she goes ahead, it will be beautiful and well done. Get an update.

MARALAL

Maralal is a Samburu center on cool forested highlands. The "Crossroads of the North," it lies between Lake Baringo and the Samburu National Reserve, and about half-way to Lake Turkana from Nairobi. Maralal boasts a colorful Samburu market, and the Maralal Game Sanctuary lies just outside of town. You can visit "Kenyatta House," where Jomo Kenyatta was last detained before becoming Kenya's first president. Maralal is home of the Maralal International Camel Derby, an annual charity event. Near Maralal is one of the most breathtaking scenes in all of Kenya—the Losiolo Escarpment. You stand at the edge of a colossal amphitheater for this end-of-the-world view. You can see forever, and the land drops dramatically down to the Suguta Valley below.

MARALAL SAFARI LODGE

Maralal Safari Lodge, Box 45155, Nairobi
☎ *211124, FAX: 214261*

Maralal Safari Lodge is "where the animals come to you." Both the dining room and veranda have views over the water hole and salt lick, and wildlife is less than nine meters from where you eat. Eland, impala, zebra, buffalo, and plenty of warthogs, monkeys and baboons mingle together at close range. Scores of interesting birds are attracted by numerous bird feeders and the water hole. Animals are free to wander in the grounds and guests must look both ways before returning to their cottages. Animals have the right of way!

The lodge is within the Maralal Game Sanctuary. Samburu game rangers lead you on game or bird walks in the cedar forests and hills. A leopard blind is near the lodge, there are camel rides, and arrangements can be made to visit a Samburu village.

The lodge can accommodate up to 62 people in 12 cottages which are built like Swiss chalets of local cedar and stone. Each room has a comfortable sitting area around a fireplace. French doors open on to the sanctuary with a view of the lovely hills beyond. The rooms have cathedral ceilings and a loft for a third bed.

There are ensuite bathrooms. Gardens and exotic plants add to the charm of this small, personal lodge.

Getting there

The lodge has an airstrip or you can drive from Nairobi via Nyahururu and Rumuruti.

MARALAL — LOIYANGALANI

This is the last long leg on the way to Loiyangalani on the east side of Lake Turkana. Scenery changes from the high forests of Maralal to barren, hot and dusty plains. There are oases of mountains and ravines from Baragoi to South Horr. Then it is a long rough ride over dark lava plains. Where is the lake?

DESERT ROSE LODGE

Desert Rose Ltd. Box 44801, Nairobi
☎ *228936, FAX: 212160 Tariff Pending*

A new luxury lodge is being planned in the hills between Baragoi and South Horr. This will be the first lodge built north of Maralal in the last 20 years. We saw photographs of the site and architectural plans for the lodge. It looks as though it will all be very lovely.

The lodge will be built on the site of an old hunters' camp where there are lots of acacia trees and a huge rock about 7.6 meters high. There are views up towards the top of mountains and a stream running below.

The enormous rock will be a focal point of the lodge and will actually be used as a wall in the dining room. The plans are for A-frame buildings of cedar and local brick. There will be four double rooms with full bathrooms ensuite. A natural pool is planned, with water flowing down rocks. There is a permanent water supply, and the lodge will have solar power.

Activities from this lodge will be mainly walking—enjoying the vistas, the birds and the vegetation. We were told that there is a thick cedar forest, caves, natural springs, rock pools in rivers and abundant bird life. However, not much game is left in this forest reserve. The site is at 1372 meters and is quite exposed. It will be chilly in the evenings, and a big open fireplace is planned between the

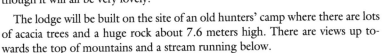

lounge and dining room. A bar and veranda area will overlook the pool and the view.

Emma Chen and her husband Yoav, have been the inspiration and driving force behind this venture. As a child, Emma fell in love with these hills. Now, with a lot of hard work, she and Yoav are beginning to turn a dream into reality. The Chens will manage the lodge when it opens.

Emma and a partner have been operating Desert Rose Limited Camel Safaris in Northern Kenya for some time. When the lodge opens, the camel safaris will originate from here. Guests will have the option of combining a stay at the lodge with a camel safari. There is an airstrip nearby for easier access.

LAKE TURKANA

Lake Turkana stretches for 288 kilometers up to the northern Kenyan border. It is surrounded by semi-desert and volcanic rock. The heat is intense and can rise to 60° Centigrade. The lake has been called the Jade Sea because of its unusual blue-green color. Strong winds blow, and the lake can become very rough. There are more Nile crocodiles in this lake than anywhere else in the world.

Lake Turkana, formerly Lake Rudolf, has now been named for one of the tribes who live on its shores. It was in this area that Richard Leakey uncovered the three-million-year-old fossils of "Homo Erectus." This prehistoric site is now known as the "Cradle of Mankind." At Koobi Fora there is a museum, and you can see excavation sites.

LOIYANGALANI

This small settlement on the southeastern shore of Lake Turkana focuses on the Oasis Club.

THE OASIS CLUB

Muthaiga Travel Ltd., Box 34464, Nairobi
☎ *750034, FAX: 750035*

A trip to the Oasis Club can be an awesome experience. The desert looks like a desolate moonscape: there is a certain grandeur in the surreal shapes, and monochromatic colors contrast vividly with the jade of the lake. The Oasis Club brings relief. This cool haven, set back from the lake, is nourished by waters from a natural spring. The spring also fills two swimming pools, and there are forests of doum palms and lush green foliage.

There are 24 very basic concrete cottages—no frills and no fans. Each has its own small veranda and bathroom. The dining room and bar have far more character. They are stone and thatch structures open to distant views of Lake Turkana. Local materials have been used in the colorful, natural decor.

Visitors' Quotes:

> *"Here you can shake off the shackles of civilization."*
>
> *"This place is for the traveler, not the tourist."*
>
> *"The pool is like a warm bathtub—you get cool when you come out!"*

The hotel sells the only cold beer for hundreds of kilometers! Food combines tasty German fare with the nightly "Nile" perch from the lake. The owners will help you plan your activities. From the club you can go sport fishing, take a boat to South Island, gape at mounds of crocodiles, go bird watching, prospect for semi-precious stones and crystals, or take a trip to the nearby oasis used in the filming of "Mountains of the Moon." You can also visit the El Molo tribe which has existed unchanged for centuries in this difficult terrain. You could also take an expedition to Koobi Fora (within easy reach by air, but a long haul by car).

FERGUSON'S GULF

The other place to stay on Lake Turkana is Ferguson's Gulf on the western side of the lake. To reach this side of the lake, you would take the tarmac road from Kitale. The trip is easier, the views are less spectacular.

LAKE TURKANA LODGE

Lake Turkana Lodge Reservations, Box 74609, Nairobi
☎ *760226, FAX: 760546*

This lodge has definitely seen better days. There are rather primitive cabins with verandas facing the lake, a shaded swimming pool, and access to the lake shore. The area is popular with bird watchers and fishermen, and you can often see hippos in the lake. Trips can be taken to Central Island with its crater lakes and to Koobi Fora on the eastern shore. (Update: We hear the lodge is temporarily closed)

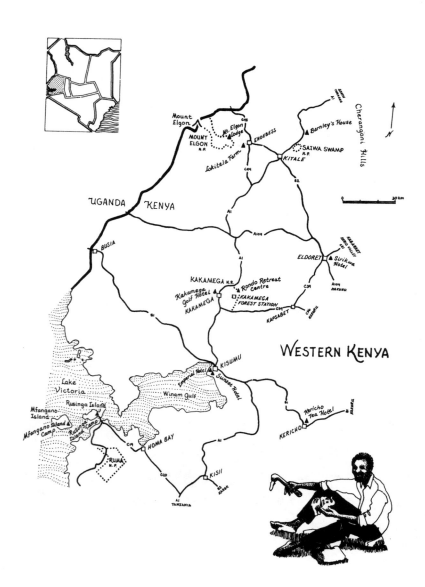

WESTERN KENYA

Western Kenya is the most densely populated part of Kenya. It is comprised of the fertile *Western Highlands* and of Kenya's slice of *Lake Victoria*. The Western Highlands extend from Kisii and Kericho in the south to the fertile farming areas of Eldoret and Kitale, which are farther north towards Mt. Elgon. The regional capital, Kisumu, is on the shore of Lake Victoria and is the third largest center in Kenya. The weather is usually hot and humid and has a lively market.

Western Kenya is not on the usual tourist circuit and, for this reason, does not have as many tourist hotels as you find in the game parks or on the coast. Areas of interest to visitors in the *Western Highlands* include:

Tea Estates

Concentrated primarily around the Kericho area, the tea fields undulate into the distance—smooth and uniform in the distinctive light-green "table" of tea bushes.

Kakamega National Forest Reserve

Surrounded by extensive agriculture is this finger of equatorial forest. This tropical jungle, dark, dense and moist, is home to a multitude of birds and butterflies. There are also many reptiles and small mammals. Because this is a unique habitat in Kenya, many species found here are not seen anywhere else in the country. The forest is a paradise for birders. There are guides and several nature trails.

Saiwa Swamp National Park

This is a small and seldom visited park. The main attraction is the rare sitatunga deer, a semiaquatic antelope with splayed hooves. There are wooden walkways and raised viewing blinds, many birds and monkeys.

Mt. Elgon National Park

Mt. Elgon is an extinct volcano which straddles the Kenya-Uganda border. With a summit just over 4200 meters above sea level, Mt. Elgon offers plenty of opportunity for walks and hikes. It is well-known for Kitum Cave where elephants mine the salty rock and thousands of bats make their home.

Cherangani Hills

These high and forested mountains have dramatic scenery and offer wonderful opportunities for walking and trekking.

The towns of Western Kenya hold little of interest for the tourist although there are small but worthwhile museums in Kisumu and Kitale. Most of the accommodations in this region are not in themselves sufficient to prompt a special visit. They are simply mentioned here because they are places to stay if you do want to visit the attractions of the area. The outstanding exceptions are Mfangano Island Camp and Rusinga Island Camp, which are both worthy of special trips.

LAKE VICTORIA

Lake Victoria has an area of almost 70,000 sq. km. The second largest fresh water lake in the world, romantic Lake Victoria featured in early explorers' search for the source of the Nile. Three countries—Kenya, Uganda and Tanzania—border on the lake. Lake Victoria is not a part of the Rift Valley and is a relatively shallow lake. Its shores are host to the bilharzia parasite—don't swim!

FLYING SAFARIS TO LAKE VICTORIA

A novel experience is being offered from the Masai Mara—a flying safari to an island in Lake Victoria and a chance to catch giant Nile perch. You fly out of the Mara in the early morning in a single-engined plane. About 45 minutes later, after flying over forests, farms and villages, you pass the hills surrounding Lake Victoria and come to land on either Mfangano Island or Rusinga Island.

MFANGANO ISLAND CAMP

Governors' Camp - Musiara Ltd., Box 48217, Nairobi
☎ *331871, FAX: 726427*

Mfangano Island Camp is a private paradise in the vastness of Lake Victoria. Simply getting there is an adventure. At dawn you squeeze aboard the tiny single-engine "GOV" plane at Musiara Strip in the Masai Mara—then fly west over the escarpment, above the cultivated green checkerboard of the Kisii area, past mountains and over water to land on Mfangano Island. Here you are met and taken aboard one of the camp's motorboats to speed around the island past coves and Luo fishing villages to the secluded bay which shelters Mfangano Island Camp.

Enchantment at first sight. Terra-cotta cottages sit in natural gardens on emerald lawns or appear partly hidden on rocky banks under giant fig trees. A jetty extends from green grass and circular stone steps. The shore is interesting with jutting dark rocks, driftwood, and colorful canoes. Behind it all rise steep forested hills with massive boulders for summits, protecting this magical place from the rest of the world—from time and worry.

The buildings are constructed in the local Luo tribe style, with reddish clay walls and thatched roofs lined with banana leaves. They all have spectacular views over water and are open to the lake breezes. Just steps up from the jetty is the airy lounge with comfortable low rush chairs. The dining area, built higher on the rocky hillside, also has open sides and looks down across the lake. The six spacious cottages, each slightly different in shape and design, have many windows with net, not glass for covering. You are always a part of the environment—feeling the breeze, listening to the waves lap sealike on the shore, or delighting in the evocative call of fish eagles.

The style of service at Mfangano is very personal, friendly and accommodating. You are made to feel part of a privileged family—one of the managers might join you for dinner; you decide your own agenda for the day, and always there are unobtrusive staff members around to make your stay supremely comfortable. The atmosphere is relaxing and laid-back.

From the Visitors Book:

> *"Absolutely beautiful, a rare treat—an island lost in time. Charming decor and delightful fishing."*

> *"Robinson Crusoe doesn't have a patch on this. Bloody Fantastic."*

> *"I'm not leaving!! I'm not! I'm not!"*

An artist's hand has clearly been at work in the layout and decor of the camp. Two cottages sit in gentle lawns close to the water while others are between natural rock formations reached by winding stone paths. The interiors are interesting and delightful. Kenyan art and handicraft items have been used in imaginative ways to achieve a harmonious effect. You are drawn to wander around your cottage examining musical instruments on walls, Kisii carvings on tables, quaint pottery holders for the fresh flowers. It is as personal as someone's home.

It is amazing that there can be such a variety of good food served in this remote spot: soups and pasta; roasts and fish; plenty of salads, and a decadent array of desserts. The fish cakes at breakfast are a specialty, and the coffee is excellent.

Meals are served in the open-sided dining room with views over the lake. There are linens painted in natural colors, fresh flowers, a breeze and the sound of waves breaking.

Mfangano Island Camp emphasizes enjoyment of the lake. There are powerboats as well as motorized canoes for fishing and lake exploration, and a traditional dhow offers a tranquil and timeless alternative.

The professionally manned powerboats can take a maximum of four clients to fish for the giant Nile perch. The exhilaration of speeding across water to different islands and from one bay to the next is nicely contrasted with the slow and expectant trolling for perch in the quiet waters. How exciting to catch a big one (some are over 45 kg.)—but even if the fish aren't biting, being out in the boat is rewarding enough on its own. Giant fig trees line the shores, villagers do their washing on the banks, fish eagles swoop for the fish you throw them, and otters may be playing in the water. There are colorful canoes, romantic fishing dhows and mountain peaks in the distance. The boatman may point out the sacred forest where sacrifices are made when rain is needed.

In the quiet of the evening you can choose to fish for tilapia. The bright canoe rocks gently near the reeds, the wine is chilled and the clouds tinted in sunset colors.

You can also choose to take a day trip from the Mara to Mfangano Island. Fly and boat in for breakfast, go fishing for perch, and fly back to Governors' after lunch.

Special Offerings

Boat rides, fishing, bird walks, visits to local fishing villages, small lake beach at camp, hikes on the island—caves.

Off Notes

We had to leave.

Safari Journal — Thursday finale!

Joan shrieks at the thunder cracks overhead. Lightening must have struck the top of the hill. We are feasting on an elegant dinner in the open sided dining room and looking out over the lake. The storm is awesome and beautiful. Jagged forks of lightening streak across the sky, silvering the lake, and silhouetting a magnificent, gnarled old fig-tree. The jetty and the boats are brilliantly lit for an instant and then we start counting slowly ~ waiting for the thunder. How many miles away is the storm now? I feel so small in this vastness and power. I smile into my wine.

RUSINGA ISLAND CAMP

Lonrho Hotels Kenya Ltd., Box 58581, Nairobi
☎ *216940, FAX: 216796*

Rusinga Island Camp is part of the Lonrho chain of hotels, and flights to this camp depart from the Mara Safari Club. You arrive right at the doorstep of the camp. Climb out of the plane, walk through a hedge, under an enormous fig tree, and you are there. Not that there is very much there—and this is part of its charm.

A wide stretch of lush lawn grows to the water's edge with just a few huge trees, a wonderful open-sided thatched lounge, three rustic cottages, and a small souvenir shop. That's all. Oh yes, and the most important features—a jetty, fishing boats, a standing fish scale, and that immense lake just waiting.

Most visitors only come for half a day—do some fishing, eat a single meal and then fly back to the Mara. You can also choose to spend the night in this serene and peaceful spot. The papyrus-thatched rondavels (offering accommodation for a total of six people) are simple, attractive, and comfortable. There are ensuite bathrooms, electricity, and a separate screened sitting area. It is wonderfully relaxing to dine and chat under the impressive high thatch roof watching the light fade from the sky and the lake.

The fishing for Nile perch from Rusinga is reputed to be especially good, and it is not uncommon for fish over 45 kg. to be caught. There are twin-engined shaded boats with up-to-date tackle. In-depth guidance is provided by the expert fishermen who accompany you.

Rusinga Island Camp seems to be home to about a million birds, and along the shore you are likely to see otters and giant monitor lizards. It is an easy walk to the famous but otherwise unremarkable site of the Mary Leaky Proconsul Man discovery.

WESTERN HIGHLANDS

These highlands are very fertile and densely populated. They form the agricultural heartland of Kenya. Most of the towns in this region are small, agricultural centers with little to attract the tourist. The hotels in these towns generally service business travelers and conferences, and are not usually of the same standard as the better known "tourist" hotels in other parts of the country. Instead of staying in these "city" hotels, the traveler might find more of interest in alternate forms of accommodation such as hosted homestays.

BARNLEY'S HOUSE

Mrs. Barnley, Box 332, Kitale
No telephone

Jane Barnley's hosted homestay is a short way off the main road from Kitale to Turkana, near the Saiwa Swamp. Jane is a warm hostess and an excellent cook—two reasons to stay in her small, cozy home. She and her daughter, Julia, serve delicious English style meals such as steak and kidney pie and steamed ginger pudding with hard sauce.

Her old settler's house is surrounded by a lovely English garden and is also home to the Barnley's six dogs. There are two comfortable guest bedrooms with twin beds, family bureaus, armoires and a fireplace in each. Since there is no electricity, you shower by candlelight among the hanging plants. The small living room, filled with books and magazines, invites guests to relax and read by the fire after tea.

Mrs. Barnley has a gift for making people feel welcome. She and Julia eat with guests and are full of helpful advice about what to see in the area. They can arrange for an extremely knowledgeable guide to take you to the swamp for bird watching. Barnley's box lunches are the best in Kenya! With advance notice, you can also stop at Barnley's for a mouth-watering meal. Campers may use the property.

The Kitale area is a good base for exploring Mt. Elgon and the Cherangani Hills. It makes a convenient stop en route to the western side of Lake Turkana.

LOKITELA FARM

Mr. and Mrs. A.C. Mills, Box 122, Kitale
No telephone

Here you are guests of Tony and Adrianne Mills on their 350-hectare farm. There are three unassuming guest rooms each with a bathroom. Although there is a private guests' lounge, you are more likely to join the Mills on their spacious veranda or around the large fireplace in their living room. Meals are taken with the Mills and you are made to feel very much part of the family. As Tony says, "It is our home, not a hotel—there is no late night room-service or masseuse."

The up-country farmhouse looks over a pretty garden with large Nandi Flame trees. Beyond you can see fields of maize—the principal crop on the farm. Mt. Elgon dominates the horizon. You are very aware of being on a farm and can see around the farmyard, admire the dairy cattle, or wonder at the maize "as high as an elephant's eye." The house is hung with farming trophies; early farm noises greet the day; and the food at table is wonderfully farm fresh. Best marmalade we've had!

Tony is voluble in expounding his views on Independent Kenya. Staying at Lokitela farm provides insight into the life-style of the colonial white farmer in Kenya. As one visitor wrote in the guest book, "...a part of Kenya and a way of life that few visitors will experience." This is a place where there is no phone; the generator is switched off at night; the furniture has seen many days; and the bath water is brown. But predinner drinks are offered by the fire; early morning tea can be served in bed; and the hospitality is warm and welcoming.

Lokitela has many well-loved animals. The cats get saucers of milk at teatime; the parrot greets you; and there is a tribe of well-trained dogs. Visiting children can help milk the cows. There are horses to ride and paths have been mowed in the riverine forest for riding, walking and bird watching. About 300 species of birds have been recorded on the farm. This, combined with the proximity of the Kakamega Forest and Mt. Elgon, makes this a particularly attractive place for ornithologists. If guests do not have their own transportation, Tony can arrange to take them to areas of interest in his 4-wheel drive which he has personally customized for the enjoyment of his guests—complete with viewing hatches.

RONDO RETREAT CENTER

*The Reverend Godfrey Dawkins, Box 14369, Nairobi
or Box 2135 Kakamega*
☎ *(0331) 41345, FAX: (0331) 20145 (Mon–Fri)*

 If you want to explore the Kakamega Forest, this is the best place to stay. The center is a nonprofit religious retreat operated by the Trinity Fellowship Project and has only recently been opened to tourists. It is set in beautiful gardens in the middle of the Kakamega forest. There are enormous trees and a myriad of birds. It is extraordinarily peaceful.

This delightful place has an interesting history. The main house was built in the 1920s by a sawmiller for his wife. She apparently asked for her home to be at the base of the "biggest tree in the forest." The giant Elgon Olive still stands in the gardens. This place has also served as an orphanage and a youth center, and it was the setting for the film *The Kitchen Toto*.

Today, the retreat can accommodate up to 24 people. Guests can choose to stay in the main house, or in self-contained log cottages in the gardens. The cottages have been decorated with flair, and have sitting rooms and kitchens. In the main house there are lovely antiques as well as local paintings, crafts and fabrics. Guests gather to eat in a beautiful dining hall where good food is served and there is silver on the table. After dinner, guests retire to coffee by the fire.

You can take walks in the garden and set off on paths into the forest. This is "a place to be still," to reflect and to relax. You take off shoes before entering the main building. No alcohol is served, and guests are requested not to smoke indoors. Tea is served on the verandah or in your cottage. There is no telephone, but electricity is provided by a generator.

Guides can be arranged for bird-watching and forest walks. Several exotic species of birds found in the Kakamega forest are not seen anywhere else in Kenya. There are a host of butterflies, and monkeys cavort in the trees. The Rondo Retreat Center is 23 km. from Kakamega town and a 4-wheel drive vehicle is needed when it rains.

IMPERIAL HOTEL

Imperial Hotel, Box 1866, Kisumu
☎ *41485*

This is a newer hotel in Kisumu and has a small swimming pool. We did not visit this hotel.

KAKAMEGA GOLF HOTEL

Msafiri Inns, Box 42013, Nairobi
☎ *330820, FAX: 227815*

For want of other options, this is where most travelers to Kakamega stay. It is often busy with conferences and birders. This three-story hotel is adequate and rather ordinary. It has a pleasant garden and a golf course. Hotel residents become temporary members of the adjacent sports club.

KERICHO TEA HOTEL

African Tours and Hotels Ltd., Box 30471, Nairobi
☎ *336858, FAX: 218109*

Situated in the rolling spring-green tea estates of Kericho is the historic Kericho Tea Hotel, built in the 1950s by the Brooke Bond company. Sadly, it is past its prime—an example of faded colonialism.

The double-story building itself is gracious and charming, conjuring images of an earlier grandeur. There are large public rooms with impressive wood floors, giant fireplaces and plenty of windows. Now, however, the smell of floor polish pervades; huge and inappropriate posters of beach scenes decorate walls; and the place has a scrubbed, but threadbare appearance. Accommodations in the main building range from single rooms to two bright and spacious suites which flank the outdoor dining terrace and have views over the gardens. There are also four sturdy stone cottages with fireplaces. Each cottage has two rooms. Conference facilities are available.

Outdoors, the overwhelming impression is of greens and reds: the red tiled roofs, the spacious green lawns with red cannas and Nandi Flame trees, and beyond, the incredible green of tea bushes. There is a nicely sited and playable tarmac tennis court and a disappointing swimming pool surrounded by stained cement walls. Birds twitter; the pace is slow and peaceful. You can almost feel all that green growing around you.

KITALE CLUB

Kitale Club Box 30 Kitale
☎ *20036*

This is one of the oldest full service clubs in Kenya. There are lovely views of Mt. Elgon. The Club is known for its golf course and also has a swimming pool and sauna. There is a restaurant and a bar which is popular with residents in the area.

Besides the old cottages, there are also new ones which are more comfortable and have fireplaces.

The room tariff includes a low daily membership fee which allows guests to use the sporting facilities.

MT. ELGON LODGE

Msafiri Inns, Box 42013, Nairobi
☎ *330820, FAX: 227815*

This very run-down lodge has seen better days. It was once a home with beautiful grounds at the foot of Mt. Elgon. Today you need much imagination to recall its past splendor. The lovely shell is all that remains. The rooms are tatty and cry for renovation. The suite over the front is spacious and full of character. But the decor...(sigh). The restaurant, we hear, does not always have a ready supply of food or even water. Today the impressive grounds and gardens are the best thing going for this lodge. This gracious old building deserves to have past glories restored.

SIRIKWA HOTEL

African Tours and Hotels Ltd., Box 30471, Nairobi
☎ *336858, FAX: 218109*

This is the main hotel in Eldoret. Eldoret is seldom on the tourist route. This highrise town hotel has 105 rooms, conference facilities and a large outdoor pool. The rooms are threadbare and the food disappointing.

SUNSET HOTEL
African Tours and Hotels Ltd., Box 30471, Nairobi
☎ *336858, FAX: 218109*

If you find yourself in Kisumu, we hear that this hotel has the best view. From your room, you are likely to see the sunset and Lake Victoria. There is also a swimming pool. We did not visit, and cannot comment on the upkeep or ambiance.

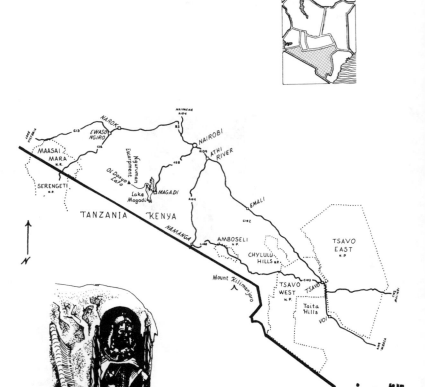

SOUTHERN KENYA

SOUTHERN KENYA

South of Nairobi, along the southern border of Kenya, lies some of the most amazing and majestic land in the world. It includes Mt. Kilimanjaro, Africa's most famous mountain, the southern end of the Rift Valley, and three major wildlife reserves: Tsavo National Park; Amboseli National Park, and the Masai Mara National Reserve, which is part of the world-renowned Serengeti ecosystem.

The Masai Mara National Reserve is 1510 square kilometers of incredible wide open vistas and verdant riverine forests following the looping bends of the Mara and Talek Rivers. It is bounded on the south by the Tanzanian border and is the Kenyan extension of the Serengeti National Park in Tanzania. Ranging in height from 1500 to 2170 meters, the Mara also has some spectacular outcrops and ridgetops. The never-ending views across the grasslands are wonderful, and from Mara ridges and escarpments you see range after range of distant mountains. Looking down on the grasslands marked by thickets and clumps of trees, the land seems spotted or dappled, which is *mara* in Maa, the Masai language.

The quantity and variety of wildlife in the Masai Mara is unequalled in Kenya. This is partly due to increased human usage of the grasslands around the reserve. Beginning in 1949, these human pressures gradually encouraged the animals to find their way into the Mara. Another reason for this movement of animals was the natural increase of elephants in the scrub thickets to the south. By about 1950, when elephant herds became large enough, they opened up the woodlands along the Tanzanian border. Grazing animals were lured there by the new elephant-created grasslands. Predators followed. The result: millions of animals protected and drawing tourists, especially during the great Wildebeest Migration.

Between the Masai Mara and Amboseli lies the southern end of the **Rift Valley** with a moonscape beauty of lava rock, arid undulating plains, and the frothy pink of **Lake Magadi** and its Tanzanian cousin, Lake Natron. Both are rich soda lakes and home to interesting birdlife, including flamingo. Lake Magadi is second in world production of *sodium sesqui carbonate*, or trona. From the lake, it is possible to cross the Rift. However, it takes a four-wheel drive to mount the extremely rough dirt tracks of the **Nguruman Escarpment**, which forms the Rift's western wall. Since maps are sketchy and the bush tracks are often very faint, it is wise to include an experienced guide in your safari group. Through the changing bush and forests, it is possible to reach fantastic viewpoints with the Loita Hills, then the Masai Mara, beyond.

Amboseli National Park became Kenya's first game sanctuary in 1948, when 3260 square kilometers were set aside as a national reserve. Besides being a renowned refuge for wildlife, especially elephant, Amboseli also has perfect views of Mt. Kilimanjaro. At 5895 meters, Kilimanjaro is Africa's highest mountain, its perfect caldera crowned with one-fifth of all the ice in Africa. Although it often seems suspended between low-lying clouds and the deep blue sky, it is actually the highest free-standing mountain in the world. Thanks to movie makers and visitors from around the world, the picture of this magnificent mountain with animals grazing under thorn trees below has become a well-known symbol for Africa.

In 1973, an area of 392 square kilometers of the original reserve was declared a national park. Today, like the Masai Mara, Amboseli's grasslands are in danger of abuse by too many minibuses, though recent regulation may help. The park includes grassy savanna, the seasonal Lake Amboseli, three primordial green swamps and various viewpoints. In the dry season, the dry lake bed and erosion can make parts of the park very dusty. The remains of trees torn by elephant herds make some corners of the park resemble moonscapes or galleries of fantastic driftwood art.

The Chyulu Hills National Park is a young volcanic ridge to the east of Amboseli that extends east and west for 80 kilometers. This park is seldom visited, and the dirt tracks are very rough and require a four-wheel drive.

During the rainy season the tracks may be washed away. The 471 square kilometers of this park include beautiful valleys and peaks with views in all directions. From the northern slopes, it is often possible to see Mt. Kilimanjaro in the distance. Rains turn the hills into a soft, rolling green and give rise to underground rivers.

At Mzima Springs in the adjoining Tsavo National Park West, these waters join other subterranean rivers from Kilimanjaro to create an amazing oasis in the dry scrubland of Tsavo. These springs are a paradise for hippo, fish, and birdlife. A system of ranger-patrolled paths and an underwater viewing room make this a rewarding stop for tourists.

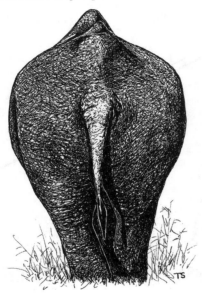

Tsavo National Park covers more than 20,800 square kilometers and includes some of Kenya's most rugged volcanic terrain. Generally very rough, rocky, and wild, Tsavo West includes some of the Chyulu Hills, the Ngulia mountains rising to 1830 meters, and various isolated granite monuments to break up the semiarid plains and bush. This sort of landscape continues into Tsavo East, though much of the eastern sector of the park is flat and empty desert.

To the southwest and surrounded on three sides by Tsavo are the Taita Hills. Rising steeply with spectacular gorges, waterfalls and forests, this striking hill system provides a dramatic backdrop for the Taita Hills Wildlife Sanctuary.

Beyond Taita to the south, the railroad marks the way to Kenya's southernmost town, Taveta. A real outpost since the railroad linked it to Voi in 1924, Taveta is between **Lake Chala**, a crater lake to the north on the Tanzanian border, and **Lake Jipe** to the southwest, a haven for bird lovers.

MASAI MARA AREA

MASAI MARA NATIONAL RESERVE

The Masai Mara is the most popular game reserve in Kenya. It is an extension of the Serengeti Plains in Tanzania, and offers the best game viewing in Kenya. On these wide open rolling grasslands you can often see an incredible variety of different animals at one time. Perhaps a cheetah mother sits on a termite mound with her punky-looking cubs, while beyond, gazelle, antelope and zebra placidly graze. Giraffe might peer curiously through the trees, while elephant pass on silent feet and vultures circle above. Every year millions of wildebeest migrate north from the Serengeti to the green grass of the Mara. This exciting spectacle usually occurs sometime between July and August.

Even when animals are not highlighting the scene, the views by themselves are worth the trip. Imagine bright oblique rays of evening light slanting under blue-black storm clouds. The rich golden expanses of waving grass are brilliant in this light, and the solitary flat-topped acacia tree is dramatically spotlighted on the crest of a hill. Beyond rise the steep smoky blues of the Oloololo Escarpment—such distances, such breathing space. At sunup you may be hanging on to the open overhead hatch as your Land Cruiser plunges down a rocky track to ford a rushing stream. Your hands feel frozen solid, and the steep climb on the other side looks impossible. You loosen your knee joints, tighten your grip and grin inanely—what fun!

The abundance of game and easy game viewing has led to an explosion of lodges and tented camps in and around the reserve. At the time of writing, there are at least 20 places to stay—more than double the number that existed six years ago. As a visitor you have many attractive choices. You can choose to stay in a luxury tent with no electricity, where animals are free to wander into camp, or you might opt for the opposite extreme—the solid walls of a lodge with a swimming pool.

Some of the camps and lodges are within the reserve itself, others are outside. To enter the reserve you must pay a park fee. Places outside of the reserve do not have to adhere to park rules and can offer game walks as well as night game drives. Animals, however, are not confined to the reserve and are also found in good numbers outside. You are also likely to see human habitation, especially Masai with their herds, when you stay outside the reserve.

Visits to a Masai *manyatta* can be arranged from many of the camps or lodges. Another popular "excursion" is a romantic hot-air balloon trip where you view animals from above and then touch down for an extravagant breakfast in the bush. Pricey but memorable. Another day or overnight jaunt offered from the Mara is a flying trip to an island camp on Lake Victoria where you fish for giant Nile perch (see Western Kenya).

You are likely to go on at least one or two game drives a day when you stay in the Mara. Early morning and evening drives are the most popular—they can also be very cool, so remember to pack some warm layers along with your hats, suntan lotion, binoculars and malaria medication.

The explosion in places to stay in and around the Mara also means that there are more visitors and more minibuses. Although you are still guaranteed to see a lot of game, there are times and places in the reserve when vehicles jostle for position around an animal (usually a cat), and the sounds of video cameras and revving engines destroy the peace. Many visitors have their hearts set on seeing "the Big

Five." After spotting lion, the minibuses rush off in search of elephant. (It is rare to see rhino here.) Remember that there are great rewards in switching off the engine—just watching and listening to the everyday life of this marvelous part of Africa.

Travelers to the Mara arrive by plane (there are several small landing strips) or by vehicle. The trip from Nairobi is long, bumpy and spectacular. Those driving by minibus tend to concentrate in the southeastern part of the reserve. The camps farther from Nairobi attract more flying customers and tend to be better equipped with their own game watching vehicles. During the rainy seasons the roads become very difficult, especially where there is black cotton soil, notorious for trapping vehicles.

GOVERNORS' FAMILY OF CAMPS

The Governors' Family of Camps provides luxury and comfort while retaining the authentic flavor of safari camping. There is still excitement—wild animals in camp, only canvas overhead—and yet you can have a hot shower and iced drinks. The high quality of food and service seem amazing in this rough, bush setting miles from civilization.

Most visitors to the Governors' Camps fly to the Governors' Musiara Airstrip just minutes from the various camps. There are four of these camps all sited among the trees along the banks of the Mara River, which loops back and forth in this western section of the Masai Mara Game Reserve. Each of these camps has its own unique character. They include:

Governors' Camp—largest and best known.

Little Governors'—our favorite camp in the Mara and the smallest of the Governors' permanent camps. Its site around a small marsh is reached by crossing the Mara River by boat.

Paradise Camp—designed to look more like a rough safari camp.

Private Camp—gives your group the feeling of being on a traditional mobile safari with a camp set up for you alone.

All of the camps give you bush camping without fences. Animals are free to wander very close and even into camp, though armed Masai guards patrol day and night to assure your safety.

Governors' emphasize high quality food and friendly attentive service. Food is generally superior with a tempting array of salads, entrees, breads, and desserts. At Private Camp, you can work with the Governors' Executive Chef to plan your own menus.

Each tent has a covered outdoor veranda with two safari chairs and a small table. Simple tent furnishings include twin beds, a wardrobe rack, a desk/dressing table and safari chairs. None of the camps uses electricity to light the tents. Candles, matches, lanterns and flashlights are provided. Screened windows let in light and air during the day and are covered at night.

All the tents at each camp have private tented bathrooms with a flush toilet and hot showers. The more rustic rely on traditional safari showers, while at the other extreme, Governors' and Little Governors' even have bidets.

Game drives in open-topped green Land Rovers are included in the tariff. Driver/guides will design the game drives to suit individual preferences and are willing to share their extensive knowledge of the birds and animals.

Little Governors' Camp is home to **Mara Balloon Safaris**. You can splurge on this unique adventure to float over the Mara at sunrise watching for game below. After landing you are served the traditional champagne breakfast in the bush.

You can also arrange to fly for a day trip to the Mfangano Island Camp in Lake Victoria, or better yet, stay overnight in one of the camp cottages. (See Mfangano Island Camp for details.)

GOVERNORS' CAMP

Governors' Camps - Musiara, Ltd., Box 48217, Nairobi
☎ *331871, FAX: 726427*

This was the first tented camp to be established in the Masai Mara National Reserve. "Main" Governors', as it is sometimes called, first opened in 1972 on the site of Teddy Roosevelt's Mara camp. It is now one of the best known camps in the Mara, and especially popular with American clients.

Safari Journal
Thursday ~ deep night

Gracious dining ... fine linens. We were lingering over coffee in the candlelit dining tent. Suddenly the quiet of the night was broken by the dramatic arrival of Maasai warriors. First we heard the spine~tingling resonance of their many-voiced chant. Then they were among us, flickering shadows, flowing and twisting and turning just as their river flows and twists and turns. Their movements were strong and fluid, accented by the deep red of their shukas. Mesmerized by the sound and movement, we followed them to the campfire. We were lucky: the trance-like dancing, which is also warrior-training, flowed on ~ finishing with the astonishing and traditional high jumping ~ a test of spirit and strength .... then they were gone, but some of their conjured spirit remains ....

Although Governors' is also one of the largest camps, you never see more than a few tents at a time. Amazingly enough, as many as 38 green tents are sited along the high banks of the looping Mara River. Tall old trees, clipped green lawns, and the quiet river give everything a feeling of tranquillity. You can watch and listen to birds, you may even see larger animals which sometimes wander into camp. It is quite possible to wake up to the sound of hippos feeding on grass outside your tent.

Quotes:

American businessman sitting in front of his tent, drink in hand,
"This is really hard to take, isn't it?"

The reception area is built of natural stone and features a small museum showing mounted photographs and bronze sculpture of wildlife.

The tented bar/lounge, open on three sides, is especially inviting with its bar built of logs. Nearby, there is a cleared area overlooking the river where breakfast and lunch buffets are served when the weather is fine.

Fine à la carte dinners are served by candlelight in the dining tent, which seems intimate and private, though it can seat 100. The meal ends with the arrival of local Masai musicians or dancers who then draw you outside to the traditional camp fire.

Accommodations

Each tent is sited on a cement foundation with a private bathroom. There are hot showers, flush toilets, wash basins, and even bidets. *Our Favorites*: For best view of river—#19, 22, 23. For privacy—#12, 12a, 14. *Note*: #25–30 are noisy, public and near parking. #1–3 are set back with no river view.

Special Offerings

Game drives, balloon safaris, fishing on Lake Victoria, museum, superior souvenir boutique, doctor, airstrip. *Please Note*: There is no swimming pool.

Off Notes

A larger camp means more people and more noise.

LITTLE GOVERNORS' CAMP

Governors' Camps - Musiara, Ltd., Box 48217, Nairobi
☎ *331871, FAX: 726427*

This is our favorite place in the Mara—getting there is half the fun. First, you cross the Mara River in a little boat pulled along a fixed rope by the boatman. Then you climb steep steps cut into the bank and walk down a shady forest path. Suddenly you step out into an open glade: Seventeen tents curve around the edge of a marsh, looking toward the plains and high escarpment of the Mara. In a word, spectacular!

There is something about this camp that is very friendly, yet private. Guests seem to enjoy mingling with the staff and with each other, and because of the smallness of the camp, you really feel special.

Little Governors', with its open views and no fences, makes it possible to be very close to wildlife. When we visited, a family of giraffe browsed just beyond the last tent, some waterbuck wandered through the marsh, and the elephant, affectionately known as "Winston," made one of his regular visits to camp.

When we visited, the food seemed particularly good, especially the "sinful" desserts. Breakfast and lunch are served buffet-style outside under tall trees with views over the marsh and towards distant ridges. Candlelit dinners are served in the cozy dining tent. In this setting it feels natural to combine the elegance of silver, crystal, and linen with canvas, safari chairs, and lanterns. After dining, guests like to sit quietly around the camp fire—liqueurs, stories and stars.

From the Visitors' Book:

> *"We came as guests and were looked after like the Royal Family."*

Accommodations
All the tents look out across the marsh. Each tent has an adjoining tented bathroom with flush toilets, bidets and running water. There is no electricity. *Our Favorites*: Spectacular view of escarpment, slightly more private, #1 and 2. Game viewing at tent flap, but quite a hike from camp center, #17.

Balloon Safari Launching
Book a ride with champagne breakfast. Or bring your camera to the launch area. The whole take-off rigmarole is tremendously exciting, and the rainbow-hued balloons are a treat to see. Other Offerings: Same as for "Main" Governors' Camp.

Off Notes
The steps down to the boat and up to the camp across the river are steep, not easy for an out-of-condition middle-aged on-holiday camper...You can hear balloons inflating for early morning flights.

Safari Journal
Friday, high noon ~

"Hey, there's an elephant in the dining area!"
The shout drew me with the other disbelieving new arrivals.
Sure enough, there was an elephant right in camp, reaching under
the screening cloth with his trunk to sample things set out for the
lunch buffet. We all wanted to get near this wonderful, _huge_ beast.
Then I was practically bowled over by a youthful camp manager
hurrying toward the dining area and looking harassed.

"Stay back, just stay back, everyone," he whisper-shouted
in his best quiet-but-projecting voice. "It's only Winston.
He doesn't bother the tents, but you have to remember not
to get in his way. After all, he _is_ wild." Winston didn't look wild
to me, but he certainly looked big. The young manager looked resigned
as Winston ate a potted plant, then stripped a small tree for desert.
I was sorry when the elephant made his ponderous way
down the path out of camp with an honor guard of camp watchmen...

GOVERNORS' PARADISE CAMP

Governors' Camps - Musiara, Ltd., Box 48217, Nairobi
☎ *331871, FAX: 726427*

Governors' Paradise Camp is located in the same general area as Main Governors' and Little Governors', but you are just that much closer to real bush camping. Each year after the long rains, this traditional old-style safari camp reappears. Governors' canvas tents are pitched directly on the ground in the uncleared bush along another twisting loop of the Mara River.

The 20 tents give you most of the same comforts of the other Governors' camps including tented bathroom with a flush toilet. However, water for washing and bathing is hand carried to the tents, and hot water is supplied on request for the overhead gravity showers. Again, there is no electricity.

The service and food that have become traditional at the other Governors' camps are brought to Paradise in an unobtrusive way.

You feel very close to nature.

GOVERNORS' PRIVATE CAMP

Governors' Camps - Musiara, Ltd., Box 48217, Nairobi
☎ *331871, FAX: 726427*

 Governors' Private Camp can be booked as your own private safari camp in the cool green Mara River forest. You can include from four to 16 people in your safari party. It must be reserved for a minimum of three nights.

The comfort of the Governors' tents, with behind-the-scenes service, gives you all of the luxurious attention of a mobile safari without the very high costs. Again, there are flush toilets and showers, but no electricity. You can plan your own camp schedule and choose your menus with the executive chef. Bar orders, except for French champagne, are included. The lounge/mess tent can be used for parties or meetings. The camp hosts know the surrounding area and wildlife and will be happy to help you plan your activities.

MARA INTREPIDS CLUB

Prestige Hotels Ltd., Box 74888, Nairobi
☎ *338084, FAX: 217278*

Mara Intrepids Club is a luxury tented camp in the Masai Mara National Reserve. With the Talek River on the South joining a small tributary of the Mara River to the West, the camp is set apart as an oasis of comfort and privacy under spreading trees.

The 27 tents are scattered among the trees and along the river banks in secluded groups of three or four. In camp you walk along flagstone pathways winding through the riverine forest. There are birds and monkeys in the trees, who are eager to share early morning tea on your veranda. You have the romantic feeling of being on your own private safari in the African bush. In fact, some tent clusters include a club tent equipped with bar, fridge and dining table. You and your party can plan a personal barbecue and camp fire with the help of the Intrepids staff.

The tents are fun! They are rustic and natural with handcrafted safari furniture of wood and leather, but they are far from basic. There are canopied beds, hand-woven rugs, full-length mirrors, electrified lanterns sitting on barrel tables and several zip-and-screened windows. Each has a private veranda and ensuite bathroom with zipdown door and separate shower. The flashlight and big black umbrella are nice touches. There is even a fascinating safari box with folding mirror and hidden compartments—Finch-Hatton, where are you?

In keeping with the traditional safari experience, breakfast and lunch are served buffet-style in an outdoor dining area. The tall trees above are alive with the sounds of more birds and monkeys. Dinner is served more formally in the open-sided dining tent.

The lookout tower near the airstrip is set up as a sundowner bar in the late afternoon, providing a good place to relax after game drives and to watch for game at sunset. A rustic swimming pool surrounded by interesting rocks offers cool relief and a lazy place to rest in the heat of the day.

There is a rustic bar with comfy leather chairs near the river. Wildlife videos are shown in the adjoining alcove. Every night, leopard bait is hung out across the river to entice this beautiful and secretive animal into floodlit view. Enjoy this exciting spectacle in comfort from the bar, or get an even closer view from the wooden deck extending out over the river.

Quotes:

> *"This camp is like an island. Did you see the bridge we drove over? Just two parallel strips of metal track...we were "intrepid" for sure..."*

Nearby, a wooden suspension footbridge spans the river. The wobbly crossing adds a charming sense of adventure to any Intrepids game drives which set off from the opposite bank. Vehicles are a well-used fleet of green Land Rovers. They have wide open top and sides and are tough and cheerful. Mara Intrepids' unique location means that you rarely see a vehicle from somewhere else. Once you leave camp you are immediately among the wildlife, and the scenery in this part of the Mara is superb—varied and memorable.

Accommodations

Most tents are twin-bedded and some have double beds. *Our Favorites*: You can hear the sound of falling water from Kiboko Cluster, and Mamba Cluster offers a nice view of the river. Chui Cluster, across the river, has more open views.

Special Dining

You can have private meals in your club tent. A barbecue can be cooked and served just for you, and you can end the evening relaxing around an open camp fire near your tents. It feels as though you are on a private fully-catered camping safari—"doing" Africa in style.

Special Offerings

Arrangements for sunrise balloon safaris, airstrip, observation tower, swimming pool, souvenir/sundry shop.

Off-Notes

Private barbecues in the cluster club tent can put a damper on your enjoyment if it is given by another party sharing the cluster and your tent is not invited. All that transpires is audible, and well-meaning staff may have "borrowed" your veranda's safari chairs to furnish the other party's camp fire area.

SEKENANI CAMP

Chartered Expeditions Kenya Ltd. and Utalii Tours
and Safaris Ltd. Box 61542, Nairobi
☎ *333285, FAX: 228875*

 The Sekenani Camp Visitors' Book is crammed with flattering superlatives and promises to return. Easy to see why. This small gem of a tented camp offers luxury, comfort and personal attention wonderfully mixed with the adventure and excitement of being in the untamed African bush.

Sekenani Camp is just outside the National Reserve (six kilometers from the Sekenani Gate). It has a most unusual setting. From the dense vegetation and deep shade of a stream bed, you climb up to a dry grassy ridge. Here, 15 tents have been thoughtfully sited so that each has a view and is far enough from its neighbor to insure privacy. From your deck you might look down over a marshy stream which attracts game, or up to the hills and plains beyond.

The tents are surrounded by natural vegetation and blend harmoniously with the scenery. The tents at Sekenani are amazing. They get our vote for being among the most luxurious in Kenya. Raised high off the ground on wooden platforms, the tents are extra large with many generous screened "windows." When you walk into the tent, you are struck by its bright airiness and most especially by the bathtub which is centered in the bathroom. Not what you expect under canvas. Nothing bashful or apologetic—a big, elegant bathtub with brass taps and individual gas water heaters.

Safari Journal ~ 6:30 a.m.

The sun is beginning to rise. I can see pink and gold tingeing the sky, and there is a steaming cup of tea beside me. I am lying in my bathtub ~ quite fantastical in a tent! From here I can see out a window to the hills beyond, and the early morning bird chorus sounds loud and cheerful through the canvas walls. Beside me is the "toothbrush stick" our Maasai guide cut for me on the bush walk yesterday. I arrived back at camp scrubbing at my teeth and with the leaves of another plant under my arms ~ absorbing and aromatic, and used by the Maasai as deodorant when they are on long journeys.

It is especially rewarding to be out in this wonderful countryside and not always have to view everything from behind glass in the "safety" of a vehicle.

Other quality touches are the fine wooden toilet seats, beautiful hand-carved and painted chests with locks and handsome polished wood floors. The bed-spreads and floor rugs are white, contributing to the light and spacious feel of the tent. A counterpoint to this "sophistication" is the absence of electricity. At nightfall, hurricane lamps glow in the tents. The dining area is built on another rise and faces a wide expanse of natural veld with hills beyond. To reach it from the tents you cross over a small ravine on a wooden bridge.

The dining/meeting space is a log and canvas structure with high peaked roof and completely open at both ends to let in air, light and distances. Extending beyond the covered dining area is a large stone terrace—a perfect place to sit and look for game or chat companionably around a log fire at night, listening for animal sounds and admiring the bright stars above.

From the Visitors' Book:

> "This is the ultimate in roughing it in elegance!"

> "Three weeks in Africa—this place was the best—good food and the warmest nicest staff. Fabulous. We will be back."

A small attractive building of natural stone looks down over a marshy pond. It houses a small shop with quality craft items and a large covered deck where you can relax while enjoying the many birds and with luck perhaps larger animal visitors.

The small size of this camp allows for great flexibility and privacy. Meal times and bush walks are arranged to suit. A tempting variety of special activities are offered at an extra charge. These range from private dinner parties or sundowners in the bush to game walks with an experienced Masai guide who will also tell you tribal uses of the plants you pass. Remember to ask about these activities if you are not briefed on them.

Quotes:

> *"A lion took a zebra just nearby. It was 1:30 p.m. so we said 'hold lunch' and took a vehicle to look for the lion." Asst. Manager.*

> *"How exciting walking with the Masai guide—his spear and his knowledge of the wild were our only protection." Guest.*

Accommodations

All tents have views and privacy. #4 and 6 have double beds. *Our Favorite*: #6 for open view and double bed.

Special Offerings

Game drives, bush banquets, game walks, talks about Masai culture, airport transfers.

Off Notes

The nearest gate into the Reserve is six kilometers away. However, you are likely to see game from the camp itself.

KICHWA TEMBO CAMP

Windsor Hotels International, Box 74957, Nairobi
☎ *219784, FAX: 217498*

Kichwa Tembo is a large and well-maintained tented camp just outside the National Reserve to the northwest. Popular with its predominantly American clientele for its setting and high standards, Kichwa Tembo has an aura of permanence and quality. Although guests sleep in tents, the camp has the trappings and comforts of a first-class permanent lodge. There are notice boards in the lobby, a large gift shop, laundry service and carefully tended and fenced grounds. Most of the camp faces broad, parklike lawns with dramatic circular cactus gardens. Beyond, there are wide open vistas of Mara savanna.

One of the Mara's largest tented camps with 45 well-appointed tents, Kichwa Tembo also has six rondavels to cater to those who prefer to sleep behind walls. The tents are set fairly close together, but they all have private views from their verandas. Many face the long sweeping Mara view while others look over more secluded forested areas alive with birds and monkeys. The tents are spacious with many screened "windows" and a large bathroom with a stone floor. *Kichwa Tembo* means elephant head in Swahili, and the elephant theme is reflected in the rugs and bedspreads.

You approach the camp on a shaded dirt road through a dense stretch of indigenous forest, home to an interesting variety of monkeys. The circular lobby with its high thatched roof and red polished floor is cool and dark, a marked contrast with the view which greets you out the other side—golden space stretching forever.

The long dining room and circular lounge have wide openings between stone pillars and also face this marvelous vista. Afternoon tea and sandwiches are served in the lounge with its heavy wooden chairs, low tables, and yellow lights in hanging baskets. The roof is lovely—thatch lined with pale golden papyrus which contrasts with dramatic black supporting beams.

There is a secluded swimming pool, its unusual shape edged by big boulders and gardens of cacti and palms. On the lawns surrounding the pool are chairs and comfortable loungers. It is quite luxurious to swim in the heat of the day, then lie in comfort with a cool drink and watch for wild animals which might be only a stone's throw away.

Safari Journal

dawn . . .

I lean against a tree to watch the sun rise over the vast plain. There is dew on the grass. Zebra and impala catch the early light ~ bright focal points in all that space. . . . . The view in front of me is wild and timeless, and yet just behind are tended flower gardens, comfortable chairs, and a swimming pool ~ the hand of man. Early morning tea is being delivered to tents. An impala spronks ~ leaping up and down, white tail showing ~ an expression of joy or a warning? The day begins . . . .

Most guests fly to the Kichwa Tembo airstrip just five minutes from the camp. There are package rates which include game drives, (the camp operates 26 Land Cruisers). You can go on a nature walk or visit a Masai manyatta. Picnic lunches are available, and there are binoculars for hire. Masai dancers perform most evenings, and it is possible to organize bush breakfasts or banquets—even a "black-tie" dinner which is served under the stars with crystal glasses etc. (P.S. you don't really need a tie).

From the Visitors' Book:

> *"The service, the game, and the tents were top notch. If all camps were like this, there wouldn't be any hotels."*

Accommodations

There are 45 tents and six cottages. *Our Favorites*: Tents H5-H14 for sweeping views, FE A and B for privacy, and D 1–12A if you can't get the others.

Other Offerings

Game drives, balloon safaris by arrangement, nature walks, Masai manyatta visits, swimming pool, games available at reception, registered Clinical Officer.

Off Notes

There are lots of tents close together... A popular camp means lots of people, and canvas is not very soundproof... That marvelous wide view also includes game drive vehicles and the occasional plane landing in the distance.

MARA SAFARI CLUB

Lonrho Hotels Kenya Ltd., Box 58581, Nairobi
☎ *216940, FAX: 216796*

If you love hippos, the Mara Safari Club is the place for you! Set along the looping Mara River at the northeastern part of the Mara, this luxury tented lodge combines the romance of tented accommodations with all the security and comforts of a grand lodge. From the effusive hostess who greets you in her stylish African dress, to the pool which is heated, the Mara Safari Club aims to please in every way.

The spacious lodge, built of dark wood logs with high peaked ceilings, is sited on the edge of the Mara River. The open-plan, multi-level design follows the curve of the river. Although the lodge includes reception, dining room, bar, fireplace, lounge and gift shop, its unusual and asymmetric shape helps to mask its size.

A wooden deck curves along the outside of the lodge over the banks of the river. Here are two pleasant and shaded seating areas with nice views of the river and the resident hippos.

The hippos! They are a highlight of staying at the Mara Safari Club. You can see and hear them in the river—often from the deck of your tent. There is something humorous and special about lying in a tent at night listening to hippo wuffles and snorts! The high, steep banks of the river and electric fences ensure that they do not wander into camp.

Each of the 40 tents is near the edge of the river bank. The tents are raised on high wooden decks, and the natural growth between them gives a sense of privacy. Stone pathways and green lawns lead from the lodge to the tent sites. The natural and rustic mix pleasantly with the established and well-tended.

Near the lodge is an attractive, heated pool with lounge chairs and stone paving partly shaded by tall trees. There is an outdoor bar and grill. Safari chairs and tables are sometimes set up near the pool for alfresco eating at lunch—very pleasant with the sounds of birds and the river below. (We wished we could have eaten all our meals outside.) Breakfast and dinner are served in the main dining room which is split into two levels with dark wood walls and matching furniture.

Safari Journal
midnight

Suddenly I was wide awake. Hippo Noises . . .
Worse than your snoring.
Wish you were here!

After the evening game drive, a fire is lit in the lounge where tea is served. In the evenings a slide-show/lecture by the resident naturalist alternates nightly with Masai dancing.

Since it is outside of the Masai Mara National Reserve, the Mara Safari Club is able to arrange for morning walks, sundowner cocktails, or bush banquets. On your game drives you are also likely to see stately Masai herders in their vivid red *shuka*.

Up to three game drives a day are included in the tariff. The Mara Safari Club has a fleet of 16 Land Cruisers modified for game viewing: seats covered in green canvas, field guide books, binoculars, a cooler filled with drinks, and well-padded, open roof for game viewing.

Most guests fly in to the all-weather strip close by.

Quotes:

> *"This place is rustic but classy, elegant but informal. It's relaxed and friendly with a nice atmosphere."*

> *"The main building reminded me of a ski lodge—big and dark."*

Accommodations

The tents are luxurious, fun and well-equipped. Four-poster beds are bedecked with a striped canopy and mosquito net, and colorful carpets are on the floors. There are thick toweling bathrobes, and the shower and sink in the ensuite bathroom are both encased in wood. The electricity is on all night—great for readers. *Best Tent:* #12 has a king-sized bed and sunken bathtub as well as a superb view of the river and the surrounding hills.

Other Offerings

Balloon safaris, bush banquets, sundowner cocktails, B.B.Q. dinners, visit to Masai village, souvenir shop, airstrip, fishing on Lake Victoria (see Rusinga Island Camp), "Off the Beaten Track Walking Safaris" (see Rekero Farm), visit to "Wanga" Rhino Sanctuary with white rhino roaming freely on private grounds. Off Notes: The interior of the lodge is rather dark.

SIANA SPRINGS

Windsor Hotels International, Box 74957, Nairobi
☎ *219784, FAX: 217498*

Siana Springs is a tranquil tented camp outside of the National Reserve. On the site of the old, well-known Cottars' Camp, Siana Springs is the closest Mara camp to Nairobi and is popular with people driving from the capital. Although it is some distance from the busy Sekenani Gate, you are likely to encounter game close to camp without necessarily driving into the reserve.

Being outside the reserve allows Siana Springs to offer a variety of walking and dining experiences in the bush. You can go on bird or game walks with Peter Blackwell, the camp naturalist. You might pass elephant on foot, or enjoy sundowners from a high rock looking down at game in the plains. After dark you can go on night game drives.

The 20-hectare Siana Springs property ranges from flat grassy spaces with random thorn trees, to areas of lush dense growth around water from natural springs. It is these springs which give the camp its name and which attract animals to the area. The veld grass has been cut between the tents, but there has been no attempt at manicured lawns or planted gardens—the natural bush has been retained. Around the camp stretch wide panoramas of the Masai Mara—golden distances, green acacia and rocky hills.

There are 38 tents which have been arranged in three separate groupings: Acacia, Bamboo and Palm. Each of these groups has its own butler who will bring drinks, clean shoes and so forth. The tent furnishings are large, solid and heavy—chunky beds and tables custom-made from pale logs of Blue Gum. Electric fans provide coolness. The bathrooms are impressive, with super-large shower heads and a separate, private toilet. Each tent has a veranda, and some command wonderful wide-open views of the Mara while others have a more intimate view of nearby trees and bush. The tents are well spread out over the extensive grounds—some are a long walk from the main buildings. An electric fence provides security. *Best Views*: Tents #10 and 8.

The casual dining area, from the Cottars' Camp days, is built in dark wood and is open on one side. Siana Springs has a rustic, bush flavor. There is extensive use of canvas and stone. Canvas-covered doors bring the feeling of camping to the public areas, and there are electric hurricane lamps. The overall image is of solid, no-nonsense camping in comfort and style. Every night the traditional camp fire is lit.

Quotes:

"This showerhead is big enough for two."

"Our evening walk took us close to a herd of elephant."

Special Offerings

Game walks and drives, bird walks, slide shows, swimming pool.

Off Notes

Quite a hike to some tents... If you want to go into the game park, the Sekenani Gate can be quite congested and slow.

MARA RIVER CAMP
Mara River Camp Ltd. Box 48019, Nairobi
☎ *335935, FAX: 216528*

This midsized, friendly and informal tented camp is outside the Reserve (20 minutes from the Musiara Gate in the northeast of the Mara). It has a lovely position on the banks of Mara River looking up at the escarpment. There are green lawns and safari chairs, big shady trees and hippos in the river. The dining area is largely outdoors under trees and has pleasant views across the river. You welcome to take bird walks with the resident ornithologist, and game drives are available.

There are 27 very basic tents. Some have good river views, while other tents are set back from the river and rather close together. In the evening a camp fire is lit and guests are sometimes treated to performances by the staff band. There is electricity, no fences and no pool.

SAROVA MARA CAMP

Sarova Hotels, Ltd., Box 30680, Nairobi
☎ *333248, FAX: 211472*

Sarova Mara Camp is a large, established tented lodge inside the Reserve. The entrance is impressive—exotic gardens and a high thatched lobby with ethnic decor. The lodge buildings are attractive and airy, a big dining area includes an outdoor terrace with wide-angle views, and there is a well-used swimming pool which they plan to enlarge.

Seventy-five tents are scattered through sizeable grounds. Many paths wind through lawns and gardens, and there are wooden walkways over wide lily ponds. Some tents are quite a hike from the main lodge. Outlooks from the tents differ—some have wide open vistas of the Mara while others feel more like being in a tended garden.

The tents are substantial, with a concrete addition for private bathrooms—secure and neighborly rather than adventurous. Sarova Mara Camp is basically a big, touristy lodge that offers a small taste of the romance of camping in tents.

FIG TREE CAMP

Mada Holdings, Box 40683, Nairobi
☎ *221439, FAX: 332170*

This is a larger camp with 30 basic tents and 30 wood cabins. It is just outside the reserve near the Talek Gate, and is reached by crossing the Talek River on a covered wooden footbridge. The atmosphere is relaxed and casual. The accommodations are basic, and tents and cabins are crowded close together in a rather hodgepodge arrangement. Some have a river view.

There is a pool, video room, outdoor barbecue area, and a large souvenir/sundries shop. Many activities are available at extra charge: game drives, game walks, moonlight bush dinners. Fig Tree Camp is a base for balloon safaris and is the closest lodge to many informal campsites along the river. There is 24-hour electricity; no fences.

OSEUR TENTED CAMP

Oseur Tented Camp, Box 8114, Nairobi
☎ *556503, FAX: 545833*

This new camp is eight kilometers outside the Reserve (through the Olemutiak Gate). A total of 32 tents is planned. To promote privacy, the camp is divided into three self-contained manyatta, each with its own dining tent and bar. The tents are basic and unpretentious, and are well-spaced in the bush. An electric fence is in place, and a pool is planned. Game walks are offered in the surrounding hills, and the camp is close to Masai *manyatta* which can be visited on foot. There is an airstrip and a nearby petrol station.

When we visited, the camp was not yet completed. There were unpleasant odors and evidence of rushed and cost-cutting construction.

TALEK RIVER CAMP

Prestige Hotels Ltd., Box 74888, Nairobi
☎ *338084, FAX: 217278*

This small rustic tented camp is inside the reserve. Eight compact tents and a small mess tent are set in natural bush along an oxbow in the Talek River. There are no fences and no electricity, but there are flush toilets and running water. Game drives are offered. Talek River Camp is a less expensive alternative to its sister camp Mara Intrepids, which is two kilometers away. Talek shares an airstrip with Mara Intrepids.

REKERO FARM

Wilderness Trails (K) Ltd./Bush Homes of East Africa Ltd.,
Box 56923, Nairobi
☎ *506139, FAX: 502739 REKERO*

Rekero Farm is the home of Ron and Pauline Beaten. It is built in the Masai Mara Conservation Area adjacent to the reserve, a vast expanse of game country where you are unlikely to encounter other tourists. From here, the Beatons run an exclusive and up-market house-hosting and foot safari operation.

The guests we spoke with were exuberant in their praise. They were sophisticated international travelers who were thrilled by the authenticity of their experience at Rekero—the privilege of being all alone in the middle of the bush with such a knowledgeable and experienced host and guide.

Said Ron during our visit, "I give clients an experience which existed fifteen years ago—in the last four days we haven't seen anyone else." Ron, whose father was the first warden of Nairobi National Park, is a veteran "White Hunter" and is permitted to carry a gun when he takes his clients walking in the Mara.

A guest commented, "You feel completely safe and confident because you are with a professional, it's part of the enjoyment."

Rekero is truly exclusive. Only one party of up to four guests stay at any one time, and activities are organized to suit them. When they stay at the farm, accommodations are in simple thatched cottages with ensuite bathrooms. If guests choose to go on a walking safari, they sleep in mosquito-proof mobile tents.

"We are not offering Hilton Hotel accommodations," warned Ron. "This is not five star amenities."

One of his charmed guests piped up, "There's nothing wrong with it. We've had hot showers all the time, and the food couldn't be better!"

Activities include game viewing by four-wheel drive or on foot. You can also visit local Masai *manyatta* or the Ndorobo hunter-gatherers.

Guests' Comments:

> *"This is the best, and we toast it."*

> *"Last night, when we camped out, they cooked the food in a tin trunk, and it tasted fabulous."*

In addition to having privately hosted guests, Ron also offers a daily walking safari. Guests are collected in the early morning from the Mara Safari Club and driven to the ridge of the Kipleleo Mountain to admire the marvelous view over the Mara before they set off for their walk and a bush breakfast. They visit the Ndorobo, have drinks at Rekero and are returned to the lodge for lunch. The Beatons also do longer five-day walking safaris, and offer four "adventure" walks a year which are more rustic, with donkeys and porters carrying the gear.

BUSH TOPS

Glen Cottar Safaris, Box 44191, Nairobi
☎ *882408*

Bush Tops is a private home near the Masai Mara National Reserve. It belongs to Glen and Pat Cottar, who can host a party of up to four people. When guests stay at Bush Tops, they have the privacy of a house to themselves, domestic staff to cook and clean, and *askari* for safety. They also have the freedom to organize their days as they wish.

Bush Tops is just west of Siana Springs Camp (which used to be Cottars' Mara Camp). The house is built on the side of a hill and overlooks a natural salt lick which is often visited by animals. The building is functional with a flat facade and a green corrugated iron roof. The interior has cement floors, papyrus-lined ceilings and basic furniture.

Guest accommodations include two simple guest bedrooms as well as a separate tent. There are flush toilets, solar-heated water, and solar-powered electricity.

Guests may choose to visit the Masai Mara National Reserve (about a 30-minute drive away), go for game walks from Bush Tops (with a Masai guide), or simply relax at the house, watching for birds and animals. It is all very low-key, relaxing and peaceful—no tourist buses, no schedules to keep. There is an airstrip close by, handy for those who prefer to fly in.

We did not visit Bush Tops and cannot comment on the comfort or food.

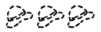

MPATA SAFARI CLUB

Mapata Safari Club, Box 58892, Nairobi
☎ *217015, FAX: 217016*

This luxurious, upmarket Japanese club hotel sits high on the edge of the Oloololo escarpment with panoramic views across the Mara Plains. The club is named after a Tanzanian artist S.G. Mpata, whose paintings enjoy great popularity in Japan.

A melding of Japan and Kenya, the Mpata Safari Club is the most pricey place to stay in the Mara area. There is an emphasis on elegance and sophistication, personal attention and luxury. Each suite has its own private outdoor jacuzzi—bubbles in the sun and the world spread out below. The Kenyan chef has been trained in Tokyo and offers world-class international cuisine. The unusual furniture, conceived by a Japanese designer was made by Kenyan craftsmen. Typically, each group of clients is hosted by one of the club's upper management team (Japanese or English speaking) who customizes the clients' stay, joins them for some meals and generally sees to client well-being. The hotel staff are almost exclusively Kenyan and bring a relaxed and friendly style to the operation of the club.

The architecture of the Mpata Safari Club is most unusual. Guests stay in separate concrete structures well-spaced along the top of the escarpment. There are 10 suites and 12 deluxe units, each with interlocking curves separating bedrooms, bathrooms and verandas. The chief feature of the deluxe rooms is the panoramic sweep of the Mara you can see from your bed. The Suites have similar views and are larger with a lounge, kitchenette and, best of all, a jacuzzi. The units are reached by stone pathways meandering between indigenous bush and trees which help to soften the towerlike concrete structures.

The soaring main clubhouse has several levels, huge windows and wonderful views. Natural materials have been used—stone for steps and floors, wood for tall posts and beams. The center of the clubhouse is a large circular shaft open to the sky and the elements with lush tropical vegetation at its rocky base. A library nook has a fireplace, a diverse collection of books in both Japanese and English, and the only comfortable, curl-up seating in the club. A spacious bar looks out over the vast view. Way below is the Mara River, the distinct circular shapes of Maasai manyattas, and the golden expanse of the Mara plains stretching to purple hills. Above, the forever sky.

Not only does the Club's name honor art, but throughout there is a flavor of the artistic and the unusual. The long wood reception counter is a carved masterpiece of curves and bends, inspired by the Mara River, which winds and shimmers far below. Fantastical African sculptures surprise and intrigue, colorful Mpata paintings hang in the suites, and everywhere there are fun, whimsical, improbable chairs—chairs which invite photography rather than sitting—giant carved wooden chairs with lethal looking protrusions, feminine little skirted chairs for straight backs—hardly two the same.

Gourmet meals are served in style in the dining room where wooden posts rise to the roof high above, large wooden chairs make a dramatic statement, and more enormous windows face the view. Menus are printed in French, and nouvelle cuisine is so attractively presented that you are reluctant to disturb the artistry. But do! It rewards the palate as well. Special dietary needs are catered to, including a taste for Japanese cuisine.

With a ratio of about two staff to every client, you are made to feel very special and very welcome. Besides receiving a great deal of individual attention, you find fresh flowers in the room, a thick white toweling gown to wear to the jacuzzi, and a hot water bottle to greet you in bed at night.

There are a variety of activities to choose from. You can go on day or night game drives in one of the Club's Land Cruisers, you may choose to have a bush breakfast or sundowners on the escarpment, you can accompany a Masai naturalist on a bush walk learning about the birds and plants you encounter, you can hike to the bottom of the escarpment and up again (with an armed escort), you can swim in the attractive swimming pool or you can take to your jacuzzi and the view.

Since the Maasai Mara National Reserve is about a 40 minute drive from the club and because there is so much to tempt you on the grounds, we recommend that you spend several nights at Mpata (pocketbook willing).

Although Mpata Safari Club was designed to cater to its Japanese Club members, bookings can also be made within Kenya, and management is keen to encourage an international mix of upmarket clients.

From the Visitors Book:

> *"Best food I've tasted in a long time, could steal the furniture, gorgeous location, super service."*

> *"Room with a view!"*

> *"You could spend the night in the jacuzzi admiring the stars."*

Off Notes

The vistas are breathtaking, but the animals are far below and it is a long drive down for close-up viewing... Even if you have a yen for your own outdoor jacuzzi with a marvelous view, it requires many, many yen to stay there.

OLKURRUK MARA LODGE

African Tours and Hotels, Box 30471, Nairobi
☎ *336858, FAX: 218109*

The new Olkurruk Mara Lodge has a spectacular site high on a rocky cliff at the top of the Oloololo escarpment. There are panoramic views over the plains and the meandering Mara River far below. This location was used in the Denys Finch-Hatton funeral scene in the film *Out of Africa*.

There are 19 thatched guest rondavels designed to create the feel of an African village. *Olkurruk* means pied crow in Masai, and the theme is carried through in the handmade bedspreads and rugs as well as in eye-catching leather wall hangings which depict local myths about the pied crow.

The public rooms have been simply and attractively decorated using natural local materials. There is an indoor/outdoor dining area, a cozy circular lounge with an open fire in the center, and the *Out of Africa* bar which has the best view of those vast distances. Beyond this bar juts a large rocky overhang where you can sit and feel suspended in space over the Mara. With binoculars you can pick out herds of elephant, or see a distant clutch of combies (mini-vans) perhaps crowded around a kill. In the early morning you might watch a colorful hot air balloon drifting below you.

Unfortunately, there are many places in the lodge where that marvelous view is obscured by vegetation. Several rondavels which would otherwise have magnificent outlooks, face bushes instead. We were told that it is frequently windy at the edge of this escarpment and that the vegetation acts as a windbreak. At this height, it can be cold at night. In the rainy seasons, it is often misty, with poor visibility.

The rooms are cozy and snug. They are more appealing in the evening than in the heat of the day when they seem a little dark and enclosed. There are pale reed walls, handwoven rugs on the painted floor and an unusual fabric ceiling which is gathered tentlike up to the peak of the rondavel. Bathroom walls are made of rough dark timber, and there are showers with plentiful solar-heated water. Decor in the rooms is imaginative and appropriate, but it is already showing some signs of wear.

It is a long haul down into the Reserve, and half or even full-day game drives are more popular than the traditional shorter game drives, offered by most lodges in the Reserve. Olkurruk operates six Land Cruisers for game drives, and an airstrip has been recently constructed nearby. There is 24-hour electricity and an electric security fence. There is no swimming pool at this time.

KEEKOROK LODGE

Block Hotels, Box 47557, Nairobi
☎ *335807, FAX: 340541*

Dating from 1965, Keekorok Lodge is a large and busy lodge located at the well-traveled crossroads within the Masai Mara National Reserve. It can accommodate almost 200 guests including many minibus tour groups. Keekorok is popular among those who prefer solid walls to tents and for its location. It is one of the easier Mara lodges to reach from Nairobi by road. The lodge is sited on a shallow rise where you can see for miles, and the sky stretches—beyond the horizon—to infinity.

With whitewashed walls in clean contrast to high-peaked black rooflines, the lodge is laid out to give all main rooms and most guest rooms a wide open view of the Mara. The main hotel building is usually a hive of activity. There are notice boards announcing activities, a lecture room, a busy gift shop and a comfortable lounge surprising in leather and tartan. The dining room is open to the terrace—allowing for fresh breezes and that view. The large stone terrace has heavy wooden chairs and tables, and overlooks mowed lawns and a swimming pool made private by bougainvillea bushes. Below are the tall trees and lush growth at the edge of the Pololet River. Beyond all of this stretches the golden vastness of the Mara plains.

Keekorok, which means place of black trees in the Masai language, is named for the trees at the river's edge. A high wooden walkway has been built here, and allows close-up views of the plants, trees, birds and other wildlife that live along the river. At one end, a small thatched sundowner bar overlooks a river pool with resident hippo. There are no fences around Keekorok, and it is not uncommon to see elephant and buffalo wander on to the perimeters of the grounds—always under the watchful eyes of the askari on guard.

Accommodations

Although Keekorok has over 70 rooms, the different wings have been laid out to minimize a sense of crowding. Rooms are simply but nicely furnished, most with tub and shower. Some have double beds and minibars. Many rooms have views of the Mara, and from most new wing rooms and the VIP House, there are even opportunities for early morning game viewing while lying in bed or from your private terrace. *Our Favorites:* #41 (a corner room which overlooks the water hole), #52–59 (for great views), and the VIP house (Kissinger stayed here, so can you!).

Safari Journal — Tuesday, after dinner

After dinner coffee on the terrace .... pinch me, this is Africa! There's some nice scent in the air and the Maasai dancers have left for their village. Everything seems much quieter. The moon and the stars are amazing. Even in the dark we can see some buffalo and that elephant we've seen come and go all afternoon. We can hear the people at the next table talking about the lion cubs they saw today and about international politics all at the same time.

Special Facilities

Game drives (there is only one hotel van, most visitors are with tour buses or in a private vehicle), early morning ballooning (by arrangement), Masai dancing, naturalist slides, lectures on Masai culture, pool, video room, conference room, souvenir shop, airstrip, petrol station.

Off Notes

Can be crowded and noisy with tour groups... You can hear balloons inflating for early morning flights.

MARA SERENA LODGE

Serena Lodges and Hotels, Box 48690, Nairobi
☎ *710511, FAX: 718103*

This popular lodge is set high on a ridge within the Reserve. It commands magnificent uninterrupted views down across the Mara plains and over two water holes. The Mara Serena's unique architecture and decor suggest a fantasy Masai *manyatta*—rounded spaces, earth tones, natural furnishings, and tribal touches.

A swimming pool has been positioned to take advantage of the wonderful view. Well-tended luxurious flower beds line the paths to the rooms which extend in a row from the main lodge. There are almost 80 rooms—small, enclosed, and rather claustrophobic. They all face views but have small windows and no balcony. The rooms are brightly colored in yellows and oranges with full bathrooms ensuite.

The public rooms are harmoniously decorated with lights in hanging pots, spears in window treatments and tribal motifs on walls. There are some thoughtful touches such as refrigerated platters keeping the buffet fresh, internal windows framing tropical plants, and an outdoor bird feeder near a stone seating area. The lodge offers a variety of special activities such as breakfast at the hippo pool, wildlife films, Masai dancing and balloon safaris.

Off Notes

At this height, and surrounded by concrete, you feel rather removed from the bush.

MASAI MARA SOPA LODGE

Kenya Holiday Management Services Ltd., Box 72730, Nairobi
☎ *337410, FAX: 331876*

The Masai Mara Sopa Lodge is built on a high ridge in the southeast corner of the Masai Mara National Reserve. The best thing about this lodge is its spectacular terrace view across a valley, with wildlife visiting a small water hole below.

To enter the lodge you descend steep stairs into an enormous round lobby and lounge leading to the dining area, another huge space. All of this is capped by a tall thatched roof that is amazing in size. Surprisingly, these huge rooms are quite dark, perhaps in keeping with the Masai manyatta decor—curving walls and the floor shades of rusty red. The open terrace with the far-reaching view is a relief from the heaviness of the main rooms.

The 60 double rooms and 12 suites are lined up along the ridge in connected thatch-topped rondavels reached by a rock-paved path, and all of them face the view. Unfortunately, the private verandas are not very inviting, but room windows do face the view. Furnishings and bathrooms are adequate, but rather tired.

The swimming pool and sports area needed maintenance when we visited. The lodge has a disco farther down the slope.

Special Facilities
Balloon safaris, conference facilities, boutique and sundry store, minibars.

Off Note
The whole lodge was in need of a thorough cleaning.

PARADISE MARA CAMP
Paradise Safaris Ltd., Box 41789, Nairobi
☎ *229262, FAX: 228902*

The Paradise Mara Camp at Hippo Point is on the banks of a bend in the Mara River just beyond the northwest corner of the Masai Mara National Reserve. This thatch and stone built lodge overlooks a well-populated hippo pool and offers morning and evening game drives which are included in the tariff.

There is a thatched lobby which opens to the river. An adjoining Lookout Bar and dining veranda is built right over the water. Hippos bellow and splash below. At night a leopard is baited across the river.

Guests stay in two-story huts built right along the riverbank. Each room has a thatch-shaded veranda overlooking the river. There are mosquito nets and adjoining shower bathrooms. Some family suites are available.

Indian vegetarian delicacies are a specialty of the lodge. The head chef presides over separate vegetarian and vegan kitchens. There is a swimming pool, and a camp fire is lit at night.

We did not visit this lodge, but we hear that it is used by large tour groups.

THE NGURUMAN ESCARPMENT

Visiting the Nguruman Escarpment gives access to a changing panorama of unspoiled African bush. The Nguruman Escarpment forms the western wall of the Rift Valley and affords stupendous views of the Rift, as well as views of Lakes Magadi and Natron. This trip is seldom made by tourists. The challenging dirt tracks are rough, and an experienced guide is advisable.

OL DONYO LARO

Ol Donyo Laro, Box 44924, Nairobi

Ol Donyo Laro is perhaps the best bush experience in Kenya. It is certainly the most exclusive. Ol Donyo Laro, which means Mountains of the Buffalo in the Masai language, is a private wilderness sanctuary in the Nguruman Escarpment.

In this totally unspoiled piece of Africa, you are shamelessly spoiled. The natural scenery is stunningly spectacular—to do it justice would take pages of superlatives, a coffee-table book of soul-inspiring photos. There you are, the only people in this vast and beautiful tract of wilderness—Africa "as she was." As to the blissful luxury—you stay in small and tasteful camps, the food is sublime, the service superb, and there are such unthinkable extravagances as a floodlit tennis court high on an escarpment, and a pool where, as you swim, you have unsurpassed views over the Rift Valley. There are beds with real down duvets, beautiful books on Africa in your tent and mahogany floors.

Throughout your Ol Donyo Laro experience, you will enjoy loving attention to detail and quality. You will be impressed by the ingenious way the camps have been designed and built to harmonize with the natural surroundings. You will marvel at the foresight and engineering which made all of this possible. This is a place visited by the rich and famous—it is also a place loved by those who know and care for Africa.

Ol Donyo Laro is not just a single camp, but an entire experience which takes you from one carefully placed camp to another. Each gives you a different taste of bush life: vistas vary, vegetation changes, climates fluctuate. Even the ambience of each camp is different. You are constantly delighted and surprised.

Only one group of up to 10 are ever accepted at Ol Donyo Laro at any one time. The group has exclusive enjoyment of this sanctuary for their reserved time: a minimum of four days and nights. For most people, the experience begins when you are met by your guide in Nairobi. Although there are landing strips near the camps, guests are strongly encouraged to make the four-wheel drive passage from the city and the smooth tarmac of the Magadi Road to faint and rough tracks leading into the wilder African bush.

Leaving Nairobi, you pass the Ngong Hills and plunge down into the Rift Valley and on to Lake Magadi. In the still heat you cross this other-worldly soda lake—impossible pinks, drifting flocks of flamingos, and reflections of clouds and the deepest blue. Ahead, the Nguruman Escarpment rises dark, the green of its steep slopes folding into sharp ridges and peaks. Each turn reveals another quiet glade, a different unsuspected vista—you feel you are on a return journey into Africa.

Ol Donyo Laro extends through 2134 meters from the Rift floor into the valleys, hills and rain forests above. The fortunate guest has the opportunity to enjoy this varied environment and can be assured of the utmost privacy, exclusivity and security. Guests are carefully screened to ensure that the natural ambience will not be disturbed.

Your host is Dougie Arnold, long-time Kenya resident. As companion and guide, he will lead you into the complex and multileveled experience of Ol Donyo Laro. There are three fixed camps and a mobile fly camp. How you move among these is customized for your group.

You may spend a night in a wilderness fly camp, sleeping in a tent close to the earth. There is a camp fire and the living night sounds of Africa all around. Sometimes this fly camp is set up in arid scrub bush, sometimes in the high rain forest.

At **Kisidai**, the jungle camp, trees and bush surround each customized tent. It is hot and green and humid; there are enormous tamarind trees, and the sounds of birds are everywhere. The mess tent is near a stream and a small dam has slowed the water to form a natural swimming pool among the trees. Dougie tells us plans are afoot to create a lounge and perhaps a sleeping area or two in the spreading tops of towering fig trees.

The timber and canvas tents are spacious and sturdy, with screening on all sides to give you the feeling of staying among the trees. Each has a well-designed bathroom with hot and cold running water and flush toilets. The shower has an innovative huge showerhead—lots of hot water and pressure. The water here and in all of the camps comes straight from mountain springs and is drinkable. At Kisidai, you notice leaves, butterflies, trees and plants, the minutiae of the surrounding life with glimpses of the high Ngurumans through the trees.

Ol Duvai Camp is much higher up, right on the edge of the escarpment with views over the Rift Valley. The vistas are vast; you can see across to the opposite side and south into Tanzania. Dominating the view is Shombole, its high volcanic peak and dry eroded sides clearly etched above the hazy golds of the Rift Valley floor. Lake Natron lies silver and pink below.

The heart of Ol Duvai is an open-sided tented lounge and dining area. There are yards of safari green canvas rising to a vaulted ceiling, chunky pale wood furniture, and sculpted stone seating comfortable with cushions. All is natural, low-key and well-made. Closer to the escarpment edge is a raised swimming pool made with rounded stones set in cement. As you swim in the mountain spring water, you can see across the Rift.

A stone path winds to a thatched gazebo on a little point with the world spread below on three sides. Guests often breakfast here. In early morning sunshine they sit and watch as mist forms below and slowly rises to eye level. During the day dozens of dust-devils whirl in tall columns on the Rift floor. Sometimes at night, a flock of flamingos might fly just overhead—floating silhouettes in the moonlight.

At Ol Duvai guests stay in customized "tents" which combine canvas ceilings with stone walls. Plenty of screens allow for views and breezes, and keep out the bugs. All is spacious and comfortable and the bathrooms boast many mirrors and more big showerheads. There is an airstrip at this camp, as well as a tennis court—floodlit, of course, for cooler night play.

Laro is the highest set camp. As the most luxurious, it is usually saved for last. Through a gateway of travelers palms you enter a perfect world. You stay in imaginative comfort in tropical gardens. Behind rise steep hills; to the side plunge forested gorges; in front, the awesome spectacle of the Rift.

You pass under a bougainvillea arch, through an open tent door—in front of you is the swimming pool with nothing beyond it but lounge chairs and the whole Rift Valley—just you and that view.

You take off your shoes to enter the drawing room. The mahogany floor gleams; there are mirrors and bookcases, groupings of sofas and chairs, bowls of flowers and old brass. Here is Victorian elegance touched by Africa—the walls are canvas, the roof a soft furry thatch and one entire side is completely open to the bush and the view.

You climb mahogany stairs to the broad veranda of your tent raised high on sturdy poles. The furniture is handmade, there are bouquets of fresh flowers and oil lamps of etched glass and brass. The bathrooms are lined in African mahogany, the voluminous bathsheets are deep-piled, and there is even a toothbrush with Ol Donyo Laro stamped in gold.

Before dinner, guests gather around a camp fire close to the escarpment edge for quiet talk and tall tales, drinks and hot snacks. At night the romantic "drawing room" is lit by an extravagance of large candles. Elegant tables are set for gourmet meals. Always the service is smooth, friendly and unobtrusive.

Nothing was spared in creating these beautiful and high quality camps. This is particularly amazing when you consider the intricate planning and engineering required in this rough and isolated terrain. The many kilometers of roads were hacked through the bush, cleared and contoured by hand. Water and electrical systems were custom designed to meet the needs of each camp. A base has been set up where fresh fruits and vegetables are grown. The steep roads to reach Laro meant that all materials and furnishings had to be painstakingly carted by four-wheel drive vehicles.

This wilderness sanctuary is huge. Some of the camps are more than an hour's four-wheel drive apart. The going can be rough and dusty. Encephalitis-free tsetse-flies may invade the vehicle and lead to a frenzied bout of slapping and mashing. You ford fast-flowing rocky streams, brave "impossible" inclines, marvel at evidence of animal passage and note the airborne color of birds and butterflies. This is what you came for—the unspoiled Africa.

Other Offerings

Flying trips to Masai Mara, Samburu, Mt. Kenya...

Off Notes

Game is there. You hear it, feel it. But you seldom see it.

AMBOSELI NATIONAL PARK

Amboseli National Park was Kenya's first established game park. Since 1948, millions of international guests, including Hollywood film companies, have been drawn to the park by the magic of Mt. Kilimanjaro—the snow-capped mountain reaching to the sky above, with wildlife grazing under flat-topped thorn trees below.

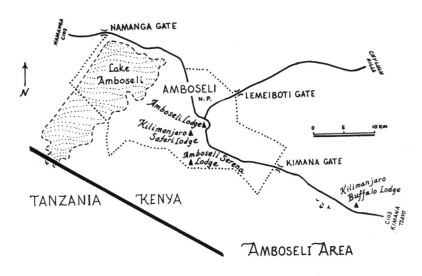

AMBOSELI AREA

Despite its proximity to the mountain, many tourists today are disappointed with Amboseli because of its dusty dirt roads and the barren expanses caused in part by the overuse of humans and animals. Years of abuse by tourist vehicles have left off-road vehicle tracks where there had been grasslands. Prolific herds of elephant have broken and destroyed trees—creating stark and stunning weathered sculptures on the landscape.

Much of Amboseli is dry and desertlike. In fact, about a third of the park is taken up by Lake Amboseli, a seasonal soda lake which, at certain times, appears to be a dead, flat wasteland. Indeed, *amboseli* is Maa for "salt dust." In dramatic contrast to these dry "desert" areas of Amboseli are riverine forests and swampy areas bright green with primordial clumps of vegetation.

In Amboseli, more than in any other park of Kenya, you are guaranteed to see many elephant. Elephant herds are easily visible across rolling grassy savannas, usually grazing their way to and from major feeding grounds or water holes.

Although Amboseli has major problems, it is heartening to consider the regenerative forces of nature. Remains of trees left by elephant are returning nutrients to the soil. According to scientists, the water table of Lake Amboseli is rising. Because there is water in the lake more often, there are also flamingos to be seen. These factors, combined with needed efforts by Kenyan authorities and conservationists to control "tourist erosion," may help to give Amboseli the opportunity for recovery. Off-road driving is now forbidden.

Many still enjoy coming to Amboseli. Always, there is the possibility of seeing the mountain. Enjoyment of Amboseli National Park is in the eye and understanding of the beholder.

AMBOSELI SERENA LODGE
Serena Lodges & Hotels, Box 48690, Nairobi
☎ *710511, FAX: 718103*

The Amboseli Serena Lodge is the nicest and most interesting lodge in Amboseli National Park. The rounded terra-cotta shape of the lodge resembles a Masai dwelling, and wildlife and Masai themes are repeated throughout the hotel.

To enter, you walk across a wooden bridge over running water, a pleasant contrast to the hot dusty roads of the park. Hanging gardens and water lilies contribute to an impression of a return to Eden. Rounded spaces, walls, windows and doorways combine with a certain cool dimness to take you away from the straight sharp edges of modern life. The emphasis is on smooth, natural harmony with the environment and the wildlife in it.

Whimsical wall-sized paintings of wildlife delightfully decorate interior walls. Hanging lights are shaded by the irregular shapes of hollow Masai gourds, adding interest to the ceiling. At check-in you receive your Masai war-club with key attached—"to fend off monkeys," the receptionist says with a smile.

The passage leading to rooms is open to the sky and traverses thick tropical gardens. The bedrooms are small. However, large wall-sized windows either look towards Mt. Kilimanjaro or towards the water hole visited by herds of wildebeest, antelope, or elephant. Bedroom walls echo the wildlife outside with another animal mural. The bathroom is modern, but the wall is curved, and a Masai spear holds up the shower curtain. The decor uses natural materials in unusual ways to suggest the Masai way of harmonizing with nature: cut sticks frame the beds, a Masai club is the door handle, hollowed gourds are the bed lights.

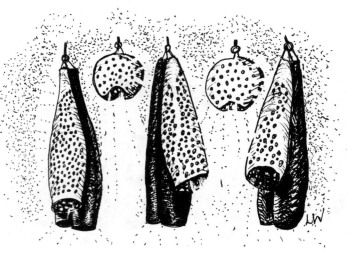

The pool, main bar and outdoor terraces overlook the surprising green grass and bush of the water hole. There are no fences. Guests have many opportunities for game viewing, even at night, when elephant families graze just a few meters away under floodlight.

To reach the dining area you cross an indoor bridge over more running water, with floating gardens and water lilies. The dining area is broken up into several adjoining rooms of different sizes, making for pleasant and intimate service. Floor-to-ceiling windows give the feeling of eating in the gardens, though the main dining room is dark, and monkeys can be uninvited "guests."

Quotes:

> *"Once in a lifetime dream come true. Endless elephants."*

> *"We enjoyed our cocktails with the gnus."*

> *"A monkey came right into the dining room and stole a piece of my pineapple."*

Breakfast and lunch are served buffet-style, and dinners are served at table with candlelight. For an extra fee, you can choose to participate in the Masai Exotic Dinner, served every other night in the terrace below the swimming pool. Waiters in Masai *shuka* serve barbecued meats and traditional foods, and there is an open bar.

The lodge invites guests to help preserve and restore the ecology of Amboseli by planting a tree in the 25 hectares of grounds surrounding the lodge. For those interested in Masai culture, Masai customs are explained informally in afternoon lectures in the Conference Room, and Masai dancers appear at the nightly camp fire.

The clientele often includes tour groups, guests usually stay for only one night, and for many it is their first experience with animals in the wild.

Safari Journal

Thursday

I went down to the open grassy terrace. I was just enjoying the breeze when this gorgeous lady elephant ambled right into the spotlight in front of me, delicately pulling and munching the long, lush grass... Other people came up, but the elephant didn't twitch an ear. She was only about ten feet from me ~ I just couldn't believe it. Sharing after dinner coffee with an elephant!

Accommodations

Bedrooms are small. There are 86 with twin beds and 10 with double beds. All have modern bathrooms with combination bathtub and shower. Rooms with double beds are smaller and have no large window. *Please note*: Best water hole views, #45–51. Best Views of Kilimanjaro, #23 & 24. Good Views of Kilimanjaro, #4–26.

Special Offerings

Game drives, bird walks, swimming pool, jogging path, playground, small airplane flights over Mt. Kilimanjaro by arrangement, folk singing guitarist at night, lectures on Masai culture, library room, souvenir and sundry shop.

Off Notes

The rooms seem very small. Seeing Mt. Kilimanjaro is a memorable part of the Amboseli experience, but there is little opportunity to see it from the public areas of the Amboseli Serena.

AMBOSELI LODGE
Kilimanjaro Safari Club, Box 30139, Nairobi
☎ *227136, FAX: 219982*

This is an older lodge located in the park. Its 118 double rooms are full of tour groups, and the lodge has seen better days. However, it has a nice lounge and terrace with views of Mt. Kilimanjaro. The best rooms are #5 & 6 and #30 & 31 for views of the mountain. It has lovely green lawns and a large swimming pool. A new reception building is under construction. The lodge shares an off-putting entry with its sister lodge, the Mt. Kilimanjaro Safari Club.

KILIMANJARO BUFFALO LODGE
Kilimanjaro Safari Club, Box 30139, Nairobi
☎ *227136, FAX: 219982.*

This older lodge was built in 1973 and needs refurbishing. It can accommodate 200 and is very often full of tour groups. It is outside the Amboseli National Park, about a 20-minute drive from the nearest gate. It is also near a Masai village. You have a fantastic wide-open view of Mt. Kilimanjaro from rooms #80-90, the Hemingway Tower Bar, and the swimming pool. The decor combines lava stone with dark wood and high ceilings. Room rondavels are spread through grounds. It is near the Kenya departure point for climbing Mt. Kilimanjaro.

Special Offerings
Light plane ride over Mt. Kilimanjaro, camel rides, bush banquets, day trips with picnics to Chyulu Hills, Taita Hills and Mzima Springs, bird walks.

MT. KILIMANJARO SAFARI CLUB
Kilimanjaro Safari Club, Box 30139, Nairobi
☎ *227136, FAX: 219982*

This older lodge resembles a large tented camp, but without canvas. There are approximately 100 double rooms in concrete and thatched cottages and a newer "K" Wing with cottages built of wood. Unfortunately, each room practically touches the next, and work is in progress on the water table which has caused flooding in some cottages. There is a pleasant dining room, but only the new rooms in "K" wing are appealing with many windows, private terraces and bright fabrics. Rooms # K-9, K-10, and K-12 have fantastic views with terraces opening out to green lawns and Mt. Kilimanjaro. This lodge is frequented by tour groups and shares the off-putting entry with the Amboseli Lodge.

TORTILIS CAMP
Tortilis Camp Limited, Box 39806, Nairobi
☎ *0154-22551, FAX: 0154-22553*

Just open in July 1994, this luxury camp of 15 tents is the newest place to stay in Amboseli. It is set on a gentle slope on Masai land at the edge of the park near the Kitirua Gate. Besides going for game drives by camp Land Rover inside the park, guests can explore outside the park on guided game walks.

Each tent has a spectacular view of Mt. Kilimanjaro from the privacy of its own veranda. The tents have been designed for comfort by one of the guide/owners, Stefano Cheli. Besides traditional safari chairs, chests and beds, each includes a private bathroom and will have hot water and electricity supplied by solar panels.

There is a good view of animals at a nearby waterhole from either the dining room or the bar. The owners, Stefano and Max Cheli and Liz Peacock, are known for providing high quality, personalized safaris. They have kept the camp small to ensure that each guest is looked after in a very special way. The owners also plan to encourage the local Masai to participate in introducing guests to Amboseli.

"Tortilis Camp is the only one of its kind in Amboseli. We offer our guests the chance to experience the real Africa. Sleeping under canvas and waking up to spectacular views, our guests can enjoy something special, a bit of luxury and seclusion away from the bustle of the main lodges." (Liz Peacock, owner)

Authors' Note

We have yet to visit this camp, but it sounds very good and is well-placed.

KIMANA

Kimana is a small village between Amboseli National Park and the Chyulu Hills.

KIMANA LODGE

Kilimanjaro Safari Club, Box 30139, Nairobi
☎ *227136, FAX: 219982*

This undistinguished lodge is located between Amboseli National Park and the Chyulu Hills. Catering mainly to tour groups from the coast, it has 112 double or triple rooms in several wooden units crowded together in a small garden/parking area. However, the attractive bar/dining room is light and airy, with the lounge and terrace overlooking a waterfall. There is a swimming pool.

COTTAR'S KILIMANJARO CAMP

Glenn Cottar Safaris, Box 44191, Nairobi
☎ *882408*

Small and rustic, this camp has four double tents and one banda. They are well spread out under fever trees near a running stream which sometimes is home to hippo. You can also fish in the stream.

The accommodation is very basic with twin beds, but there are flush toilets. There is a separate mess tent.

It is possible to take game walks with spear-carrying Masai, and you can also make excursions to the Chyulu Hills, Amboseli, or neighboring lodges.

KIMANA LEOPARD CAMP, LTD.

Kimana Leopard Camp, Ltd., Box 16004, Nairobi
☎ 732125, FAX: 732462

A cut-rate tented camp for tour groups, this camp is on the river. The tents are gnome-sized with metal beds and flush toilets. Signs abound warning guests to "watch out for leopard" and that "guests must pay for breaking furniture"!? A leopard is baited nightly.

CHYULU HILLS

The Chyulu Hills are a beautiful rolling ridge of volcanic mountains, dating back four or five centuries. This makes them some of the youngest mountains in the world. On the eastern side of the range is the black Shaitani Lava Flow, an evil-looking wasteland of lava rock created when the Chyulus were born. The lava flow is near the Chyulu Gate of Tsavo National Park West.

OL DONYO WUAS

Richard Bonham Safaris Ltd., Box 24133, Nairobi
☎ 882521, FAX: 882728

Perched on a ridge in the foothills of the Chyulus is Ol Donyo Wuas, Richard Bonham's exclusive hideaway. The setting is superb. The land falls away, stretching for miles in green and golden waves with strange shaped hills and flat-topped acacia trees for accent. Beyond and above towers the whole Kilimanjaro massif with the famous snow-capped peak unbelievably high in the sky. It is clear that this site was carefully chosen for the view.

Richard Bonham built his home here in the middle of Masai country and has added thatched rondavel-style cottages for guests. There are five cottages for a total of ten guests. The main room is a large separate stone building with a high thatch roof. It is open on one side to frame the compelling view. There are comfortable stuffed chairs and couches in faded florals, an inviting fireplace, shelves crammed with books and music, and intriguing animal pictures on the walls. This room serves as lounge, dining room and bar area. It has a lived-in atmosphere—a place to feel at home, put your feet up, help yourself to a drink.

The cottages are well spaced among bushy trees. They have been artistically decorated with local furniture, fabrics and handicrafts, and each has a veranda and fireplace. There are mosquito nets, electricity and ensuite bathrooms with hot showers and flush toilets.

Two of the cottages are extra large and each have two bedrooms and a shared bathroom—ideal for families. Our favorite two cottages are built on stilts and won our private award for rooms with the best view in Kenya. These cottages (one is known as the honeymoon suite) have outsized beds covered in wonderful soft leather bedspreads decorated with Maasai beadwork. There is also a small sitting area which, like the bed, faces the marvelous view of Mt. Kilimanjaro. The high roof comes almost down to floor level and a wide opening has been cut in the thatch to frame the view. No glass here between you and the immensity of Africa.

No glass or walls either between the long-drop and the view! Sheltered behind by trees and built at the edge of the ridge is the long-drop toilet, magazines piled at the side and one of the most spectacular views imaginable in front. Although there are toilets and showers in each cottage, the long-drop is recommended when convenient because all water has to be brought up from the pipeline below.

Ol Donyo Wuas means "The Spotted Hills" in Masai and is situated miles from any major settlement. To reach it you drive through open veld dotted with plains game towards the impressive Chyulu Range, a younger volcanic range running between Amboseli and Tsavo National Park. During the rains the Masai move in to this area. You can often see young Masai herders with their cattle at home among the wild animals. The land which Richard Bonham leases is part of a 100,000 hectare Masai Group Ranch.

Richard Bonham is the soul of Ol Donyo Wuas. He found the site, built the place, and harbors a lifetime's knowledge and love of animals and the bush. He will take you on game walks or to ride horses in the hills, perhaps to spend a night in a fly camp. You may be surprised by a bush breakfast—eggs and bacon cooked in the open and served under a tree with a mountain view. It is a joy to go on a game drive in Richard's cutaway Land Rover with a high bench seat built in the back. Again, there is nothing between you and the enormity of the scene: the game, the mountains, the tremendous sense of distance and sky. There are many options, lots of flexibility, and no other tourists to clutter up the scene.

Safari Journal — First Day

The elephant was only yards away. A huge bull with awesome tusks. I stepped carefully over the dead branch, crouching under the leaves. i watched for Richard Bonham's hand signals, feeling totally confident in his experience, his gun, and his dog. What a thrill! i looked down ruefully at my city clothes. We had just arrived, gulped down tea, when Richard, who had flown in minutes before, hustled us out to track down the elephant he had spotted from the air. The object — to take identity photos of the elephant to try to determine where he had come from. Count me in any day!

Richard inspires great confidence with his wealth of experience in the bush and is a fund of information about animals. He is known for organizing unusual safaris, and spends several months of each year leading exclusive walking and boat safaris in the remote and unspoiled Selous Game Reserve in Southern Tanzania. Ol Donyo Wuas is not the same when he is away.

Special Offerings

Horse riding, horse safaris (meeting fly camps each evening), day and night game drives, walking safaris, bird shooting available July to October, airstrip.

Off Notes

Don't go if your main object is to see the Big Five or laze by a pool... Richard is not always there. Try to book when he is the host.

ILTALAL CAMP
Iain MacDonald Safaris Ltd., Box 59224, Nairobi
☎ *503265, FAX: 506824*

Iltalal Camp is a small tented camp near the Kiliguni Airstrip in the Chyulu Hills. To get there, you must either fly to the airstrip or drive across the Shaitani Lava Flows outside the Chyulu Gate of the Tsavo West National Park. The camp shelters in a grove of ancient fig trees with Masai villages on either side. No one may stay in the camp unless hosted by one of Iain MacDonald Safaris' professional guides.

Camp activities with guide
Game drives, escorted walks by day or night, star gazing with camp telescope, and visits to Masai manyatta and wells tapping underground river.

Optional extras with guide
Leopard viewing overnight at Leopard Camp, bush picnics, visit to Tsavo West and Amboseli National Parks, fly camping, deep sea-fishing and water sports at private beach cottage on coast.

Accommodations
The tents are very basic with two twin metal beds and attached thatched bathrooms with showers and flush toilets.

Off-Notes
The camp seems musty and far from game.

TSAVO NATIONAL PARK, EAST & WEST

Tsavo National Park covers more than 20,800 square kilometers. It is Kenya's largest national park and is split into Tsavo East and Tsavo West by the busy Mombasa/Nairobi Road and the railroad.

During the last century, **Tsavo West** has been through changes connected with the great elephant herds. Thick forests were gradually turned into grasslands by elephant grazing patterns. By 1960, the elephant population was up to at least 50,000. Because of poaching, they were reduced to only 5000. Now the grasslands are changing again to new forest and scrub. Poaching has been a major problem in this park, and the Black Rhino population was reduced from about 7000 in 1969 to less than 100 in 1981. Thanks to today's conservation efforts, poaching has largely been contained.

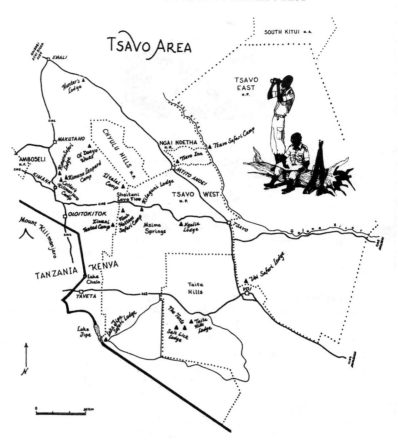

Tsavo West's approximately 9000 square kilometers also include the Ngulia Mountains and the Ndawe Escarpment, all part of the same volcanic upheavals that created the Rift Valley, Mt. Kilimanjaro and Mt. Kenya. The volcanic ridges give rise to the underground river systems forming Mzima Springs, an incredible outpouring of crystal clear water which forms a series of pools. The luxuriant growth at its edges is in marked contrast to the dry harshness of the surrounding terrain. There is an underwater viewing chamber from which you can often see hippo. Mzima Springs is the source of much of Mombasa's drinking water.

In Tsavo West, the combination of rocky hills, high viewpoints and dry scrublands creates a harsh beauty—a certain drama.

Tsavo East, far less visited than Tsavo West, is approximately 11,000 square kilometers of varied bush, arid flatland and desert. Most of the area north of the Galana River is closed to the public for security reasons. Much of this part of the park is the Yatta Plateau, a lava flow 300 kilometers long. Oases along the Athi, Tiva, Tsavo and Voi Rivers relieve the dry scrublands.

Tsavo West and East combined have 2000 kilometers of dirt tracks, some of which serve as firebreaks, all of which are important in the continuing fight against poaching. Despite this network of tracks, wildlife is not easy to see because of large distances, thick scrub and high grass. However, the stunning landscapes and the sense of isolation felt in this vastness can put you in touch with a part of the real Africa.

TSAVO NATIONAL PARK – WEST

FINCH HATTONS SAFARI CAMP
Future Hotels, Box 24423, Nairobi
☎ *604321, FAX: 604323*

A luxurious tented camp will soon open in the Tsavo West National Park. The camp is named after Denys Finch-Hatton, the enigmatic adventurer who was immortalized by Karen Blixen in *Out of Africa* and led royalty on safari in Kenya. Finch-Hatton did things in style. He brought Mozart and crystal into the bush. So will this new upmarket camp which is being lovingly planned by owner Peter Frank, previously a Regional Director with Hilton Hotels Ltd. Peter plans to live on the site and act as host.

Finch Hattons Safari Camp is built at the edge of three hippo pools which are fed by natural springs. Surrounding the camp is the vast, dry expanse of thorn scrub and volcanic lava which characterize this rather hilly section of Tsavo. Mt. Kilimanjaro forms a majestic backdrop—visible from many parts of the camp.

There are 35 very luxurious tents widely spaced on both sides of the hippo pools. The tents are raised on wooden platforms and face towards the water. Each has a spacious and shaded veranda with a Lamu-style day bed and chairs.

The tents are extra large and airy with many big screened "windows." They have wooden floors, rich kilim rugs and high quality beds and mattresses. There are minifridges in each tent and the ensuite bathrooms have stone floors, oval mirrors and showers.

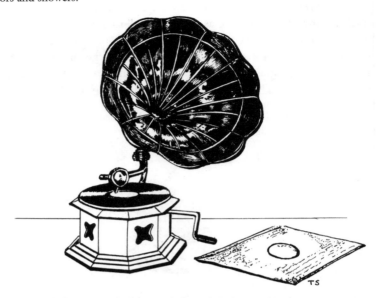

The main lodge, with its open terrace, looks over a hippo pool towards Mt. Kilimanjaro. There are lava-stone walls, and a high and intricate thatched roof. The camp has been decorated in keeping with its name—old-fashioned, British and high-class. There are leather couches, brass lamps and writing desks. On the walls are prints of old safari photos, and there is a fireplace with a big chimney. Guests will be required to dress for dinner—no shorts. There will be Mozart and crystal.

The camp is not fenced, and animals are free to wander in the grounds. There will be a battalion of busy *askari* escorting guests to and from their tents. Elephant have been seen on the camp paths, and at night hippo pass the tents to graze. (The proximity of wild animals means that children are not encouraged as guests.) The natural vegetation has been retained, and the camp paths pass through lava rock and bush. Some tents are under tall trees. There are bridges over the stream, a raised walkway and two special observation areas. At night the hippo pool is discretely illuminated. The farthest tents are quite a hot hike from the main lodge, and stocked minifridges will be most welcome.

A kidney-shaped swimming pool is surrounded by natural rock and has been elevated to keep out the wild animals. It sounds as though some thoughtful and thorough planning has gone into this camp. Peter Frank spoke of proper sewage systems, solar heating, and a "clinical" kitchen with white tiles and walk-in freezers. He wants to emphasize good food, and plans to hire an exceptional chef. Peter Frank's experience in the Kenyan tourist business, his knowledge of this area of the country, and his stated determination to make this camp "be professionally done from the beginning," all suggest that this will be a quality camp.

Special Offerings

Pool, souvenir and sundry shop, minifridge in tent, safety deposit, observation areas, game drives.

ZIWANI TENTED CAMP

Prestige Hotels Ltd., Box 74888, Nairobi
☎ *338084, FAX: 217278*

Ziwani is a pleasant tented camp on the western boundary of Tsavo West National Park, not far from the Tanzanian border. It is in an undeveloped part of the Ziwani Sisal Estate, on the edge of a small natural-looking dam in the Sante River. Clumps of papyrus grow in the dam, tall trees fringe the far banks, and lawns extend from the lodge to the water. Birds are everywhere—ducks swim past the papyrus, a fish eagle perches on a fallen tree trunk, a large marabou stork putters about in the shallows. There are monkeys playing in the trees, and you can sometimes see hippo and crocodile in the water. At night, bait is put up for a leopard on the far side of the dam. When it is clear, you can see the snow-covered peaks of Mt. Kilimanjaro high above the trees.

Ziwani has 16 tents and an attractive dining and bar area with views across the dam. This open-sided structure has a makuti roof and local "twig" chairs painted green. There is an inviting bar counter and hanging clay pots with plants. The effect is natural, pleasing and functional.

The tents are fairly close together. They are set far back from the river and have unremarkable views. From some you hear the relaxing sound of flowing water. The tents are on large cement slabs which provide generous verandas. Large *makuti*-thatched roofs keep the tents shaded. There are woven mats on the canvas floor and many "windows" to let in air and light. The furniture is made of pale wood, and there are high-quality mattresses on the twin beds. Immediately behind each tent is a private bathroom with a long-drop toilet and a safari shower. Since there is no electricity, hurricane lamps are used instead.

The camp is hosted by Tim and Rainie Samuels. Service is friendly and personal. On arrival, we were greeted with refreshing wash towels and a cold drink. Tim is a jovial person who adds warmth and informality to Ziwani.

The lunch we had was delicious, with a variety of freshly "home-cooked" dishes. Since there is no electricity, all meals are prepared on charcoal, and metal trunks are used for baking. Guests have a full English breakfast and eat a barbecued dinner at night.

At Ziwani you can go on night game drives or guided walks where you are likely to see hippo at close range in some of the river pools. You can also go on game drives in Tsavo West National Park. Most visitors are tourists from the U.K. who are driven to Ziwani from the coast. For this amount of driving and to appreciate the natural beauty and peace of Ziwani, it's worth coming for more than one night. There is an airstrip right next to the camp.

KILANGUNI LODGE

African Tours & Hotels, Box 30471, Nairobi
☎ *336858, FAX: 218109*

This lodge is worth a trip because of its magnificent setting in the heart of Tsavo West Park with views of the Chyulu Hills and the snowy peaks of Kilimanjaro. First built in 1962, Kilaguni was the first luxury lodge in Kenya.

The main lodge building is newly rebuilt and inviting with tall thatch roof and one whole side open to the view and a waterhole which attracts large numbers of zebra, buffalo, elephant, impala, baboon and warthog. Beyond the rustic reception area, the dining room and bar/lounge share the open-sided view.

> *"During dinner we watched a hyena waiting for our scraps below the railing. Hornbills and weaverbirds came to the table looking for crumbs. Even eating at this lodge is a wildlife experience."*
> (Guest Quote)

The 53 guest rooms are simply furnished and have full private bathrooms. Each room's veranda overlooks the waterhole and Mt. Kilimanjaro. All the rooms are undergoing renovation, and a separate VIP cottage and a new wing of superior rooms are under construction.

The meandering wings of the lodge set off lovely interior grounds filled with rock gardens, bougainvillea and other colorful tropical plants. The rock gardens are home to nearly tame hyraxes playing hide-and-seek among the rocks along the pathways and near the swimming pool. The pool is also scheduled for repainting, but is still operational with the "adams" and "eves" dressing room signs appropriate in this eden-like setting.

Best Accommodations

Rooms on the second floor (#14–20) for best view.

Other Facilities

Gift and sundry shop, airstrip, conference room.

NGULIA SAFARI LODGE

African Tours & Hotels, Box 30471, Nairobi
☎ *336858, FAX: 218109*

Located in the Tsavo West National Park 290 kilometers from Nairobi, Ngulia Safari Lodge has a spectacular site. The top of a rocky outcrop has been carved into two flat terraces for the lodge buildings and swimming pool. One side of the site is a sheer cliff dropping off to the Yatta Plateau below. The two-story stone lodge rises at the edge of the cliff to overlook a grassy water hole. Game from the surrounding hills are frequent visitors day and night.

You walk through reception and up to the open-sided view terrace and dining room, which echo under high ceilings with excited guests lining the balustrade to see animals at the water hole below. Bait is left each evening for rhino and leopard, and the water hole is floodlit for night game viewing.

The 52 guest rooms are located on two floors to one side of the lodge. All have twin beds with mosquito nets, balconies and ensuite bathrooms. The bathrooms are very tired and bear testimony to the fact that this lodge was built in 1969. Extra beds are available for families.

There is a small, but sparkling swimming pool in the rock gardens at the side of the dining room. Nearby, a breathtaking covered viewpoint teeters at the very edge of the cliff where the view is unbroken and without measure.

All guests are on full board, with breakfast and lunch served from the buffet. Dinner is served by candlelight.

Ngulia Safari Lodge caters to a mixed clientele of international tour groups.

Quotes:

> *"Very exciting day—changed flat tire in front of lions. 10/10 for view, service, and food—even saw the leopard at night."*

> *"Es ware alles "super" hier."*

> *"Very beautiful view, but you need new bathrooms."*

Off-Notes

It is dangerous to take walks from the lodge. There are no vehicles, so you need your own for game drives.

HUNTERS LODGE
Mada Holdings, Box 40683, Nairobi
☎ *221439, FAX: 332170*

This landmark on the road to Mombasa is 145 kilometers from Nairobi. The lodge was opened by the famous game warden, John Hunter. Today it is best known as a rest stop en route to and from the coast. There is a petrol station and a restaurant. The lodge has 20 very basic rooms. There is a dam with a bridge and a garden with peacocks.

TSAVO NATIONAL PARK – EAST

TSAVO SAFARI CAMP
Kilimanjaro Safari Club, Box 30139, Nairobi
☎ *227136, FAX: 219982*

Near Mtito Andei, this restful camp is a good overnight stop en route to the coast. Twenty-seven kilometers into the hot dryness of the little-visited Tsavo East National Park, the Tsavo Safari Camp is a green oasis on the Athi River. To get there, you park your vehicle in the camp lot and take a very short trip across the river in a rubber boat.

Tsavo Safari Camp has been in operation for 28 years and was originally a hunting camp. Today 30 tents and six bandas (for those who don't like canvas) are set close together in a row along the river. They are well-shaded by mature trees. Small gardens of indigenous flowers and exotic plants are scattered in amazingly green lawns, a sharp contrast to the dry and dusty scrub in the Park beyond. After your long drive, the camp swimming pool is a refreshing treat.

The focal point of the camp is the stone and thatch bar/dining area open on two sides to garden and river. Lionel Nutter is the long-time host—he creates a warm and personal atmosphere. Everything is very relaxed and casual. The bar has become a popular watering hole for British Kenyans who might even fly in just for the afternoon.

There are hundreds of resident birds—the camp is a real hornbill heaven. Take your chair down to the riverbank to watch the birds at sunset.

It is not easy to see game from this camp. A dik-dik here, a dik-dik there and the occasional oryx or jackal. If you're lucky you might see kudu. Since you leave your vehicle on the other side of the river, you must book and pay extra for game drives, which can be rather expensive. Another special offering is a trip up to the Yatta Plateau for sundowners and to watch the sun set behind Mt. Kilimanjaro.

Accommodations
The tents are comfortable and simply furnished. They all have large shower bathrooms with solar heated water and flush toilets. There are five family tents with extra beds.

Special Facilities
Swimming pool, game drives.

VOI SAFARI LODGE
African Tours & Hotels, Box 30471, Nairobi
☎ *336858, FAX: 218109*

Voi Safari Lodge sits high on a red rock bluff overlooking a busy water hole and a large expanse of Tsavo National Park East. The entire lodge curves along the edge of the cliff so you get that marvelous view from everywhere—dining room, terrace, pool and bedrooms.

The lodge itself is not luxurious, but it is remarkable, even spectacular in several ways. Natural rock has been used effectively in walls and floors with interesting gourd lamps in the lounge/bar, which is open to air and birds. The wooden animal carvings over the bar are often accented by the real thing when baboons peer in through the roof skylight.

You walk on bare red rock through rock gardens to the viewpoint and the swimming pool at the edge of the cliff. During the five minutes before noon, we saw three cape buffalo, eight elephants and numerous baboon and antelope from the viewpoint.

Each of the 50 double rooms has one entire wall of windows, either two or three twin beds and a rather tired bathroom with telephone shower.

The lodge is located in Tsavo East National Park, 338 kilometers from Nairobi and 161 kilometers from Mombasa. It is very popular with tourists and is often used as a lunch stop en route between Mombasa and Nairobi. There is an airstrip three kilometers away near Voi town.

Returning from the lodge to the Mombasa Road, we saw a herd of more than 75 elephant.

TSAVO INN

Mt. Kilimanjaro Safari Club, Box 30139, Nairobi
☎ *227136, FAX: 219982*

This small inn at Mtito Andei, is an easy stop on your way to Mombasa. It is right on the main Mombasa Road and about three hours from Nairobi. There is a restaurant and a pool in a garden setting. The 30 rooms are very basic—no frills.

TAITA HILLS WILDLIFE SANCTUARY

HILTON HOTELS IN THE WILD

The privately owned Taita Hills Wildlife Sanctuary is 17,000 hectares of rolling savanna accented by dramatic rocky outcroppings and small plateaus. Because there is plenty of water, many animals shelter there, and large herds of elephant and other plains game migrate to the sanctuary from Tsavo each year.

Hilton International holds a long lease on the land and has built a trio of safari lodges to harmonize with this beautiful setting. These include the Taita Hills Lodge, the Salt Lick Lodge for overnight game viewing and The Tents, a tented camp hidden in the forest along the banks of the Bura River. All are run according to high Hilton standards of luxury and service. Visitors are an international mixture of tour groups, businessmen and small private safaris arriving every day by road or by air.

Hilton is also responsible for managing the sanctuary and ensuring the safety of the animals. For this reason, there are 18 game wardens on Hilton's Taita Hills staff. Because the sanctuary is privately managed, there are very few vehicles on game drives. The wardens keep track of the animals to guard them from mishap and poaching. The wardens also pass the word to drivers, which can make game drives very exciting and satisfying.

TAITA HILLS LODGE
Hilton International, Box 30621, Nairobi
☎ *332564, FAX: 339462*

You enter the Taita Hills Wildlife Sanctuary through the impressive Taita Hills Lodge. It is here that you check in to all three lodges. It is possible to arrange a stay that includes meals or even nights at each of the different lodges.

The Taita Hills Lodge resembles a fortress and was built with sandbags of World War I cemented together to form the tall three-story ramparts. However, the rather stark outlines of the lodge are softened by dark green veils of creeper, and the walls enclose elegant public rooms leading to lawns, tropical gardens and a swimming pool.

Once you enter the fortress, you find yourself in the spectacular two-story tall central room that is the heart of the lodge. Windows reaching from floor to ceiling give light and beautiful views of gardens and the plains beyond.

Inside, there is harmony and creativity—a blending of African themes and natural materials. There are tables made with African drums, stone settees and carved panels and batiks of Masai life.

This dramatic room is particularly memorable for the wonderful hangings and furnishings especially designed and handwoven by the Nairobi-based Weaver Bird company. Wall-sized tapestries depict African wildlife and Masai themes.

The woven rugs, curtains and cushions are rich and elegant—complementing the polished stone and wood of the room. A stunning stone fireplace soars for two stories from a sunken conversation area. A small bar serves drinks and snacks. Bamboo fan-back chairs are set in the window nooks.

The 60 guest rooms are uniform double rooms with twin beds and full ensuite bathrooms. More Weaver Bird woven rugs and fabrics give the rooms some bright colored style. All rooms have a small balcony. Some look over the sanctuary plains with good views of wildlife or distant mountains. There are also two suites available with nicely decorated sitting and dining areas.

Lunch and dinner are served in the large Chala restaurant. In the evening there is often live music or entertainment by traditional dancers. The breakfast buffet is set up in a sunny room which looks over gardens and lawns on three sides and is reached by a rock pathway through the lovely central garden. This room is often used for conferences, and business services are available.

Champagne breakfasts, barbecue lunches and elegant "Out of Africa" dinners can be arranged in the bush on request.

Special Offerings

Day or night game drives in 16 minivans, balloon safaris, swimming pool, minigolf, camel rides on grounds, tennis courts, soccer or football field, darts, basketball court, video films, conference facilities, business center, and private airstrip.

SALT LICK SAFARI LODGE

Hilton International, Box 30624, Nairobi
☎ *332564, FAX: 339462*

 Salt Lick Safari Lodge is an all-night game viewing lodge. (See section on Night Game Viewing Lodges.) This lodge is especially memorable for its imaginative structure. A complex of rondavels sits on stilts over a series of water holes. These two-story towers, topped by peaked thatch roofs, are connected by open-air bridges—creating an African fantasy reminiscent of a medieval fortress.

You walk across a drawbridge which will be pulled up at night. The curved walls, the natural stone, the horn trophies, the air of general excitement and commitment, all predict an unusual experience ahead. You climb the stairs to the dining room and terrace, then find your room by traversing the outdoor walkway connecting the room towers. The curved rooms are amply comfortable with twin beds, easy chairs and ensuite bathrooms. Those on the top floor have the advantage of a dramatic soaring thatch roof. Most rooms have large windows and you often see animals from your own room.

Salt Lick Lodge has been built with game viewing in mind—you can see animals in all directions and from many vantage points. Unlike most of the other night game viewing lodges, which are built in forested areas, Salt Lick commands some spectacular open views. You might see elephant while on the walkway from your room. There are game viewing terraces on the ground and upper levels, and you can cross through a carpeted underground tunnel to a blind that puts you among the animals. Fantastic!

The lounge has an unusual free-standing stone fireplace—you can pop in for a quick warm-up during your night game vigil. Candlelit dinners are served buffet-style in the ring-shaped dining room. The stone chimney from the ground floor lounge fireplace lances through the central space to the high peaked roof above like a sleek piece of modern sculpture. Hot and cold drinks and snacks are available all night long. It is FUN to be locked up in Salt Lick.

THE TENTS
Hilton International, Box 30624, Nairobi
☎ *332564, FAX: 339462*

Perfectly at home in the thick forest on the banks of the Bura River, 12 forest green tents are a slice of Eden under canvas. Green shade and the refreshing sound of rushing water envelop every tent site with coolness and privacy. Birdsong and the flit of bright feathers are everywhere. Each tent has twin beds with forest green Hilton blankets, safari chairs, verandas and ensuite bathrooms with flush toilets. You go back in time for your wood-heated hot water and the soft glow of hurricane lamps at night.

Pathways through the trees and wooden bridges over water wind from site to site in an undefined circular way. They lead back to the heart of the camp, the fanciful James Stewart House, a natural tree sort of house, constructed for the movie *A Tale in Africa* starring Jimmy Stewart, as you may have guessed.... It is the gathering place, where you can have small snacks and drinks night or day. You dine with the sounds of Africa around you and the stars overhead—often a Kenyan barbecue and other ethnic dishes are served buffet-style. Night sounds are terrific, you hear lots of animals over the water and bird sounds. However, an electrical fence and spear-carrying night guards ensure that you sleep securely.

LAKE JIPE

This volcanic lake straddles the border with Tanzania. The shore is flat and thick with reeds, making it a haven for birds. Grogan's Folly, a run-down castle in the medieval style, was built by Ewart Grogan, a shady entrepreneur who planted the sisal on the plantation where the castle stands. Beyond Lake Jipe are the North Pare Mountains of Tanzania.

LAKE JIPE SAFARI LODGE

Lake Jipe Safari Lodge Ltd., Box 31097, Nairobi
☎ *227623 Telex: 25508*

This lodge is in Tsavo West National Park close to Lake Jipe. Due to annoying lake flies, the lodge has been built at quite a distance from the shore, and you cannot see the lake from the rooms. If you can brave the mosquitoes, however, the pool area does have a spectacular view of the lake and the Pare Mountains in Tanzania.

Except for the pool, this lodge lacks charm. The lounge and dining areas are in a huge rondavel, tour group stickers on windows mar the view, and the food is below average. Accommodations are in thatched rondavels which are crowded together, have no verandas and offer little privacy. There is a public veranda with a view, but, because of the mosquitoes, it is not always furnished, and you may have to arrange for chairs to be carried out.

You must drive to reach the lake. It is beautiful on Lake Jipe—the views of the mountains are superb, but the boats and service used for these trips are not. Friends who went out complained that the boat was leaky and that they were not provided with drinks.

THE KENYAN COAST

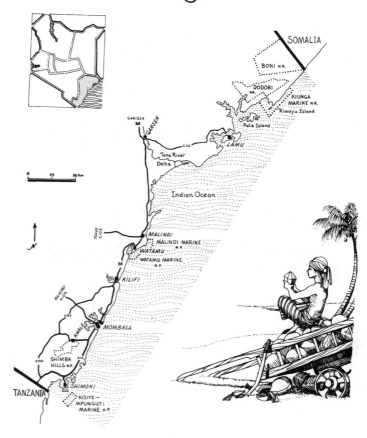

SOMALIA

BONI N.R.

DODORI
N.R.

KIUNGA
MARINE N.R.

Kiwayu Island

Pate Island

GARISSA
B8

GARSEN

C112

LAMU

Tana River
Delta

Indian Ocean

0   25   50 Km

TSAVO
C103

MALINDI

MALINDI MARINE
N.P.

WATAMU

WATAMU MARINE
N.P.

B8

KILIFI

NAIROBI
A109

C107

KWALE

MOMBASA

C106

SHIMBA
HILLS N.P.

A14

TANZANIA

SHIMONI

KISITE —
MPUNGUTI
MARINE N.P.

N

THE KENYAN COAST

The harsher beauty of most of Kenya's interior is tempered by the soothing south-sea-island delights of Kenya's coral coast. The lush, tropical bush of the coast is brilliant with many birds and fragrant blossoms of frangipane and hibiscus. The vivid colors of bougainvillea and stands of graceful palms frame long stretches of white coral sand lapped by the gentle warm water of the Indian Ocean. It is hot and humid, but the pace is languid. A Swahili proverb much-used at the coast says it all: "*Haraka haraka haina baraka*"—or, literally, "haste, haste has no blessing."

Stretching 480 kilometers from Somalia in the north to Tanzania in the south, the Kenyan Coast has been known to the world since A.D. 110 when a stop at the port of Mombasa was recorded by a

Greek explorer named Diogenes. Ptolemy, another Greek, included details of the Kenyan coast in his A.D. 150. "Map of the World."

Since then, Arabs who had come to trade settled, intermarried, and mingled coastal tribal and Arab ways. They created a new Swahili language and culture which is still very much alive today in Old Town Mombasa and on Lamu and Wasini Islands. They built beautiful cities embellished with carvings and monuments, and they valued fine arts and crafts.

Portuguese explorers and traders brought a garrison to Mombasa at the end of the 16th century and built the formidable Fort Jesus, which still stands. In the 19th century, British interest in exploration and in abolishing the slave trade led to Kenya coming under British influence. There are still British colonial monuments and ruins along the coast.

Now the Kenyan coast is known for its fine beaches and resorts and generally even-tempered weather. The hot and humid weather is pleasantly cooled by the monsoon trade winds blowing off the Indian Ocean. Despite the winds, the beaches are protected with approximately 240 kilometers of coral reef. Although you can often see white breakers beyond the reef, the water on the shore side is usually quite calm—better for windsurfing than for surfing. Swimming between the reef and shore is also generally safe from strong currents and protected from nasties such as shark. The water ranges from 27–35 degrees centigrade.

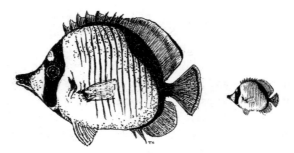

The beauty of the coral and the amazing colors and shapes of these tropical fish invite goggling or scuba diving. The national marine parks and reserves off Shimoni, Mombasa, Watamu, Malindi and Lamu protect these marine treasures. Kenyan reefs have been favorably compared with those of Australia and the Red Sea.

There are many ways to explore the Kenyan reef. On certain beaches you can swim and even walk out to the reef through tidal pools. Some hotels maintain glass-bottom boats. You can snorkel from these or from other smaller boats. Private boatmen are eager to take you to the reef and sometimes even to rent equipment. Prices are negotiable. Snorkeling is fun and easy, even for novices—a beautiful and memorable experience. Try it!

There is a big tidal variation along this coast. On some beaches high tide leaves only a narrow strip of sand, and in places the water reaches right up to the edge of hotel property. At low tide the water sometimes recedes back beyond the reef, leaving would-be swimmers high and dry. However, almost all hotels have their own swimming pools, and it seems that the majority of guests are just as happy to nab a beach lounger by the pool or in the shade of a palm tree to work on their tans and relaxation.

On the most popular tourist beaches, there are many hawkers trying to sell their wares. Informal displays of carving, jewelry, and bright cotton kanga are set out along the sand; a small shack professes by its sign to be a "Massage Parlor"; and women want to braid your hair with beads. As you stroll the beach, you are likely to be approached by friendly but persistent vendors. Some hotels employ security guards or police to try to discourage these hawkers. It is unadvisable to walk along the beach displaying wealth with fancy jewelry or cameras.

Although the climate is generally easy to take all year long, the monsoon winds blowing across the ocean determine the seasons. The kaskazi is northeasterly and lasts from October to March. November is usually the month of occasional rains during the *kaskazi*. The kusi is the stronger and colder of the two winds, lasting from April until September. During this wind, rain is to be expected from May until June. Even during the months of "rain," however, there are often fine days at the coast. Hotel rates are usually lower at this time of the year. Some of the hotels catering primarily to overseas tourists even close.

Over the course of the year, especially during the kusi, a great deal of seaweed is washed up on to the Kenyan beaches. The amounts and location of the weed can vary from day to day, affected by the winds and currents. There are occasions when there is so much seaweed that it is difficult to walk on the beaches or to swim in the ocean. Several hotels employ staff to rake and bury the seaweed in the sand—this helps, but it is still waiting for you in the water! Seaweed afflicts some beaches more than others. For example, Watamu on the North Coast is badly affected, while Diani on the South Coast is somewhat less so.

Sport fishermen from all over the world come to Shimoni in the south, where big game fishing for marlin and sailfish is at its best in the Pemba Channel. However, many of the big resorts along the coast can give expert and novice fishermen an unforgettable day "hunting the big ones." On the North Coast, Watamu and Malindi are the "in" places to go, and there are many fishing tournaments.

Beyond the sybaritic beach experience, you can still see wildlife in nearby forested areas such as Shimba Hills National Reserve, Arabu-ko-Sokoke Forest and the Tana River Delta. Travel agents, specially trained hotel staff, and homestay hosts can help you arrange safaris into these areas.

In all ways the island of Mombasa is the hub of the Kenyan Coast. It is a major seaport. There is an international airport, the train from Nairobi brings many visitors to the Mombasa Railroad Station, and Mombasa is where the road from Nairobi meets the coastal highway. Mombasa, separates the North Coast from the South Coast.

The **South Coast** is reached by crossing on the Likoni Ferry. There are a string of resorts on a series of beaches, the best known and most developed being Diani Beach. South of Diani is less developed.

The **North Coast** has concentrated groupings of hotels near Mombasa, Malindi, and to a lesser extent, Watamu. Farther north towards the Somali border are the islands of the Lamu Archipelago. The ancient Swahili town of Lamu is well known and often visited by tourists.

The Kenyan Coast is a popular destination for package tours from Europe. Resort management and clientele often reflect specific nationalities, with German and Italian predominating.

There is a sophisticated infrastructure of resort hotels ranging from the luxurious to the more basic. Many hotels offer similar services, facilities and activities. The hotels range from the exotic (high-thatch roofs, whitewashed arches, Lamu-style furniture) to the more prosaic (cement accommodation wings, balconies angled towards a possible sea view, plastic loungers).

There are also some resorts with private villas or condos (complete with cook, if desired), as well as opportunities for more personalized homestays. You can even opt for the romance of staying in a grass shack on the beach. In addition there are private homes which can be rented through agents. However, as these require self-catering, they are not covered in this book.

MOMBASA

Mombasa City Codes ☎ *011 - #, FAX: 011 - #.*

Mombasa, the second largest city in Kenya, is on Mombasa Island. It is a steamy, tropical, low-rise city with asymmetrical streets, a languid pace, and a diverse and intriguing population. Mombasa is mostly a Swahili town. Women chatter by in dark *bui-bui* or wrapped in brilliant multicolored *kanga*. There are dozens of intricate mosques and temples, pungent open markets, mazes of narrow lanes crowded with street stalls. Mombasa is a port and a commercial center, not a resort town. It is rather seedy and romantic, not slick and efficient. There are no beaches in Mombasa and the hotels tend to be modest and somewhat old-fashioned. Tourists in Mombasa have mostly been "bused" in for shopping and sight-seeing.

Mombasa has a long and complex history, best appreciated by a visit to **Fort Jesus** and the **Old Town**. Fort Jesus, begun by the Portuguese at the end of the 16th Century, dominates the entrance to Mombasa Harbor, and commands good views over the Old Town. The fort is now a national monument and houses an interesting museum. The Old Town is a maze of narrow streets, mosques and crowded buildings, some with impressive carved doors or intricate balconies.

THE CASTLE HOTEL

The Castle Hotel, Box 84231, Mombasa
☎ *223403, Telex: 21008*

This city hotel is centrally placed in Mombasa Town and harks back to an earlier era. There is a big open dining veranda with whitewashed pillars, tiled floor and potted plants. This is a good spot for a cool drink and watching street life. Tour buses bringing sight-seers into Mombasa often use the Castle Hotel as a drop-off and pick-up point. This adds to the bustle and activity of the open veranda and also signals an increase in drink prices.

The 60 rooms at the Castle have few frills and are rather worn. There are high ceilings with fans, and the furniture is tired and old.

NEW OUTRIGGER HOTEL

New Outrigger Hotel, Box 82345, Mombasa
☎ *20822, Telex: 21368*

This hotel is above Kilindini Harbor, with views over the water. There are palm trees, tropical shrubs and a swimming pool. Rooms have balconies facing the sea, air conditioning, and telephones. The hotel is under Belgian management. We did not visit this hotel and have no firsthand information on the ambience or upkeep. The brochure speaks of French cuisine and a beach.

THE MANOR HOTEL

The Manor Hotel, Box 84851, Mombasa
☎ *314643, FAX: 311952*

The Manor used to be the British governor's mansion in Mombasa. This downtown hotel has lost most of its colonial charm and is now quite run-down. The lobby is big and dark, with dim lights and worn floor tiles. The side porch, with its arches and views of the busy street, is more pleasant. The staff are very friendly. The food is substandard, and the rooms are dingy with noisy air conditioning, many mosquitoes and mildewed towels.

MANSON HOTEL

Manson Hotel, Box 83565, Mombasa
☎ *222420*

This is a newer business hotel in Mombasa. We did not visit but hear it is adequate.

THE OCEANIC HOTEL

The Oceanic Hotel, Box 90371, Mombasa
☎ *311191*

Advertised as the "largest hotel on Mombasa Island," this multistory cement hotel is near the Likoni Ferry and overlooks the Likoni Bay. It is not a "beach hotel." The style recalls the 1950s and the hotel is large, rather shabby and run-down.

COAST : MOMBASA & SOUTH

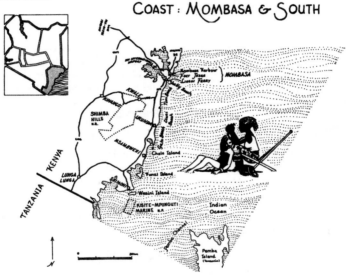

SOUTH OF MOMBASA

Heading from Mombasa to the south coast, travellers must take the Likoni Ferry. This is usually a hot and colorful experience with little stalls lining the road as you wait for your ferry and a stream of pedestrian traffic in various garb passing your window. There are bags of cashew nuts for sale, fresh coconuts as a thirst quencher—lots of noise and color.

The coastline which extends from Mombasa down to the Tanzanian border is generally less developed than the north coast, the exception being the long stretch of Diani Beach which has many tourist hotels.

You will not see the ocean from the road which heads south. Sign-posted roads off to your left lead to the various beaches. In the case of the less developed beaches you will find yourself driving down winding dirt roads under tall coconut palms. You pass little settlements—thatched houses made of coral rock and dried mud, children and chickens in the road, women draped in bright kanga.

SHELLY BEACH

This is the first beach after the Likoni Ferry. The beach is narrow and rather uninviting.

SHELLY BEACH HOTEL

Shelly Beach Hotel, Box 96030, Mombasa
☎ *451001, FAX: 451349*

The hotel sports a great deal of concrete. The beach looks unappealing. Plastic loungers surround a crowded pool and there is little shade. The hotel has many facilities to offer and seems to be full of inexpensive package tour groups. Shelly Beach Hotel is close to the ferry and to Mombasa Town.

TIWI BEACH

Tiwi is a relatively quiet stretch of beach bordered by private homes and rental cottage complexes. These cottages, some of which have communal pools, are typically self-service. There is a camping site which edges the beach and is popular with overlanders. There are fewer foreign tourists here and not as many vendors trying to sell their wares. Unfortunately, this lovely spot has suffered a rash of security problems over the past few years.

FALCON BAY LODGE

Falcon Bay Lodge, Box 2084, Mombasa
☎ *2553, FAX: 2565*

There is something mysterious about Falcon Bay. It opened in 1990, but it still is not quite finished. It does take guests, but the staff is small and a bit vague about how many. They have plans for 50 bungalows, but there are only eight completed. However, the rooms are modern, well-furnished with very nice bathrooms and air conditioning. There is a quiet beach with beach chairs on rockers, and a sand-underfoot bar and grill. Wood sculpture placed along paths adds a touch of whimsy. The "Big House" has an interior courtyard pool, sitting and dining area, and four bedrooms—would be great for family or party groups. Resort pool and tennis courts are "under construction." Ask for sea-view rooms.

DIANI BEACH

This is the most popular and the most sophisticated beach south of Mombasa. There are many hotels, shops and services. The beach itself is a long stretch of white sand fringed by palms and other indigenous bush.

Although there are many hotels on Diani Beach, most of them are low-rise and are set in quite large properties with gardens and trees. There are also many private homes along the Diani beachfront. Therefore, although this is a popular and busy tourist spot, you do not feel overwhelmed by cement and people. There is still a nice sense of nature, most of the hotels have a laid-back, relaxed atmosphere, and in certain places you can still walk along the beach where there will not be throngs of people.

Many hawkers are on Diani Beach selling their wares. There are opportunities for windsurfing, diving and snorkeling. You can take small boats out to the coral reef—less spectacular here than farther south at Kisite Marine National Park or north at Watamu and Malindi.

There is quite a variety of accommodations to choose from. You can be personally hosted in a private home where you are the only guests, you can stay at a sophisticated, gleaming hotel with several restaurants and evening entertainment, or you can select a relaxed, low-key family-style hotel.

THE INDIAN OCEAN BEACH CLUB

Block Hotels, Box 47557, Nairobi
☎ *335807, FAX: 340541*

The Indian Ocean Beach Club is possibly the most upmarket hotel on Diani Beach and probably the most expensive as well.

It definitely has the best setting on the beach. Located at the northern-most part of Diani, close to the winding Tiwi River mouth, the club looks over wonderfully clean golden sands and good surf. There are enormous old baobabs, and right next to the club, nestled in a forest of these ancient trees, is a 16th-century Arab mosque.

The club has been designed as a Swahili village, with clusters of whitewashed cottages arranged on both sides of the large main buildings. There are 100 rooms, all of which face the Indian Ocean. Some cottages are single-storied with makuti-thatched roofs while others, housing a few rooms, are double-story with flat roofs in the Swahili-style. The main building, with its grand red-tiled roof and wooden shutters, is more reminiscent of colonial Kenya. The overall effect is a rather busy mélange of architectural styles.

The public rooms are simple and elegant. "Spices," the large and airy upstairs dining room, seems to have no walls, just a series of arched-top windows lined in wood. Instead of glass, there are wooden shutters, opening to reveal glorious views of palms, white sand, and blue ocean—all only steps away. Below this restaurant is an open-sided breakfast area and a large free-form swimming pool with water flowing over the edges.

The Indian Ocean Beach Club does not intend to be just another hotel-on-the-beach. Arriving guests are greeted with scented towels and then, instead of queuing up at a long reception counter, will be ushered to chairs at individual welcoming tables. There are message boxes outside of each room and a 24-hour valet service. Many watersports are included in the tariff such as windsurfing, sailing, goggling, and there are guided bird walks up the Tiwi River. In addition to the large main pool, three small plunge pools are scattered around the grounds.

The rooms also evidence quality and detail. There are king-sized Lamu beds, cushioned window seats, nice stone-tiled floors, dark mangrove beams set in white ceilings, and the hotel logo of a fish painted on the tiles above the bath. There are also fancy extras—direct-dial telephones, hair-dryers, and air conditioning which automatically turns off when you open the door. However, the rooms are disappointingly small, and the bathrooms astoundingly compact. The rooms feel cozy and somewhat enclosed rather than spacious and airy. The arrangement of the cottages is such that some rooms are very close together—ideal for families or groups.

To an appreciable extent, it is the club's location which makes it so special. The baobabs are truly awesome—enormous bulges in undreamed of shapes—hundreds of years old. They provide interest and focal points to the grounds which are still rather lacking in shade or color. Because there is a gap in the reef, waves are able to reach the shore, and even at low tide, the water is deep enough for swimming. This is quite unusual along this coast. With exposed sandbanks and indigenous vegetation, the gentle meandering channels of the Tiwi River add a special interest. Children were leaping down sheer cliffs of sand into the river, then floating gently upstream in the clear ocean water of the incoming tide—great fun.

Special Offerings

Free sports facilities (tennis and squash) including green fees at the Nyali Golf Club, unlimited water sports (extra charge for deep sea fishing and scuba diving), free courtesy shuttle bus to Likoni and Diani, fully equipped conference room with air conditioning, gift boutique, beauty center, children's club.

Off Notes

Cottages are close together... Rooms are cozy rather than spacious... Some lack of privacy in ground-floor rooms.

ALLIANCE HOTELS ON DIANI BEACH

Three Alliance Hotels make up a large resort near the southern end of Diani Beach. Each of the hotels has its own personality. When you stay at one of the hotels, you may choose to use the restaurants and facilities of all three. A shuttle bus connects the hotels if you'd rather not walk.

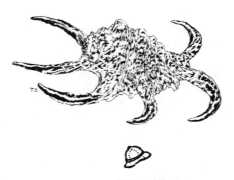

JADINI BEACH HOTEL

Alliance Hotels, Box 49839, Nairobi
☎ *337501, FAX: 219212*

This is our favorite of the three Alliance Hotels. Since it was remodelled in 1990, it looks bright and fresh. The hotel has many windows and is open to sea breezes. You can see the ocean from practically everywhere.

The hotel's many restaurants and public areas seem to line the beach. Walking around Jadini Beach Hotel gives the feeling of moving along a lively and colorful boardwalk with the beach and ocean always in view. The pool is small but sparkling. It is surrounded by white plastic loungers and overlooks the beach.

There are several places where you can eat. The main restaurant is large and bright with windows on three sides looking out to sea. White tile floors and colorful blue and pink fabrics lend a cheerful appearance. There are ceiling fans and a special area with child-sized furniture. Nearby is an ice cream parlor and a lobster bar. You can also choose to go to restaurants in the other Alliance Hotels.

Jadini Beach Hotel can accommodate 172 guests. The bedrooms face the ocean and have large sliding windows and high ceilings. They are attractively decorated, up-to-date and feel spacious and full of light.

SAFARI BEACH

Alliance Hotels, Box 49839, Nairobi
☎ *337501, FAX: 219212*

The Safari Beach Hotel is touted as the most deluxe of the Alliance Hotels. However, staying there does not give the feeling of being near the sea. The bedrooms are behind the main reception area with no ocean views and quite a walk from the beach. Even the public rooms only offer glimpses of the ocean.

The most impressive part of the hotel is its lobby—spacious under high thatch. Nearer the beach is a pleasant and good-sized pool where you can have snacks and indulge in ice creams.

The 186 rooms are located in separate two-story thatched rondavels set well back among trees in the hotel's extensive grounds. The rooms are generous and fairly comfortable with the usual modern conveniences and especially nice bathrooms. However, furnishings are rather faded, air-conditioners are tired, and a swim is a long walk away.

There is a well-equipped Sportsman Club built far from the beach, behind the accommodation rondavels. It has a small pool, three tennis courts, a squash court, and modern machines for body building. You can slake your thirst at the Sportsman's snack bar.

Off Note

There was a strong "whiff" of mildew when we visited the Island Grill à la carte restaurant.

AFRICANA SEA LODGE

Alliance Hotels, Box 49839, Nairobi
☎ *337501, FAX: 219212*

This is the most basic of the Alliance Hotels, with a variety of accommodation styles including small individual rondavels set close together and very far back from the sea. The rooms are clean with ensuite bathrooms, but with unimaginative decor. Renovation has begun. The pool is very small, and white plastic loungers crowd its perimeter. There is a dank disco, though dancing to live music poolside at the Jadini Beach Hotel is the bigger draw.

As well as 158 rooms, the lodge also boasts a six-bedroom Directors' Cottage with private living room, terrace, garden and fully-equipped kitchen, complete with cook if desired.

LAGOON REEF HOTEL

Reef Hotels, Box 61408, Nairobi
☎ *214322, FAX: 332702*

Lagoon Reef is near the southern end of Diani Beach. This hotel feels slightly more intimate than some of its larger neighbors. The hotel, situated on 20 acres, has spectacular grounds and an interesting pool. Near the beach is a huge 50-year-old baobab tree which attracts many monkeys. The free-form pool, built like a lagoon, has an island with jungle vegetation. Tropical gardens cascade down the long slope towards the beach.

The lobby, with its high thatch roof is cool and exotic. There is the sound of water and interplay of light and shadow. Wooden bridges lead over large lily ponds, and there are bird songs from a small aviary. The main dining room is at the same level as the lobby—the ocean and pool are a long way down a rather steep slope. This hill has been nicely landscaped and paths meander down towards the pool. At night the gardens are illuminated.

There is more informal dining near the swimming pool. An open-sided bar right at the edge of the beach overlooks the ocean. Across the road, built in the forest, are two hotel tennis courts.

Accommodations

There are accommodations for almost 300 people in thatched blocks, three stories high. All rooms have balconies and big windows, and most have garden or pool views. There are fans and air conditioning. Mosquito nets are available on request. There is a choice between superior, standard and family rooms. *Our Favorites*: the superior sea-front rooms on the top floor. Like its neighbors, Lagoon Reef attracts tour groups.

KASKAZI BEACH HOTEL
LTI - Kaskazi Beach Hotel, Box 135, Ukunda
☎ *(0127) 3170, FAX: (0127) 2396*

The Kaskazi is one of the newest large hotels on Diani Beach. Its luminous white marble, graceful arches and established gardens suggest a magical palace right out of the Arabian Nights:

> *"Aladdin asked the spirit of the lamp to build him a palace near the sea...the next moment a magnificent white building with beautiful arches and cupolas emerged from the dry coastal land, the sound of the fountains filled the air, and there were people and music everywhere..."*

Like the tale, the hotel's decor is light, bright and airy. Jewel-bright cushions, drapes and upholstery accent the intricate wooden shapes of Swahili-style furniture. There are touches of stained glass, patterned brass and cool tiling.

The open-air reception sets the scene with towering high thatch roof, a vast expanse of white tiled floor, and a scattering of rich color in upholstery and decorative tiles—exotic, elegant and airy. Even from reception there are tantalizing views of the blue ocean framed by white arches. A winding marble stairway follows an indoor waterfall to the colorful Lamu Lounge. Just beyond are rock garden dining terraces overlooking a large free-form swimming pool, the romantic ruins of an old mosque and the sea.

The graceful proportions of the mosque's arched window have been reproduced in the balcony arches of the guest rooms, which rise in tiers on three sides of the terraced rock gardens. Most rooms have some sort of balcony sea view. Children are welcome.

Breakfast buffets and dinners are set up in the table d'hote restaurant or on the terrace. The Aladdin Grill is an elegant restaurant for more romantic à la carte dining, and there are snack-bars at poolside and beach. A weekly program is announced which includes nightly entertainment such as tribal dancing, acrobats, games and dancing to the hotel's resident band. On some evenings dinner is set up and served around the flood-lit pool. Music is played on and off during the day, volleyball arranged on the beach, and watersports often enliven the pool.

Kaskazi has a somewhat more sophisticated and elegant atmosphere than many of the other hotels on this beach. We visited this hotel when it was still new and looked sparkling—we hope it wears well over time. It was too soon for Kaskazi to have established a reputation, but it is certainly visually beautiful.

Accommodations

There are 193 rooms at Kaskazi. Each room has one double and one single bed, small ensuite bathroom, air conditioning, ceiling fan, minibar and telephone. Some rooms have connecting doors. There are wonderful views in Central Rooms #432–440, in South Wing Room #331, and in North Wing Room #358.

Special Offerings

There are air-conditioned conference facilities, two floodlit tennis courts, and centers for sea sports at the beach.

Off Notes

The main dining area is very crowded when the hotel is full. Furnishings, although bright and attractive, are not particularly high quality. This stretch of Diani Beach is rather narrow and rocky, and is not especially good for swimming in the ocean.

LEOPARD BEACH HOTEL

Leopard Beach Hotel, Box 34, Ukunda
☎ *(1261) 2111, FAX: (1261) 2113*

This hotel was built in 1974 and combines modern lines with African high-thatch architecture. Its rooms and suites are at the top of a rocky cliff with public areas at different levels leading down to the beach.

The small beach has interesting rock formations and tall palms. You need shoes to protect your feet from the coral bottom when swimming.

A unique feature of this hotel is that you only see one level at a time, it is large but seems small and intimate. The pool is lower down on the cliff, built into a terrace which juts out with good views of the small bay. A disco is also cut into the cliff. Rock gardens and lily ponds combine cool color with beckoning corners and nooks.

The cuisine is billed as international with Italian flavors. Meals are taken in a very large dining area where some tables overlook the sea.

Standard rooms are very tired. The reason for choosing this hotel would be to stay in one of the very reasonably priced, beautifully located, and commodious suites. Wonderful choices are Master Suites #1 and 7 (especially #7!), each with private sitting area and terrace with magnificent sea view and private garden (can rent with master bedroom only, or with additional double bedroom).

Other good choices are Jr. Suites #15, 16, & 18 which share a sitting area and terrace. Cottage #19/20 (two double rooms connecting) is also a good possibility. These all have minibar; TV in English, Italian and German; and excellent private bathrooms (with bidet) for each bedroom.

TWO FISHES HOTEL

Two Fishes Hotel, Box 23, Ukunda, Mombasa
☎ *(1261) 2101*

The most remarkable feature of this large hotel is the unusual swimming pool meandering through the lounge area and out into the grounds. There are bridges over the narrow channels of water and a slide leading to a lower pool. A few large painted plaster animal figures are scattered in the gardens. The hotel seems popular with children and has a low-key, informal atmosphere. The main lobby and lounge area look dated with furnishings in orange and brown, and amateur murals on the walls. When we visited, the hotel was less than spotless.

The 199 rooms are located in three-story thatched buildings. Some rooms are close to the beach and have ocean views.

DIANI REEF GRAND HOTEL

Sonotels Kenya Ltd., Box 61753, Nairobi
☎ *227571, FAX: 227585*

This hotel was built in 1981, and it is huge! It is a rambling complex of 300 rooms, seven restaurants and many lounges and public rooms. There are two swimming pools, a romantic lagoon with pedal boats, and a beachfront terrace where there is dancing every night under the stars. There is also a disco, a casino, a shopping arcade, a children's playground, a gymnasium, video room, beauty shop and a conference hall for 300.

The beach area is wide and very pleasant. Breakfast is served buffet-style in a room floating on the garden lagoon with ocean views. There are tropical flowers, rock gardens and the familiar but beautiful tall swaying palms.

With a choice of seven restaurants, you can select among French, Italian, Polynesian, Middle Eastern, African, Indian Ocean and International cuisines.

The choice is more exciting than the food. There are also two floodlit tennis courts, air-conditioned squash court, archery range, bocce, and a fitness track.

Accommodations

Older rooms are too-much-used and tired, but due for redecorating. All have air conditioning, minibar, radio, telephone. The newer Deluxe Wing is better and is closest to the sea. Ask for rooms #720/721 & 925–927. Rooms #820, 924, and 923 form suites, but can be reserved as doubles.

Off Notes

Several of the public rooms are fighting mildew problems and have a very musty smell.

DIANI SEA LODGE

Welcome Inns Ltd. Kenya, Box 37, Ukunda
☎ *(0127) 2114, FAX: (0127) 2287*

This is advertised as a "bungalow hotel" with 135 Swahili-style bungalows set far back from the beach in established gardens. All have a terrace, shower and AC. Some have an extra bedroom. Closer to the beach is a ten-room apartment with sea views.

The main building has shops, a disco, a bar and a restaurant which looks towards the kidney-shaped pool and the sea beyond. There is also a toddlers' pool, a children's playground, and a pool bar which serves snacks. Sports options include tennis, table tennis, minigolf and billiards as well as the usual selection of watersports and activities. Shady lawns with wooden loungers stretch down to the beach.

The hotel is run by German owners.

DIANI SEA RESORT

Welcome Inns Ltd. Kenya, Box 37, Ukunda
☎ *(0127) 3081, FAX: (0127) 2287*

This brand new resort hotel is part of the German Welcome Inn-Hotels. The architecture is very plain, with the central wing distant from but facing the sea, and two side wings angled towards it. The hotel has 340 beds, standard and family rooms, and several suites. The dining area is at the top of a long sloping central garden. Exposed pathways shimmer in the sun.

Rooms are spacious with air conditioning and private bathrooms with showers. Light-giving French doors open to a terrace or garden. The pool at the foot of the central garden area has an island and water slide. There are sports and resort facilities. This hotel has yet to develop any character, but at least it is new and clean.

LEISURE LODGE

Leisure Lodge, Diani Beach
☎ *(0127) 2011*
or book through travel agents in Germany

This large resort on Diani Beach is a classy Hotel-Club-Casino combination specializing in catering to a tour-group clientele from Germany. Leisure Lodge has a hotel section which is closer to the ocean, as well as a more exclusive Club set in gardens far from the beach.

A huge reception area leads into a glitzy shopping arcade, followed by a Casino. Beyond are terraces, bars, and restaurants, some with sea view. There is red tile underfoot and the cooling peaks of high thatched domes above.

The hotel has more than 200 double rooms in several multilevel blocks stretched along the property to one side, some with good sea views. All have air conditioning and ensuite bathrooms. There is one hotel swimming pool.

Although farther from the sea, the club is very exclusive and more upmarket than the hotel. Entry to the club is carefully restricted. The 116 rooms are more luxurious with elegant decor. There are 16 deluxe suites and two swimming pools. Pretty walkways pass over lily ponds. There are lawns, colorful flower beds and a dining terrace.

Special Offerings

Guests of both hotel and club share resort facilities: casino, restaurants, beach lounger rental, windsurfing with lessons, a PADI Diving School, four floodlit tennis courts, a golf course, horse riding on the beach or inland, beauty salon, massage parlor, and bus service to Mombasa.

PARADISE OCEAN VILLAGE CLUB

Universal Safari Tours, Box 49312, Nairobi
☎ *221446, FAX: 218686*

Clients at this smaller resort are mainly from France, and menus and notices are written in French. The atmosphere is low-key and European.

There is an attractive open lobby, but it is a long walk to the ocean. Guests stay in Spanish style cottages (white stucco and arches) lining the narrow gardens. Each cottage has a veranda and shares a living room. The rooms are rather small and dark with very basic decor.

The appeal is in the casual, open-sided dining and lounge areas near the beach, and in the natural vegetation which has been retained—baobab trees and jungle-like vines. There is a cool lounging area close to the rather small pool. You dine under thatch at the edge of the sandy beach. Along with bright bougainvillea, there are checked tablecloths and an emphasis on food. Your choices include an attractive fruit and juice bar, a lobster and seafood grill and a restaurant serving game meat.

Many activities are included in the tariff (goggling, windsurfing, archery). There are some organized activities such as water polo in the pool, and musical evenings.

GOLDEN BEACH

Golden Beach, Box 31, Ukunda, Mombasa
☎ *(0127) 2625, FAX: (0127) 2321*

This is a huge concrete highrise with 138 rooms. There is little charm and loud decor—it feels rather like a convention center. Although the beachfront is extensive, the buildings are far from the beach. There are many sports activities, a big pool and gardens. The hotel is frequented mainly by German tour groups.

ROBINSON BAOBAB CLUB

Robinson Baobab Club, Box 84792, Mombasa
☎ *(1261) 2026*

Built in 1974, this is one of the oldest hotels on the beach. It can accommodate 300 people. The clientele is predominantly German, and bookings are made in Frankfurt. The hotel has a magnificent site high on a rocky promontory, well-treed, and with views down over the ocean. There are some nice touches—a waterfall by the lobby, interesting Lamu furniture, dining tables next to big open windows with sea views. However, closer inspection reveals drawbacks—there is a maze of rooms, heavy doses of mildew, and loudspeakers broadcasting rousing music.

SOUTHERN PALMS BEACH RESORT

Southern Palms, Box 363, Ukunda, Mombasa
☎ *(0127) 3721*

This is a new beach resort going up near the northern end of Diani Beach. Southern Palms will have 180 rooms in three-stories. There is to be a large pool, sports and conference facilities and nightly entertainment. Rooms will have Swahili-style decor and balconies facing the sea. They will also have air conditioning, mosquito nets, and large double beds. An extra Lamu-style divan will add to the Swahili theme.

TRADE WINDS HOTEL

African Tours and Hotels Ltd., Box 30471, Nairobi
☎ *336858, FAX: 218109*

This hotel can accommodate approximately 200 people. Public rooms and old wing rooms have sad decor and are substandard. A newer wing with Arab-style windows is set farther back from the beach. There is a large but poorly maintained swimming pool and a nice beachfront.

DIANI HOUSE

Diani House, Box 19, Ukunda, Mombasa
☎ *(0127) 2412, FAX: (0127) 2391*

Diani House is a coastal taste of colonial Kenya. Located about halfway along Diani, this pleasant home with grassy slopes rolling down to the beach is a nostalgic reminder of what the Kenyan coast was like before the mushrooming of resort hotels. Sitting on the cool veranda with dogs at your feet, you feel transported back in time.

When you stay at Diani House you are hosted by Annelise (Lulu) Archer and John Clark. This lively young couple helps you to feel completely relaxed and at home, and they will organize activities or outings to suit. They have a boat for fishing, snorkeling, or visiting nearby islands. You can also windsurf. Side trips to the Shimba Hills National Park for game viewing or into Mombasa for shopping or sightseeing can easily be arranged.

Diani House can accommodate a maximum of eight guests. The bedrooms are spacious and simple. Lulu has decorated them with individuality using Kenyan furniture, fabrics and crafts to make them colorful and attractive. There are bookshelves piled with books and scattered rugs—the ambience is casual and homey rather than luxurious. There are fans (no air conditioning) and each bedroom has a large bathroom ensuite. In place of glass, there is dark meshing over the windows, but from the veranda outside there are nice views down over the garden towards the ocean.

Safari Journal — last, late evening

At dinner there were candles, music wafting out of the living room, and a selection of wines. There was a pleasant breeze, a bushbaby ran along the edge of the veranda and we could sense the ocean through the night. Conversation flowed. Could have spent a week just talking to John and Lulu, to hear more about their wonderful and diverse experiences growing up in Kenya — from game safaris to movie sets.

The almost five hectares in size grounds are impressive with palms, baobabs, and bougainvillea are also a refuge for all manner of birds and small wildlife. There are colobus monkeys in the trees, a bushbaby helps itself from a feeder, and everywhere there are birds.

Fresh home-cooked food is served with an emphasis on the wonderful seafood and tropical fruits available. Meals are casual and usually enjoyed alfresco on the long veranda.

NOMAD

Nomad, Box 1, Ukunda, Mombasa
☎ *(0127) 2155, FAX: (0127) 2391*

Nomad is a return to basics on Diani Beach. You pass new shopping malls, discos and highrise hotels and then turn down a long, winding dirt road shaded by old trees: a staggering contrast. Guests have a choice of staying in one of the three new large family cottages or in the older small bandas. The setting is idyllic—only grass and tall palm trees between you, the beach, and the ocean beyond.

Staying in the bandas at Nomad is like camping on the beach—except the "tents" are made of sticks. The cottages, on the other hand are bright and spacious with sliding glass doors on to private verandas and the beach just steps away.

Nomad began as a restaurant 15 years ago, and is still a popular place to eat. The food is simple and excellent. There are two restaurants. The main restaurant (high thatch roof, sides open to views and breezes) serves à la carte meals in the evenings with an emphasis on seafood. On Sundays there is a curry and Jazz lunch.

The ultracasual "Nomad's Beach Bar" is basically a *makuti* roof supported by a tree trunk with sand underfoot. Customers are often in swimwear, and the ocean is only steps away. The menu ranges from sandwiches to wonderfully fresh seafood platters. The Diani Boutique adds color and activity to the scene.

Nomad is popular with British Kenyans. It has a relaxed and friendly atmosphere. The staff have been there a long time, there is a loyal repeat group of guests, and children are welcome. As the manager said, "This is the exact opposite of a package tour place...there are no jumping Masai for entertainment...here you can completely relax, you don't even have to talk to anyone else." The only pool is the Indian Ocean. Deep sea fishing is available, and there is a diving school.

Accommodations

Nomad can accommodate a maximum of 50. The three family cottages each have one double room and a family suite which can sleep four. Two cottages have an upstairs garret which can sleep two. Rooms are bright and attractive and are equipped with an electric kettle and a large mosquito net enclosing both beds and a fan. Bathrooms are large and modern. The bandas are small, basic and dark—some are family units with a very small second bedroom. Each has a bathroom en suite. There is electricity, but no fans. Even if you don't stay at Nomad, at least stop by for a meal.

GALU BEACH

Situated south of Diani, Galu Beach is less built up, with fewer hotels and no shopping malls. There are dirt roads and indigenous bush. The beach is smaller and more private than Diani, and has fewer beach vendors or boating activities. Coral rock means more difficult swimming along some portions of this beach.

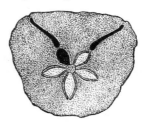

NEPTUNES HOTELS ON GALU BEACH

Neptune Village, Box 696 Ukunda, Mombasa
☎ *(0127) 3061, FAX: 3019*

Side by side are two Neptune resorts—the older "Neptune Cottages" and the bright new "Neptune Paradise." Between them they have over 250 units in two-story rondavel-style cottages with very tall peaked roofs—they look like a gnome's village come to life!

Since the plots are very deep, it's a long walk to the ocean. The cottages are set back in gardens, or overlooking the pool rather than the sea.

Neptune Paradise, the new and smaller resort, has a clean "decorated" feel to it. There are scores of chairs and loungers in pastel hues with coordinating fabrics, the bar is built in the shape of a boat with bar stools to look like dolphins. The open-sided beach bar and the thatched dining area are built close to the beach, and there is a big pool with a swim-up bar. Muzak plays, and there is a TV and table tennis under thatch. Images of Florida and ice-cream parlors come to mind.

Accommodations

The rooms are clean, attractively decorated and well-equipped with minibars, phone, radio, tables and chairs. Most rooms look into the backs of others. Those closest to the pool have the best views and the most noise.

PINEWOOD VILLAGE
Pinewood Village, Box 190, Ukunda, Mombasa
☎ *(0127) 3720, FAX: (0127) 3131*

Pinewood Village is a new complex of 20 townhouses in the coastal forest near the end of Galu Beach. These two-story white villas are compactly arranged along narrow grounds stretching to the beach. Staying at Pinewood Village is more like renting your own condominium than staying at a traditional ocean resort hotel. You have a living room and a fully-equipped kitchen with staff to cook and clean. Privacy and individuality are combined with the security of being part of a complex.

Set well back from the sea, the villas have views of coastal bush rather than the ocean. They share a lovely curved swimming pool which has a swim-up thatched bar. Landscaped steps beyond the pool give way to gardens and lawns, then Galu Beach.

The villas are solidly built and attractively furnished, giving a sense of quality and attention to detail. Fresh whitewash dominates—a dramatic contrast with the dark ethnic furniture and bright fabrics. Arches abound. The effect is clean, spacious and uncluttered—more aesthetically pleasing than comfortable.

Upstairs, however, all is comfort. Big beds with ceiling fans above are encased in voluminous mosquito nets. Again there are pleasing fabrics and bright whitewash. The bathrooms are elegant with tiles imported from Italy. With central air conditioning, the bedrooms are also the coolest rooms in the villa. (There are fans, but no air conditioning downstairs.) The bedrooms open on to large terraces where you might glimpse colobus monkeys in the trees.

Each villa also has its own direct dial telephone. Some villas have connecting doors which allow a larger family or group the opportunity of sharing a doubled living space with four to six double bedrooms upstairs.

A cook steward is assigned to each villa and, if you choose, will cook and serve all of your meals. You are responsible for providing the food. Supplies can be purchased at the mini supermarket in the main building. Fresh seafood and vegetables are on sale at the resort's own small open market. There is also a charming restaurant and bar in the main building which is reached by a wooden bridge over a lily pond.

There is a certain thoughtfulness at Pinewood Village—accommodation for drivers and ayahs is included in the tariff, kitchen staples are placed in your villa, and cold beers can be purchased at the store.

Other Facilities
Floodlit tennis court, squash court, games room, air-conditioned video/TV room, and a terrace which can be used for conferences and parties. The management will organize tours to Mombasa, sea sports, and

shopping or entertainment trips to Diani Shopping Center, only eight kilometers away.

CHALE PARADISE ISLAND

Chale Paradise Island, Box 4, Ukunda, Mombasa
☎ *(0127) 2127, FAX: (0127) 3319 Msambweni*

This small island south of Galu Beach is astoundingly beautiful with a lovely natural sandy bay, dramatic rock formations and a great variety of indigenous trees. Chale Island is now being developed, though many had hoped it would become a protected reserve. The developer is full of vision and energy—he sees Chale Paradise Island as a luxury tented health spa. The tents will be large and full of antique Lamu furniture, the rough rocks will be covered with sand for barefoot walking, the pure natural sulphur mud will be amazingly regenerative. There was talk of masseurs, health food and attentive service. It seemed a pity that the tents were being constructed cheek by jowl, that day trippers were expected, and that the development tractors were driving over coral. What price tourism? Update: Chale Paradise Island is advertising bookings and on-site birthday and wedding ceremonies.

MSAMBWENI

A bumpy dirt road leads past palm groves and mud houses to Msambweni. This is a relatively unspoiled stretch of beach edged primarily by private properties. There are rocky outcrops, low cliffs and patches of coral on sandy bays.

BEACHCOMBER CLUB

Beachcomber Club, Box 54, Msambweni
☎ (0127) 52074
or Lets Go Travel, Box 60342, Nairobi
☎ 340331, FAX: 336890

Simple, pleasant and unique, the Beachcomber Club is tucked away on an unspoiled stretch of Msambweni, south of busy Diani Beach. What makes Beachcomber Club special is its relaxed and tranquil atmosphere, its wonderfully sited dining areas (and accompanying good food), and its location above a private sandy cove edged with dramatic rock formations.

Accommodations are 16 very simple rooms on two stories. There are basic bathrooms ensuite, private balconies and electric fans, but no air conditioning. The rooms are set back from the beach, overlooking trees and tropical gardens, with glimpses of the ocean beyond. The attraction of Beachcomber Club is not luxurious accommodations, it is the privacy, friendly atmosphere and great setting. Manager Tamsin Corcoran is charming and well-known for her cuisine.

The settings for dining are worthy of Tamsin's specialties! The upper dining and bar area is simple, airy and attractive, with wonderful views over dark, sculpted rocks and the sandy bay beyond. Breakfast and dinners are served there. For lunches and drinks you climb down narrow rocky stairs towards the beach. Just above the sand you come to Tamsin's whimsical bar and grill. Built in a shallow rocky "cave," it meanders among the rocks with views over the beach, the sound of breaking waves and fresh sea breezes. Tamsin's huge, brightly colored cushions of local *Kanga* cloth add comfort to the rocks—exotic and fun! A few tables with chairs are set out on the beach in the dappled shade of bushes. Old wooden dugout canoes soft with patterned cushions invite naps and quiet reading.

Tamsin's artistic talent is also evident in the rustic but attractive gift "shop" and reception area where she displays an unusual and appealing mix of Kenyan items for sale. She has enthusiastic plans for redecorating the guest rooms.

Near the upper dining area and partly shaded by trees is a small swimming pool with water coming out of a concrete shell.

The beach here invites exploration. There is contrast and some drama—rocks, bays and undeveloped stretches of beach. At high tide, waves break in front of the Club. To swim at low tide you must climb over coral rock to the ocean beyond. All quite a contrast to the long sandy beaches and calm sea of Diani Beach.

Beachcomber Club can offer a variety of water activities such as windsurfing, scuba diving, glass bottom boats to the coral reef, and deep sea fishing. Nearby is a micro-light plane, horse riding and tennis. The club is a popular spot for British Kenyans and families.

Safari Journal ~ Saturday afternoon

Lounging on Kanga cushions in the cave bar at Beachcomber Club. Great Pimms, great views. Waves break below, fresh breezes blow. So poetic!

CLUB GREEN OASIS (FORMERLY BLACK MARLIN)
Club Green Oasis, Box 80, Msambweni
☎ *(0127)52030*

This spread-out resort bakes on a cliff. The beach below is rocky, disappointing and small. The clientele is mostly German and French tour groups. The sea-view pool schedules adult water polo and exercise. There are horses for riding. Accommodations are a series of rather scruffy small villas and rondavels scattered in huge lawns. The Barracuda Villa Rooms #110, 111, & 112 would make up for a lot just because of the private sitting room and wonderful view!

Update: We hear that parts of the hotel have burned down and that it has opened under a new name: Club Green Oasis.

SEASCAPES BEACH VILLAS

Seascapes Limited, Box 45541, Nairobi
☎ *334280*

Seascapes is ideal for people who want to escape hotels, but still want the option of eating meals in a restaurant instead of cooking. In a dramatic cliff-top setting, 16 thatched double-story Arab style villas share a central swimming pool. Each white villa has three large double bedrooms with bathrooms ensuite, a lounge-dining area, a fully equipped kitchen and sun-balconies. There are fans, but no air conditioning. Sea breezes are free to blow through the unglassed windows. Each villa comes with a cook and cleaner.

The setting of Seascapes makes it unique. The wide expanse of beach is far below, down many stairs. Although it is quite a hike, once you are on the beach, there are no crowds or beach vendors, just long stretches of sand. The villas are well spread out on 12 acres of landscaped grounds. Stone paths lead through lawns. There are palm trees and bougainvillea.

The swimming pool is fairly small and has an adjoining bar and bistro/snack restaurant. There is also a shop where you can purchase groceries and produce for your cook to prepare. Tennis and squash are free to villa residents. At Seascapes you have a sense of privacy, although you can be communal around the pool and bar. The best villas for the view are #1 and #11.

FUNZI – SHIMONI – WASINI

After Msambweni the coast road passes open green swamps, tall palm trees, then fields of sugar cane. About 80 kilometers south of Mombasa is Shimoni, known for game fishing and coral caves. In view of the shore is Wasini, a narrow rocky island with no roads and no running water. On the island is a small Swahili village, exposed coral gardens, some Muslim ruins, and the Wasini Island Restaurant with a reputation for wonderful seafood. Day-long dhow trips to the island give you a look at Swahili culture and a gourmet lunch.

The snorkeling in this area is superb. Boats can take you to the Kisite-Mpunguti Marine National Park—magnificent coral reefs less visited than those further north. You can use your own snorkeling equipment and hire a small local dhow to get to the reef. Or, you can go to the other extreme and splurge on an outing with Shimoni Aqua-Ventures Ltd. where equipment, expert underwater guiding and instruction, and even a fabulous five-course seafood lunch are included. (Contact Shimoni Aqua-Ventures at Indian Ocean Beach Club ☎ *(0127) 3730 ext 179)*

PEMBA CHANNEL INN

Pemba Channel Fishing Club, Ltd., Box 86952, Mombasa
☎ *313749, FAX: 316875*

The Pemba Channel is world famous for some of the best big game fishing in Africa. The Pemba Channel Inn is small, delightful and very personal. It is the capable manager, Sandra Ruysenaars, who gives the Inn its special character. Her warmth and good humor put her guests at ease, her cooking is outstanding, and she has made this once rather spartan fishing lodge an attractive and comfortable place to stay.

The Inn is built on the high banks above the channel. There is no proper beach, but there is a pleasant view of water, boats and Wasini Island. The Tanzanian mountains seem to loom just at the end of the water. You can cool down in the large, beautifully tiled swimming pool.

The Inn has a central clubhouse—large and sprawling with open sides. There are overstuffed chintz cushions on wicker sofas, bowls of shells, and freshly picked flowers. Marlin trophies, photos and lists of amazing catches add substance to enjoyable conversations recounting special experiences fishing or snorkeling in the channel.

A feeling of professionalism and purpose touches everything connected with the big game fishing here. The teamwork and the experience of the all-Kenyan boat crews help Pemba Channel boats to bring in more catches over 500 pounds than any other boats on the Kenyan coast. There are three boats, each of which is fully equipped for three people to fish at a time. Each boat has tackle in the 130, 80, or 50 lb. class. An experienced fisherman always goes with the boat to give advice or to instruct novices. Children under eight years are not allowed. There is an eight-month fishing season from August to the end of March. Being in the lee of Pemba Island, the seas are normally calm.

The ship-to-shore radio crackles! You know firsthand the fortunes of each deep-sea fishing boat right up to the moment of weighing in the catch. The understated pride, the world-class significance of what is done, laces everything at the Pemba Channel Inn with a fizzing excitement.

Pemba Channel Inn can accommodate a total of 14 guests in a series of simple white bandas scattered on the grounds. The rooms are bright and spacious with cheerful fabrics, a standing fan, and mosquito nets. The ensuite bathrooms have huge showers with welcome water pressure. Sandra has made the rooms personal with magazines, baskets of toiletries, and flowers. Each banda has a small veranda—some with views over the water.

Thanks to Sandra's culinary skills, dinners at Pemba Channel Inn are memorable adventures in gourmet dining, often served on the terrace under the stars. You have the feeling that everything is done for your personal delight—especially the individual chocolate souffle!

Just minutes away from Pemba Channel Inn is a colorful coastal market which is spread out on the site of the old British colonial outpost. Nearby, you can examine some of the terrible "black holes" of the slave trade, which are still said to be haunted.

Please Note
The Inn is closed April–July 31. Reservations which include fishing boat booking will bump bookings for lodgings only.

Off Note
No real beach.

SHIMONI REEF LODGE

Reef Hotels, Box 61408, Nairobi
☎ *214322, FAX: 332702*

Best known for its PADI Diving Center, this small lodge mainly attracts divers. It is built on the high banks of the Wasini Channel, and the bar and restaurant overlook the water. The atmosphere is very casual and tranquil. There are ten rather run-down cottages with thatched roofs, fans and private flagstone verandas. There are grassy areas, trees and a free-form swimming pool that has seen better days.

SEA ADVENTURES LTD.

Sea Adventures Ltd., Box 56 Shimoni
☎ *Shimoni 12*

If you plan to go big game fishing for more than one day, you can stay with the Hemphills. Pat Hemphill and his son, Simon, have years of fishing experience, and operate two boats equipped for big game fishing. They specialize in light tackle fishing and offer special "kids days."

Guests stay either in the Hemphills' home or a guest cottage. There are four double rooms, and meals are taken with the Hemphill family. Rates include fishing.

FUNZI ISLAND CLUB

Funzi Island Club, Box 90246, Mombasa
☎ *225546, FAX: 316458*

The canoe speeds up and heads straight at a wall of mangroves. The instinct is to duck, but suddenly you are in a narrow waterway overhung by trees—dappled light on the water, the splash of jumping fish. Land on sand and race up the hot midday slope to the cool dark welcome of a big thatch banda.

Shades of Graham Greene: A wonderful antique victrola is scratching out a tune—a call to dance on the straw matting in bare feet with chilled wine in hand. There are giant polished mangrove root tables, fish trophies mounted on makuti walls, visitors books and photos of guests having a good time. Out in the bright glare donkeys plod, pulling water for the tents. Dogs tease. All seems rather a mirage, a step out of time, blurred and softened at the edges.

Funzi Island is peace and privacy at a price. There are only seven tents—wonderful whimsical tents set far apart—large and light-filled. There are kingsize Lamu beds with tie-dye covers made by your hostess, Robina. In front of the tents are big shaded veranda areas and water-filled footbaths for sandy toes or birds. There are many delightful and ingenious touches such as the large tree nuts used to operate the bush shower.

Although the tents themselves are wonderful, they do not command any special views—sand and scrubby bush—no panoramas over water. We visited on a very hot and rather airless day and did not spend the night, so have no sense of whether breezes provide sleeping comfort.

Funzi Club is best known for fishing. One or two day fishing trips can be arranged in Funzi Club's "Jungle Cat," which is equipped with tackle, fighting chairs and an experienced crew. Beyond the reef are big game fish—marlin, sailfish and yellow fin tuna.

However, you don't have to like fishing to enjoy yourself here. Your host, Tony Duckworth, is a knowledgeable ornithologist and can lead bird walks as well as canoe trips up the river estuary and between the mangroves. He gloats, delighted at having spotted a white-backed night heron. (Mean something to you birders?)

If you're not much into fish or fowl, you might prefer to lounge (with drink and food at hand) on the "African Queen" in the middle of a peaceful bay, or land on a sandy spit of beach for a picnic and a swim. The choice is yours—no timetable, no set agenda. All just very languid and lazy.

There is a minimum of a three-night stay at Funzi Club. Robina commented that some people leave in tears, and an entry in the visitors' book read "Robinson Crusoe refuses rescue." The lunch we had was excellent—lots of ultrafresh seafood and great salads. To quote Tony, the price includes "Full board and drinks on the sideboard." We regretted that we could only spend a few hours at Funzi Club—didn't get to test out the Lamu beds or enjoy more of the wry humor of our host.

Funzi Club also offers a selection of day trips for people who have lodging elsewhere. The Club closes over the low season months. Funzi Island is 60 kilometers south of Mombasa along the main coast road.

SHIMBA HILLS NATIONAL RESERVE

The Shimba Hills run parallel to the coast south of Mombasa. It takes less than an hour to drive from Mombasa up into this hilly reserve. At 500 meters above sea level and covered by beautiful forest, the Shimba Hills National Reserve is a refreshing contrast to the coast. There is not a great deal of game in the reserve although there are elephant, buffalo and giraffe. The park is best known as being the only place in Kenya where you might see the rare sable antelope.

SHIMBA HILLS

Block Hotels, Box 47557, Nairobi
☎ *335807, FAX: 340541*

Shimba Hills is a pleasant overnight game viewing lodge (see section on Night Game Viewing Lodges). It is nestled in the Shimba Hills Game Reserve only miles from the tropical scenery of the Kenyan Coast. Compared with the sticky humidity at sea level, Shimba Hills is cool and refreshing—welcome jungle greens after the glare of sand and sea. After you leave your vehicle, a lush scenic walk leads you into the stunning open treehouse ingeniously built into the forest—three rooms even have trees growing through them!

Every aspect of the building is designed to be in harmony with nature. The dining room is a covered veranda overlooking the floodlit pond—you can watch game during dinner. Walkways and balconies provide picture perfect views of exotic trees, birds, monkeys, and even herds of elephant drinking at the waterhole below. The trees are labeled for the fledgling botanist. To minimize the mosquito population, the pond is home to a school of Gambusa Fish.

Typically, you arrive at Shimba Hills in time for tea, a sundowner game drive, or a chance to enjoy jungle life and sounds at one of the three bar areas. The most unique is the Jungle Bar at the end of a long, winding wooden walkway. At night floodlights illuminate the waterhole.

Shimba Hills can accommodate up to 80 people. All rooms have standing balconies facing the water hole. The rooms, although small, are light and cheerful with big windows and nice fabrics. There are ceiling fans and ample electricity. Guests share clean, bright communal toilet and shower facilities which are constructed of wood and stone.

Weddings have also been held at Shimba Hills, with the ceremony performed at the end of the Jungle Bar Walkway. The bridal suite is very large with an outstanding view of the water hole, ensuite dining area, and private bathroom.

Accommodations

There are 24 doubles, five triples, and two self-contained suites. All the doubles and triples have twin beds. The suites have double beds. All rooms have ceiling fans and mosquito nets are provided on request. The rooms are sprayed, and there are screen and glass windows. Suites are #19 and #20. The rooms with trees growing through them are #22, 23, and 16. No children under 7 are allowed.

Special Offerings

Sundowner game drive, pre-dawn game drive, souvenir and sundry shop.

Off Note

Not noted for abundance of game.

COAST: MOMBASA & NORTH to MALINDI

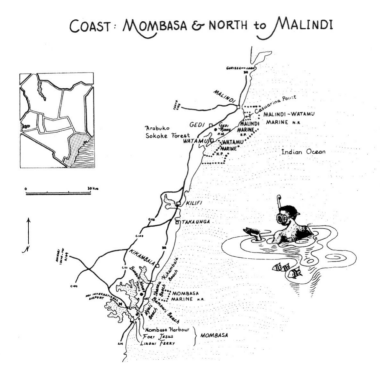

NORTH OF MOMBASA TO KILIFI

Mombasa City Codes ☎ *011 - #, FAX: 011 - #.*

The coastline stretching north of Mombasa is heavily developed with resort hotels. The concentration of hotels peters out as you move towards Kilifi and then intensifies again in the Malindi area. Heading north from Mombasa towards Kilifi, the resort beaches are Nyali, Bamburi, Shanzu, and Kikambala.

If you want a change from beach activities you can visit the *Bamburi Quarry Nature Trail,* an impressive and heartening example of land reclaimed from a cement quarry. There is also the *Mamba Village* crocodile farm and *Bombolulu,* a handicrafts center which employs disabled people. Golfers might choose to try their skill at the *Nyali Beach Golf Club.*

NYALI BEACH AND ENGLISH POINT

English Point looks across towards Old Town Mombasa, and Nyali Beach begins the coral sand beaches north.

NYALI BEACH HOTEL
Block Hotels, Box 47557, Nairobi
☎ *335807, FAX: 340541*

The Nyali Beach Hotel is the grand old hotel of the Mombasa coast. In 1931, the 1300-foot Nyali Bridge opened to link the Port of Mombasa with the northern mainland. After World War II, the Kenyan Government invited Harry and Eva Noon to build a hotel at the coast developing some of the prime land on Nyali Beach. Beginning with a rough clearing or *nyali,* they dealt with every problem and setback, determined to build an elegant and comfortable hotel. In December 1946, the Nyali Beach Hotel opened to become the first of Kenya's beach hotels with a reputation for hospitality and excellence that endures to this day.

Your first impression is of cool whitewashed walls and tiled floors. There are ceiling fans, potted palms, pale marble and white wicker furniture. Light streams through paladian windows to emphasize the blue-green color of cushions where hotel cats doze. A large brass samovar catches the light, and there are pots of tropical foliage. The atmosphere is easy, there is a sense of comfort and tradition. You have the feeling that you are waiting for Humphrey Bogart and Sidney Greenstreet to appear.

Although the hotel opened with only 57 rooms, today it can accommodate approximately 450 people and do it with style. Nyali attracts honeymoon couples, families with children, and tourists from all over the world. There are many choices of accommodation, 26 acres of grounds and gardens, many varieties of water sport and activities. Guests can sample aerobic workouts, beauty treatments, deep sea fishing, golf and tennis.

Marine "safaris" take you to the reef in glass-bottom boats, and you can safari to see big game in Tsavo National Park. There is the jungle environment of Shimba Hills and the lure of Old Town Mombasa nearby. In fact, Nyali Beach is perhaps the closest resort hotel to the shopping, sightseeing, and restaurants of Mombasa.

There are two swimming pools, one olympic-sized with a huge outdoor terrace overhead. The other is the appealing Lagoon Pool, free-formed, near the beach, surrounded by lush tropical flowers and palms—a perfect place to enjoy the sea view from a wooden terrycloth-cushioned lounger. With a drink and seafood bar nearby, you can easily spend the day.

Variety is the spice of life at Nyali Beach Hotel, and that applies to the seven eating areas. The cuisine varies from the gourmet splendor in the oceanside Mvita Grill to the open-air fruit bar and Parrots' snackbar at the beach. A wonderful breakfast is served every day in L'Orangerie with active chefs preparing eggs and pancakes to order!

The hotel issues a daily entertainment and sports program. Two shopping arcades boast seven boutiques and shops for every possible need. For romantic nights, you can dance at the Nyali Blues Disco or even under the stars on an outdoor terrace within sight of the sea.

Accommodations

There is a wide range of accommodations from luxury suites to elderly cottages in slightly overgrown gardens. Wings of rooms and cottages are spread through the grounds. Some guests stay in the main building which has spacious older rooms. In the most recent addition, the "new wing," there are three luxury suites and 54 superior ocean view rooms.

All rooms have modern bathrooms with both bathtub and shower, air conditioning, mosquito nets on request, telephones, and 24-hour room service.

Special Offerings

Conference facilities, a games room, library, customized weddings, organized children's activities.

MOMBASA BEACH HOTEL

African Tours & Hotels, Box 30471, Nairobi
☎ *336858, FAX: 218109*

This is a larger hotel with five-story accommodation blocks facing the sea. It is built on an attractive rocky point with old trees. Many stairs lead to the beach. There are three conference centers, a shopping arcade, five restaurants, and a waterpark with slide. The pool is surrounded by a concrete terrace with plastic lounge chairs. There are many recreational choices. The rooms are bright and airy, and many have good sea views.

REEF HOTEL

Reef Hotel, Box 82234, Mombasa
☎ *471771, FAX: 71349*

The Reef is a large resort hotel which can accommodate about 350 guests. There is no sense of the ocean from the main rooms or pool. The layout is rather confusing with many passages and paths before you reach the beach. There are rows of rooms and lots of concrete. The hotel offers a plethora of facilities and activities: bingo, videos, conference facilities, hair salon, fitness center, tennis, several restaurants, organized pool activities, water sports. The rooms have air conditioning and fridges. A range of room types are available, including a five-bedroom villa with private pool.

THE TAMARIND VILLAGE
The Tamarind Village, Box 95805, Mombasa
☎ *471729, FAX: 472106*

The Tamarind Village in Nyali is a beautiful and luxurious condominium complex which looks over the harbor towards the Old Town of Mombasa. It shares a driveway with the Tamarind Restaurant, justly famous for its wonderful seafood and setting.

The Tamarind Village has 22 privately-owned apartments. About half of these can be booked through central management. There are one, two, and three bedroom apartments, each with a private entrance, enchanting views, and outdoor terraces. The apartments are serviced and have fully equipped kitchens. As well as the option for self catering, the Lido Bar near the pool serves breakfasts and light lunch dishes. Room service to the apartments can also be arranged. And, of course, you can always splurge next door at the Tamarind Restaurant.

Safari Journal — afternoon ...

This is the life! Here I sit in a cool jacuzzi, with a glass of champagne. Below me is the Mombasa harbour with a few dhows, sails slack in this still heat and the water looking incredibly blue. There are about ten of us lounging, joking, and toasting in this oversized jacuzzi ~ a wedding party. It seems the perfect activity in this beautiful and luxurious place. I pinch myself and take another sip.

What makes the Tamarind Village so special is its lovely site and exotic and luxurious appearance. It is built in Swahili style and has a series of arches, open-sided walkways with tantalizing water views, and open grillwork walls in Moorish designs. All is in startling, sparkling whitewash alive with the exuberance of bougainvillea spilling over balconies and peeping into corridors. The complex is built along the side of a hill in six levels—balconies jut out at different heights, some shaded by thatch, others by log beams letting through slants of sunlight. Although this is a large, multilevel building, the interest and variety in the layout and design make each apartment personal and unique. There is a clean simplicity, an exotic elegance about the place.

The apartments vary in size, but all have master bedrooms, with bathrooms ensuite. There are telephones and air conditioning. Since they are privately owned, there are different styles of decor, and some are much nicer than others. We found #41,#45,#54 and #65 to be well-appointed and comfortable. Each apartment has a terrace and some have lovely views down across the water. A few have private outdoor jacuzzis.

The landscaping and swimming pool deserve special mention. Paths wander down through flowering rock gardens and lawns, creepers climb up walls and drape over balconies. The large contoured pool is glorious, with a swim-up bar, unheated jacuzzi and great views over the harbor. Next to the pool under a thatch roof is the sit-up Lido Bar with a selection of snacks and light dishes.

Other Facilities

Air conditioning, telephone connection to 24-hour switchboard, fax facility, fully serviced apartments, swimming pool with jacuzzi, nearby stores.

BAMBURI BEACH

This is the next beach up the coast. It is a busy strip full of large and small tourist hotels.

WHITESANDS
Sarova Hotels, P.O Box 30680, Nairobi
☎ *333233, FAX: 229388*

Accommodating up to 700 people, this is the largest resort hotel on the Kenyan Coast. This low-rise complex is widely spread out on well-maintained and spacious grounds. There is a clean and exotic flavor to Whitesands—yards of cool white marble, rows of arches and a wonderful use of water. Public areas seem to float on aquatic gardens, bridges cross meandering swimming pools, and birds dip into lily ponds, shattering arabesque reflections.

There is an attractive wide beachfront with lawns and tall palms. Many of the rooms overlook the ocean and beach.

Whitesands gives the impression of being a well-maintained and efficient operation. There are many standard resort facilities and activities, as well as some more unusual offerings such as Swahili lessons and events like coconut tree climbing. There are three attractive swimming pools and a fun water slide. A separate entertainment pavilion doubles as a late night disco. Whitesands is a popular conference center.

The lounges and dining areas are in four separate open-sided pavilions with colorfully decorated pillars and ceilings. Although accommodation blocks separate them from the sea, the public rooms overlook aquatic gardens and are reached by stepping stones and bridges. The full-board meals are repetitious buffets—commingling smells and long lines. For a change of pace, there is a coffee bar, the pool grill, and an à la carte restaurant. The wonderful Tamarind Restaurant is only a short cab ride away.

Accommodations

The rooms have air conditioning, nice bathrooms, and private balconies. Many have lovely views and are only steps from the beach. Double beds, larger triple rooms, and suites can be requested. Set way back from the sea is a sumptuous VIP cottage. *Our Favorites:* # 1036 and 1037—quieter, ground floor, close to beach.

Other Offerings

Watersports, tennis courts, games room, fitness center, children's playground.

SEVERIN SEA LODGE

Severin Sea Lodge, Box 82169, Mombasa
☎ *48500*

This is one of the larger hotels on Bamburi beach. It has a rambling layout and some unique features such as a dhow restaurant moored on a little stream, and a conference center which resembles an Islamic mosque. There are two swimming pools and a high thatched rondavel bar which sports game trophies.

The rooms are in two or three story whitewashed bungalows with thatched roofs. The rooms are better than average—all with mini-bar, telephone, and air conditioning. The 90 new comfort rooms, each with one double and one single bed, have Lamu-style furniture and nice bathrooms with double sink and hairdryer. Most rooms are set back from the sea, but standard rooms 400 and 402, and comfort rooms 177 and 178 have good ocean views. There is a busy entertainment program from water polo to jazz bands.

Off Note

There is no beachfront at high tide.

BAMBURI BEACH HOTEL

Bamburi Beach Hotel, Box 83966, Mombasa
☎ *485611*

This hotel has a small beachfront and is crowded with package tours. There are many sports activities and a night club.

KENYA BEACH HOTEL

Kenya Beach Hotel, Box 95748, Mombasa
☎ *485821*

This is a narrow garden complex of 100 rooms in two and three-story blocks. The beachfront is not very wide. The hotel is Swiss-run and clean. There is a large pool, an extensive cement terrace and open-air dining close to the beach.

OCEAN VIEW BEACH HOTEL

Ocean View Beach Hotel, Box 81127, Mombasa
☎ *485601*

Concrete and run-down. Sunbathers on plastic loungers crowd the constricted lawns facing the beach. There is a scuba diving center.

NEPTUNE BEACH HOTEL

Neptune Beach Hotel, Box 83125, Mombasa
☎ *485701*

This is a family hotel with 80 rooms. A pleasant entry leads to a long and narrow plot busy with shops, Disney ice cream bar, sun loungers, and colorful furniture. There is a thatched bar by a circular pool. Undistinguished rooms are set back from the beach.

PLAZA HOTEL

Plaza Hotel, Box 88299, Mombasa
☎ *485321*

A highrise on a thin plot. There are slow elevators and tired wall-to-wall carpeting. Pool.

TRAVELLERS BEACH HOTEL

Travellers Beach Hotel, Box 87649, Mombasa
☎ *485121*

This newer hotel is divided into two sections to skirt a private beachfront property. The hotel is long and narrow. There is a white and clean lobby with a high roof, stream, and swimming canal which connects with the pool. There are lines of shops, several restaurants, and many sports. Fully equipped rooms have a double and one single bed and a TV. There is a rather unreal shopping mall atmosphere about this hotel. It's a long way to the sand.

fets—commingling smells and long lines. For a change of pace, there is a coffee bar, the pool grill, and an à la carte restaurant. The wonderful Tamarind Restaurant is only a short cab ride away.

Accommodations

The rooms have air conditioning, nice bathrooms, and private balconies. Many have lovely views and are only steps from the beach. Double beds, larger triple rooms, and suites can be requested. Set way back from the sea is a sumptuous VIP cottage. *Our Favorites:* # 1036 and 1037—quieter, ground floor, close to beach.

Other Offerings

Watersports, tennis courts, games room, fitness center, children's playground.

SEVERIN SEA LODGE

Severin Sea Lodge, Box 82169, Mombasa
☎ *48500*

This is one of the larger hotels on Bamburi beach. It has a rambling layout and some unique features such as a dhow restaurant moored on a little stream, and a conference center which resembles an Islamic mosque. There are two swimming pools and a high thatched rondavel bar which sports game trophies.

The rooms are in two or three story whitewashed bungalows with thatched roofs. The rooms are better than average—all with mini-bar, telephone, and air conditioning. The 90 new comfort rooms, each with one double and one single bed, have Lamu-style furniture and nice bathrooms with double sink and hairdryer. Most rooms are set back from the sea, but standard rooms 400 and 402, and comfort rooms 177 and 178 have good ocean views. There is a busy entertainment program from water polo to jazz bands.

Off Note

There is no beachfront at high tide.

BAMBURI BEACH HOTEL
Bamburi Beach Hotel, Box 83966, Mombasa
☎ *485611*

This hotel has a small beachfront and is crowded with package tours. There are many sports activities and a night club.

KENYA BEACH HOTEL
Kenya Beach Hotel, Box 95748, Mombasa
☎ *485821*

This is a narrow garden complex of 100 rooms in two and three-story blocks. The beachfront is not very wide. The hotel is Swiss-run and clean. There is a large pool, an extensive cement terrace and open-air dining close to the beach.

OCEAN VIEW BEACH HOTEL
Ocean View Beach Hotel, Box 81127, Mombasa
☎ *485601*

Concrete and run-down. Sunbathers on plastic loungers crowd the constricted lawns facing the beach. There is a scuba diving center.

NEPTUNE BEACH HOTEL
Neptune Beach Hotel, Box 83125, Mombasa
☎ *485701*

This is a family hotel with 80 rooms. A pleasant entry leads to a long and narrow plot busy with shops, Disney ice cream bar, sun loungers, and colorful furniture. There is a thatched bar by a circular pool. Undistinguished rooms are set back from the beach.

PLAZA HOTEL
Plaza Hotel, Box 88299, Mombasa
☎ *485321*

A highrise on a thin plot. There are slow elevators and tired wall-to-wall carpeting. Pool.

TRAVELLERS BEACH HOTEL
Travellers Beach Hotel, Box 87649, Mombasa
☎ *485121*

This newer hotel is divided into two sections to skirt a private beachfront property. The hotel is long and narrow. There is a white and clean lobby with a high roof, stream, and swimming canal which connects with the pool. There are lines of shops, several restaurants, and many sports. Fully equipped rooms have a double and one single bed and a TV. There is a rather unreal shopping mall atmosphere about this hotel. It's a long way to the sand.

SHANZU BEACH

After the long straight stretches of Nyali and Bamburi, there is a more intimate curve to Shanzu Beach. Even at low tide there is usually enough water for a swim here. There are major hotel properties on this beach.

SERENA BEACH HOTEL
Serena Lodges and Hotels, Box 48690, Nairobi
☎ *710511, FAX: 718103*

Imaginative arabesque architecture makes the Serena Beach one of the most interesting hotels on the coast. The buildings are a delight of whitewash, arches, and grillwork. There are lush garden courts, and a spectacular arrangement of pools. Water is a major theme of this hotel. A free-form swimming pool sparkles in the sun, there is the sound of fountains, and cool garden pools compliment white marble and colorful flowers. Beyond, the sea laps the beautiful white sand of Shanzu Beach.

The reception area sets a striking mood for the hotel. The high white ceiling has contrasting mangrove beams, and there is an entire wall of elegantly carved and arched wall niches. Lamu-style furniture with bright cushions and hanging brass lanterns continue the Swahili motif.

Although the hotel has space for more than 300 guests, its spacious grounds and rambling low layout mean that you never get the feeling of being in a large busy hotel. The management limits the size of tour groups. All the public areas look over lawns and tall palm trees towards the sea.

Serena Beach Hotel has been accepted as one of the "Leading Hotels of the World." There is something extra special about the appearance of this hotel and the services it offers. The public rooms and dining areas are particularly lovely. A host of water sport activities are included in the tariff. Champagne is poured at breakfast, and afternoon tea served on the beach.

There are several restaurants. The elegant Fountain Restaurant has white arches, cool dripping fountains, and intricately carved Lamu furniture. The restaurant spills out on to a terrace overlooking the ocean. Right on the beach, is the less formal Jahazi Grill which specializes in charcoal-grilled seafood and barbecues. Here you can eat with sand underfoot or climb to the open upper level which is built like a dhow with sails overhead. There is an air-conditioned piano bar with complimentary hot hors d'oeuvres at the cocktail hour.

The new pool at Serena Beach is lovely. Situated in the center of the hotel grounds, it is truly a focal point—eye-catching when you come out from reception. Free-form in shape, this tiled pool has cascades, and the water flows over the edges. There is also a wading pool and swim-up bar.

Safari Journal — Arrival

Through the white washed Arab archway, I can see brilliant bougainvillea and palm trees, graceful and tall next to a series of blue-green pools. Water cascades down from the lagoon-like swimming pool, and beyond that I can see the white foam of the waves breaking on the reef I can't wait to explore!

Accommodations

Guest rooms and suites are in separate whitewashed buildings which are only two or three stories high. They are rather charming, with thatched roofs, carved balconies and various shaped arches. The rooms are located in the grounds on both sides of the main buildings.

The older section is closer to the sea and has smaller rooms. This section was designed to represent an old Swahili village. Some rooms are tucked behind others. The new section, although built further back from the sea, guarantees a glimpse of the water. These rooms are bigger with far superior bathrooms.

There are several suites and some family rooms. Two VIP suites are especially luxurious with private jacuzzis. There are both twin and double bedded rooms.

All of the 166 rooms are furnished in Lamu style, and although the decor is interesting, the old wing rooms are small and rather cramped. Swahili arches frame mirrors and windows. Each room has a balcony and ensuite bathroom with tub. There is air conditioning, a minibar, hair dryer, and direct dial telephone. *Our Favorites:* #221 in New Wing—corner room with great sea view and sunning balcony. Front rooms in old section have good sea views (#116 and 121 sleep four).

Special Offerings

Swimming pool, water sports center (windsurfing, sailing and snorkeling free to hotel guests), scuba diving, deep sea fishing, dhow cruising by arrangement, four floodlit tennis courts, air-conditioned squash courts, minigolf, pool table, table tennis, conference room, hairdresser, free shuttle bus to Mombasa.

Off Notes

All standard bedrooms feel somewhat cramped, too small for the grand reputation of the hotel.

HOTEL INTERCONTINENTAL MOMBASA

Hotel Intercontinental Mombasa, Box 83492, Mombasa
☎ *485811, FAX: 485437*

This hotel is somewhat unique on the Kenyan coast. It is more formal and glamorous than the laid-back tropical hotels more commonly found on these beaches. The Intercontinental features wall-to-wall carpeting, elevators, and an indoor piano lounge. Men arrive in business suits—it is not a place to wander around with sandy feet.

It has been well decorated—tasteful and with an eye to quality. The lobby is impressive with its high, huge atrium, marble floors, and fountains. There are 192 rooms on four floors. The carpeted rooms are comfortable, and are equipped with every modern convenience: telephone, color TV, minibar, air conditioning. You are reminded that you are at the beach when you open the sliding glass doors onto your private balcony which is angled to give you a good view of the wonderful pool below and a glimpse of the sea.

The large pool has water flowing over the edges and a swim-up bar. It is set in lovely grounds filled with gardens and palm trees bordering the beach.

Accommodations

In addition to the standard rooms there are two presidential suites, one executive, and six junior suites. Best Sea Views: Standard rooms # 340-343, 312-315, 411, and 439.

Other Offerings

Many restaurants, conference facilities, banquet halls, a casino, and a sports center with health spa.

OYSTER BAY BEACH HOTEL

Oyster Bay Beach Hotel, Box 10252, Bamburi, Mombasa
☎ *485531, FAX: 485963*

Perched on a rocky cliff, this new hotel of 35 suites overlooks an attractive lagoon-shaped pool and the ocean beyond. The beach here is very small. An elaborate jetty for watersports is under construction.

The hotel's clean modern architecture is dazzling white next to dark rock, bougainvillea color, and blue-green sea. Curving balconies provide a large shaded terrace with a sea view for each suite. There is Lamu-style furniture, and sitting rooms have fans. Bedrooms have air conditioning and nice private bathrooms with bidet. Two bedrooms per suite are possible.

The dining room is on a terrace above the pool, a seafood grill is in the planning, and there is 24-hour room service. The pool is surrounded by rock gardens with a waterfall and swim-up bar. Resort activities are planned.

THE AFRICAN SAFARI CLUB

African Safari Club, Box 81443, Mombasa
☎ *485906/7/8, FAX: 485909*

North of Mombasa there is a chain of very clean, very safe, high standard hotels owned and operated by this German travel company. In all the hotels, the public rooms tend to be spacious and dramatic. Accommodations are in simple and basic rooms, each with small bathroom including shower, toilet and basin. The hotels have an attractive choice of restaurants, shops and sports facilities, with some of these being shared by two or more hotels. Each has a swimming pool and some kind of beach access. They are fanatic about security and usually have larger-than-average well-fenced grounds. If you enjoy a real German atmosphere and cuisine, these hotels will please.

The hotels are Bahari Beach with sister hotels Silver Beach and Silver Star at English Point; Coral Beach, Palm Beach, Shanzu Beach, Paradise Beach, Malaika, Dolphin, and Flamingo Beach at Shanzu; Club Sea Horse and the nearby Manarani at Kilifi Creek; and Watamu Beach.

In addition Mara Buffalo Camp in the Maasai Mara and Masai Safari Lodge near Nairobi National Park are part of this chain.

Reservations can be made through one of their European offices or by contacting African Safari Club in Mombasa.

KIKAMBALA BEACH

Kikambala is a long straight beach, 28 kilometers north of Mombasa. We found no hotels on this beach which we would especially recommend.

LE SOLEIL

Le Soleil, Box 84737, Mombasa
☎ *(01251) 2195, FAX: (01251) 2164*

This is a modern condominium-style complex. It is built on a narrow plot with most of the rooms set back quite a distance from the ocean. Le Soleil is a family resort with standard rooms, suites, and three bedroom villas. There are equipped kitchens for self-catering and a choice of restaurants. The large pool has a swim-up bar. The rooms were less spacious or well-furnished than expected. Although this was a new complex, there were already signs of poor maintenance.

MOMBASA SUN AND SAND

Mombasa Sun and Sand, Box 2, Kikambala
☎ *(01251) 2621, FAX: (01251) 2133*

This is a sprawling thatched resort with tall palms and lots of bougainvillea. It caters to large package tours (queues for meals), has a conference center for 200, and offers many sports activities. There are two pools, one is seawater. Accommodations are in small cottages with thatched roofs and air conditioning. Some have nice sea views. The hotel looks tropical and exotic, but is rather run down.

THOUSAND PALMS

Club Thousand Palms Ltd., Box 84 Kikamabala via Mombasa
☎ *(0125) 32165, FAX: (0125) 32161*

A very ordinary package-tour hotel. The public toilets were dirty when we visited.

WHISPERING PALMS HOTEL

Whispering Palms Hotel, Box 5, Kikambala
☎ *(01251) 2004, Telex: 21018*

This hotel is rather a hodge-podge with heavy concrete structures as well as thatch. There are three small pools, peeling paint and pay-as-you-go sports. It caters to package tours and has a cut-rate atmosphere.

KILIFI

Kilifi Creek is a major break in the coastline between Mombasa and Malindi. Before 1991 there was no bridge spanning this wide creek, and travelers crossed by car ferry. There are few hotels in Kilifi, but many interesting private homes. It is a popular sailing and boating center.

BAOBAB LODGE

Baobab Lodge, Box 40683, Nairobi
☎ *222229, FAX: 332170*

This small and casual lodge is built on top of a rocky cliff overlooking the ocean at Kilifi. Rondavels are scattered around a nicely shaded property. There are 26 attractively decorated rooms with Masai murals on the walls and spacious verandas. Most rooms do not offer sea views.

There is a lovely pool with a swim-up bar and views over the ocean, but there is not much of a beach. Steps down through the rocks and past baobab trees lead to a small cove with more coral than sand underfoot. The lodge offers diving, and owns a glass-bottom boat. You can walk to the reef at low tide. There is a relaxed and low-key atmosphere—a dart board hanging on a tree, private shady places to lie and read, and a cool, open-sided dining area under high thatch.

KILIFI BAY RESORT HOTEL & VILLAGE

DEINSA S.A., Box 3092, CH 6901 Lugano
FAX: 0041-091-228490
or
Box 156, Kilifi
☎ *(0125) 2511, FAX: (1252) 225*

This Italian hotel can accommodate 85 and is typically booked in Europe. De-signed and decorated with flair, it feels spacious and exotic. There are high thatched roofs, large open air verandas, carved Lamu-style furniture, and lush and colorful tropical vegetation. Public buildings are set well back from the beach and look over the pool and past palm trees to the ocean beyond. Accom-modations are in three-roomed bungalows, some close to the beach. Stone steps lead down to a long beach with a thatched shelter for shade. Invigorating music was being played for scuba diving lesson in the pool.

TAKAUNGU HOUSE

Wilderness Trails (K) Ltd./Bush Homes of East Africa Ltd.,
Box 56923, Nairobi
☎ *506139, FAX: 502739*

On a private curve of beach, far from the hotels of Mombasa and Malindi, is Takaungu House. Located south of Kilifi, the house is named after the neigh-boring small village of Takaungu—supposedly the oldest slave port in Kenya.

Phil and Charlotte Mason are your hosts. Guests stay in a very old slave trad-er's house with thick whitewashed walls, giant roof beams, and shutters on the windows. It is close to the ocean. The Masons themselves stay nearby on the property in a newly constructed Arab-style house.

Takaungu House is special because of the wonderful setting, the atmosphere of tranquillity and timelessness, and the delightful hosts. The small bay is edged with dark rocks and has golden sand seldom marred by human footprints. The big old baobab trees and the hoary stone ruins bear silent witness to history, Af-rica, and inspired imaginings. The house was recorded on a map drawn on the HMS *Stork* as she passed in 1844.

We ate a delicious home-cooked lunch in the cool of the old house. A horse peered through the door, blocking the bright light which shimmered in from the heat and ocean outside. He reluctantly obeyed Charlotte's entreaty not to enter. You can ride horses when you stay with the Masons. You can also use their boats.

Phil operates a boat yard, and you may choose to join him sailing or perhaps explore the nearby creek in their dingy—have a barbecue on the beach of an island. There are three guest bedrooms, each with functional bathrooms. The house is comfortable and lived-in—lots of books, slip-covered couches. There is a very small swimming pool. The Masons can arrange to pick you up from the airport—Mombasa, or Malindi. The tariff includes all food and activities except deep sea fishing. They close for May and the first half of June.

MIRELLA RICCIARDI'S KILIFI HOME

Safcon Travel Services, Box 59224, Nairobi
☎ *503265, FAX: 506824*

At this time of writing, the accomplished photographer, author and traveller, Mirella Ricciardi, is planning to join the ranks of those offering hosted accommodations in small, select, private settings. In Mirella's case, the setting is her interesting and attractive home in Kilifi.

There are actually two houses, perched high on the banks of the Kilifi Creek. Steps lead down to a small private sandy beach, and massive baobab trees add a timeless feel. The newer house has an impressive high-thatched roof with a large opening through which bougainvillea spills. Below is a wide veranda. There are no windows—just big arched openings and metal grillwork. There is an artist's touch everywhere—carvings on wooden pole supports, relief designs in the plaster work.

The house has two bedrooms downstairs, a sleeping loft up a ladder and one bathroom. There are no fans, and it can be hot and plagued by mosquitos. The other house is an older coastal home and is currently being redecorated. It has a wonderfully spacious living/dining room with lovely views of trees and water. There are two rubber dinghies and dogs. Mirella is a strong-minded woman with a penchant for ambiance, lively conversations and good cuisine.

KILDINI

Kesana, Box 39672, Nairobi
☎ *749062, FAX: 741636*

This spacious and airy Arab-style house belongs to Michael and Jean Skinner (who own Juani Farm in Molo). Kildini has three double bedrooms and can cater for up to six people. The house is surrounded by delightful gardens, and there is a swimming pool. Steps lead to a private beach on Kilifi creek.

The Skinners can host your stay and show you neighboring points of interest. The house can also be rented with house staff on a "self-service" basis. We did not visit Kildini, but did see photographs of this very attractive and exotic-looking house. Apparently it is right on the creek, not far from the new bridge.

WATAMU

Watamu, south of Malindi is best known for the Watamu Marine National Park—a spectacular coral reef alive with tropical fish and only a short boat ride, or energetic swim at low tide. The beach is really a series of wide sandy bays separated by rocky outcrops. The area is distinctive with its craggy rock islands dotting the bays. Dark and jagged with narrow necks, they invite exploration. At low tide it is possible to walk out to many of these strange isolated formations. Crabs skitter out of sight, and impossible shapes have been sculptured by the sea. Rock pools ring the islands revealing their treasures of shells, seaweed and bright fish each day when the tide is out.

The coastline is more interesting than some of the popular long sandy stretches such as Diani Beach south of Mombasa. Watamu has only a handful of hotels, but there are many private beachfront homes. At certain times of year, (especially May until the end of September) a great deal of seaweed is washed on to the Watamu Beaches.

There is much to see and do in the Watamu area:

Watamu Marine National Park
This is one of the better places on the Kenyan coast for snorkeling.

Big Game Fishing
Many people come to Watamu for the big game fishing.

Mida Creek
Peaceful daily dhow trips are offered on Mida Creek. This broad stretch of water lined by tidal mud flats and mangroves is home to a multitude of birds and is a noted migratory stop. These dhow trips are operated through Ocean Sports, but any Watamu hotel can book them for you.

Gede Ruins
This Swahili City was mysteriously abandoned in the 14th Century. Today you can wander through the 18 hectares of these interesting and thought-provoking ruins. Sightseers can also visit the Giriama Village nearby to see drumming and dancing.

Arabuko-Sokoke Forest
This is the largest remaining stretch of lowland coastal forest in East Africa. It shelters rare trees and animals and is of particular interest to birdwatchers.

Watamu Village
Explore this fishing community—many souvenir sellers.

HEMINGWAYS

Hemingways, Box 267, Watamu
☎ *(0122) 32624, FAX: (0122) 32256*

    Hemingways is an intimate, privately owned hotel built right at the edge of the beach—the ocean can be seen from most rooms. The impression is one of pristine whitewash and spacious stone terraces. There are two sparkling blue swimming pools, and a multitude of very tall coconut palms continually wave in the breeze. The hotel exudes a casual "upmarket" elegance. It is known for deep-sea fishing and is also a romantic and relaxing getaway, popular with honeymooners. What makes Hemingways special is its attention to detail, service and pampering touches. You will be delighted by the vases of roses everywhere, the welcome basket of strawberries in your room and the interesting menus.

A newcomer to Watamu, Hemingways was built in 1988 on the site of the old "Seafarers" Hotel. The hotel was raised nine feet so that it would look down on the sea. From the beach there is a fortresslike wall giving a rather forbidding aspect to the hotel, but when you are above, on the terrace or sitting in the dining room, you have lovely views down over the ocean and across the bay with its intriguing rock formations.

The bar, dining room, and reception area are in huge white rondavels with dramatic soaring thatched roofs, so distinctive of the area. The main dining room has a sunken central area for buffet, band and dance floor. Tables are arrayed around the raised circumference as well as in a "minstrel's gallery" on a higher level. Tables near windows have lovely views. Candlelight dining is out-side on the terrace during the gentle *Kaskazi* (seasonal northeast wind) from late November to Easter. During the rest of the year, when the stronger *Kusi* blows, all meals are served in the main restaurant.

Hemingways places an emphasis on dining. There is elegance in the starched tablecloths, fresh flowers at each table, and candlelit dinners. As well as a set menu, there are à la carte choices. You can also be served unusual and tasty snacks at poolside. We had breakfast crepes smothered with strawberries and yo-gurt—a real treat. Afternoon teas are included in the tariff.

The bar is a large and pleasant room with big doors opening out to the ocean terrace. It sports impressive fishing trophies such as a 750 lb. blue marlin. There is a friendly sit-up central bar and comfortable rush chairs around tables. The feeling is airy, natural, and uncluttered. The hotel's intimate nature combined with its popularity among British Kenyans and fishermen means that the bar is a place where new friends are made and fishing tales are swapped over many a drink. We were reminded by the manager that the name Hemingways conjures not only images of Africa and fishing, but of drinking as well.

Many clients come to Hemingways for the deep-sea fishing. The hotel owns several twin-engine boats and charters others. Full-day and half-day fishing trips are offered for both novice and skilled fishermen from August to May. The main billfish are sailfish and marlin.

Quotes:

> *"The original dream for Hemingways was freezing cold drinks, really good food and sport." Garry Cullen, Managing Director.*

> *"It's a class act all the way" A happy American fisherman return-ing from a deep sea fishing trip with his family. His young son was handed a framed polaroid photograph of the family with the fish they'd caught. Staff were asking which fish they would like pre-pared for their dinner.*

Accommodations

After recent renovations, the hotel has a capacity for 175 guests. There are two wings: an older sea-view wing which has double rooms, and a brand new "superior" wing which includes triples and suites. The bedrooms of the older wing are disappointingly small for a hotel of this caliber. They are, however, close to the ocean, and afford the best sea views. The new wing is two and three-stories high and angles back from the beach. You can see to the ocean beyond the gardens and swimming pools.

Safari Journal — Friday

We sit in comfort on the stone patio in front of the bar.
Below, the big blue Hemingway's sign hangs above
the fish weighing area. The tension mounts; the crowd
is full of camaraderie at many binoculars focus on the sea.
The deep sea fishing boats rock over the waves
flying catch flags. Six white flags... six fish over 30 lbs,
one black flag ... one Kingfish. The bar will be lively tonight!
Yesterday, honeymooners from London caught
a big sailfish ~ the sail an incredible, deep iridescent blue,
the novice fisherman all smiles

I can't wait ~ my husband and eleven year old son
have been out since 6:00 a.m. Their first fishing trip ever.
Did the seasick pill work? Hope my son caught something.

All rooms have air conditioning, mosquito-nets, fans and a safe for valuables. All of the rooms except the suites have a balcony and a shower. The suites have bathtubs in addition to showers and a large sitting area instead of a balcony. Sliding glass doors open the rooms to light and air and distant sea views. *Our Favorites* for being closest to the sea—old wing #103-109 (ground floor) and new wing #145 (ground floor), #373 (top floor). Even in the bedrooms at Hemingways you are treated to many thoughtful extras—there is a poem and rosebud on your pillow at night and a bottle of Hemingways' mineral water next to your bed.

Special Options

Fishing (deep sea and inshore), snorkeling trips in a glass-bottom boat, windsurfing, diving, dhow trips on Mida Creek, free trips to Malindi for shopping and to the nearby Gede ruins, free transfer to and from Malindi Airport, day-room facilities with shower (extra charge), video room, small boutique and sundry shop.

Off Notes

Limited shade, terraces get hot... Old wing bedrooms are small... Small, barred windows and fussy curtains tend to hide the wonderful views from the old-wing bedrooms... Remember that during the off-season the beaches can be full of unsightly seaweed. Rough seas will mean that deep-sea fishing is suspended.

TURTLE BAY BEACH CLUB

Turtle Bay Beach Club, Box 457, Malindi
☎ *(0122) 32080, FAX: (0122) 32268*

Turtle Bay is a larger family-style hotel which operates on an all-inclusive resort system similar to a Club Med. Included are meals, snacks, most drinks and a range of sporting activities (watersports as well as tennis, mini golf etc.) This hotel is appealing for its relaxed ambiance, its range of activities for families, and the pleasantly shaded area overlooking the beach and ocean.

The focal point of the hotel is the pool area. The large rectangular pool has a diving board. To the side, and sheltered by makuti thatch, are table-tennis, darts and snooker. There is also a giant chess set with wooden African playing pieces. A thatched bar and restaurant at poolside serves a snack and à la carte menu. It is open-sided and has views of the ocean through a stand of palm trees. Stretching from the pool to the beach is an area well-shaded by mature palms and other indigenous trees where guests can lie on padded lounge chairs placed on the sand. There are pleasant sea breezes, lovely views of the beach and ocean and shelter from the hot sun.

The hotel is built on a slope—there are winding paths and series of wide cement steps. Low-rise accommodation blocks are reached through tropical gardens vivid with bougainvillea. Some rooms have good ocean views, but most are set further back, only glimpsing the sea through palm trees. The main dining area is open to gardens and fishponds—but has no sea-view or sea breezes. The food tends to be rather unremarkable—generous safari buffets predominate. There is evening entertainment ranging from bingo nights in the large and rather functional lobby lounge, to acrobatic performances around the pool with the night sky and waving palms for an added touch of the exotic.

Children (ages 4–12 years) can join the Children's Mini Club with various activities and programs (videos, swimming, painting etc.) under supervision.

Water activities at Turtle Bay include windsurfing and scuba diving. Glass-bottom boats make the short trip out to the marine park for snorkeling. We hear that there is now an expert who will accompany you on your snorkeling trips, pointing out and explaining items of interest as you swim along.

This hotel is popular with families and is also booked by European tour groups—predominantly German.

Accommodations

There are 154 rooms, all with private balconies, ceiling fans and ensuite bathrooms. Most rooms are in fairly large low-rise white structures. There are also deluxe rooms which are somewhat larger and newer. These rooms are in smaller thatched three-story units. *Best Sea Views*: Deluxe Rooms #43,44, and 45. Beach Block #1–5.

OCEAN SPORTS

Ocean Sports Ltd., Box 100 Watamu
☎ *(0122) 32288, FAX: (0122) 32266*

Ocean Sports opened in 1957 and was the first hotel at Watamu. This small family-run hotel is popular with British Kenyans. The hotel is ultracasual and re-laxed—bare feet and first names. It appeals to families and does a lot of repeat business.

As its name suggests, there is an emphasis on ocean sports. There is a diving school and opportunities for deep-sea fishing. The bar is alive with fishing tales and heavy with fishing trophies. (It boasts more impressive catches than its up-market neighbor, Hemingways, but has been at it a lot longer.)

The bar and dining rooms have good views over the ocean, and there is a large outdoor terrace just steps off the beach. A good basic seafood menu is offered. There is a smallish pool and many paths winding among colorful bougainvillea. Ocean Sports offers dhow trips on Mida Creek. Tennis and squash are also available on the premises.

Ocean Sports has character. It is low-key and has an established air—quite a contrast to some of the glitzier, more uniform large hotels which cater primarily to package tours from Europe.

Accommodations

A series of cottages are built along a small hill behind the main hotel. There are 25 standard rooms and four air-conditioned rooms. The rooms are basic and quite spacious, each with a private bathroom. There is a charming lack of uniformity. One cottage is a quaint little double story "house," another has four double rooms and a large shared veranda. Afternoon tea is served on your private veranda. Some cottages glimpse the sea through vegetation.

Off Note

Rooms are quite far from the sea and across the parking area.

BLUE BAY VILLAGE
Blue Bay Village, Box 162, Watamu
☎ *(0122) 32626, FAX: (0122) 32422*

This is another Italian hotel with architectural and decorative flair. It has wonderful soaring thatch, fresh whitewash, and opulent use of Lamu furniture and rich fabrics. This hotel has an unusual central "courtyard" which is spacious and open to the sky. It is dominated by a pool and surrounded by boutiques, a restaurant, lounge areas and a simply beautiful high-roofed lobby. The restaurant serves Italian cuisine and has a window wall overlooking the ocean.

You walk on to the beach through a large carved door. Built at the edge of a bay, Blue Bay Village uses two beaches If one is marred by seaweed, the other is usually clean white coral sand. Beach loungers are arranged on the sand and a volleyball net invites some exercise.

Accommodations are separate thatched cottages in verdant gardens. Most do not have ocean views. Although the clientele is almost exclusively Italian, this hotel can be booked in Kenya.

BARRACUDA INN
Barracuda Inn, Box 59, Watamu
☎ *(0122) 32061 Telex: 21347 BARCDA KE*

The Barracuda Inn is an Italian managed "village" resort with 64 rooms. There are high thatched roofs and whitewashed walls. Guests stay in cottages which are built in rows running back from the beach. Barracuda Inn is on Blue Bay Lagoon (around the corner from Blue Bay Village). Guests tend to congregate around the large swimming pool. Sports offerings include tennis, squash, gymnastics and ping-pong.

TEMPLE POINT VILLAGE
I Viaggi Del Ventaglio,
Via de Amicis 43, 20123, Milano, Italy
☎ *5818644 (Milano)*
or Box 296, Watamu
☎ *(0122) 32057, FAX: (0122) 32289*

This is a stylish thatched village with two swimming pools and accommodations for 180. You must either book through Italy or take your chances as a walk-in guest. The two-story cottages have ceiling fans, mosquito nets, Lamu furniture, and are attractively decorated in the Swahili-style. There is a dramatic view of the Indian Ocean from the bar and restaurant. Unfortunately, rough coral rock prevents guests from ocean swimming in front of Temple Point, but hotel boats will take you to a private sandy beach nearby. There are tennis courts and water sports.

MRS. SIMPSON'S

Mrs. Simpson's, Box 33, Watamu
☎ *(0122) 32023*

Mrs Simpson has been hosting guests at her rambling and informal beach home for nearly 20 years. She has lived in Kenya since 1923, and at her advanced age is still active in marine conservation.

There is room for seven people on a full-board basis, but Mrs. Simpson often takes more, and somehow finds everyone a bed, mosquito net, lamp and sheets. In her words, she "runs the house as a party." The guests are a mixed group of families, researchers and young world travellers who are happy with basic but friendly accommodations. They all eat together with Mrs. Simpson, and afternoon tea is a communal affair. As Mrs. Simpson says, her house "is not a smooth place"—showers are cold, some share bathrooms, and some guests even sleep on the roof.

Her trained staff can take people goggling or birding in the Arabuko-Sokoke Forest, and guests can rent the house sailboat. The house is very informal and full of old worn furniture and books. Guests were complimentary about the meals and especially enjoy the company of Mrs. Simpson, who is a keen naturalist.

MALINDI AND VICINITY

Malindi city codes ☎ *0123 - #, FAX: 0123 - #*

Malindi is the second largest city on the Kenyan coast. There are trendy boutiques and shops, many restaurants, and a colorful outdoor market. It is famous for the Malindi Marine National Park and deep sea fishing. Many of the beach resorts have a significant Italian influence.

Most of the hotels are strung out along the beachfront to the south of Malindi's town center. Those closest to town resemble city hotels. There are also many hotels which are further inland and have no beach access. We did not visit all of these hotels.

INDIAN OCEAN LODGE

Safcon Travel Services, Box 59224, Nairobi
☎ *503265, FAX: 506824*

This prestigious lodge in Malindi accommodates guests in sumptuous Arab-style houses. The lodge has four acres of private property and is built on a promontory overlooking the ocean. There is great beauty and a sense of the exotic about this unusual and exclusive lodge. Your first impression is of wonderful color contrasts—brilliant white arches against a vivid profusion of bougainvillea and the deep blueness of the Indian Ocean gleaming beyond. Timeless baobabs twist with ponderous grace.

Indian Ocean Lodge offers something similar to a private homestay since your hosts, Peter and Joanna Nicholas, live here and are familiar with the surrounding area and its history. The difference is that the lodge looks more like a perfectly arranged museum than a "worn at the corners" family home. You want to stop and admire the lovely Swahili furniture, the carpets, the wall decorations.

The lodge guarantees exclusivity. A maximum of only eight guests are accommodated at a time. The guests stay in spacious quarters with four-poster beds, sitting areas, and private patios or balconies. All has been tastefully decorated in keeping with the Arab style of the buildings. There is an indoor-outdoor feel about the lodge—open arches, outdoor stairways, breezes blowing and bright clear light streaming into rooms. The whitewash dazzles the eyes.

There is a swimming pool within the walled property, and you must climb down many steps to the sea. A boat belonging to the lodge can be used for fishing or snorkeling. The rates include your hosts collecting you from the airport and driving you within a 40 kilometers radius for shopping or sightseeing. They will also accompany guests to tennis, golf, squash, windsurfing, or scuba diving. Deep-sea fishing can be arranged at an extra charge. Full board rates include alcohol, soft drinks and daily laundry.

The atmosphere and ambiance of a privately hosted stay depend to a large extent on the hosts. Unfortunately, since we could not arrange to spend the night or sample the food at the Indian Ocean Lodge, we can comment only on the physical nature of the lodge—which is truly outstanding.

MALINDI BEACH CLUB

Malindi Beach Club, P.O. Box 868, Malindi
☎ *20928, FAX: 30103*

The Malindi Beach Club stresses privacy and a Swahili atmosphere in its 24 newly renovated rooms. With its private beach fronting Malindi's marine park, you can sample all marine sports, take advantage of nearby disco and casino, play golf or tennis, go for morning horse rides along the beach, or just enjoy palm-shaded courtyards and terraces, some with a sea view.

The peaceful harmony of an Arabian village is suggested by an irregular grouping of white two-story structures, accented by arches, black grillwork, and balconies. Tile pathways meander through shaded gardens and into courtyards. There are two saltwater swimming pools, a club house, bar, piano and barbecue. The restaurant menu features fresh seafood and Italian cuisine. The Swahili theme is accented inside with fine antique pieces of brass, chests and oriental carpets. All is well coordinated and tastefully done.

The rooms have Swahili decor with tile or wood floors, air conditioning, mosquito net, refrigerator-bar, telephone, and private bathroom.

KILILI BAHARINI

Francorosso International Spa, Via Veneto, Rome, Italy
☎ *(06) 4457055*

The unique layout of the Kilili Baharini gives it an intimate and personal atmosphere. The spacious thatched villas are arranged in groups of three or four around a small swimming pool. There are a total of three such groupings, each with its own "private" pool. Nearer the ocean is a larger communal pool and a dining and bar area.

The landscaping is exotic with many trees and flowering shrubs. The villas are oversized, with loads of veranda space and Lamu furniture colorful with kanga cushions. A high platform above the veranda is reached by ladder and is yet another private space to relax. The place has flair and offers an exotic and unique concept. Most clients are Italian.

KINGFISHER LODGE

Kingfisher Group, Box 29, Malindi
☎ *21168*

Kingfisher Lodge is the Malindi home base for the exclusive family-run business which also includes luxury tented safaris and big game fishing. The extended Paul family (British Kenyan) are experienced hosts, guides and fishermen.

The inland lodge has four deluxe cottages set in beautifully maintained gardens around a sparkling swimming pool. These thatched cottages have spacious bedrooms with air conditioning and ceiling fans. Delicious home-cooked meals are served in the open-air dining rondavel next to the pool. Tennis, squash, golf and windsurfing are included in the tariff. Local trips by arrangement at extra cost.

WHITE ELEPHANT SEA LODGE
Turisanda: International Tour Operator,
Via Poerio 2/A 20129 Milano

Classy and elegant, this smaller lodge caters almost exclusively to Italians. It can not be booked within Kenya, but if there is space, they will accept walk-ins. Beautiful furniture and unusual artwork distinguish the White Elephant. There are hunting trophies on the walls, elephant hide covers the reception desk, and beautiful views of flowers and water are framed by carved doors and windows. An aura of nostalgia and refined taste pervades. You may wish you spoke Italian.

There are 40 spacious rooms with Lamu furniture and air conditioning. Rooms do not have sea views.

THE DRIFTWOOD BEACHCLUB
The Bunson Group, Box 45456, Nairobi
☎ *337604, FAX: 723599*

Like its name, the Driftwood has been around for a long time, gaining character and some forgivable grunge. This low-key and personal family-style hotel is a long-time favorite of British Kenyans. It is known for its relaxed and friendly atmosphere, popular bar and good food. The attractive dining room and bar are open to breezes and sea views, and the beach is only steps away.

Accommodations are in individual bandas. The rooms are rudimentary. Some have sea views and air conditioning. Rooms closest to the ocean are #21, 22 and 25. There are two luxury family villas, a pleasant pool and a diving center.

Appreciate the Driftwood for its character.

SILVERSANDS VILLAS

Silversand Beach Cottages Ltd. Box 91, Malindi
☎ *20407*

This is a small, family run hotel on a long, narrow plot. The hotel can accommodate 62 guests in a series of cottages and larger family villas. Although most of these are some distance from the beach and breezes, they are surrounded by gardens.

The rooms have parquet floors and Lamu style furniture and each has a private patio. There are ceiling fans and air conditioning, and there are bidets in the bathrooms. Reserve the "Malindi" villa if you want to be closest to the beach.

Two swimming pools are in the central garden area along with a large makuti-roofed restaurant with adjoining bar. Especially appealing is the natural thatched bar and restaurant built right on the beach—checked cloths on the tables and sand underfoot.

KIVULINI BEACH HOTEL

Kivulini Beach Hotel, Box 142, Malindi
☎ *20898 Telex: 21335*

This hotel is built on the edge of a rocky cove with an attractive walkway by the sea. The clientele is predominantly Italian. Accommodations are 36 thatched rondavel cottages with private verandas. Kivulini Beach hotel has eye-catching wooden furniture, a free-form swimming pool and a well-stocked gift shop. The hotel is about five kilometers from town and reached by a sandy road through natural bush.

COCONUT VILLAGE

Coconut Village, Box 868, Malindi
☎ *20938, Telex: 21459*

Coconut Village is an Italian resort with flair. There are two-story thatched beach villas with Arab style furniture. Some rooms have sea views. The pool and restaurant are set back from the beach. There is a casual atmosphere and nightly entertainment.

EDEN ROC HOTEL
Tropicana Hotels Ltd. P.O. Box 350 Malindi
☎ *20480*

This large city-style hotel in Malindi town has been recently renovated and looks fresh and clean. It caters primarily to inexpensive German package tours. There are sea views from the lobby and some rooms. It is a long walk through gardens, down terraces and past two swimming pools to the beach.

AFRICAN DREAM VILLAGE
African Dream Village, Box 939, Malindi
☎ *20442, FAX: 20119*
or Pan Travel Viaggi Turistici, SA 6900, Lugano, Switzerland
☎ *(091) 232043, FAX: (091) 226286*

Set in natural tropical gardens, the large African Dream Village can accommodate approximately 120 guests in a high-thatch complex on the beach near Casuarina Point and the Malindi Marine Park. Public rooms and restaurants are airy, a semi-circular swimming pool curls around a swim-up bar. Rooms are air-conditioned with private bathrooms. There are many sports activities, a disco, and a conference center. This hotel caters primarily to tour groups from Europe.

BLUE MARLIN
Blue Marlin, Box 54, Malindi
☎ *20440 Telex: 0987/21410*

This city hotel on the Malindi beach front has 145 basic rooms with air conditioning. There are sports facilities and two pools. It is a long walk through the grounds to the beach.

BOUGAN VILLAGE
Bougan Village, Box 721, Malindi
☎ *21205, FAX: 5242139 (Italy)*

This large Malindi resort on 16 acres is quite a distance from the beach. For guests who want the beach experience, there is continuous bus service as well as a beach snack bar. Rooms and bungalows are located in gardens and have ensuite bathrooms and Lamu-style furnishings. The thatched club has a res-

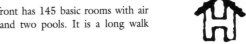

taurant, two bars and a swimming pool. There are two tennis courts in the park. The influence here is Italian, with disco dancing at night.

DORADO COTTAGES

Hotel Bldgs. Ltd., Box 868, Malindi
☎ *20252*

Pretty thatched whitewash cottages are closely spaced in bougainvillea gardens around two pools. There are currently 22 cottages and more are planned. Each cottage has a living room, bedroom and kitchen with refrigerator but no stove. Two extra beds can be added. There are fans. Full-service dining is in an older house overlooking the beach. The beach access is down a hill from the site. The cottages do not see the ocean. It is under Italian management and caters to tour groups.

LAWFORDS HOTEL

Lawfords Hotel, Box 54, Malindi
☎ *20440*

See "Blue Marlin." This is next door, run by the same company and even more down-market.

PALM TREE CLUB

Palm Tree Club, Box 180, Malindi
☎ *20397 Telex: OVERTURCO 21214*

This large Italian resort is right next to the Malindi golf course about 600 meters from the ocean. There is a shuttle for continuous transportation to and from the beach.

The circular construction of the main building surrounds a large swimming pool. Double rooms overlook the pool or are located in separate cottages on the extensive grounds. Tall thatched roofs ensure coolness, and there is an interesting combination of Lamu-style furniture, zebra-skin rugs, African wood carvings of tribal fetish statues and bouquets of tropical flowers. Each room has a full bathroom.

In addition to a restaurant with à la carte menu, there are sports facilities for tennis, golf, and bowling. Riding stables on the grounds provide horses for the resort riding school or for free riding in the forests or on the beaches. Italian films are shown regularly.

SCORPIO VILLAS

Scorpio Enterprises Ltd., Box 368, Malindi
☎ *20194, FAX: 21250*

This is a maze of large cottages set close together. The ocean is nowhere in sight but can be reached by hiking along a small footpath. The cottages are furnished in Lamu style and have equipped kitchens with fridges. There is a restaurant and three swimming pools.

STEPHANIE SEA HOUSE

Stephanie Sea House, Box 583, Malindi
☎ *20720*

A primarily Italian resort, Stephanie Sea House has 80 beds. A pool and raised restaurant overlook the beach and ocean. Cottage rooms are set far from the sea and close together. There is high thatch and Lamu-style furniture.

THE TROPICAL VILLAGE

The Tropical Village, Box 68, Malindi
☎ *(0123) 20256, FAX: (0123) 20788*
or Pan Travel Viaggi Turistici, SA 6900, Lugano, Switzerland
☎ *(091) 232043, FAX: (091) 226286*

The Tropical Village is another Swahili-style hotel on the beach which caters to European tour groups. There are tropical gardens, whitewash and thatch, Lamu furniture and a free-form swimming pool. The "village" accommodates approximately 60 in several double story buildings.

A focal point is the large open-sided restaurant serving seafood and Italian specialties. There are many sporting activities and nightly entertainment.

MALINDI TO TANA RIVER

Up the coast from Malindi (and south of Lamu) are two unusual and more remote places to stay. One is a tented camp sheltered by dunes, and the other offers grass shack beach accommodation. There is also a large Italian resort complex under construction—Angel Bay.

CHE-SHALE

Che-Shale, Box 857, Malindi
☎ *20676*

At Che-Shale, the accommodations are a step above camping, the food is superb, and the location a remote and sandy beach. It is romantic and rustic. Built on a deserted beach, 20 kilometers north of Malindi, Che-Shale is reached by 4-wheel drive or you can ride there from the Kibokoni Riding Center.

COAST: MALINDI to LAMU & NORTH

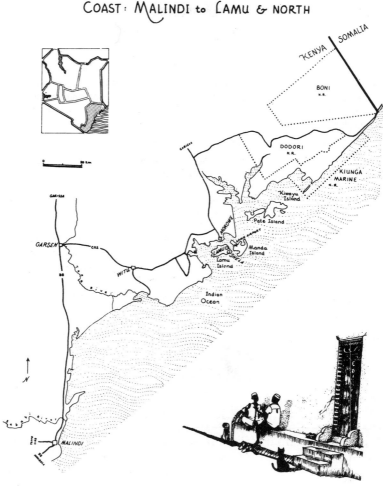

Accommodations in ten small makuti-mat shacks are spread among the sand dunes. The location is bright and hot with little natural shade or ground cover. The sand underfoot can burn, and eyes crinkle in the glare.

The cool makuti restaurant serves world-class seafood with a gourmet Italian taste. We enjoyed deep-fried seaweed, fresh cracked mangrove crab, and char-grilled sea fish. The bar is interesting and comfortable with Lamu beds, brass accents, and huge floor cushions covered in kanga cloth.

It is pleasant to swim in front of Che Shale—the beach is sandy and deserted, and at certain tides sandbars stretch out into the ocean. There are plenty of opportunities for long walks and bird-watching, and fishing and sailing can be arranged. The wide beach curves to a rocky point where you can snorkel. At low tide it is possible to take a 4-wheel drive vehicle along the sand to discover and explore even more remote bays.

Accommodations

Each makuti shack has a double bed and basic bathroom with chemical toilets and safari pull shower. There is an electrical generator which provides light for the tents until midnight. A shaded veranda in front of each shack has a daybed—private and peaceful. *Shack Choices:* # 9 & 10 for sea views, # 5 for bird-watching, # 1 for honeymooners, and #3,5,9 for triple occupancy.

Off Notes

Hard to book through local Italian owners in Malindi... Tour group day-trippers can come for lunch at a separate restaurant... Angel Bay Resort, a large Italian complex with shops and condominiums, is being constructed nearby.

Che-Shale closes from the end of April to the middle of July.

TANA DELTA CAMP

Robin Hurt Safaris, Box 24988, Nairobi
☎ *882826, FAX: 882939*

Tana Delta Camp is a unique and unusual experience. It takes time and resolve of purpose to get there. When you finally arrive, you feel privileged to be in such an isolated and unspoiled place—a mixture of beach and creek, sandy beaches and mangrove-lined waterways and only a handful of other guests.

Tana River Delta is a small, tented camp where a branch of the Tana River meets the sea. The camp, sheltered behind high sand dunes, looks out over a broad stretch of river. Climb over the dunes, and on the other side, surf pounds onto miles of deserted sandy beach.

It is not simple to get to Tana River Delta. Most guests are met in Malindi by the camp vehicle and drive north for over three and a half hours through thick thorn scrub and doum palms. You might see topi, buffalo, waterbuck. When you reach a tributary of the Tana River you transfer to the "African Queen" and putter down the river for another half-hour in this converted dhow. The terrain changes from savannah to mangroves and salt bush. You pass hippos and crocodiles, and there are masses of birds. It is very hot.

You round a corner into a broad stretch of the delta and head for the camp, well-camouflaged under thatch on a bushy sand bank. There are only eight permanent tents. The heart of the camp is an open-sided rondavel which includes lounge, dining area and bar. The tents are quite close together, but natural bush has been left between them for privacy. Each tent has its own veranda, some have a glimpse of the water, and those set further back are hotter and have bush views.

Your hosts are Renaldo and Jill Retief from Malindi. Renaldo is keen to share his knowledge about the area, wildlife and history. Jill is in charge of camp cuisine—you dine mainly on fresh seafood.

There is lots to do at Tana Delta Camp. You can explore the waterways in motorized fiberglass canoes—fish, marvel at all those birds, or even go to the main mouth of the river where there are fishing villages. You can visit the raintree forest on the Tana which was a location for Lucas Film's *Young Indiana Jones Chronicles*. You are guaranteed to see hippo in the river, and this area is a favorite nesting site for crocodile.

This is an ideal place for walking. Remember to cover up and to bring mosquito repellant. You can walk for miles along deserted ocean beaches, or head inland to open acacia woodland. You can go walking in the dunes with a tribesman and look for birds and game such as the rare Tana River bushbuck. You are certain to see baboon. This area used to be a hunting block, and apparently there are still elephant and lion not far away. Over 200 species of birds are found in the area and there is a bird feeding table at camp.

There are some therapeutic mud-flats where you can immerse yourself in mud before being taken into the sea for a wash-off. A thatched shelter has been built on the surfing beach, and a cold box might be brought there so you can have a refreshing drink before tackling the feet-burning sand on the dunes. Being so close to the river delta means that the sea can sometimes be muddy.

Quotes:

> *"It was absolute magic going over the top of the dunes and seeing mile after mile of beach without another soul... I loved the total pristineness of it... I didn't know beaches like that existed anymore."*

Accommodations

The tents have ensuite bathrooms with flush toilet and showers. There is a local, coastal flavor to these comfortable tents. Bright *kanga* fabrics have been used in the decor, and the beds are made from mangrove poles. Large netted windows let in light and the occasional sea breeze. Tents #1 and 4 have a glimpse of the Tana River.

Other Offerings

Arrangements can be made for deep-sea fishing. There is an airstrip for charters (shortens the trip by two hours).

Off Notes

The main drawback of Tana Delta Camp is also its main advantage—its remoteness. You have to make time for Tana Delta... The drive from Malindi is rough, dusty and bumpy... It can be very hot, and a swim is a hike away... Tsetse flies and mosquitoes dine well.

Please Note

The minimum stay is four days/three nights... The camp is closed in the low season.

LAMU AND NORTH

In this most northern coastal area, the emphasis is on exploring Swahili culture in the streets of Lamu or at the sites of historical ruins or monuments. You can also return to nature—explore a coral reef, sail on a dhow, or a stay in a romantic grass shack on a secluded beach.

To reach Lamu Island you must cross by boat. There is no motorized transport on the island. Visitors tend to stay either in Lamu Town for closer contact with the Swahili culture, or in the nearby fishing village of Shella, where there are better hotels and access to a swimming beach. You can also elect to stay in beach resorts further away or in private homes.

LAMU ISLAND – LAMU TOWN

As an interesting and historic city of Kenya, Lamu Town attracts many visitors. Situated on Lamu Island with only donkeys and dhows for transport, this ancient town has narrow winding streets, open sewers, historic mosques, a fort, colorful markets and many eager local guides.

There are not yet any hotels which we would strongly recommend in Lamu Town. However, if you choose to stay in the town, here are some possibilities which came to light during our research:

PETLEY'S INN

Petley's Inn, Box 4, Lamu
☎ *(0121) 48107, Nairobi,* ☎ *29612*

This old, well-known hostelry is on the waterfront near the museum. It is steeped in Lamu tradition. Though the hotel was quite run-down when we visited, it was beginning to undergo renovation under new American management. The new owners plan to retain, restore, and install many old Lamu elements. If all goes well, it may be charming and interesting when finished. Surprisingly, there is a small swimming pool taking up most of the second floor! There is also a rooftop restaurant.

LAMU PALACE HOTEL

Lamu Palace Hotel, Box 83, Lamu
☎ *(0121) 3272*

This is a fairly large new hotel on the waterfront. The advantages of this hotel are its proximity to downtown Lamu and the fact that it has air conditioning throughout. It has a Lamu-style decor. There is a restaurant with an extensive menu. The bedrooms seem small and enclosed.

STONE HOUSE

Stone House, Head Office, Box 81866, Mombasa
☎ *223295, FAX: 221925*

A new offering since we visited Lamu, Stone House provides bed and breakfast in an 18th century house. The house derives its name from Lamu's historic stone houses with their Swahili Islamic architecture. The rooms are all doubles and have Lamu furniture, a telephone and a private bathroom. The house has its own water supply—a boon in Lamu town. There is a restaurant which offers seafood and Swahili delicacies. Stone House is advertised as being "small" with a "serenely quiet and private" atmosphere and "personal and friendly service."

YUMBE HOUSE

Yumbe House, Box 81, Lamu
☎ *(0121) 3101*

Yumbe House is in an old-style building deep in Lamu Town. It is quite basic and has the feeling of a well-set-up youth hostel. Rooms have private bathrooms and can hold up to three beds. There is a rooftop lounge with city and harbor views. Breakfast is included.

LAMU ISLAND – SHELA

You have a nicer choice of accommodations at the fishing village of Shela, a short dhow ride from Lamu Town, and the site of its closest swimming beach. Although Shela Beach is good for swimming and some watersports, there has been danger from thieves and thugs.

PEPONI HOTEL

Peponi Hotel, Box 24, Lamu
☎ *(0121)3029, Telex: 21471 PEPONI*

For many years people visiting Lamu have passed the word: "Peponi's is the place to stay."

The hotel is right at water's edge in Shela Village, a few kilometers walk, or a pleasant 20-minute dhow ride away from Lamu Town. This privately owned hotel has been in the hands of a Danish family, the Korschens, for 25 years.

Part of the appeal of staying at Peponi is arriving by water. Most guests fly to Lamu Airstrip on Manda Island and then board the hotel's large wooden dhow. Immediately you are transported back to a slower, more peaceful time. You chug past Lamu Town, then by beautiful gardens and villas. After landing, you walk along a sandy beach to reach the hotel.

You are dazzled by whitewashed terraces, blazing bougainvillea, and tall waving palm fronds. There is color and life in the busy open-air public bar, the riot of exotic flowering shrubs, and the bustling boating activity in front of the hotel. On the other hand, peace and relaxation are found in the residents' section of the hotel with its quiet and established air. There is a solid, timeless feel about Peponi—nothing slick or nouveau. It invites indolence: reading, sitting on deck chairs admiring the view, sipping a drink on the terrace, just watching boats.... It lives up to its Swahili name. *Peponi* means place where there is coolness, rest and relief from trouble...

There are only 25 rooms at Peponi Hotel, and the atmosphere is intimate and low key—no sense of bustling, mass tourism. There is an interesting layout of rooms. On one side of the main building, a row of rooms faces a lawn with tall palm trees and a low stone sea wall clothed with bougainvillea. There is a more unusual arrangement on the other side of the hotel, where rooms are at different levels and reached by meandering paths between flowering trees. Some rooms are up narrow flights of open-air stairs, others are tucked below, overlooking sand and water. All rooms have a private veranda with comfortable chairs and pleasant views. The newer rooms have been attractively decorated with bright carpets, modern art, and cane furniture. The older rooms are simply and solidly furnished, dim and cool with high ceilings and "casablanca" fans—echoes of a colonial time.

The dining room is simple and elegant—predominantly white with dark wood furniture. Colorful old Dutch plates and bowls brighten the white stucco walls, and there are attractive Lamu chairs with woven string backs. A wall-size painting of an intricate Swahili arch adds an exotic touch. Along one entire side of the room are windows with French doors leading out to a comfortable terrace overlooking the water. In addition to the formal dining room, there is an outdoor grill restaurant with raked sand underfoot and a tangle of bougainvillea overhead. The hotel specializes in seafood and has both a table d'hote as well as an à la carte menu. The drunken prawns were a treat!

Safari Journal

Sunday begins . . .

Lars, the second generation manager owner, told me Peponi's was "the sunrise place." And it is. I came down from my room above the white roof top terrace just at dawn when the birds started calling. Everything is so quiet and peaceful. The water is like glass. The air is still and the light a bright haze. The little dhow across the way with its brown triangle sail leaves hardly a ripple as it glides out to sea. Even this early you can feel the heat starting to build and swell. The California couple swim just in front of the main building. They stroke straight out, cutting through the calm water, right through the moorings of the hotel boats. She turns against the current ~ I see her stroking, but the current holds her still. Then they turn to swim back. The steward just arrived with my early morning coffee ~ rich and freshly brewed...

After a day's sight-seeing in Lamu Town climbing up narrow and pungent streets in the heat, peering into dark shops, squeezing past donkeys and absorbing a sense of history and the exotic, it is a pleasant relief to return to the tranquillity, beauty and security of Peponi...and a cold drink—the lime juice is wonderful.

Accommodations

The 25 rooms vary somewhat in size. There are high Lamu-style beds (king, double, or twin), en suite bathrooms, 24-hour electricity, mosquito netting, and ceiling fans. The four newest rooms are nearer the water and seem brighter with a more colorful and interesting decor. *Our Favorites:* New Wing: #24, #25. Old Wing: #19, #20. Also check out the view from the room they call "Top."

Bathing Beach

A short walk around the rocks from Peponi leads to a long beach backed by dunes. This is the closest bathing beach to Lamu Town and dhows bring visitors here. Hotel guests are warned not to take anything valuable to the beach because of thugs and thieves.

Local Tour Guides & Boatmen

Local residents are always available for hire at the hotel's outdoor bar to guide you through Shela and Lamu Town or to take you where you want to go by boat. Their knowledge is worth it, and so is their protection from others wanting you to hire them!

Hotel Dhow Service to Lamu Town

Free 9 a.m. shuttle with return at noon. Takes about 15 minutes.

Walks

Transportation on Lamu Island is by foot, by donkey, or by boat. The walk to Lamu Town takes about 40 minutes with interesting views of water traffic and villas along the way. Walk along beach. Explore Lamu Town or Shela.

Water Activities

Through the hotel you can arrange to go snorkeling, waterskiing, or deep-sea fishing. For a special treat, enjoy a lobster feast on a dhow by day or moonlight. There is a windsurfing concession at the hotel beach.

Off Notes

Too much "local color" at the bar can be wearing on guests seeking tranquillity... Watch out for strong currents in the water... Swimming from the hotel beachfront seems uninviting during the day due to boat traffic.

Note

The Peponi Hotel closes in May and June.

KIJANI HOUSE

Kijani House, Box 266, Lamu
☎ *(0121) 3235 or 3237*

Kijani House is a small garden hotel with four double and three triple rooms spread among three charming Swahili houses. The houses have traditional coral walls with high makuti roofs. They are surrounded by large tropical gardens full of flowers.

The grounds go down to a jetty where fishermen secure their boats after fishing, and a walk along the water is very picturesque. It is possible to walk the three kilometers to Lamu Town, or to walk 300 meters up the beach to Peponis Hotel, then farther on to Shela Beach.

The bedrooms are spacious with high ceilings. Mellow Lamu-style wooden furnishings complement the pristine white of walls and linen. Four-poster beds support a canopy of mosquito netting, and copper vases full of flowers are on antique bureaus. There are ceiling fans for comfort, and full bathrooms. There are more Lamu-style wooden chairs and loungers on each private terrace.

You eat with other guests at communal tables in an open-air dining area shaded by the cool thatch roof. There is also a bar and lounge area under thatch. There are two well-kept freshwater swimming pools on the property convenient to guest accommodations. The Swiss management can arrange for excursion trips by motorboat, dhow, four-wheel drive vehicle, or airplane. Ask for Room #1 for best view of the water.

ISLAND HOTEL

The Island Hotel, Box 179, Lamu
☎ *(0121) 3290*

The Island Hotel is located in the heart of the village of Shela. It is basic and clean, though some of the 14 rooms are not very private since some walls do not extend to the ceiling. All rooms have private bathroom and fan. There are nice views of Shela rooftops from the top-floor restaurant, which is partly open to the sea breezes.

BEACH RESORTS NEAR LAMU

North of Lamu are a choice of romantic beach resorts known for secluded beaches, watersports and total relaxation.

KIWAYU SAFARI VILLAGE

Kiwayu Safari Village, Box 55343, Nairobi
☎ *503030, FAX: 503149*

Kiwayu is on the northern part of Kenya's coastline near the Somali border and 120 kilometers from Lamu. There is an airstrip just minutes away. You can fly direct from Nairobi or from Lamu.

Kiwayu Safari Village was our favorite place on the Kenyan coast. It combines great natural beauty with exotic accommodations, marvelous food, and perfect peace and privacy.

The setting is superb—the "Village" nestles under a tall stand of coconut palms on the white-sand beach of a sparkling secluded bay. Although situated on the mainland, it feels as though you are on a private island. At the far end of the bay, more tall palms signal the presence of a local village, but other than this, there is no other sign of human habitation.

Across the water is Kiwayu Island, the waves breaking white against dark rocky cliffs—such a contrast to the gentle lapping of sea on golden sand at your feet. This place was originally a hunter's camp, and elephant used to come on to the beach, sometimes to swim across to Kiwayu Island. From elephants to models—now Kiwayu Safari Village attracts international fashion photographers—perfect models posing in perfect scenery.

Kiwayu Safari Village lines the shore. At the center of the curving beach, and just above the waterline, a long spacious lounge/bar adjoins an equally long dining area. Both have high thatch roofs overhead, grass matting underfoot, and a few wooden poles to keep the two apart. The place is rustic and natural—ideal for letting the breezes and the view be part of the scene. Do not let this description conjure up spartan images. In the lounge enormous floor cushions covered in colorful *kangas* are piled upon each other in abandon, inviting you to flop—order a cold Pimms. The tables are large logs of grey weathered driftwood, bright shells are artistically arranged, irresistible snacks are brought with the drinks. Lights are low, and you hear the sound of the waves lapping on the beach. All is delightfully decadent in this dream setting.

Guest cottages are well spaced along the beach on both sides of these public rooms. Each has been ingeniously positioned to ensure complete privacy, and the ocean is just a quick dash across the sand.

"Cottage" is too meager a word to describe these luxurious and spacious grass villas. The enormous bedroom has a bigger than king-size bed, high off the floor, spread with bright fabric and draped with mosquito netting. Outside is a private lounging area with hammocks and chairs filled with colorful cushions. There is a separate dressing area with a double sink (two enamel basins) and separate rooms for a flush toilet and a fresh water shower. Walls, floor and roof—all are made of grass matting or palm leaves. There are no doors or windows, just wide open spaces in the walls which let in the air and frame views of sand and water. Growing trees are often built right into the decor and framework of the cottages. A driftwood mangrove tree stands grey on the matting, an amusing "towel rack." There is electricity. The water is unheated—not a hardship when you return hot and salty from the beach. You are likely to find hermit crab visitors in your shower—some carrying the size and type of shell you would pay dearly for in a shell shop. The whole place is wonderfully harmonious with its surroundings—nothing jars or is incongruous.

Safari Journal
Late

We recline on fat cushions spread on grass matting.
The stars above are brilliant. We agree on Orion's Belt
but debate the Southern Cross. Contentment after dinner.
Susan ordered a bottle of wine to celebrate the last
of the bumpy rides in small boats. Joan said crab
was her favorite food, that this was the best she'd ever
tasted, and then proceeded to astound us with how much
she could put away. We are joined by a young man
in charge of describing our options for the following day.
Do we want to go snorkeling, on a picnic tea to an
island, have a windsurfing lesson, walk over the dunes
to explore lovely bays on the other side …
or simply laze about? Wish I had the time
to do it all.

Dining at Kiwayu Safari Village is a delight—giant crab claws, platters of lobster, perfect salads, amazing fish soup. The emphasis obviously is on fresh seafood, but if you don't care for seafood and give them advance warning, they will prepare something else.

The majority of guests spend most of their time relaxing, eating and drinking. However, included in the tariff is a whole host of water related activities from windsurfing and laser sailing to goggling and creek fishing. Deep-sea fishing is also available for an additional fee.

There are miles of unspoiled beaches to walk, washed up shells to admire and a choice of swimming in the calm bay water or the wilder surf on the other side of the dunes. There are many boating trips you can take—go to Kiwayu Island or glide between mangroves along narrow channels of water. The snorkeling is magnificent: colorful coral and brilliant fish on unspoiled reefs—best of all, there is no one else there but you!

This is a wonderfully romantic spot and is popular with honeymooners. Many guests are repeat customers. Most visitors come for about a week. Some lucky ones stay longer.

Quotes:

> "*We bring people back to nature. There are no doors, no windows, no locks, no keys.... The secret is the space and solitude...*" Manager.

> "*I see palm trees growing in the middle of the house.... I got shells from the beach for the cook to decorate.*" Nine-year-old visitor from abroad.

> "*I loved being able to step out of my room, walk just a few paces across the sand, and be right in the water.*"

Accommodations

There are 22 cottages. One is a twin cottage for two doubles. The other cottages are planned for two with one big bed standard. This can be replaced by two single beds on request, and a third bed can easily be added. Overhanging eaves and shaded verandas insure privacy as does the distance between the cottages. Grass mat shades can be lowered over windows. Most of the cottages are right on the beach, close to the water. *Our Favorite Views*: #7, 11, and 19.

Special Offerings

Deep-sea fishing, creek fishing, dhow sailing, laser sailing, windsurfing, goggling trips, mangrove trips, souvenir shop, four-wheel shuttle, airstrip.

Off Notes

Pricey to fly to paradise... No fans, no air conditioning, and no hot water for those who need their creature comforts... Hermit crabs in the shower may not be your ideal way of getting back to nature.

Please Note

Kiwayu Safari Village closes from mid-April for a couple of months (dates may vary).

BLUE SAFARI CLUB

Bruno Brighetti's Blue Safari Club, Box 41759, Nairobi
☎ *338838, FAX: 218939*

Blue Safari Club is an ultraexclusive island paradise. It has long been an idyllic retreat for a rich and famous international clientele who seek peace and privacy. The Blue Safari Club is a handful of luxury grass huts scattered on white sandy beaches and surrounded by tall palm trees and blue waters. It is located on the northeastern tip of Manda Island, nearest neighbor to Lamu. There are no roads—you arrive by boat.

At Blue Safari Club you are the personal guests of the Brighetti family who selected this romantic spot more than 20 years ago. Bruno and his son Marco, with their outgoing friendliness, cater to your every whim. Here you do exactly as you desire. Meals are served when you are ready; the bar is always open, you can arrange snorkeling, fishing, or sailing as the spirit takes you.

The club is limited to 24 guests, and the Brighettis prefer to entertain only one party at a time. The privacy and preference of each guest is of paramount importance to all the staff. The atmosphere is casual but reserved. There is a studied informality here—mammoth floor cushions artfully arranged and beautiful people with "chic" kangas draped over swimwear.

Safari Journal

Monday ~ beautifully Blue Monday!

*Handsome Marco Brighetti, broad shouldered, tanned,
and young, came to pick us up for the boat ride
to Blue Safari ~ what a romantic name.
After days of dirty Lamu dhows and motor boats,
the Brighetti's aqua-blue fiberglass boat seemed a
marvel of cleanliness. The gray morning brightened
as we sped through mangrove-lined waterways,
bouncing a little when we hit incoming waves.
The water changed from green-gray to deep blue
as we made a final sweeping turn toward a white
sandy point, beautiful with palms ~
there it was ~ Blue Safari . . . .*

The heart of the Blue Safari Club is the open-sided dining area, lounge banda and bar. These casual, breezy structures, built from all-natural materials have a certain elegance and artistic flair, thanks to Bruno's wife, Gianna. Grass matting, shells and driftwood are used for decor. But, hidden high-tech is also there—you can watch a video or listen to music. Guests dine with the Brighettis. Fresh seafood and fish are part of every simple gourmet meal, and the pasta is perfect.

Quotes:

> *"I feel so spoiled. It's like having my own private island in the sun."*

Accommodations

Guests stay in small round bandas of woven grass and thatch. These are well spaced in two rows, with the preferred front row at water's edge. Smooth grass matting serves as walls and floors. Curtains and bedspreads are of bright kanga cloth and a veranda in front of each banda has Lamu-style lounge chairs with woven seats.

Each banda has a private bathroom reached through a short roofed and matted walkway. Bathrooms are simple with an open shower and unheated water. There is 24-hour electricity. Mosquito nets are lowered and bandas sprayed at night.

Special Offerings

(Many of these are included in the tariff) Snorkeling and scuba diving (14 tourist-free reefs to choose from), windsurfing, waterskiing, sailing, sculling, deep-sea fishing, cabin cruiser or dhow trips, motor boats, canoes, underwater photography, bird-watching, miles of private beach, free boat shuttle to airstrip, gift shop.

Off Notes

Bandas seem small and often hot (the new fans should help)... Top row bandas lack view.

KIPANGANI SEA BREEZES

Kipangani Sea Breezes, Box 232, Lamu
☎ *(0121) 3191*

On the opposite end of Lamu Island from busy Lamu Town, ten spacious grass huts rest casually under palm trees on a sandy bay. It is private, secluded, and extremely low-key—popular with honeymooners. A sprawling beach lounge is the heart of Kipangani. It lures you with colorful cushions, low tables and hammocks. The roof is thatched and tall for coolness, and it is open to breezes and sea views. The seafood we had at dinner was marvelous.

All watersports are available, but at an extra charge. We found the location (or our time there) very hot and still with many mosquitoes. Little crabs scrabble on makuti floors and keep you company in the showers.

After our visit we heard from the new management, promising many improvements for this resort. Go and see.

QUICK SAFARI
GUIDE FOR KENYA

Robert Young Pelton is a frequent traveler to Africa. He has compiled the following chapters as an overview of the places and animals worth seeing in Kenya.

Elephants

Like most people who visit Kenya for pleasure you will have an image and an understanding of what will happen on your trip. Rather than school you in the ways of safariing it might be more helpful to deal with the most important aspects of planning a safari. Kenya is the most popular destination with Masai Mara the most popular park. Samburu, Nairobi and Tsavo are the number two spots. Any major trip will include three to four game areas with a few stops at smaller attractions like Lake Nakuru or Thomson's Falls.

The Northern Circuit is the most desolate and awe inspiring, however you will not see many animals and it is very hot. Samburu, Marsabit, Meru and Mt Kenya are good choices. Very few people go as far as the Turkana area. There is always danger of armed bandits, and the constant pressure from poachers and drought conditions have reduced the wildlife dramatically.

The Coastal route that usually takes in Amboseli, Tsavo Shimba or Tana is a good second choice. Usually time at a beach resort near Malindi or historic tours in Mombasa round out a more exotic safari.

The Southwestern route is by far the most popular. Streams of minivans hit the highlights between Nairobi and their final destination the Masai Mara. Nakuru, Aberdares and Naivashu are usually put on the agenda here. Many second timers, simply skip the long minibus rides and fly directly from Wilson airport in Nairobi directly to a tented camp in the Mara.

HOW TO SAFARI

Traditional safaris: Although the traditional safari was a tented hunting safari supported by large trucks and scores of porters, most people are content with the politically correct wild game park version. Most Americans will book a tour before they leave totally trusting where and when they will be shuttled around. Not all safaris are the same. To help you understand the basic choices here is a brief guide to choosing a safari:

Minibus tours: It is easy to rack up a few game parks in one trip if you are traveling by minibus from Nairobi. Ideal for first timers who want to see the country but the distances between stops can be numbing. You will have the chance to visit a couple of markets, have your picture taken next to colorful tribespeople and get to know your fellow travelers but you will be under pressure to keep up with the schedule. Many roads are pure mud in the rainy season and blinding dust when they are dry. Consider flying directly to a tented camp and picking up a camp driver (who will know the park better).

Self Drive: Many expats based in Kenya drive out to the parks on weekends. The problem is that once you are committed to driving yourself around the parks you lose the constant chatter of a well informed guide. The spectre of robbery, breakdowns, bandits also appears. Unless you know a local, not advised.

Custom tented safaris: The ten plus ultra of African travel. One step above the fixed tented camps, a custom safari can be designed to take you where and when you want to go. Birdwatchers, animal lovers or people who can afford to keep their own schedule choose this method over the package tours. Abercrombie and Kent and Downey and Kerr are the best choices. Do not confuse a custom tented safari (which is in effect staying at fixed tented sites in established venues like Kichwa Tembo in the Mara) with a custom itinerary where you and your outfitter set up your own schedule and campsites.

Hyrax

Camel or Horseback safaris: The adventurous can choose camel safaris in the northern parks complete with Samburu or Rendille wranglers or horseback adventures along trails in the central or west part of Kenya. Private ranches also offer horseback game viewing rides. These trips are usually a group affair so inquire as to how many riding partners you will have. Not designed to be too strenuous, you will be exposed to the sun and the elements for the 15–25 miles a day you cover. Cooking and all camp work are taken care of by the outfitter. Camels offer a less comfortable but more romantic version of the classic safari. The fact that people will actually pay money to sit on a cantankerous camel amazes many but some people will go to any length to make Africa romantic. I would think that romance is the last thing these travelers think about at the end of a long day being bumped and humped on camels.

Balloon safaris: Not technically a safari but a morning's outing in the major game areas. Balloon trips were started in 1988 and are guaranteed to create a memory you won't soon forget—depending on the weather of course. It will also make a sizeable dent in your wallet (about $250–$400 a person). But the memory of floating over the primeval plains of Africa capped off by a champagne breakfast will last much longer than that sordid weekend in Las Vegas or that new sportscoat.

Flying tours: Although they sound exotic, flying tours use the transportation infrastructure to its greatest advantage. You will pick up a small charter plane directly on arrival and in one to three hours be in camp sipping on a gin and tonic. The camp will provide a driver, all supplies and load you onto your next charter. Flying tours allow you to go fishing for giant Nile perch in Lake Victoria or fly fishing in Lake Turkana.

Homestays and lodges: The most sophisticated of all Kenyan safaris. Arrange your trip to stay in some of the most elegant and dramatic ranches, homes and lodges. Use local drivers and wranglers for safaris by car or horse. Fly between major parks and hire transportation when needed.

Other safari ideas: Who said a safari to Kenya means watching animals from a zebra striped minibus? You can go scuba diving, mountain climbing, trout fishing, canoeing, deep sea fishing or even just lie on some of the best beaches in the world. Ask your travel agent for some ideas and get going.

WHAT SHOULD I WEAR?

This first question is the one that all hard core adventurers ask when setting out to parts unknown.

Although situated directly on the equator, Kenya has a diverse range of climates from very hot and dry to cold and wet. We have provided the various altitudes of the parks to give a rough idea.

Near the coast, plan on hot, sticky and wet. The Indian Ocean is very tropical and very hot. You'll be most comfortable in loose cotton, with protection from the sun.

The Eastern region below 3000 feet tends to be hot, dry and dusty. Take a hat, cotton pants, long sleeve shirts, sunglasses and sunscreen.

The Highlands between 3000–5000 feet has cool to hot days and chilly nights. Rain showers can be frequent. Add a sweater and a rain jacket.

The Montane area above 5000 feet is wet and cold. Add gloves, wool hat, heavy rain gear, stronger footwear and heavy pants.

WHAT SHOULD I DO?

The items of special interest to Americans on safari are the "bring em back alive" gear.

Binoculars: Preferably 10 X 40 for birders or wide field for animal watching.

Camera with telephoto lens: The ideal lens is a 300 f2.8 that will cost you more than your entire safari. Failing that try a 200 f4 or ideally a 80–200 zoom with an 2.8 aperture. What the camera salesman won't tell you is that most of your best shots at sunrise or sunset will render any slow or long lens useless.

Fast and slow film: Ideally one camera body for each would be perfect. ASA 50 or 64 film for daylight shots and 100–400 for dusk and early morning shots with telephotos. Do not be afraid to use negative film or to "push" (expose film at one stop faster) a roll if need be.

Video Camera: Still shots just don't do justice to the plains of Africa. Make sure you buy a unit that has a telephoto (at least a 12 times zoom). Buy a car charger adaptor and bring at least four batteries. Use a soft bag or folded jacket as a tripod and remember that the winds will render most sound recording useless unless you shield it well.

Handbooks: Take the two compact hardbound, bibles of East African safaris: *National Parks of East Africa* by J.G. Williams and *A Field Guide to the Mammals of Africa* by Theodor Haltenorth and Helmut Diller or if you prefer *A Field Guide to the Larger Mammals of Africa* by Jean Dorst and Pierre Dandelot. Other choices include the colorful Insight Guides *East African Wildlife Safari Special* from Houghton Mifflin, the *Safari Companion* by Richard D. Estes from Chelsea Green Publishing. and *Adventuring in East Africa* by Allen Bechky from Sierra Club books. Bird lovers will bring along *A Field Guide to the Birds of East Africa* by John Williams and Norman Arlott.

Goodies: Bring along candies and gum for the long hot drives and gifts for villagers like pens, baseball cards or balloons. Don't forget small creature comforts like lip balm, sunscreen and a shortwave radio. I always recommend a walkman with tapes of your favorite classics or movie soundtracks to make your own Africa movie on location.

You can buy all of the books and goodies in Nairobi but once you're in the parks your selection is limited and you will be paying tourist prices.

WHAT YOU MIGHT NOT EXPECT

1) There are other people there.

The plains will be dotted with white and zebra striped buses. Once one driver spots a cat or an unusual event like a recent kill, dozens of buses will converge. After a while you will realize that the magnitude of the event can be described as a five bus leopard or even a 12 bus kill. Use your film accordingly. If you are not a fan of rush hour ask your driver to take you to less dramatic but more reflective events like watching a hippo blow bubbles (usually a one bus event).

2) You can't do what you want.

You will quickly learn that your driver is in charge. You will be rounded up at an ungodly hour in the morning, given a cup of bad coffee and then driven out in the chill of morning for your first game drive. If you are on a deluxe drive you can leave whenever you want. If you are with other folks you will get two drives—one in the morning and one at sunset. You will then have the entire day to sit, or catch up on the sleep you are missing.

Night drives are forbidden in all parks. Foot or horseback safaris are only part of private ranch vacations. Night walking safaris are usually the best way to get shot as a poacher.

3) You will actually get bored.

After your first three or four days you will learn to be more discriminating. No longer motordriving zebras and giraffes at 5 fps, you will begin to carefully nurse each shot as if you were a sniper with two rounds. One solution is to get one of each in the first few days but then spend more time just watching. Animals actually do more than just pose for tourists' cameras. Those amazing postcards you will end up buying in the gift shop are the results of wildlife photographers spending years tracking just one leopard or lion family.

4) There is little hardship "on safari."

Safaris through Kenya require little roughing it and even less bushsmarts. Every action, need and desire will be capably handled by your guide. Even if you are on a tented safari you will probably be disappointed that your tent comes with running water and electricity. If you really decide to rough it on a custom tent safari, it gets even less rough as every whim from digging your toilet to mixing your drink is handled by a staff of up to 12 people.

Since we have exploded some myths about being on safari, here are a few tips that will help you get the most from your cosseted experience in the wilds of Africa:

1) Enjoy Africa.

Tell your driver what you want to do. Don't be a seat warmer. If you want to just park, turn the engine off and enjoy the African wildlife, tell him. He will override you in certain instances, as in the impending charge of a bull elephant, but your driver wants you to have a good time.

Like most visitors you will develop a special memory of Africa—maybe it will be the light, the wide open spaces or the feeling of being carefree and completely happy. In any case, it is a rare person who doesn't daydream about returning to Africa once experiencing a Kenyan safari.

2) Leave before dawn.

Although most game drives leave at dawn, try to get out earlier. The early morning is the best time for game viewing not only because of the activity of the animals, but the coolness and brilliant sunrise can be the most dramatic part of the day. Starting out before sunrise ensures you are in position before dawn and you will miss the rush hour traffic of the less informed travelers. Carnivores will use the early day to hunt and will then rest in the shade until dusk to preserve fluids and lower body heat. Use the time before dawn to put some distance between you and the lodge. Then sit and wait for the magical moment when the light appears and the animals come to life. Most game drives will try to leave at dawn cutting into the magical time of sunrise and you may miss the drama of the plains unfolding. Plan for plenty of action shooting and ask where the lion prides have been spotted.

Gerenuks

3) Map out your day.

Do not let your driver wander aimlessly or worse yet chase other vehicles looking for photo opportunities. Tell your driver to come clean and tell you where the animals are. Many will pretend to be Columbus discovering the new world every time they see an animal. They spent last night swapping notes with the other drivers so make them work for their tip. Tell your driver what you are looking for and that you are not creature counting. Most drivers will assume that you will be happy chasing willy nilly all over the park as you check each and every animal off in your guidebook.

Tell him specifically what you want and when you want to photograph. For example leopards in the early morning or lions making a kill. All though no one can promise any animal or any event, patience and planning will help.

4) Be patient.

If you truly want spectacular photos or memories, plan on spending a lot of time waiting and watching. Get up before the crowds, stay out longer, drive further, stake out a vantage point from which to watch a pride of lions go through their day. Sitting and waiting means you can watch the play unfold instead of rattling around looking for the next photo opportunity.

5) Understand the animal's behavior.

Although a game preserve is not a zoo it is not unusual to find the same animals frequenting the exact same spots in the park. For example a hippo pool has and probably always will be the spot to see hippos. You may bump into one at night as it forages but chances are if there were hippos there 10 years ago they will be there 10 years from now.

The Mara is well known for its many prides of lions—all named, researched, tracked and observed day after day by the drivers that work out of the camps.

6) Pick a good camp with permanent drivers.

You will get your money's worth by picking a camp that has permanent drivers. Most people pick up a driver and a car in Nairobi and drive in. Fly in camps like Kichwa Tembo have a stable of drivers and cars that can take you exactly to where every cheetah and every pride of lions were last seen. You may not be surprised to find out that most drivers are good actors. The look of surprise and discovery is usually feigned. What they don't want you to know is that they all know to keep the leopards and lions as "safari toppers" to give you a feeling of discovery. The reality is that in the major parks the location and number of most individual carnivores are not only well known but animals usually have names to help the drivers tell them apart.

7) Work the light.

The best light is the golden light found about one to two hours before sunset. Second best are the first glancing rays of light found 1/2 hour after the sun breaks across the horizon. Remember your automatic camera will be going crazy trying to balance backlighting, dark thunder clouds or any other dramatic high contrast shots. Bracket or give it a couple of stops over and under.

Familiarize yourself with the park and the direction of the rising and setting sun. Plan to visit areas like gorges when the sun is shining on the side you wish to photograph. Conversely don't be afraid to shoot against the light during the very early and very late stages of the day. Don't even bother to take pictures during the day unless you are clicking off photos for sighting records. As with the great hunters, one shot, one animal should be your motto. Watch, wait and if it doesn't happen there's always the gift shop.

8) Get up close.

Most drivers will discourage you from getting close to animals. There are two reasons for this. First of all, animals are distracted from their normal eating, mating, hunting and familial patterns every day of every year by hundreds of minivans. If every visitor was to get right up close the stress would be too much. Secondly, that stress can result in some very nasty attacks by elephants, water buffalo or carnivores—not out of hunger but pure frustration by being aggravated all day.

Never, never feed any animals. Maintain at least 50–100 yards and try to follow behind. Drive slowly. Make no noises or disturbing sounds. You are there to observe not to affect nature.

Sitting patiently is always the best way to view wildlife. In many cases cheetahs, baboons or other less shy animals will actually walk onto your vehicle to gain a vantage point.

Animals with newborn should be given a wide berth, injured or hungry animals as well.

WHAT TO WATCH OUT FOR

Many people have a healthy fear of travel to Africa for any reason. The fact that 800,000 visitors will make the trip to Kenya and that most make it back with no more than a sunburn or rash from their camera strap should give you a certain level of comfort.

However it is important to stress that there are dangers. And they are not from the sharp toothed animals. The biggest danger is exposure to a variety of bacteria, diseases and microscopic germs. I always tell people that the most dangerous creature in Africa is the mosquito. Malaria is a danger and every precaution should be taken.

Take your Larium faithfully, wear long sleeve shirts and wear insect repellent especially during the last few hours of the day when malarial mosquitoes are most likely to bite.

Use a mosquito net and coils if possible. If you are bitten do not go crazy—not all mosquitoes carry malaria. However do not scratch insect bites because they have a higher chance of being infected.

Be careful what you eat. Although Kenyans do their best to put on a Western spread, there are flies, organisms and other nasties who breed in the hot temperature. Try to eat only food that has been cooked, peel fruit, do not use ice, drink bottled products or boiled tea or coffee.

It is not unusual to have diarrhea because of the heat, different bacteria and jet lag. Drink plenty of fluids, drink moderately and take mild medicines such as Kaopectate to relieve the discomfort. If the diarrhea persists, see a doctor.

Rather than tell you all the woes of travel in the tropics I suggest you consult with the Center for Disease Control, your doctor and read many of the excellent books on tropical travel available in your travel specialty book store.

DANGEROUS ANIMALS

Many visitors ask why some drivers will not let them leave the vehicle when in the parks while the Masai wander around with sandals and a simple spear. Your driver has not told you how many Maasai are killed or maimed by elephants, lions, hippo, crocodiles, snakes and other cute animals. You only need to see how invisible a lion can be in two foot grass to understand the fear these predators put in the local people.

The most imposing animal is the elephant. Many times they will be agitated, swinging their head from side to side and shaking their ears. If an elephant is not happy to see you it will usually make one false charge and then come running head down with the business end of its tusks pointed at you. This usually happens if you are in areas that have poachers. During severe droughts elephants will charge out of thick brush without warning.

There are also numerous poisonous snakes, so watch where you walk. Long vicious thorns of the acacia bush can pierce right through hiking boot soles, and numerous other dangers make staying in your vehicle the best way to enjoy your safari.

Be careful, be cautious.

KENYA'S, BIOSPHERES, NATIONAL PARKS & NATURE PRESERVES

Eland

Kenya is the country of choice when most people think of taking their first safari. Politically stable, geographically diverse and serviced by international airlines, Kenya has the lion's share (sorry for the pun) of North American traffic to Africa. Many will tell you that Tanzania is more dramatic, South Africa more pristine, Namibia,

Botswana and Zambia more exotic—few countries can offer more diversity than Kenya.

There is something classic about a Kenyan safari—the colonial elegance of the hotels and game parks, the history and romance of following in the footsteps of Beryl Markham, Isak Dinesen, Robert Ruark and Ernest Hemingway. Movies have drawn thousands to live out their celluloid fantasies: *Born Free, Out of Africa, The Lion King* and other classic African stories still continue to inspire a dream of going on safari in millions of Americans.

Kenya sits smack dab on the equator and yet offers a fantastic range of environments only a few hours apart: the sweet hot smells of the Indian Ocean and Arab history of Mombasa and Lamu, the cool wet alpine regions of Mt Elgon, the dramatic forever views across the rift valley, desolate volcanic regions, endless horizons of the Western savannas, even snowcapped Mount Kenya.

Be forewarned that there is a very high wall between the tourist experience awaiting the Western tourist and the cultural realities of Kenya. The closest most visitors will come to the local people will be to meet a tour driver (most likely a member of the Kikuyu tribe who lives in Nairobi). Sometimes Samburu or Maasai tribespeople will be seen and occasionally will barter for goods. There is little contact with the crushing poverty and population problems of modern Kenya. The population is exploding at an alarming rate forcing people further afield for food and shelter. Poaching, encroachment and crime are all symptoms of this problem. Yet tourism remains the only bright spot and potential solution to these problems. Tourism provides jobs, foreign currency and a very profitable method of supporting this country. It would be hard to imagine what would happen if there were no game parks, no tourism and no hope for Kenya.

Most people will book a safari with a North American company who will then contract with a local company like Abercrombie and Kent in Nairobi. You will be met at the airport by a smiling, professional guide who will make your trip effortless and one of the most enjoyable you have ever experienced. Every day your minibus will be cleaned and spotless, your bags carried to and from your room. Every morning, afternoon and evening there will be endless buffets of rich heavy food of what Kenyans think Westerners want to eat. Your guide will laugh at your jokes and point out animals that you cannot even see with your binoculars. At the end of your safari your head will be spinning with amazing sights, your camera will have gone through more film than you shot in the last two years and you will take care to leave just a little dust on your safari jacket to show the folks back home.

Sable Antelope

Kenya has been careful to preserve and maintain its diverse range of parks and reserves despite strained resources. The pressure from marauding Somali poachers, hungry farmers and opportunistic teen-agers have played havoc on rhino, elephant and leopard. Kenya has employed a shoot-to-kill policy which has been the only way to com-bat the constant attacks by heavily armed intruders. Visitors will see little of this violent interface unless they head into the Northern re-gions. Towards the south and central areas there is little problem and the government maintains an efficient system of park management. No vehicles are allowed out in the parks after dark but other than that minor restriction there is little to remind the visitor of the constant threat facing African wildlife. People looking for more unique experiences should stay at private game ranches listed in the book.

BIOSPHERES

Kenya is home to four of the world's biospheres (there are over 271 around the globe). Biospheres are areas deemed to contain unique landforms, landscapes and systems of land use. They are intended to provide large protected areas ideal for scientific study of their unique qualities and interdependencies.

KIUNGA BIOSPHERE RESERVE

250 sq kms
0–30 m above sea level

Coastal preserve that includes offshore islands and coral formations. Dugong and green turtle coexist with a large population of reef fish. Birds include various gulls and terns.

Swimming, sailing, waterskiing and diving are permitted.

MOUNT KULAL BIOSPHERE RESERVE

7000 sq kms
(South Island National Park 39kms)
378 –2416 m above sea level
An area near the southeast of Lake Turkana

Vegetation ranges from mountain forest to desert with rain forest, mist forest, grasslands, dry evergreen forest, woodlands, bushlands and saltbrush scrublands. Fauna includes giraffe, zebra, elephant, cheetah, lion, black rhino, leopard, ostrich, crocodile and gazelle.

MALINDI/WATUMU BIOSPHERE PRESERVE

261 sq kms
Malindi Marine National Park 6
Watumi Marine National Park 10
Malindi Marine National Reserve 213
Watumu Marine National Reserve 32 sq kms

Best time to visit the parks is at low tide. Snorkeling can be a wonderful change from the hot and dry job of being on safari. Whale Island is a nesting ground of Roseate and Bridled Terns from June to September.

MOUNT KENYA BIOSPHERE RESERVE
MOUNT KENYA NATIONAL PARK

715 sq kms
1600–5199 m

A park begun in 1949 that includes glaciers, bamboo forests, alpine moorlands and a favorite of mountain climbers who like a mild challenge. Rich alpine and subalpine region that is the only spot of the equator where you can find snow year round. Unusual species of plants like the giant rosette plants. Home of the rare golden cat usually seen only at high altitudes. Crowned by the twin peaks, Batian (5199 m) and Nelion (5188 m). Home to the giant Mount Kenya mole rat and the Mount Kenya mole shrew. Climbing, hiking and mule pack expeditions can be booked in advance through tour operators. Includes Mount Kenya National Park.

The bunker at the 2193 m Mountain Lodge offers very close contact at the waterhole with nighttime visitors.

NATIONAL PARKS

Established in 1945, Kenya's National Parks are designed to protect flora and fauna from encroachment by man. Although designed to provide educational and recreational use by Kenyans, they are the primary generators of foreign income as tourists from around the world come to experience the classic African safari in comparative luxury.

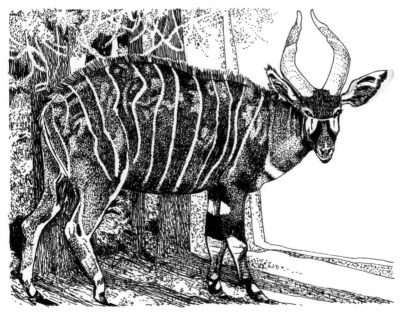

Bongo

National Parks feature comfortable fixed tented camps and lodges. Vehicle traffic and viewing is allowed during the daytime only. Marine parks allow swimming, sailing and waterskiing

Kenya protects about 7.6 percent of its areas in parks and reserve areas and is under the control of the very military Kenya Wildlife Preserve.

ABERDARE NATIONAL PARK

766 sq kms
1829–3994 m

Established in 1950 this rich montane park with cool highlands is the home of the rare bongo, trout filled rivers, bamboo forests and sylvan waterfalls. The high altitude creates a cool alternative to the typical savanna of most Kenyan parks. The elevated viewing lodges of historic Treetops (where the guest and viewing book have been filled out faithfully each night since the fifties) and the newer Ark are the prototypical game lodges that many people think of when dreaming of an exotic safari. Built around floodlit saltlicks, visitors can do their game viewing while enjoying bloody marys in the bar. These lodges provide one of the few closeups of elephants and other game from their ground level viewing blinds. There has been a lot of pressure from encroaching development resulting in lower game counts and aggressive behavior by wildlife. The elusive bongo is best spotted in the upper bamboo zone and hypericum scrub. Eland can be found in the open moorlands. Aberdare is also ideal for bird-watchers.

AMBOSELI NATIONAL PARK

3810 sq kms
1155 m

One of the oldest parks in Kenya also suffers the most from the amount of traffic created by its success. Created in 1948, it was turned over to the Maasai in 1961, and then in 1970 a sanctuary around Lake Amboseli was created for wild animals only. In 1977 it became a national park. Five wildlife habitats range from semiarid to wetlands. Amboseli is famous for its dramatic scenery and open plains. Although the image of Amboseli is usually herds of elephants against the rich blue silhouette of 5894m high Mount Kilimanjaro, there are currently only about 600 elephants left in the park. The unforgettable mass of high Mt. Kilimanjaro dominates the landscape and is recommended for its scenic drama.

HELL'S GATE NATIONAL PARK

68 sq km
2777 m

Also known as Njorowa Gorge, Hell's Gate offers one of the most scenic and exciting walks in Kenya leading through a gorge lined with sheer, red cliffs.

Fischer's Tower is a challenging rock climb and home to colonies of rock hyrax or *dassies.*

Excellent for succulents, birds of prey and other bird species.

FORT JESUS NATIONAL PARK

A 17th-century Portuguese fort on the Indian Ocean in Mombasa. There is a historical museum at the site.

GEDE NATIONAL PARK

An ancient city of Islamic origin, it is estimated to be from the 13th century. There is some partial restoration work on the great mosque and wells.

Roan Antelope

LAKE NAKURU NATIONAL PARK

188 sq kms (80 sq miles)
1753–2073 m

Created in 1961 as a bird sanctuary with over 400 species of birds stopping here, many from Europe and East Asia. The park was expanded in 1974 to include a large savanna area to the south. A shallow blue-green alkaline lake famous for its flocks of pink lesser and greater flamingos and 450 bird species. The *tilapia grahami* fish has been introduced to provide food for the pelicans who also call Lake Nakura home.

The blue-green color is because of the presence of blue-green algae called *spirulinga*. The level of the lake goes up and down with the amount of rainfall and the color is dependent on the conditions for the growth of algae. There have been up to two million flamingos on the lake at one time. When disturbed the birds lift gracefully into the air in a solid moving pink carpet.

Nakura has proven to be an excellent and safe sight for the Rothschild giraffe and black rhino. Usually a lunch stop on most safari itineraries, there is much to see along the shore. It is an excellent spot to photograph hippo, reedbuck, Defassa waterbuck and giraffe. It is also unique for its forests of cactuslike Euphorbia trees.

LAMBWE VALLEY NATIONAL PARK

120 sq kms 48 sq miles
1200–1600 m

Tall grassland and acacia thickets created to protect the roan antelope ideal for topi, oribi, hartebeest and buffalo. Zebra, ostrich and giraffes have been introduced from Samburu because of the plentiful vegetation available.

MERU NATIONAL PARK

870 sq km (CHK 1813?)
1036–3040 m

The park made famous by the books of writer and painter Joy Adamson and later by her surrogate daughter, Elsa the lioness, the star of *Born Free*. Rarely visited, the horny bushland with riverine forests offers the visitor a quiet and unfrequented corner of Kenya. The unusual doum and raffia palm are found here as well as ostrich, gerenuk, lion, leopard and elephant. The park is hot, lonely and best visited during the dry months when the game concentrates around the northwest plains with its marshes and year-round rivers. Meru is a good choice if you are looking for gerenuk or the lesser kudu *(Tragelaphus imberbis)*. Meru is also a good spot for the more sedentary sight of giant baobabs.

Baobobs *(Adansonia digitata)* are constantly under siege by hungry elephants who will spend hours carefully stripping the bark from the trees to get at the tender pulp inside. Elephants also like to search for the nuts of the doum palm. *(Hyphaene coriacea)*

MOUNT ELGON NATIONAL PARK

170 sq kms 68 sq miles
2336–4321 m

Mount Elgon is an extinct volcano. Its 4300m high peak is actually in Uganda. Wet montane forest and the fantasylike afro-alpine moorlands are Mt Elgon's claim to fame. Koitobas (flat topped basalt columns, like Alberta's hoo doos) and lava tube caves are also unique to this mountainous region. Elephants have entered the Kitum cave every two to three days since recorded history to dig out the salt with their tusks. Many people believe that the elephants actually dug the 200-meter-long caves since they have no qualms entering the dark caves in herds to eat the salt.

Large forests of Podocarpus and Juniper are found as well.

MOUNT LONGONOT MOUNTAIN PARK
152 sq kms (61 sq miles)

An extinct volcanic cone on the southern side of Lake Naivashu. Thrusting straight out of the rift valley floor, the cone is home to a wide variety of birds and wildlife. The leleshwa tree is found here in abundance—the Maasai tuck the leaves of the leleshwa under their arms to use the leaves as a deodorant.

NAIROBI NATIONAL PARK
117 sq kms
1533–1760 m

One of the last bastions of the rhino just eight miles south of downtown Nairobi. Good spot for cats. No elephants due to the lack of food and danger to nearby civilization but the impressive number of large mammals and the 500 species of bird life make this an excellent day trip from Nairobi. Primarily savanna or plains, there are areas of highland forest, acacia and riverine environments. Few people realize that the park is not entirely enclosed and that animals migrate into and out of the park with the rainy seasons. The best time to visit is at the height of the dry season. Animals will usually be found near the Mbagathi River and near the artificial dams created. If you are a birder, visit during the wet season. The park maintains an orphanage which can provide some interesting photo opportunities not available in some of the larger parks.

NDERE ISLAND NATIONAL PARK
4.2 sq kms

Twenty miles (30 km) from Kisumu on the north side of Winam Gulf, Ndere Island became a sanctuary in 1986.

Main attractions are herds of impala, magnificent lake views and birds.

OL DONYO SAPUK NATIONAL PARK
18sq kms
1524–2134 m

Montane forest with rhino, monkeys and leopard that also features a spectacular view from the 2134 m summit of Ol Donyo Sapuk mountain. Once the rains begin there are many butterflies.

OLORGESAILIE NATIONAL PARK

Site where Dr. Richard Leakey discovered a prehistoric living site of "hand axe" man. 67 kms from Nairobi along the Nairobi-Magadi road.

SAIWA SWAMP NATIONAL PARK
1.9 sq kms .76 sq miles
1860–1880 m

One of the tiniest national parks in Kenya is the last domain of about 100 sitatunga antelope. Swampy vegetation is also home to giant forest squirrel, spotted necked otter and nocturnal potto. The sitatunga are slowly increasing in number and spend their day half submerged in the floating plants. Brazza's monkey can be found in small numbers here.

SIBILOI NATIONAL PARK & CENTRAL ISLAND NATIONAL PARK

1570 sq kms 1000 sq miles
Central Island 5 sq kms
South Island National Park 39 sq kms

Arid and remote region of doum palms and yellow spear grass on the eastern shores of Lake Turkana. A crocodile population of about 12,000 (called the largest population of crocs in the world) can be found on the crater filled Central Island. Also home to the Koobi Fora paleontological site and museum. Not very popular due to its proximity to the Ethiopian border and lack of accommodations.

TSAVO NATIONAL PARK

21,283 sq kms
(Tsavo East 11.747, Tsavo West 9,065
and Chyulu National Park 471 sq kms)
229–2438 m

Much of Kenya's largest national park is a hot waterless region with a large diversity of landscapes. Less than 20 inches of rain falls per year on this dry region. Whether it's the rocky gorges of Lugard Falls with its water carved rocks or the natural catchment at Mudanda Rock between Voi and Manyani, there are many dramatic sights for the explorer. Large mammals including elephant, antelope, hippos, black rhino, giraffe and eland are the primary reason to visit Tsavo. Tsavo was the original sight of the big game hunters in search of record setting ivory; Dennis Finch-Hatton and Baron Bror von Blixen popularized Tsavo. The great tuskers of yesterday began to decline due to attracted poachers and in the great drought of 1970–71 reduced the elephants to a population of under 4500. The great herds of elephants were counted at 35,000 in 1973. The rhino that are left are kept in a gated area near Ngulia Hill.

Do not plan on seeing Tsavo in the usual two to three days allowed most parks. If you must choose between east and west, remember Tsavo West has the most dramatic scenery and is the best choice.

MARINE NATIONAL PARKS

The best time to visit the marine parks is during the dry seasons of January–March or June–October. The rains bring runoff which silts up the coastal areas. The winds and stormy weather can also reduce visibility and make snorkeling uncomfortable.

KISITE MARINE NATIONAL PARK/ MPUNGUTI MARINE NATIONAL PRESERVE

39 sq kms (Kisite 28sq kms and Mpunguti 11sq kms)
sea level–5 m

Three islands are breeding grounds of sooty and roseate terns. The coral reefs off Kisite offer the best snorkeling. Located near the Tanzanian border

MOMBASA MARINE NATIONAL PARK

10 sq kms

Located about 8 km from Mombasa town opposite the Hotel Intercontinental. This park was established in 1986 for the protection of the area's beautiful coral reefs and fish which form the main attraction. It is surrounded by a 200 sq. km Marine National Reserve where traditional fishing is allowed only under license.

Bush Duiker

NATIONAL RESERVES

NATURE AND FOREST RESERVES

Managed by the Forest Department, these areas are not as strictly controlled but are equally as important. Most people do not realize that the most famous game area in Kenya is not a national park but a nature preserve.

ARABUKO-SOKOKE FOREST RESERVE

417 sq kms (161 sq miles)
0–100 m

Surrounded by habitation and farmland here you can find rare birds like the Sokoke scops owl, butterflies, Zanzibar duiker, the yellow-rumped elephant shrew and others.

ARAWALE NATIONAL RESERVE

533 sq kms (213 sq miles)
85–100 m

Hunter's hartebeest or the hirole seems to prefer the thorny bushland of Arawale on the eastern banks of the Tana River.There are no accommodations or facilities in this remote part of northeastern Kenya.

BISANADI NATIONAL RESERVE

606 sq kms
320–660 m

Dense riverine forests and swamps surrounded by arid thorny bushland. The park provides a dispersal area for animals from Meru National park in the wet season.

BONI NATIONAL RESERVE

1339 sq kms 535 sq miles
0–100 m

Unique coastal lowland groundwater forest in Kenya known for its large numbers of elephants in the dry season. It is also used as a buffer to allow passage to the Dodori National Reserve where the elephants can wade out to Elephant Island at low tide.

BUFFALO SPRINGS NATIONAL RESERVE

131 sq kms
900–1000 m

Riverine forests of doum palm and acacia.

DODORI NATIONAL RESERVE

877 sq kms 350 sq miles
0–100 m

An oceanfront reserve consisting mostly of mangrove swamp, groundwater forest and lowland dry forest provides a breeding ground for topi. Linked with Boni and Kiunga Marine National Reserve. Elephants can be seen wading out to an offshore island at low tide. In the water can be found dugong and green turtle.

KAKAMEGA NATIONAL FOREST RESERVE

97 sq kms 39 sq miles
1520–1680 m

The easternmost area of Congo-West Africa equatorial rain forest was gazetted in 1985. Excellent area to discover amphibians, primates and mammals. Animals typically found in tropical areas: fruit bats, giant water shrew, colobus monkey and bush tailed porcupine are found in this unusual park.

KAMNAROK NATIONAL RESERVE

88 sq kms

KERIO VALLEY NATIONAL RESERVE

66 sq kms

KORA NATIONAL RESERVE

1787 sq kms (700 sq miles)
250–440 m

George Adamson chose this site to reintroduce captive leopards and lions into the wild due to the number of rocky outcrops. George Adamson was killed by bandits here in 1988. This riverine park adjoining the Rahole area is not known for large numbers of large mammals and predators and is primarily a scientific study site.

LAKE BOGORIA NATIONAL RESERVE

107 sq kms (44 sq miles)
1000–1600 m

Bushland and riverine forest. Primarily created to protect the Greater Kudu found on the western slopes of the Laikipia Escarpment. Thermal areas that include steam jets and bubbling springs are another attraction of this area. The water is very hot and the ground around the springs can collapse. Lake Bogoria is a shallow soda lake that is fed by the hot sulfurous springs.

LOSAI NATIONAL RESERVE

1806 sq kms.
625–1750 m

Thorny bushland and impenetrable forest once home to rhino and elephant now off limits to tourists.

MARSABIT NATIONAL RESERVE

2088 sq kms (840 sq miles)
420–1700 m

Little visited area in Kenya's former Northern Frontier District. The odd combination of arid dunes next to a small microclimate of lush evergreen forest on the western slope of Mount Marsabit makes this region a curiosity worth visiting. Forest merging with grasslands provides habitat for elephant, kudu, oryx, klipspringer and 13 species of bat. Marsabit is famous as the home of Ahmed whose fiberglass replica stands in the courtyard in Nairobi's museum. Ahmed had massive curving tusks. He had his own around-the-clock bodyguard for the last years of his life and was frequently visited in his old age by tourists. He died at the ripe old age of 65 and is one of the few giant tuskers in the northern area who never fell to poachers.

Volcanic craters and fresh water lakes abound. The image of a green forested mountain rising up from the dry savanna, black lava deserts and volcanic cones make Marsabit a photographer's paradise. Marsabit is the home of the biggest tuskers in Africa. Giraffe can be seen in the forests up on the mountain and the sound of the striped hyena is common at night. A trip to the rim of Dida Galgalla desert could result in the spotting of an aardwolf, Somali ostrich or any number of birds of prey.

Grant's Gazelle

MASAI MARA NATIONAL RESERVE

1800 sq kms
1500–2170 m

Justifiably reserved for the end of most safaris the Mara, as it is called by guides, is the capper in most safari itineraries. The Mara tends to provide spectacular numbers of not only grazers but the cats and other hard to spot animals. The Mara river and the Siria or Oloololo escarpment act like natural boundaries. The Mara also is ideal for photographers with its gently rising flatlands, scenic gorges and dramatic escarpment. The weather in the Mara is also ideal being cool at nights and warm during the day. Dramatic rainshowers sail across the sky and the last golden rays of the sun will turn the Mara into one of the world's most dramatic tableaus. The abundance of predators and wide open spaces also means it is one of the few places in Africa where you can have a fairly reliable chance of seeing a lion kill if you are patient.

Established in 1961, this is the premiere game preserve now famous for being the most northerly portion of the Great Migration. Between July–October the reserve is home to a quarter of a million zebras and one and a quarter million wildebeests. The Mara is also home to Kenya's largest population of lions. Very popular with tourists and feeling the pressure of too much wildlife. Established in 1961 it shares an unmarked boundary with Tanzania's Serengeti National Park. No human settlement is allowed but the Mara technically belongs to the Maasai who are traditional cattle grazers. The safety of the park and its surroundings attracts unusual numbers of large mammals and predators creating havoc for the Maasai. They complain that the animals that wander out of the park cause death and injury not only to their cattle but to the tribespeople. In the north wheat farms necessary to the sustenance of the nation are also encroaching. The final and most problematic danger may be from the tourists themselves. Hundreds of minivans range all over the park 365 days a year creating stress for the animals and a feeling of being inside a giant zoo which the Mara may one day become.

MWEA NATIONAL RESERVE

68 sq kms
1000–1100 m

Thorny brushland and boabob. Few animals but buffalo, lesser kudu and elephant can be spotted.

NASOLOT NATIONAL RESERVE

92 sq kms
750–1500 m

Thorny bushland near the Uganda border. Little game due to poaching.

NGAI NDETHYA NATIONAL RESERVE

212 sq kms
650–750 m

Thornbush, boabob. The migration path between Tsavo East and Tsavo West.

NORTH KITUI NATIONAL RESERVE

745 sq km
428–675 m

Bushland and riverine forest next to Meru National Park. Good spot for hippo and crocs along the Tana River.

RAHOLE NATIONAL RESERVE

1270 sq kms (508sq miles)
250–480 m

The dry thorny bushland on the north side of the Tana river was an experiment to see how local tribes could coexist with indigenous wildlife. It is known for its scenery but there is little game viewing and no facilities.

RIMIO (KERIO VALLEY) NATIONAL RESERVE

66 sq kms

SAMBURU NATIONAL RESERVE

165 sq kms

800–1230 m

Arid hilly region with riverine forests along the Nyiro River. Across the river is its twin reserve; Buffalo Springs. Doum palms, acacia *(Acacia albida)* woodland and scrubland create the vast arid look of Samburu. This region is becoming one of Kenya's most popular stops after the Mara. The sight of the strangely branched doum palms create an unusual look to the region. The light and vast openness creates a lonely panoramic beauty. Samburu's popularity is also due to its being only 213 miles from Nairobi or a short air trip from Wilson airport. The permanent water supply acts like a magnet for the numerous species found here. Other animals have adapted to the waterless scrub of Samburu, for example the gerenuk *(Litocranius walleri)* who gently nibbles at the low brush. Gerenuks are always craning for the tender shoots missed by other grazers. In fact gerenuk is Afrikaans for long neck. Crocodiles and storks are common sights along the river. The lodge has been baiting leopards across the river for years so leopards will be common. Also the evening feeding of crocodiles affords one of the few chances tourists will have of seeing crocs slithering out of the water to feed on scraps. There is also excellent bird-watching with numerous weaver birds, the marial eagle and the blue legged Somali Ostrich.

SHABA NATIONAL RESERVE

239 sq kms (96 sq miles)

700–500 m

Many visitors say Shaba is more dramatic than nearby Samburu but the penalty is less obvious and shyer wildlife in similar landscapes with riverine forests with acacia trees and doum palms. Penny Springs is named after Joy Adamson's leopard Penny. Adamson died here in her Shaba camp in 1980.

SHIMBA HILLS NATIONAL RESERVE

310 sq kms 124 sq miles

120–450 m

A scenic park just 10 miles inland featuring *Brachystegia* woodland, coastal bushland, riverine forests and grasslands. Sable antelope are the main attraction here since you won't see them anywhere else in Kenya. There is also elephant, bush pig, waterbuck, reedbuck and warthog. Parklike country with open grass lands is interrupted by coastal rain forest. Roan antelope have been introduced and are doing well.

SOUTH KITUI NATIONAL RESERVE

1833 sq kms

Bush grasslands and acacia woods. Near the north boundary of Tsavo East National Park. Closed to tourism.

SOUTH TURKANA NATIONAL RESERVE
1091 sq kms
900–2270 m

Dense thorn bush, riverine forests are home to elephant and greater kudu. Rarely visited due to pressure from Somali poachers.

Baboons

TANA RIVER PRIMATE RESERVE
169 sq kms 68 sq miles
40–70 m

Rarely visited, the Tana is Kenya's largest river. A small area of riparian forest has been saved from human destruction and to protect the remaining 800 or so crested mangabeys *(Cercocebus galeritus galeritus)* a subspecies of the rare mangabey. Unusual for its population of what should be a typically West African habitat it also protects the rare red colobus *(Colobus badius)*. These are just four of the seven primates found here. The area is one of the few remaining stands of tropical dense forest near the Indian Ocean. The rare Hunter's hartebeest *(Damaliscus hunteri)* has been spotted here on occasion along with 248 bird species.

MARINE NATIONAL RESERVES

MOMBASA MARINE NATIONAL RESERVE

200 sq kms

Traditional fishing is permitted under license.

GAME SANCTUARIES

SALT LICK TAITA HILLS GAME SANCTUARY

113 sq kms 914 m

Situated on the main Voi-Taita road below the Taita Hills, Salt Lick is linked by a game corridor to Tsavo West National Park. Formerly a sisal plantation, the grasslands and woodlands of the reserve now attract zebra, buffalo, waterbuck, reedbuck, impala, eland, gazelle and elephant.

WORLD HERITAGE SITES

An international group of important natural and cultural sites. These are administered internationally and have no formal protection or supervision. Fort Jesus, Hell's Gate, the Masai Mara National Reserve and Mount Kenya are examples of important sites.

ANIMALS OF KENYA

For wildlife lovers Kenya has the favorable combination of vast savannas and a myriad of species. The end result is the feeling that you are literally watching a panoramic display of the food chain in action. Kenya's highly organized tourism industry, comfortable lodges and excellent transportation enable you to visit many different parks and ecosystems in the typical two week safari. One of the real pleasures is checking off wildlife as you dash around the parks taking in more species in a day than most North Americans see in a lifetime. There are over 100 species of grazers alone, but all visitors will see a wide variety of carnivores, impressive animals like elephant and rhino, hundreds of birds, and a myriad of reptiles, insects and amphibians. We would refer you to more in depth tomes if your interest is serious wildlife study but for the casual observer here are the common residents of Kenya's major game parks. The animals are listed by their common name, scientific name and, for fun, their Swahili name (so you can impress your driver and friends back home).

you can impress your driver and friends back home).

ANTELOPE, ROAN

Hippotragus equinus
KORONGO

A large horselike antelope found in small herds and identified by the male's and female's thick, backswept and heavily ridged horns (the males being the larger). The roan antelope is not common but can be seen in the Shimba Hills preserve. Lighter than the smaller Sable antelope. The coat is short and smooth and the ears are long and narrow. The tail reaches the heels, the lower half tasseled.

ANTELOPE, SABLE

Hippotragus niger
PALA HALA

Owner of the most dramatic horns found on an antelope, the sable survives by using its massive horns to fend off predators. Dark colored, and found in herds of up to 30 animals. Can be found in savanna woodland and grassland. They eat grasses and only need water about once every two days. The upper body is usually chestnut brown to black with the facial mask pattern mimicking the body color.

BABOON

Papio cynocephalus
NYANI

There are seven subspecies of baboon but the yellow and the olive baboon (*papio anubis*) are the most common. Yellow baboons are the most common in East and Central Africa; the olive prefers the cooler highland areas of East Africa. Baboons are gregarious and obnoxious in many of the parks. Some sit patiently waiting for the tour buses to leave in the morning and then throw a fit if they do not receive food. They live and travel in large groups of up to 150, sleep in trees and are the favorite food of the leopard.

BONGO

Tragelaphus euryceros

BONGO

A rare and interesting antelope seen in dense forest and near water. The bongo will stand on its hind legs and dig with its horns. Solitary, shy and an impressive photo for any visitor. They are found in the densest primary and secondary forests, bushy and bamboo jungles in plains up to 4000m. At night they may leave dense cover to browse in clearings and plantations. The bongo's chief enemy is the leopard. When cornered by hunters or dogs, it defends itself bravely and can be very dangerous.

BUFFALO WEAVER

Dinemellia dinemelli (white–headed)

Bubalonis niger (red–billed)

These gregarious birds create the thousands of woven nests hanging from the acacia and baobab trees in the more arid areas. These very noisy 10" tall birds make sounds ranging from the loud falsetto croaking and chattering calls of the red–billed buffalo weavers, to the harsh parrot–like calls and chattering of the white–headed variety. They are common in Tanzania, Kenya and northeastern Uganda. Often seen in areas of thornbush.

BUSHBUCK

Tragelaphus scriptus

PONGO

A rather large, dull and commonly seen member of the antelope family. Bushbucks are nocturnal, solitary and will flee through the bush when surprised. Despite its size the bushbuck is a favorite prey of pythons who strangle and then can consume a smaller animal whole. Averaging about 30"–36" high at the shoulder the bushbuck can usually be found in forests, riverine thickets and bush where they have plenty of thick cover.

CAPE BUFFALO

Syncerus caffer

Mᴮᴼᴳᴼ

To hunters the wounded male mbogo is the most dangerous of the big five (lion, leopard, elephant, rhino and buffalo). Solitary male cape buffalos are known for their bad temper and unpredictable ability to charge vehicles when they come too close. Found near water the buffalo is made even more dangerous by its habit of surprising campers who seek water after dark. One hint is when walking in dense brush listen for the distinctive chirp of the ever-present tick birds.

CHEETAH

Acinonyx jubatus

Dᵁᴹᴬ

Elegant, calm and determined, the cheetah can surprise many a visitor by its utter disregard of humans by using vehicles as lookouts. Leopard-size in body, they are greyhound shaped except the head which is short–muzzled, small and rounded, with ears short and roundish. The cheetah uses its speed to overtake and trip prey. Cubs are a common sight since they stay with the mother for an entire season. Lions, leopards and hyenas will often kill and eat young cheetahs; sometimes they will also attack the adults.

CROCODILE, NILE

Crocodylus niloticus

Mᴬᴹᴮᴬ

Although the crocodile has undergone the same persecution as his prehistoric friend the rhino, it seems that they have stabilized in fair numbers in the parks. Once hunted for shoes, belts and handbags, the crocodile is found in the lower riverine regions of Kenya. The five meter (16.5 feet) crocodiles still consume numbers of unwary Kenyans every year. They sit patiently submerged in waterholes waiting for prey to bend down to drink, then leap out of the water and drag the kicking victim to death. They literally tear the victim to pieces and then stuff the chunks in their dens at the side of rivers. Be careful approaching any river or any riverbank. Two other smaller species of crocodile are found in East Africa, the long–nosed and the dwarf crocodile, but neither is dangerous to man.

DIK DIK, KIRK'S

Rhynchotragus kirki

DIK DIK

Kirk's is the smallest antelope found in Kenya's arid regions. (Gunthers dik dik is found in the Marsabit) They have no need of drinking water and can be found around the base of hills and kopjes. They often stand on their hind feet to get at succulent branches. The dik dik is easy to identify by its diminutive size and gentle shy demeanor. Their calls of excitement, warning and fear are a ringing "Zick–zick," hence the name Dik Dik. Mates become life partners living together with latest and previous young. Enemies include all larger predators as well as some monitor lizards and large snakes.

DUIKER, COMMON or GREY

Sylvicapra grimmia

NSYA

Found in dense brush or woodlands, usually nocturnal. Females are larger than males. When agitated will snort and wheeze. Found in many different ecosystems ranging from montane bamboo forests to arid lowlands. The bush duiker is reportedly faster than the forest duiker. It often outruns and outdodges dogs while dashing between hiding places.

EAGLE, TAWNY
Aquilla rapax

They are often seen along the rivers. Nests are made in the tops of trees. The tawny eagle often associates with vultures and can be seen at recent kills and around camps. They can vary between dark brown to light coffee in color (a more common sight in Northern Kenya) and have a relatively short, rounded tail, with legs feathered. Their voice sounds like a raucous, yelping cry. Found throughout East Africa but most frequently in northern Kenya.

ELAND, COMMON
Taurotragus oryx
POFU

The largest antelope identified by its long curving horns. Usually found grazing in the early part of the day in small herds of 5–50 animals. It avoids swamps, forests and deserts. Eland use the same water conservation measures as gazelles and oryxes to cope in waterless areas. They access high foliage by breaking off branches with their horns. Their greatest predators are lions and spotted hyena.

ELEPHANT, AFRICAN
Loxodonta africana
TEMBO

The future of elephant is one of the major issues of African wildlife preservation. Facing few predators, most elephants used to die from poachers' bullets before they reached an old age. Today their wide range, massive food consumption and limited area makes them incredibly destructive on every habitat they thrive in. The great herds of the '50s are gone but the elephant is resilient. Poaching has insured that the giant tuskers of the northern part of Kenya have been genetically culled from Africa. Elephants are matriarchal and are found in close knit herds, while the old cranky bulls can be found wandering in solitude. The elephant must stay on the move to find the 250 kg of green material it needs to consume to survive every day. Elephants will push over or pull down large trees to get at the high branches. They also love domestic crops and can destroy acres of corn, bananas or sugarcane in one night. The long life (over 100 years) and wide ranging nature of Kenya's elephants are a growing problem in the Masai Mara where many Masai are killed by elephants every year.

FLAMINGO
Phoenicopterus ruber
HEROE

Lesser Flamingos are a much smaller and richly colored species. They can be identified by the dark carmine colored bill. They consume the algae and diatoms found in the warm shallow lakes like Lake Nakura (up to two million have been counted here at one time) and other water areas. The greater flamingo is a bottom feeder and also eats molluscs and crustaceans. A much larger and paler bird than the lesser flamingo, from which it is easily distinguished by its paler pink bill. Both types are commonly found on alkaline lakes throughout East Africa, but are very infrequent visitors to coastal areas.

GAZELLE, GRANT'S
Gazella granti
SWALA GRANTI

This large, commonly seen gazelle can be found going against the traditional migration patterns of the East African plains. They can be found in short glass plains during the dry season and the savanna woodlands in the rainy season. December–February and August–September is the best time for calves. They do not need to drink at water holes to survive and are usually in herds of 10–30 animals.

GAZELLE, THOMSON'S

Gazella thomsoni

SWALA TOMI

Probably the most frequently encountered gazelle in Kenya game parks. "Tommies" are found in large groups on the Serengeti and move between the woodlands savanna and the floodplains every year. They survive well because they can feed closer to ground than the larger grazers like the wildebeest. Tommies also will go to water when available. During very dry periods they can be found in herds of over 400 animals. The young are commonly stalked by lions, cheetahs and leopards.

GENET

Genetta genetta

KANU

A nocturnal animal rarely spotted since it prefers rocks and trees as its habitat. Genets are good climbers, especially downward. They defend themselves by catlike arching of the back, erecting hair on the tail and spinal crest, and scratching and biting while on their back. They also eject an evil smelling anal secretion. Genets feed on small rodents, birds, lizards, snakes, frogs, eggs, insects, spiders, seafood and fruit.

GERENUK

Litocranius walleri

SWALA TWIGA

Found in the arid north of Kenya the gerenuk can be recognized by its giraffe-like features. It is commonly seen feeding by standing on its hind legs and nibbling at acacia bushes. One of the most desert-adapted antelopes, it prefers open landscapes. Wedge-shaped hooves, powerful lower limbs and modified lumbar vertebrae allow gerenuks to stand bipedally and graze high up more securely than other antelopes.

GIRAFFE

Giraffa camelopardalis (Masai)

Giraffa reticulata (Reticulated)

Twiga

There are three subspecies of giraffe in Kenya. The Masai with its softer pattern is the most common and found in the parks south and west of Nairobi. The Reticulated has more clearly defined patches and is darker in color. They are common in the north in more arid parks like Samburu and Buffalo Springs. The Rothschild giraffe from Uganda is the rarest and the tallest and is now only found in Lake Nakura (they were introduced by AFEW). They lose their white socks and five horns when interbred with Masai or Reticulated giraffes. Giraffes feed on acacia leaves and are able to pick between the needle sharp thorns. They feed in the early morning and late in the day. During the heat of the day they can be found sitting or standing in the shade. Males are larger than females and although adults have few predators, it is not uncommon to see claw marks and torn tails from hungry lions.

GUINEA FOWL

Numida mitrata

The guinea fowl look like well dressed dowagers rushing to a linen sale. Common in bush country, arid thorn-bush areas, neglected cultivation, open parklike country and savanna woodlands. The helmeted guinea-fowl (*Numida meleagres*) is about 20" high and makes a loud cackling call. The attractive spotted plumage is offset by the bird's scabby blue head and bony horn. A series of loud, shrill cackles and a loud "kak, kak, kak, kak, kak" is the typical call you'll hear.

HARTEBEEST

Alcelaphus buselaphus

KONGONI

Found along the edge of woodlands and longer grasslands the hartebeast have shorter horns than most antelopes. Their long horselike faces make them easy to identify. Males are darker with more pronounced markings than females. Calves are pale tan without markings. Males often stay with their mothers until sub–adults (2.5 years) before joining bachelor herds. Found in the savanna regions, the hartebeest must drink at least once a day or feed on melons and tubers during dry seasons. Socially they mix with zebra and wildebeest.

HIPPOPOTAMUS

Hippopotamus amphibius

KIBOKO

Ugly, ungainly and never far from water, hippos are the overweight denizens of the savanna. Most people are shocked to discover that the hippo is the largest killer of humans in East Africa. Tourists are even more surprised to find out that hippos are commonly found wandering around campsites at night when they come up to graze. Hippos like to live in herds of 10–50 animals and spray their droppings on the rocks around the waterholes and in the water flipping their tails around in a fanlike motion to get maximum coverage. They also can be found fighting to establish dominance. Their razor sharp tusks often rip large gashes in their soft pink skin. Known to inhabit lakes, rivers and swamps with sufficient water, hippos also may be observed under ideal conditions in the crystal clear waters of Mzima Springs in the Tsavo National Park, Kenya.

HORNBILLS (Red/Yellow-billed)

Tockus erythrorhynchus/flavirostris
TOKOS

Hornbills can be seen darting from tree to tree in the Mara. The gregarious hornbill is famous for being a prototypal chauvinist bird. The male actually seals the incubating female into a large nesting hole in dead trees. The male then feeds the female and the young through a small opening. When old enough to fly, the offspring and the female chip their way out. The average size for these medium to large birds is between 17"–20" tall. Hornbills are characterized by their large curved bills.

HUNTING DOG

Lycaon pictus
MBAWA MWITU

A rare and colorful sight in Kenya. They will run down their prey in teams until the quarry falls over from exhaustion. The pack will then tear the animal to pieces. Wild dogs hunt game as small as hares and as large as zebra. Persecution, disease and reduction in wildlife habitats and populations have caused a decline in wild dog numbers, raising fears they could soon become extinct. Wild dogs are often in competition with hyenas who try to steal their kills.

HYENA

Crocuta crocuta
FISI

The spotted hyena is one of the few animals that can create fear in the African night. They have been known to attack sleeping humans and are fierce aggressors around camps and villages. The calls of the hyena are unique and chilling; they can make up to 17 different sounds from what sounds like insane laughter to barking to howling screams. The hyena kills live prey as well as eats carrion. It is not unusual to see them coated in dried blood skulking around campsites.

HYRAX

Heterohyrax brucei

Pimbi

Every guide will tell you that the hyrax is the closest living relative to the elephant (in bone structure only). The rock hyrax lives in communes in the many rocky out-croppings on the savanna. The tree hyrax is known for its blood curdling scream at night. Small, tailless creatures with long bodies and short legs that resemble rodents more than ungulates. Bush and rock hyraxes live in colonies composed of a male with a harem of several related females and their offspring.

IMPALA

Aepyceros melampus

Swala Pala

The distinctive impala is known for its gravity defying leaps and bounds as it scurries away at the approach of predators. The impala can jump up to 10 feet high and as long as 36 feet. They can be found grazing in bachelor herds or in harems of between 20–100 females. Often confused with Grant's or Thompson's gazelle, the impala is identified by its lyre shaped horns. The horns are used to advantage when bachelor males fight for control of harems.

JACKAL

Canis mesomelas

Bweha

The jackal has a reputation for its cunning and speed. In reality the jackal is a dog and a scavenger surviving mainly by stealing carrion from vultures. It only hunts small rodents, large insects and domestic livestock. Jackels scavenge at lion and hyena kills. Leopards, with a well–known preference for dog meat, are the main predator of adult jackals and eagles are a threat to young pups around the den.

KLIPSPRINGER

Oreotragus oreotragus

Mʙᴜᴢɪ Mᴀᴡᴇ

Found on kopjes and steep rock faces. They can spend their entire lives within an area as small as 25 acres depending on availability of forage. Sure footed and sturdy they will scamper goatlike up steep rock faces when disturbed. They depend on steep, rocky terrain as a refuge against predators. Water independent, they graze on leaves, shoots, berries, fruits, seed pods, flowers, evergreens, succulents, herbs and green grass.

KUDU, GREATER

Tragelaphus strepsiceros

Tᴀɴᴅᴀʟᴀ Mᴋᴜʙᴡᴀ

The second tallest antelope with spectacular horns. Found in Marsabit National Reserve. Kudu live in small herds and prefer to stay in hilly areas with bush cover. Males are usually solitary. Adept at concealment, it is one of the few large mammals that thrives in settled areas. Herds typically include one to three females and their offspring but averages vary from five to up to 15 depending on the season.

KUDU, LESSER

Tragelaphus imberbis

Tᴀɴᴅᴀʟᴀ Nᴅᴏɢᴏ

Found in pairs, the lesser kudu is smaller, has more stripes and smaller horns (only the male has horns). The lesser kudu uses thickets for camouflage, foraging on up to 118 different plant species. Herds tend to be larger in the rainy seasons. It seldom browses acacias and remains on all fours while feeding. When running the tail is fanned and raised and extremely conspicuous.

LEOPARD

Panthera pardus

CHUI

The crowning achievement of most safaris is the sighting of a leopard high in a tree or poised on a kopje. Leopards are shy, solitary and nocturnal animals that can be seen with some regularity in the Mara. Even though the stunning sight of a leopard is enough to attract every vehicle in the park the leopard will gaze back calmly. The sight of a rotting antelope carcass hanging in a tree is usually evidence of a leopard nearby. Leopards also like to walk around campsites late at night and are often discovered in areas of human habitation. Employing infinite patience and stealth, leopards try to get within five yards of quarry before pouncing.

LION

Panthera leo

SIMBA

There is little to compare with your first sight of a magnificent male lion. Perhaps no other animal makes you feel glad you are in a steel vehicle. Almost invisible in the tall golden grass, lions easily stalk and kill any hoofed animal they choose. In fact lionesses can easily take down a full sized buffalo by gripping its nostrils in a suffocating death grip. They will then lovingly lick the nose and hind quarters before feeding. Lions hunt in groups with the females doing most of the dirty work. The males will slowly move the prey towards the hiding females. Many times it seems they are practicing since they lack the speed of the cheetah or the viciousness of the hunting dogs.

Lions are most active in the late afternoon and can be found sitting under trees or on rock outcrops.

MONGOOSE, BANDED

Mungos mungo

KICHECHE

Mongooses can be seen in groups usually scattering when vehicles approach. The banded mongoose is greyish–brown and medium–sized (about 18") with transverse dark bands along its body. They prey on bird eggs, insects and fruits. They live in burrows and make a host of noises when agitated or fighting. Both sexes are territorial, repelling same-sex intruders. One male lives with several related females rearing their young communally.

MONKEY, VERVET

Cercopithecus aethiops

NGUCHIRO

The vervet monkey is identified by its black face and smaller size (48"–56") than the baboon. Many of these inquisitive and noisy monkeys can be found around the camps looking for scraps or handouts. They are often found in riverine vegetation especially groves of fever trees which provide both safety and sustenance year-round. Vervets help propagate their food plants by dispersing seeds in their droppings. They are gregarious animals and are often found in large groups.

ORIBI

Ourebia ourebi

TAYA

Found in the Masai Mara the oribi is easy to confuse with duikers. Found in pairs the oribi will bound when surprised in a stiff legged pouncing action. Oribi prefer open grassland tall enough to hide in but not too tall to see over. Settlement, agriculture and hunting have greatly reduced the oribi habitat and range.

ORYX

Oryx beisa

Choroa

Found in arid regions the oryx or beisa has been hunted for its massive horns (some reach up to 45 inches in length) They feed at night and very early in the morning. Found in very arid regions like the Marsabit and Tana river region, they are easy to identify since both males and females carry the dramatic upsweeping horns. The oryx drinks regularly when water is available but can get by on melons, roots, bulbs and tubers for which they can dig with their sharp hooves.

OSTRICH

Struthio camelus massaicus
    (Maasai ostrich)

Struthio camelus molybdophanes
    (Somali ostrich)

Mbuni

Even from a distance it is easy to spot the ungainly ostrich. The females are a drab brown and the male is all formal in his black and white plumage. The male's skin turns bright red during breeding season. Ostriches use their large feet to evade predators and can reach speeds of up to 30mph. Ostriches prefer the lush, open grasslands of the savanna plains, dry thorn bush country and semi–desert.

PYTHON

Python sebae

Nyoka

The python is Africa's largest snake. Thick bodied reptiles, they grow to a length of 6 meters (20 ft.). They are typically found near water except in the higher regions. Pythons, contrary to popular belief, will not attack unless provoked.

REEDBUCK

Redunca redunca

TOHE

A common large antelope found in the lower floodplain and grasslands. Active at night they can be seen picking at low brush in the late afternoon and dawn. Found in Amboseli, Nairobi and Tsavo the reedbuck is usually found close to water. The common reedbuck lives in monogamous pairs in territories of 86 to 148 acres. Reedbucks run in a distinctive rocking canter, well adapted to high grass and hillsides, displaying their white tails and whistling when excited.

RHINOCEROUS, BLACK

Diceros bicornis

KIFARU

The major difference between white rhino and black rhino is their lips (white is the bad translation of *weit* or wide mouthed); black rhino have pronounced triangular upper lips. Sadly you will only see black rhino in Kenya. An attempt to introduce white rhino resulted in the slaughter of the remaining five white rhinos and one ranger in Meru National Park in 1988. Many people believe the days of the rhino are numbered since there are only around 500 left in Kenya. That is down from over 22,000 in 1970. Poaching still continues (primarily by the Chinese for questionable medicinal purposes) and the price of one horn is more than most Kenyans will make in ten years. If poachers are not enough to ensure their demise, rhinos have terrible eyesight, usually run when provoked, have a heck of a time procreating, and live solitary lives.

SECRETARY BIRD

Sagittarius serpentarius

It's easy to spot the tall gawky birds that strut purposely and slowly through the low grasslands. The 40" high bird has a conspicuous crest that looks like a tiara or halo. The reason the leggy birds walk so carefully and silently is because they are after their favorite meal of snake. They are widely distributed but not commonly seen throughout East Africa on open plains, bush country and farmlands. Though usually silent, during breeding season they can produce remarkable croaks and even a lion-like cough.

SITATUNGA

Tragelaphus spekii

Nzohe

The Sitatunga antelope is found only in the Saiwa Swamp National Park. Their total population is just over 100 in all of Kenya. Unusual for their elongated hooves and facility in swimming, the Sitatunga are able to traverse marshy lands easily. Sitatunga feed on swamp vegetation up to their shoulders, come ashore to graze on green pastures and enter the forest to browse woody vegetation. They will stand on their hind legs to reach high flowers and males sometimes break branches with the backs of their horns.

TOPI

Damaliscus topi

Nyamnera

The topi has short curved horns and a very distinctive sad face. It likes greener grasses and shoots. The morning is a good time to watch the males face off in bachelor herds. Similar to the hartebeest the topi has a rich red coat with dark hind quarters, front legs and face. Their number and habitat been greatly reduced by human hunting and habitat destruction.

VULTURE
Gyps africanus

Vultures are medium to very large birds (26"–34") with long wings, short tails and relatively small naked or down covered heads. Luckily vultures have no sense of smell. They eat what is left by hyenas and jackals (usually waiting patiently like aged undertakers in the background). Vultures actually need other predators to rip open the carcass so they can begin the job of picking and peeling what is left. You can often hear their harsh squawking croaks while they are feeding on the carrion. Sometimes after they eat they cannot fly so they will hop away and digest their meal.

WARTHOG
Phacochoerus aethiopicus
Ngiri

Easily the ugliest hooved animal on the face of this planet. The warthog is actually a sweet lovable pig once you get to know it. They live in large burrows in termite mounds and actually have the presence of mind to enter backwards to facilitate a quick exit when disturbed.

A warthog family running at full speed is a humorous sight indeed. Its puny tail sticks straight up and it is usually followed by its tiny long-legged offspring. The warthog defends itself with its razor-edged tusks that actually sharpen against each other as it eats.

WATERBUCK, COMMON or DEFASSA
Kobus ellipsiprymnus
Kuru

Probably the least exotic looking savanna animal to North American visitors. These deer-like antelope have a subspecies (Defassa Waterbuck) found only west of the Rift Valley. They are usually found within a few hours walk of water and can be seen anytime day or night. Males have horns.

WILDEBEAST, COMMON or GNU
Connochaetes taurinus
NYUMBU

The most common grazing animal on the Kenya Plains. The estimated 1.3 million wildebeest or gnus still make the great Serengeti migration each year. They need fairly fresh grasses because of the inability to crop closely and cannot stray more than 15km from water. Not known for their intelligence, gnus will never seem to make the right moves when chased by predators. Even left to their own devices they will do strange things like roll around, buck and run around in circles without any prodding.

ZEBRA
Hippotigris quagga
   (Burchell's or Plains Zebra)
Hippotigris grevyi (Grevy's Zebra)
PUNDA MILLIA

One will ask if the zebra is a white donkey with black stripes or vice versa. The zebra is one of the more striking examples of African adaptation. Zebras are never found in forests or bush so their stripes can only confuse when they are great numbers. Of the two species, Burchell's are the ones with the heavy bands while Grevy's have thinner, fingerprint style stripes.

Burchell's zebra are found in the west and south and Grevy's in the north. Both species are the favorite food of lions and hyenas.

HOTEL CHAIN CHARACTERISTICS

In the course of our travels, we have noted certain characteristics within hotel chains. These are listed below. We have not included chains with fewer than five properties in Kenya.

African Tours & Hotels Ltd.
Most properties located in outstanding sites. Rather poorly maintained.

Block Hotels
Large variety of properties. Somewhat varied in standards and quality.

Mt. Kilimanjaro Safari Club
Smaller, older properties in the Amboseli/Tsavo region. Tour groups.

Lonrho Hotels Kenya Ltd.
Reliably high standards. Large variety of properties.

Musiara Ltd. (Governors)
Consistently excellent. Intimate and imaginative. High quality food and service. Perfect and pricey.

Msafiri Inns
Generally lower standards. Less frequented by international travelers.

Sarova Hotels
Variety of properties. Varying standards and quality. Newest Sarova hotels imaginative and colorful. Dining unexceptional.

Serena Lodges & Hotels
Imaginative decor done in various African themes. Reliably high standards. Rooms consistently on the small side. Great gardens.

Chains with fewer than five hotels in Kenya include:

Alliance Hotels

Hilton International

Inter-Continental Hotels

Prestige Hotels Ltd.

Windsor Hotel International Ltd.

FIELDING'S TOP "TOPIS"

We visited more than 230 places. We "tip" our topis to the 93 best Kenyan hotels, lodges, tented camps, ranch/sanctuaries, homestays and grass shacks on the beach. "Phantom" hats have been awarded to places which are not yet fully operational. Three "tipped topis" were the most hats awarded to any one place. Throughout the book, all hotels listed in large print are well worth a visit.

THREE HATS

Blue Safari Club
Borana Lodge
Finch Hattons Safari Camp
Hemingways Kiwayu Safari Village
Kongoni Valley Game Ranch
Larsens
Lewa Downs
Little Governor's Camp
Loldia House
Mpata Safari Club
Mfangano Island Camp
Mundui
Ngare Niti
Ol Donyo Laro
Ol Donyo Wuas
Ol Malo (phantom hats)
Serena Beach Hotel

Mara Intrepids Club
Pemba Channel Inn
Sikenani Camp Tortilis Camp
(phantom hats)

TWO HATS

Aberdare Country Club
Island Camp
Kichwa Tembo
Mara Safari Club
Mt. Kenya Safari Club
Nairobi Serena Hotel
The Norfolk Hotel
Ol Pejeta Lodge
Peponi Hotel
Rekero Farm
Rondo Retreat
Safari Park Hotel
Samburu Intrepids Club
Sarova Shaba Lodge
Segera Ranch
Takaungu House
The Tamarind Village
Windsor Golf & Country Club

TWO & ONE-HALF HATS

Colcheccio Ranch (phantom hats)
Giraffe Manor
Governor's Camp
Indian Ocean Beach Club
Indian Ocean Lodge

ONE & ONE-HALF HATS

The Ark Forest Lodge
Diani House
Funzi Island Fishing Club
Grand Regency Hotel (phantom hats)
Longonot Ranch Olerai House
Rusinga Island
Siana Springs
Taita Hills Lodge
Tana Delta Camp
Wingu Kenda

ONE HAT

Amboseli Serena Lodge
Delamere Camp
Deloraine
Jadini Beach
Kilaguni Lodge
Lake Naivasha Club
Malindi Beach Club
Mara Serena Lodge
Mayfair Court Hotel
Naro Moru River Lodge
Nyali Beach
Olkurruk Mara Lodge
Outspan Hotel
Salt Lick Safari Lodge
Shimba Hills
Sweetwaters Tented Camp
The Tents (at Taita)
Whitesands

ONE-HALF HAT

Beachcomber Club
Chale Paradise Island
(phantom one-half hat)
Che-Chale
Elsamere
Fairview Hotel
Hotel Intercontinental Mombasa
Kaskazi Beach Hotel
Keekorok Lodge
Kilili Baharini
Kingfisher Lodge
Kipangani Sea Breezes
Lagoon Reef Hotel
Lake Baringo Club
Leopard Beach Hotel
Pinewood Village
Saruni
Tsavo Safari Camp
White Elephant

NAIROBI CIRCUITS

1. Get to the Nairobi Game Park at about 4 p.m. of your first day. After entering through the Main Gate, notice the spread of land and horizon with the Nairobi skyline off to your left and the distinctive "four-knuckle" peaks of the Ngong Hills to the right.

   Go for the scenery, and you will enjoy coming across the animals more. You may see giraffe, zebra, impala, Thomson's gazelles, warthog, baboon, rhino, an assortment of birds and just maybe, lion! Remember, the park closes at 7 p.m.

2. On another day, take the Langata Road. Near the turnoff to Langata Road South, follow the signs on the right to the Arts and Crafts Village at the Ostrich Farm. Feed the tame ostriches and watch handicrafts being made: jewelry, soapstone and wood carvings, basket weaving, spinning and weaving, flamingo and feather tying, and more. This is a unique shopping experience. Back on Langata Road, turn onto Langata Road South and follow the signs and visit Utamaduni, an upmarket craft center.

   Continue down Langata South Road following signs to the African Fund for Endangered Wildlife (AFEW) Giraffe Center. Continue with Circuit 3 or 4 below.

3. Do Circuit 2, but treat yourself to prebooked lunch at Giraffe Manor. Proceeds go to AFEW.

4. Cross to Karen Road either on Bogani Road or Langata Road. Visit Karen Blixen Museum. Have lunch in a Karen garden at Charlie's Restaurant. After lunch, follow signs to the Kazuri Bead Factory—visit factory, buy inexpensive but colorful ceramic jewelry and pottery. Return or continue with Circuit 5.

5. Follow Karen Road to Langata Road. Turn left to Karen Village. Visit Marco Polo, a craft shop. Continue on Dagoretti Road to visit Rockhound for fine mineral crafts.

6. Visit Limuru for tea or lunch with Mrs. Mitchell. Visit small church at beginning of road to her estate.

SOME INTERESTING OVERLAND CIRCUITS

1. NAIROBI–BARINGO–MARALAL–SAMBURU–MT. KENYA–NAIROBI

Best to use a four-wheel drive vehicle, but a minibus will do it. Requires about five hours travel time between overnight stops. Road is roughest from Maralal to Samburu.

Take Limuru Road passing through highland tea plantations. (Take old road following signs for Kentmere Club for most scenic ride.) Eventually will join A104. Stop for view of Mt. Longonot at edge of Rift Valley (second stop is best.) Continue to Nakuru. Take B4 to Lake Baringo. Stop for picnic lunch, perhaps inside the park at Lake Nakuru. Spend at least one night at Lake Baringo. The night before, ask for box lunch on day of departure.

Just north of Baringo, turn right at Lorok fork to connect with C77 to Maralal. Notice beautiful views of Lake Baringo as road climbs. Turn left on C77 to go north. Enjoy the sight of Samburu herdsmen and people dressed and on their way to market.

Spend two nights at Maralal Lodge, which is in a small game park with salt lick. Visit Kenyatta's house, bring pens for street boys at colorful Samburu market. Make arrangements for guide to Losiolo View Point for second day and request box lunches.

On second day, collect box lunches, get guide and go to View Point, about a 20-minute drive.

"You will be astounded, and you will never want to leave. After driving through an evergreen forest, a small village and rolling farmland, you begin to see over the curve of the rolling pasture. Suddenly, the road ends, and the world you have been driving through drops away. Thousands of feet straight down the land seems to twist and roll into wave after wave of rocky hills, twisting valleys and broken outcrops. A golden haze sets off pockets of green pasturage dotted with antlike flocks of sheep. The haze turns misty blue as the eye reaches for distant mountain ranges and a nonexistent horizon. The air is very clear and seems to vibrate like a silent bell. There is magic and majesty in this place that cannot be denied, that once recognized, will be known forever. You want to be silent, you want to dance and share it with kindred souls. You will never want to leave.

"Soon, local people arrive. They are polite and will leave you alone, but they would also love to socialize, and they belong in this place. If you want, share the remains of your lunch boxes (there is always too much). You may want to walk or climb a little. You may just want to sit and commune with the view. You will never want to leave."

(From a Safari Journal)

Eventually, return to lodge. You will feel light and refreshed. Request lunch boxes for the following day road trip.

From Maralal, return South on C77 to left turn on C78 toward Wamba. Enjoy high plateau views of many mountain ranges, including Mt. Kenya if it is clear. Before Wamba, turn right to go south and east on C79 to the A2. Turn right to go south toward the border town of Isiolo. (Have lunch at any view point that pleases. Share anything extra with herdsmen.)

Heading south, you can opt for a stopover (at least two nights) in the Samburu Game Reserve Area (See Northern Kenya Section.)

Continuing south from Isiolo, you have Mt. Kenya and attendant ranges directly in front of you, a glorious view in the clear highland air. Stop for pictures of Mt. Kenya before the road turns south, as the best view of the mountain is from the north.

You can stopover at several homestay ranches in the Mt. Kenya Area before reaching the high ranch country town of Nanuki. You could stop for a fresh trout lunch under the trees (with attendant Colobus monkeys) at Kentrout Trout Farm at Timau, several miles north of Nanyuki (there are signs on the road). You can stop at the Mt. Kenya Safari Club, the Aberdare Country Club, Sweetwaters, Ol Pejeta, Naro Moru River Lodge, the Outspan Hotel or just return to Nairobi.

2. NAIROBI–NYERI–NANYUKI–MT. KENYA–SAMBURU

Driving straight through to destinations, the driving times are approximately as follows: 1.5 hours to Nyeri, 3.5 hours to Nanyuki, and 5 hours to Samburu.

Take the A2 north on the Thika Road.

Stop in Nyeri to have coffee, lunch, or tea on the garden terrace of the Outspan Hotel. You might be enticed to spend the night. Visit the Baden-Powell Museum on the grounds.

Or, if you prefer to bypass Nyeri and the Outspan Hotel, turn right just after Karatina.

Continue north to Nanyuki on the A2. On clear days you get good views of Mt. Kenya looking to the right as you travel from Nyeri. The shoulders of Mt. Kenya's broad base fill the horizon even on cloudy days. The road winds from lowland pineapple plantations to hilly farmland to the spreading wonder and far horizons of the Laikipia Plateau. The rolling ranchland surrounding Nanuki is anchored by the looming mountain.

At Nanyuki, stay in Mt. Kenya Safari Club (see detailed write-up in accommodation section. Note: men need coat and tie for dinner) or choose a ranch homestay or the self-help cabins at Timau's Kentrout.

Or simply continue up the A2 to Isiolo and stay in the Samburu Game Reserve Area. (See accommodation section.) It is best to stay in the Samburu Game Reserve Area at least two nights to allow one full day of game viewing.

Take time (requires two to three hours) at some point to drive up the Sirimon Route to the first hut on Mt. Kenya. (four-wheel drive is necessary, especially if there has been rain.) Follow signs to the Mt. Kenya National Park and enter at the Sirimon Gate. You can also choose to walk up from this point. Since the track is broad enough for vehicles, no guide is needed. You can choose to bring a picnic lunch.

Return to Nairobi. (About 1.5 hours to Nyeri, 3.5 to Nanuki, and 5 hours to Samburu.

3. NAIROBI–MTITO ANDEI–CHYULU HILLS– AMBOSELI–NAMANGA–NAIROBI

This is a good two-day trip for either minivan or four-wheel drive. It takes about 3 hours to Kilaguni, 3–4 hours from Kilaguni to Amboseli, and about 4 hours from Amboseli to Nairobi.

Take A109 south toward Mombasa. On a clear day, you can begin to see Mt. Kilimanjaro off to the right just after clearing Nairobi. Turn right into Tsavo West at Mtito Andei. Follow signs for Kilaguni Lodge. Arrive in time for lunch at 1 p.m. Visit Mzima Springs and Hippo Pools in the afternoon. From the lodge, enjoy views of Mt. Kilimanjaro and watching various animals visiting waterhole. Arrange with lodge staff to join convoy through Chyulu Hills at 8 a.m. next morning.

Travel in convoy toward Mt. Kilimanjaro with Chuylu Hills to the right. Cross Shaitani lava flow. You will see Masai herdsmen and villages or manyattas. Could choose to stay at Finch Hattons Camp or continue on to Amboseli National Park.

Stay at Amboseli Serena or possibly at the Tortilis Camp (see accommodation section for details). After entering the park, your game drive to the lodge will probably include sightings of Amboseli's big herds of elephant. At the lodge, request box lunches for following day.

The next day, go for early morning game drive. Return for breakfast. Game drive out to connect with C103 heading toward Namanga (border town with Tanzania). Enjoy seeing animals and Masai gatherings in villages and along the road.

From Namanga, take A104 back to Nairobi.

4. SAIWA SWAMP–MT. ELGON–CHERANGANI HILLS VIA KERIO VALLEY

It takes approximately six–seven hours to first stopover at Barnley's.

Drive to Nakuru via A104 (approximately 2.5–3 hours). Turn north to Baringo. Continue to just before Marigat. Turn left (direction Kabarnet) onto C51. Some of the most beautiful landscapes in Kenya are along this road, and there are several places to stop for scenic vistas, and a picnic. The road is very smooth. After reaching Eldoret Lake, take B2 (direction Kitale). From Kitale, take A1 (direction Kaperguria) to Barnley's (just past Saiwa Swamp National Park).

During the next two days, visit Saiwa Swamp National Park, then explore Cherangani Hill Area and Mt. Elgon.

Return to Nairobi by passing through Eldoret, then taking new tarmac road (C54) through the Eldama Ravine and Chepkorio. This route is 165 kms, and trucks are not permitted. Take a picnic and find one of the beautiful view points towards the Kerio Valley and Tigen Hills. You will pass forests and green pastures. The scenery is spectacular.

5. LAKE MAGADI VIA OLORGESAILIE PREHISTORIC SITE

An Acheulian Site discovered by Louis and Mary Leakey in 1942, Olorgesailie is an interesting stop on the way to Lake Magadi, an amazing pink soda lake, a frequent feeding stop for Kenya's giant flamingo.

At Olorgesailie, you can see animal bones and hand axes. There is a small museum and four "self-help" bandas (no bedding, do your own cooking).

Leave Nairobi on the Langata Road. 1.6 kms after the Main Gate Entrance to the Nairobi Game Park, turn left onto Magadi Road. At 24.1 kms, you will have a spectacular view over the Rift Valley. You will descend from 1700 meters altitude of Nairobi to the 600 meters altitude of Lake Magadi. Take lots of water. The heat can be unbearable. At 56 kms a track leads left 1.5 kms to Olorgesailie Prehistoric Site.

Return to Nairobi by retracing route.

6. RIFT VALLEY LAKES CIRCUIT (4+ NIGHTS)

A. DELAMARE CAMP

Depart Nairobi for Nakuru on A104. Stop at one of the viewpoints at the edge of the Rift Valley. Spend the first night at Delamere Camp (tented camp) about one and a half hours from Nairobi and before Nakuru. You turn right off the main road and circle under the road. The camp is beautifully sited at the edge of Lake Elmenteita. Enjoy bird walks, sundowners on the cliff and the night game drive. Ask for packed lunch the night before you leave.

B. DELAMARE CAMP TO LAKE BARINGO VIA LAKE BOGORIA

From Delamere Camp continue to Nakuru and turn north on the Baringo road (B4). Continue—the road is good. The turn to Lake Bogoria is to the right near Marigat and before Lake Baringo. Have your picnic at the Hot Geothermal Springs—at the end of the paved road and on the edge of the lake. Boiling hot water gushes into the air and whirlpools rumble and bubble (take extra care with young children). Sometimes thousands of flamingo ring the lake in pink. Forested hills rise all around. It is an isolated, beautiful and primeval setting. (If you have a four-wheel drive and lots of time, you can go to the camping site under giant fig trees at the far end of the lake—rough road and lovely spot.)

Drive to Lake Baringo and the pick-up point for Island Camp. The last stretch of the road is especially rough. Leave your vehicle (there is an askari to look after it) and catch the boat to Island Camp. Spend at least two nights in this wonderful spot and be sure to take the boat trip into the swamp. (Another, less romantic accommodation option is Lake Baringo Club.)

C. RETURN TO NAIROBI: OPTIONS

Depart Island Camp after breakfast. (Depending on your plans for the day, ask for a picnic lunch the night before). There are several options of stops/side excursions on your return to Nairobi.

1. Turn right just after Marigat and drive up the well-tarred road to Kabarnet (C51) home of President Moi. Marvelous views and viewpoints on this winding road up to the top of the escarpment. You could go to the Kabarnet Hotel for a drink or lunch—good views from here over the other side of the escarpment. Retrace your route and head towards Nakuru.

After this you could:

a. Make it back to Nairobi before dark.

b. Go to Menengai Crater in Nakuru for an amazing view over one of the largest craters in the world. Then spend the night at Lake Nakuru or Lake Naivasha or try to get back to Nairobi.

2. Instead of Kabarnet go directly to Menengai Crater in Nakuru—have your picnic here and then head for Nairobi or spend the night at Lake Nakuru or Lake Naivasha.

3. Go to Lake Nakuru National Park. See the flamingos and enjoy the many warthogs and waterbuck. You may be lucky and see leopards in the Fever Trees. Admire the forest of Euphorbia trees. Picnic in the park—several picnic sites (watch out for monkeys and baboons who also enjoy a picnic). Plan to stay the night at a Nakuru lodge if you have already done Options 1 and/or 2. If you have gone directly to Nakuru from Island Camp, you might consider heading to Lake Naivasha for the night. There are many choices of places to stay at Lake Naivasha—select what suits you. If you have the time, you might choose to stay a night at Lake Nakuru and the next one or two nights at Lake Naivasha.

At Lake Naivasha:

a. Try and get out on the lake in a boat if you can.

b. A walk on Crescent Island among wild animals is always a treat.

c. Consider driving around Hell's Gate—dramatic scenery and plains game.

d. Stop at Elmenteita Weavers (just past the entrance to Lake Naivasha Club) for lovely kikoys and other craft items.

e. If you need replenishment before heading back to Nairobi, consider stopping for a snack or a meal at La Belle Inn in Naivasha town.

INTERESTING EATING

NAIROBI AREA

To be certain of seating, make reservations.

1. For romance, elegance, and good food...

   Ibis Grill Norfolk Hotel • ☎ *335422.*

   Mandhari Restaurant, Serena Hotel • ☎ *725111.*

   Galleria Restaurant, Nairobi Casino • ☎ *7426000.*

2. For beautiful views over the city, have lunch at...

   Chateau Restaurant, Hotel Inter-Continental • ☎ *335550.*

3. For seafood and Swahili fare...

   Nairobi Tamarind Restaurant • ☎ *220473* or *338959.*

4. For superior Indian cuisine...

   Haandi Restaurant, The Mall in Westlands • ☎ *448294/5/6.*

   Dawat Restaurant, Shimmers Plaza, Westlands • ☎ *749338.*

   Nawab Tandoori Restaurant, Muthaiga Shopping Center • ☎ *740292.*

5. For gourmet nouvelle cuisine with Japanese flair...

   Zephyr, Rank Zerox House, Westlands • ☎ *750055.*

6. For traditional African lunch twice a week...

   Fairview Hotel • ☎ *723211.*

7. For pleasant outdoor dining...

   Toona Tree, Nairobi Casino • ☎ *742600.*

8. For special pastries at a gourmet coffee shop...

Orna's, ABC Place, Westlands • ☎ *445368.*

9. For barbecued game meat, lots of tourists, and disco and evening entertainment...

Carnivore, Langata Road • ☎ *501775.*

THE COAST

1. For seafood with seaview...

Mombasa Tamarind Restaurant • ☎ *474600.*

Also try the float-away feast on the *Tamarind Dhow*.

2. To eat in a cave or at the beach bar...

Ali Barbour's on Diani Beach • ☎ *2033.*

3. For gourmet Italian in Arabian Nights setting...

La Malindina, Malindi • ☎ *20045.*

HOTEL BOOK:
Hats, Money Bags,
Double Occupancy
Rates

The rates quoted here are based on 1995 high season double occupancy. Sometimes this will include full or half board, breakfast, or no meals depending on what is usual for each specific area.

Kind of accommodation (such as "Hotels" or "Tented Camp" etc.) is indicated in the book by an icon in the outside margin. An asterisk (*) denotes a "small print" hotel.

Where hotel and lodge prices include game drives or fishing, this has been noted. Many private homestay prices include a variety of otherwise pricey extras, eg. game drives, escorted walks, horse riding, etc.

The following letters are used to note the type of accommodation:

Hotel..H

Hotel (Night Game Viewing Lodge)..H-NGVL

Homestay...HS

Ranch/Sanctuary.. R/S

Tented Camp ....TC

Grass Shacks/Tents on the Beach ....GS/ToB

Accommodation	Type	Hats	$ Bags	Price
1. NAIROBI				
City Center				
Grand Regency Hotel	H	🎩👢	💰💰💰	$275
Hotel Intercontinental Nairobi	H		💰💰	$195
Nairobi Hilton	H		💰💰	$150

367

Accommodation	Type	Hats	$ Bags	Price
Nairobi Safari Club	H		🛍️🛍️🛍️	$226
* New Stanley Hotel	H		🛍️🛍️	$110
* Six Eighty Hotel	H		🛍️	$74

Beyond City Center

Accommodation	Type	Hats	$ Bags	Price
The Norfolk Hotel	H	🎩🎩	🛍️🛍️🛍️	$255
Nairobi Serena Hotel	H	🎩🎩	🛍️🛍️🛍️	$210
Mayfair Court Hotel	H	🎩	🛍️🛍️	$100
Fairview Hotel	H	🌿	🛍️	$70
* Jacaranda Hotel	H		🛍️	$82
* Boulevard Hotel	H		🛍️	$80
* Panafric Hotel	H		🛍️	$84

City Suburbs

Accommodation	Type	Hats	$ Bags	Price
Windsor Golf & Country Club	H	🎩🎩	🛍️🛍️	$184
Safari Park Hotel	H	🎩🎩	🛍️🛍️	$150
Utali Hotel	H		🛍️	$80
* The Kentmere Club	H		🛍️	$32
* The Blue Post Hotel	H		🛍️	$20
The Giraffe Manor	R/S	🎩🎩🌿	🛍️🛍️🛍️🛍️	$450

2. RIFT VALLEY

Lake Naivasha

Accommodation	Type	Hats	$ Bags	Price
Lake Naivasha Club	H	🎩	🛍️🛍️	$120
Elsamere Conservation Center	H	🌿	🛍️	$90
* Safariland Club Ltd.	H		🛍️🛍️	$110
* Crater Lake or Lake Songasoi Tented Camp	TC		🛍️🛍️🛍️	$220
Kongoni Game Valley Ranch	R/S	🎩🎩🎩	🛍️🛍️🛍️	$300
Loldia House	R/S	🎩🎩🎩	🛍️🛍️🛍️	$326
Mundui	R/S	🎩🎩🎩	🛍️🛍️🛍️	$360
Longonot Game Ranch	R/S	🎩🌿	🛍️🛍️	$196
Olerai House (Acacia)	HS	🎩🌿	🛍️🛍️🛍️	$280
* Lakeside House	HS		🛍️🛍️	$180
* Morendat House	HS		🛍️🛍️🛍️	$210
* The Wagon Wheel	HS			

Gilgil

Accommodation	Type	Hats	$ Bags	Price
River House	HS		🛍️🛍️	$140

Lake Elmenteita

Accommodation	Type	Hats	$ Bags	Price
Lake Elmenteita Lodge	H			
Delamere Camp	TC	🎩	🛍️🛍️	$176

Lake Nakuru

Accommodation	Type	Hats	$ Bags	Price
Lake Nakuru Lodge	H		🛍️🛍️	$160

Accommodation	Type	Hats	$ Bags	Price
Sarova Lion Hill	H		💰💰	$136
Rongai & Molo				
Deloraine	R/S	👒	💰💰	$160
Juani Farm	HS		💰💰	$116
Lake Baringo				
Island Camp	TC	👒👒	💰💰	$170
Saruni	TC	👒		
Lake Baringo Club	H	🥾	💰💰	$102
Kabarnet				
Kabarnet Hotel	H		💰	$34

3. CENTRAL HIGHLANDS — MT. KENYA AREA

Nyeri - Nanyuki & Beyond

Accommodation	Type	Hats	$ Bags	Price
The Aberdare Country Club	H	👒👒	💰💰	$126
Mt. Kenya Safari Club	H	👒👒	💰💰💰💰	$319
Naro Moru River Lodge	H	👒	💰💰	$114
Outspan Hotel	H	👒	💰💰	$112
* Thomson's Falls Inn	H		💰	$20
The Ark Forest Lodge	H-NGVL	👒🥾	💰💰💰	$264
Mountain Lodge	H-NGVL		💰💰	$184
Treetops	H-NGVL		💰💰	$158
Sweetwaters Tented Camp	TC	👒	💰💰	$148
Lewa Downs	R/S	👒👒👒	💰💰💰	$310
Ngare Niti	R/S	👒👒👒	💰💰💰	$300
Borana Lodge	R/S	👒👒👒	💰💰💰💰💰	$500
Ol Pejeta Lodge	R/S	👒👒	💰💰💰	$233
Segera Ranch	R/S	👒👒	💰💰💰	$300
Sangare	R/S		💰💰💰💰	$390
* Mogwooni Bandas	R/S		💰💰💰	$200
* Mokorindo Cottage	R/S			
Wingu Kenda	HS	👒🥾	💰💰💰	$300

Meru National Park

Accommodation	Type	Hats	$ Bags	Price
* Meru Mulika Lodge	H		💰	$76
Kindani Camp	TC		💰💰💰	$250

Embu

Accommodation	Type	Hats	$ Bags	Price
* Izaak Walton Inn	H		💰	$24

4. NORTHERN KENYA

Samburu Area

Samburu National Reserve

Accommodation	Type	Hats	$ Bags	Price
Larsens	TC	👒👒👒	💰💰	$178

Accommodation	Type	Hats	$ Bags	Price
Samburu Intrepids Club	TC	🎩🎩	💰💰	$170
Samburu Serena Lodge	H		💰💰	$182
Samburu Lodge	H		💰💰	$144
Shaba National Reserve				
Sarova Shaba Lodge	H	🎩🎩	💰💰	$160
Buffalo Springs National Reserve, Introduction				
* Buffalo Springs Lodge	H		💰💰	$120
Marsabit				
The Marsabit National Park				
Marsabit Lodge	H		💰	$64
Matthews Range				
Kitich Camp	TC		💰💰💰	$200
Rumuruti - Wamba - Maralal Area				
Ol Malo	R/S	🎩🎩🎩	💰💰💰💰	$460
Colcheccio Ranch	R/S	🎩🎩🎩		
Ol Ari Nyiro Ranch	R/S		💰💰💰💰💰	
Maralal				
Maralal Safari Lodge	H		💰💰	$112
Maralal - Loyangalani				
Lake Turkana				
The Oasis Club (East Shore)	H		💰💰	$150
Lake Turkana Lodge (West Shore)	H			
5. WESTERN KENYA				
Lake Victoria				
Mfangano Island Camp	H	🎩🎩🎩	💰💰💰💰	$900 (fishing & flight)
Rusinga Island Camp	H	🎩🎩	💰💰💰💰	$800 (fishing & flight)
Takawiri Fishing Camp	H		💰💰	$195 (or $650 fishing & flight)
Western Highlands				
Barnley's House	HS		💰	$40
Lokitela Farm	HS		💰💰💰	$330
Rondo Retreat Center	HS	🎩🎩		
* Imperial Hotel	H		💰	$46
* Kakamega Golf Hotel	H		💰	$40
* Kericho Tea Hotel	H		💰	$48
* Mt. Elgon Lodge	H		💰	$50

Accommodation	Type	Hats	$ Bags	Price
* Sirikwa Hotel	H		🪙	$60
* Sunset Hotel	H		🪙	$50

6. SOUTHERN KENYA

Masai Mara National Reserve

Governors' Family of Camps, all include game drives

Accommodation	Type	Hats	$ Bags	Price
Governors' Camp	TC	👒👒🥾	🪙🪙🪙	$325
Little Governors' Camp	TC	👒👒👒	🪙🪙🪙	$325
Governors' Paradise Camp	TC		🪙🪙🪙	$325
Governors' Private Camp	TC		🪙🪙🪙🪙	$650 (x2 as 4 must book)
Mara Intrepids Club	TC	👒👒🥾	🪙🪙🪙	$256 (with game drives)
Sekenani Camp	TC	👒👒🥾	🪙🪙🪙	$300 (with game drives)
Kichwa Tembo Camp	TC	👒👒	🪙🪙🪙	$242 (with game drives)
Mara Safari Club	TC	👒👒	🪙🪙🪙	$308 (with game drives)
Siana Springs	TC	👒🥾	🪙🪙🪙	$242 (with game drives)
Mara River Camp	TC		🪙🪙	$140
Sarova Mara Camp	TC		🪙🪙	$176
* Fig Tree Camp	TC		🪙🪙	$150
Rekero Farm	HS	👒👒	🪙🪙🪙🪙	$440 (with game drives, walks)
Bush Tops	HS		🪙🪙🪙🪙	$400 (with game drives)
Mpata Safari Club	H	👒👒👒	🪙🪙🪙🪙	$680 (jacuzzi & game drives)
Olkurruk Mara Lodge	H	👒	🪙🪙	$180
Keekorok Lodge	H	🥾	🪙🪙	$124
Mara Serena Lodge	H	👒	🪙🪙🪙	$208
* Masai Mara Sopa Lodge	H		🪙🪙	$180
* Paradise Mara Camp	H		🪙🪙	$240 (with game drives)

Nguruman Escarpment

Accommodation	Type	Hats	$ Bags	Price
Ol Donyo Laro	R/S	👒👒👒	🪙🪙🪙🪙	$1000 (with game drives)

Amboseli National Park

Accommodation	Type	Hats	$ Bags	Price
Amboseli Serena Lodge	H	👒	🪙🪙🪙	$208
Amboseli Lodge	H		🪙🪙🪙	$210

Accommodation	Type	Hats	$ Bags	Price
Mt. Kilimanjaro Buffalo Lodge	H		🛍️🛍️	$190
Mt. Kilimanjaro Safari Club	H		🛍️🛍️🛍️	$210
Tortilis Camp	TC	👒👒👒	🛍️🛍️🛍️	$264

Kimana

* Kimana Lodge	H		🛍️🛍️	$170
* Cottar's Kilimanjaro Camp	TC		🛍️🛍️🛍️🛍️	$400 (with game drives)
* Kimana Leopard Camp Ltd.	TC		🛍️	$80

Chyulu Hills

Ol Donyo Wuas	R/S	👒👒👒	🛍️🛍️🛍️🛍️	$440 (with game drives, walks)
* Iltalal Camp	TC		🛍️🛍️	$160 (with game drives, walks)

Tsavo National Park

Tsavo National Park West

Finch Hattons Safari Camp	TC	👒👒👒	🛍️🛍️🛍️	$376
Ziwani Tented Camp	TC		🛍️🛍️	$126
Kilaguni Lodge	H	👒	🛍️🛍️	$144
Ngulia Safari Lodge	H		🛍️🛍️	$144
* Hunters Lodge	H		🛍️	$20

Tsavo National Park East

Tsavo Safari Camp	TC	🦶	🛍️🛍️	$170
Voi Safari Lodge	H		🛍️🛍️	$144
* Tsavo Inn	H		🛍️	$80

Taita Hills Private Reserve

Taita Hills Lodge	H	👒🦶	🛍️🛍️🛍️	$224
Salt Lick Safari Lodge	H	👒	🛍️🛍️🛍️	$290
The Tents	TC	👒	🛍️🛍️🛍️	$290

Lake Jipe

Lake Jipe Safari Lodge	H		🛍️🛍️	$126

7. THE KENYAN COAST

Mombasa

New Outrigger Hotel	H		🛍️	$65
Castle Hotel	H		🛍️	$75
Manor Hotel	H		🛍️	$40
Manson Hotel	H		🛍️	$80
* Oceanic Hotel	H		🛍️🛍️	$120

Accommodation	Type	Hats	$ Bags	Price
		South of Mombasa		
		Shelly Beach		
* Shelly Beach Hotel	H		💰	$29
		Tiwi Beach		
Falcon Bay Lodge	H			
		Diani Beach		
Indian Ocean Beach Club	H	🎩🎩👢	💰💰	$180
Alliance Hotels:				
Jadini Beach Hotel	H	🎩	💰💰	$164
Safari Beach	H		💰💰	$184
Africana Sea Lodge	H		💰💰	$130
Lagoon Reef Hotel	H	🎩	💰💰	$150
Kaskazi Beach Hotel	H	👢	💰💰	$104
Leopard Beach Hotel	H	👢	💰💰	$156
Two Fishes Hotel	H		💰💰	$128
Diani Reef Grand Hotel	H		💰💰💰	$220
Diani Sea Lodge	H		💰	$55
Diani Sea Resort	H		💰	$55
Leisure Lodge	H		💰💰	$176
Paradise Ocean Village Club	H		💰💰	$115
* Golden Beach	H		💰💰	$142
* Robinson Baobab Club	H		💰💰	$130
* Southern Palms Beach Resort	H		💰💰	$108
* Trade Winds Hotel	H		💰💰	$120
Diani House	HS	🎩👢	💰💰	$195
Nomad	GS/ToB		💰	$80
		Galu Beach		
Neptune Hotels on Galu Beach:				
Neptune Cottages	H		💰💰	$145
Neptune Paradise	H		💰💰	$158
Pinewood Village	HS	👢	💰💰💰	$230
Chale Paradise Island	GS/ToB	👢	💰💰	$146
		Msambweni Beach		
Beachcomber Club	H	👢	💰	$76
Seascapes Beach Villas	HS		💰	$80
		Funzi - Shimoni - Wasini		
Pemba Channel Inn	H	🎩🎩👢	💰💰	$150
Shimoni Reef Lodge	H		💰💰	$122
Sea Adventures, Ltd. (includes fishing)	HS			
Funzi Island Club	GS/ToB	🎩👢	💰💰	$190

Accommodation	Type	Hats	$ Bags	Price
Shimba Hills National Reserve (Night Game Viewing)				
Shimba Hills	H-NGVL	🎩	💰💰	$118
North of Mombasa to Kilifi				
Nyali Beach & English Point				
Nyali Beach Hotel	H	🎩	💰💰💰	$220
* Mombasa Beach Hotel	H		💰💰	$142
* Reef Hotel	H		💰💰	$152
The Tamarind Village	HS	🎩🎩	💰💰	$190
Bamburi Beach				
Whitesands	H	🎩	💰💰	$160
Severin Sea Lodge	H		💰💰	$146
* Bamburi Beach Hotel	H		💰	$96
* Kenya Beach Hotel	H			
* Ocean View Beach Hotel	H		💰💰	$120
* Neptune Beach Hotel	H		💰💰	$134
* Plaza Hotel	H		💰	$76
* Travellers Beach Hotel	H		💰	$82
Shanzu Beach				
Serena Beach Hotel	H	🎩🎩🎩	💰💰	$176
Hotel Intercontinental Mombasa	H	👣	💰💰	$195
Oyster Bay Beach Hotel	H			
The African Safari Club	H			
Kikambala Beach				
* Le Soleil	H		💰	$90
* Mombasa Sun & Sand	H		💰💰	$124
* Thousand Palms	H		💰	$57
* Whispering Palms Hotel	H		💰💰	$145
Kilifi				
Baobab Lodge	H		💰	$78
Kilifi Bay Resort Hotel & Village	H		💰	$90
Takaungu House (Phillip & Charlie Mason)	HS	🎩🎩	💰💰💰	$280
Mirella Ricciardi's Kilifi Home	HS			
Kildini (Michael & Jean Skinner)	HS			
Watamu				
Hemingways	H	🎩🎩🎩	💰💰💰	$208
Turtle Bay Beach Club	H		💰	$90
Ocean Sports	H		💰💰	$120
Blue Bay Village	H		💰💰	$156
* Barracuda Inn	H		💰💰	$100

Accommodation	Type	Hats	$ Bags	Price
* Temple Point Village	H		🎩🎩	$101
Mrs. Simpson's	HS			

Malindi & Vicinity

Accommodation	Type	Hats	$ Bags	Price
Indian Ocean Lodge	H	🎩🎩🔑	💰💰💰💰	$500
Malindi Beach Club	H	🎩	💰💰	$146
Kilili Baharhini	H	🔑		
Kingfisher Lodge	HS	🔑	💰💰💰	$208
White Elephant Sea Lodge	H	🔑	💰💰💰	$200
The Driftwood Beachclub	H		💰	$50
Silversands Villas	H		💰💰	$130
Kivulini Beach Hotel	H			
Coconut Village	H		💰💰	$135
Eden Roc Hotel	H		💰💰	$100
* African Dream Village	H		💰💰	$140
* Blue Marlin	H		💰	$56
* Bougan Village	H			
* Dorado Cottages	H			
* Lawfords Hotel	H		💰	$50
* Palm Tree Club	H			
* Scorpio Villas	H		💰💰	$140
* Stephanie Sea House	H		💰	$70
* The Tropical Village	H		💰💰	$140

Malindi to Tana River

Accommodation	Type	Hats	$ Bags	Price
Che-Shale	GS/ToB			
Tana Delta Camp	GS/ToB	🎩🔑	💰💰💰💰	$480

Lamu & North

Lamu Island, Lamu Town

Accommodation	Type	Hats	$ Bags	Price
Petley's Inn	H		💰	$35
* Lamu Palace Hotel	H		💰	$56
* Stone House	H		💰	$20
* Yumbe House	H		💰	$32

Lamu Island, Shela

Accommodation	Type	Hats	$ Bags	Price
Peponi Hotel	H	🎩🎩	💰💰💰	$220
Kijani House	H		💰💰	$124
Island Hotel	H		💰	$80

Beach Resorts Near Lamu

Accommodation	Type	Hats	$ Bags	Price
Kiwayu Safari Village	GS/ToB	🎩🎩🎩	💰💰💰	$380
Blue Safari Club	GS/ToB	🎩🎩🎩	💰💰💰💰	$900
Kipangani Sea Breezes	GS/ToB		💰💰	$130

SWAHILI GUIDE FOR SAFARI ENJOYMENT

The official languages of Kenya are Swahili and English. Most Kenyans, and especially those in the tourist business, are fluent in English. However, it is fun to use some Swahili as well. Please note: there are also many tribal languages in Kenya.

COMMON WORDS & PHRASES

Hello	*Jambo*
Mr.	*Bwana*
Mrs.	*Bibi*
Elder	*Mzee*
How are you?	*Habari?*
Good, very well	*Mzuri*
Bad	*Mbaya*
Fine	*Sawa*
Thank you very much	*Asante sana*
Please	*Tafadhali*
Goodbye	*Kwaheri*
May I come in?	*Hodi*
Welcome	*Karibu*
Danger	*Hatari*
Friend	*Rafiki*
A Shop	*Duka*
How much?	*Bei gani*

COMMON WORDS & PHRASES

Money	*Pesa*
Expensive	*Ghali*
Now	*Sasa*
Slowly	*Pole pole (pol ee, pol ee)*
Sleep well	*Lala salama*
Here	*Hapa*
Where	*Wapi*
Come	*Kwende*
Let's go	*Twende*
Quickly	*Haraka*
Why	*Kwa nini?*
What	*Nini?*
Who	*Nani?*
A bug, insect	*Dudu*

EATING & DRINKING

Beer	*Pombe*
(For cold drinks, add baridi sana to your order.)	
Cold	*Baridi*
Hot	*Moto*
Coffee	*Kahawa*
Tea	*Chai*
(Coffee or Tea with milk is often expressed as "white".)	
Water	*Maji*
Milk	*Maziwa*
Sugar	*Sucari*
Ice	*Barafu*
Food	*Chakula*
Meat	*Nyama*
Fish	*Samki*
Chicken	*Kuku*
Fruit	*Matunda*
Vegetables	*Mboga*

NUMBERS

One	*Moja*
Two	*Mbili*
Three	*Tatu*
Four	*Nne*
Five	*Tano*
Six	*Sita*
Seven	*Saba*
Eight	*Nane*
Nine	*Tisa*
Ten	*Kumi*

SAFARI ANIMALS

Lion	*Simba*
Leopard	*Chui*
Cheetah	*Duma*
Elephant	*Tembo*
Rhino	*Kifaru*
Buffalo	*Nyati*
Hippo	*Kiboko*
Giraffe	*Twiga*
Zebra	*Punda milia*
Impala	*Swara*
Hartebeest	*Kongoni*
Hyena	*Fisi*
Baboon, monkey	*Nyani*

INDEX

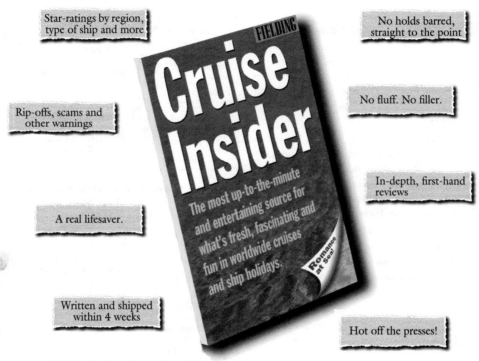

Order Your Fielding Travel Guides Today

BOOKS	$ EA.
Amazon	$16.95
Australia	$12.95
Bahamas	$12.95
Belgium	$16.95
Bermuda	$12.95
Borneo	$16.95
Brazil	$16.95
Britain	$16.95
Budget Europe	$16.95
Caribbean	$18.95
Europe	$16.95
Far East	$19.95
France	$16.95
Hawaii	$15.95
Holland	$15.95
Italy	$16.95
Kenya's Best Hotels, Lodges & Homestays	$16.95
London Agenda	$12.95
Los Angeles Agenda	$12.95
Malaysia and Singapore	$16.95
Mexico	$16.95
New York Agenda	$12.95
New Zealand	$12.95
Paris Agenda	$12.95
Portugal	$16.95
Scandinavia	$16.95
Seychelles	$12.95
Southeast Asia	$16.95
Spain	$16.95
The World's Great Voyages	$16.95
The World's Most Dangerous Places	$19.95
The World's Most Romantic Places	$16.95
Vacation Places Rated	$19.95
Vietnam	$16.95
Worldwide Cruises	$17.95

To order by phone call toll-free 1-800-FW-2-GUIDE

(VISA, MasterCard and American Express accepted.)

*To order by mail send your check or money order,
including $2.00 per book for shipping and handling (sorry, no COD's) to:
Fielding Worldwide, Inc. 308 S. Catalina Avenue, Redondo Beach, CA 90277 U.S.A.*

Get 10% off your order by saying "Fielding Discount"
or send in this page with your order

Favorite People, Places & Experiences

ADDRESS:	NOTES:

Name

Address

Telephone

Name

Address

Telephone

Name

Address

Telephone

Name

Address

Telephone

Name

Address

Telephone

Name

Address

Telephone

Name

Address

Telephone

Favorite People, Places & Experiences

ADDRESS:	NOTES:

Name

Address

Telephone

Name

Address

Telephone

Name

Address

Telephone

Name

Address

Telephone

Name

Address

Telephone

Name

Address

Telephone

Name

Address

Telephone

Favorite People, Places & Experiences

ADDRESS:	NOTES:

Name

Address

Telephone

Name

Address

Telephone

Name

Address

Telephone

Name

Address

Telephone

Name

Address

Telephone

Name

Address

Telephone

Name

Address

Telephone

Favorite People, Places & Experiences

	ADDRESS:	NOTES:

Name

Address

Telephone

Name

Address

Telephone

Name

Address

Telephone

Name

Address

Telephone

Name

Address

Telephone

Name

Address

Telephone

Name

Address

Telephone

Favorite People, Places & Experiences

ADDRESS:	NOTES:

Name

Address

Telephone

Name

Address

Telephone

Name

Address

Telephone

Name

Address

Telephone

Name

Address

Telephone

Name

Address

Telephone

Name

Address

Telephone

Favorite People, Places & Experiences

	ADDRESS:	NOTES:

Name

Address

Telephone

Name

Address

Telephone

Name

Address

Telephone

Name

Address

Telephone

Name

Address

Telephone

Name

Address

Telephone

Name

Address

Telephone

Favorite People, Places & Experiences

Name

Address

Telephone

Name

Address

Telephone

Name

Address

Telephone

Name

Address

Telephone

Name

Address

Telephone

Name

Address

Telephone

Name

Address

Telephone

Favorite People, Places & Experiences

ADDRESS:	NOTES:

Name

Address

Telephone

Name

Address

Telephone

Name

Address

Telephone

Name

Address

Telephone

Name

Address

Telephone

Name

Address

Telephone

Name

Address

Telephone

Favorite People, Places & Experiences

ADDRESS:	NOTES:

Name

Address

Telephone

Name

Address

Telephone

Name

Address

Telephone

Name

Address

Telephone

Name

Address

Telephone

Name

Address

Telephone

Name

Address

Telephone

Favorite People, Places & Experiences

Name

Address

Telephone

Name

Address

Telephone

Name

Address

Telephone

Name

Address

Telephone

Name

Address

Telephone

Name

Address

Telephone

Name

Address

Telephone

Favorite People, Places & Experiences

ADDRESS:	NOTES:

Name

Address

Telephone

Name

Address

Telephone

Name

Address

Telephone

Name

Address

Telephone

Name

Address

Telephone

Name

Address

Telephone

Name

Address

Telephone

Favorite People, Places & Experiences

ADDRESS:	NOTES:

Name

Address

Telephone

Name

Address

Telephone

Name

Address

Telephone

Name

Address

Telephone

Name

Address

Telephone

Name

Address

Telephone

Name

Address

Telephone

Favorite People, Places & Experiences

ADDRESS:	NOTES:

Name

Address

Telephone

Name

Address

Telephone

Name

Address

Telephone

Name

Address

Telephone

Name

Address

Telephone

Name

Address

Telephone

Name

Address

Telephone

Favorite People, Places & Experiences

ADDRESS:	NOTES:

Name

Address

Telephone

Name

Address

Telephone

Name

Address

Telephone

Name

Address

Telephone

Name

Address

Telephone

Name

Address

Telephone

Name

Address

Telephone

Favorite People, Places & Experiences

ADDRESS:	NOTES:

Name

Address

Telephone

Name

Address

Telephone

Name

Address

Telephone

Name

Address

Telephone

Name

Address

Telephone

Name

Address

Telephone

Name

Address

Telephone